PERSIAN VOCABULARY

PERSIAN
VOCABULARY

BY

ANN K. S. LAMBTON

C.B.E., B.A., PH.D.

Professor of Persian in the
University of London

CAMBRIDGE UNIVERSITY PRESS

CAMBRIDGE

LONDON · NEW YORK · MELBOURNE

Published by the Syndics of the Cambridge University Press
The Pitt Building, Trumpington Street, Cambridge CB2 1RP
Bentley House, 200 Euston Road, London NW1 2DB
32 East 57th Street, New York, NY 10022, USA
296 Beaconsfield Parade, Middle Park, Melbourne 3206, Australia

Hard covers ISBN: 0 521 05518 0
Paperback ISBN: 0 521 09154 3

First published 1954
Reprinted 1961 1966 1969 1975

First printed in Great Britain
at the University Printing House, Cambridge
Reprinted in Great Britain by
Alden and Mowbray Ltd at the
Alden Press, Oxford

PREFACE

This volume was originally planned simply as a vocabulary to my Persian Grammar (published separately in 1953), and was to contain only such words as occurred in the Grammar. However, in view of the difficulty with which students were faced, at the time I wrote, in obtaining dictionaries at prices within their means (a difficulty since by no means entirely or satisfactorily removed), it seemed that a useful purpose might be served by including in the vocabulary a somewhat wider range of words.

The consequent additions have been based not on a scientific word-count, but rather on my own experiences in teaching with the Grammar as a text-book. It may well be that critics will now judge the volume to have fallen between two stools, and that they will find many words omitted which they themselves would regard as essential while, conversely, they condemn some of the words included as of rarer occurrence.

Nevertheless I venture to hope that the vocabulary in its present slightly enlarged form will be useful to the student, and that its shortcomings are merely those inseparable from any selective vocabulary as opposed to a complete dictionary. The student is again warned in general, as he was in the Introduction to Part I of the Grammar, that the vocabulary is not intended to obviate reference to complete dictionaries, which alone will give him a full list of the meanings of the words, and in particular that classical meanings, where they differ from the modern usage, are not included.

Lastly it remains for me to record my gratitude to Mr Hakim Ilahi for reading through the text and to Mr N. C. Sainsbury for his generous help in proof-reading.

A. K. S. L.

LONDON
4 *June* 1954

CONTENTS

NOTE ON TRANSCRIPTION

1. The transcription used in this volume is that used in the Grammar and described in the Introduction to that volume. The system adopted is recapitulated below:

ا   *alef* or *alef hamze:*

     (i) in a medial or final position it is transcribed by *a*;

     (ii) in an initial position it represents a glottal plosive and is not represented in the transcription; it may be vowelled *e*, *a*, or *o*; when followed by ى (*i*) or و (*u*) in an initial position it is not represented in the transcription.

آ   *alef madde* is transcribed by *a*.

ب   *b*   (voiced bilabial plosive).

پ   *p*   (voiceless aspirated bilabial plosive).

ت   *t*   (voiceless aspirated dental plosive).

ث   *s*   (voiceless alveolar fricative).

ج   *j*   (voiced post-alveolar plosive).

چ   *c*   (voiceless post-alveolar fricative).

ح   *h*   (glottal fricative).

خ   *x*   (voiceless velar uvular with scrape; approximating to *ch* in the Scottish word 'loch').

د   *d*   (voiced dental plosive).

ذ   *z*   (voiced alveolar fricative).

ر   *r*   (voiced alveolar with weak roll or tap).

ز   *z*   (voiced alveolar fricative).

ژ   *ʒ*   (voiced post-alveolar fricative; corresponding to *j* in the French word 'jour').

س   *s*   (voiceless alveolar fricative).

ش   *ʃ*   (voiceless post-alveolar fricative; corresponding to *sh* in the English word 'show').

ص   *s*   (voiceless alveolar fricative).

ض   *z*   (voiced alveolar fricative).

ط   *t*   (voiceless aspirated dental plosive).

ظ   *z̧* (voiced alveolar fricative).

ع   *ain* (glottal plosive; corresponding to the check in the voice substituted for *t* in Cockney and other dialects in such words as 'bottle'); (i) in an initial position when followed immediately by a vowel it is omitted from the transcription; (ii) in a medial or final position it is transcribed by '; preceded by *a* and followed by *i* the combination tends to become $\widehat{ai}$ rather than a'*i*.

غ   *ɣ* (voiced or voiceless uvular plosive according to phonetic context)

ف   *f* (voiceless labio-dental fricative).

ق   *q* (voiced or voiceless uvular plosive according to phonetic context غ and ق are not differentiated by most speakers, and are pronounced as a voiceless uvular plosive, formed by the back of the tongue coming into contact with the rearmost part of the soft palate, unless between two back vowels, when they tend to be pronounced as a voiced uvular plosive).

ك   *k* (voiceless aspirated palatal, made by the front of the tongue, excluding the tip, coming against the hard palate, if followed by *i*, *e*, *a*, $\widehat{ei}$, or a consonant, or in a final position; voiceless velar plosive if followed by *a*, *o*, *u*, $\widehat{ai}$, or $\widehat{ou}$).

گ   *g* (voiced palatal plosive, made by the front of the tongue, excluding the tip, coming against the hard palate, if followed by *i*, *e*, *a*, $\widehat{ei}$, or a consonant, or in a final position; voiced velar plosive if followed by *a*, *o*, *u*, $\widehat{ai}$, or $\widehat{ou}$).

ل   *l* (voiced alveolar lateral; corresponding to the *l* in the English word 'light').

م   *m* (voiced nasal bilabial).

ن   *n* (voiced nasal alveolar; followed by ب *b* in the same word it is pronounced *m* and so transcribed).

و   (i) *v* (voiced labio-dental fricative);

        (ii) after an initial خ *x* in Persian words it is not pronounced and is therefore not represented in the transcription; exceptions to this are خوب *xub* 'good', خون *xun* 'blood', خوك *xuk* 'pig', خوشه *xuſe* 'cluster of grapes', خوزستان *xuzestan* 'Khuzistan');

        (iii) *u* (approximating to the vowel in the English word 'booed'; in the words, دو 'two', تو 'thou', بوته 'bush', and in numerous words derived from Turkish و is transcribed by *o* and corresponds to a vowel rather more rounded than the vowel in the English word 'book').

ه   (i)   *h* (glottal fricative);

(ii) in a final position in certain words when preceded by the vowel *e*, ه is not pronounced and is therefore not represented in the transcription. This ه, which has been termed the 'silent' *h* in the Grammar, is found as a verbal, adjectival and nominal suffix, and in lieu of ة in certain Arabic words.

ی   (i)   *y* (semi-vowel, as *y* in the English word 'yes');

(ii) *i* (approximating to the vowel in the English word 'beat');

(iii) in cases where ی represents the *ezafe* it is transcribed *ye*.

2. Diphthongs are shown in the transcription by a ligature mark, thus: $\widehat{ei}$, $\widehat{ai}$, $\widehat{ui}$, $\widehat{ou}$, and $\widehat{ai}$..

3. ≍ (*fathe*) is transcribed by *a*, ⌐ (*kasre*) by *e*, and ≛ (*damme*) by *o*.

4. The sign ء is known as *hamze*:

(i) written over a bearer in Persian words or preceding the Abstract, Adjectival, or Relative ی *-i* added to words ending in ١ *-a* or و *-u*, it merely indicates a junction of vowels, and is not represented in the transcription;

(ii) *hamze* placed over the 'silent' *h* and representing the Indefinite, Adjectival, or Relative ی *-i*, or the personal ending of the 2nd person singular, is transcribed by *i*;

(iii) *hamze* placed over the 'silent' *h* and representing the *ezafe* is transcribed *ye*;

(iv) in Arabic words the *hamze* is of two kinds: the *hamzat ol-qat'* and the *hamzat ol-vasl*. The former is pronounced as a glottal plosive. In a medial position it is represented in the transcription by '. In an initial position it is omitted from the transcription. In a final position the *hamze* is seldom articulated vigorously and is therefore in most cases omitted from the transcription. If the *hamzat ol-vasl* follows a word ending in ١ *a*, و *u*, or ی *i*, these vowels are shortened and are represented in the transcription by *a*, *o*, and *e* respectively.

5. *Tanvin*. The vowel sign ≍ of the accusative case in Arabic, when the noun or adjective is indefinite, is written double and takes an *alef*, thus ١ً, unless the word ends in ة or *hamze*, in which case it is written ةً and ءً respectively. It is transcribed by *an*.

6. Sun Letters. When the Arabic definite article ال is prefixed to a word beginning with one of the sun letters (i.e. ز, ر, ر, ذ, د, ث, ت, س, ش, ص, ض, ط, ظ, ل, or ن), the *l* is assimilated to the sun letter. This is represented in the transcription by a doubling of the sun letter, e.g. الساعه *as-sa'a* 'immediately'.

7. The purpose of the transcription is that it should be a guide to the standard pronunciation of words; no attempt has been made to cover the variations found in different parts of the country. There is, for example, a marked tendency to substitute *e* for *a* in certain words. This has been indicated in the transcription in some cases, but no consistent policy has been followed. کشمکش is thus transcribed *kefmakef*, whereas شنکش has been transcribed *fenkaf*, although its pronunciation by many speakers is rather *fenkef*. Since, however, there is, on the whole, no consistency by speakers in the substitution of *e* for *a* it seemed preferable, where both variants are found, in general to maintain *a* in the transcription.

8. Certain inconsistencies will also be found in words derived from Arabic roots of which the second and third radicals are the same. In general, where the second and third radicals are in a final position and not separated by a vowel, both have been shown in the transcription, as for example عوام *avamm*; but it should be pointed out that when the Persian *eẓafe* or some suffix is added to such words the doubled consonant is not always (or even usually) pronounced as a doubled letter, thus عوامانه *avamane* for *avammane*. There are a few cases of a doubled consonant in other than a final position not being reflected in the pronunciation, notably عمو *amu* 'paternal uncle' for *ammu* (but in عمه *amme* 'paternal aunt' the double *m* is given its full value).

9. Some explanation is perhaps required concerning the transcription of compound words. In general in the case of nouns and adjectives these have been transcribed as one word, e.g. باصفا *basafa* 'pleasant', برآورد *baravard* 'estimate', but in the case of compound verbs, the verbal and the non-verbal elements have been kept separate, e.g. برگشتن *bar gaftan* 'to return'.

10. I am conscious that the system chosen will not seem wholly satisfactory either to those who favour a strict transliteration or to those who prefer a purely phonetic transcription, the more especially since, as indicated above, I have allowed myself some small freedom in its application. In extenuation I would emphasize that my transcription is intended not as a substitute for the Persian but merely as a guide to the pronunciation.

A. K. S. L

4 *June* 1954

PERSIAN—ENGLISH

VOCABULARY[1]

PERSIAN—ENGLISH

١

	آب	*ab*, water; juice; آب سالی *absali*, year of plentiful or abundant rainfall; آب و هوا *ab o hava*, climate; باب انداختن *be ab andaxtan*, to launch (a ship).
	آباد	*abad*, inhabited, cultivated, populous, flourishing; a suffix denoting place of abode.
	آبادی	*abadi*, village; flourishing and populous condition.
	آبان	*aban*, eighth month of the Persian solar year.
	آبپز	*abpaz*, boiled (of food).
A	ابتداء	*ebteda*, beginning.
A	ابتکار	*ebtekar*, initiative.
A	ابد	*abad*, eternity without end.
A	ابر	*abr*, cloud.
A	ابراز	*ebraz*, expressing, expression.
	آبرو	*abru, aberu*, good name, reputation; آبروش ریخت *aberuʃ rixt*, he has lost 'face'.
	ابرو	*abru*, eyebrow.
	ابریشم	*abriʃom*, silk.
	ابریشمی	*abriʃomi*, silken.
	ابزار	*abʒar* (colloq.), instrument, tool.
	آبکشن	*abkaʃ*, strainer.
	آبگوشت	*abguʃt*, kind of clear soup.
	آبگینه	*abgine*, mirror.

---

[1] Where possible the derivation of foreign words has been indicated as follows: A = Arabic, F = French, R = Russian, and T = Turkish. In the case of compound words where one part, at least, is non-Persian, the derivation has also been given, thus AP indicates that the first part of the compound is derived from Arabic, while the second part is Persian and PA that the first part of the compound is Persian and the second Arabic. AP has also been used where both parts of the compound are Arabic but the structure of the compound Persian, as in combinations such as صورت حساب *surate hesab* 'bill, account.' The following abbreviations have been used in the transcription: *b. = budan*, *d. = daʃtan*, *k. = kardan*, and *ʃ. = ʃodan*.

A	ابلاغ	*eblaɣ*, sending, conveying, announcing, notifying, communication, notification.
A	ابلاغیه	*eblaɣiye*, communication, official notice.
A	ابلق	*ablaq*, piebald.
	آبله	*abele*, small-pox.
	آبله رو	*abeleru*, pockmarked.
	آبله کوبی	*abelekubi*, vaccination.
A	ابن	*ebn*, son.
PA	آب‌نبات	*abnabat*, kind of candy, boiled sweet.
A	ابوی	*abavi*, my father, father.
	آبی	*abi*, irrigated (of farming); blue; aquatic (of animal).
	آبیاری	*abyari*, irrigation.
A	ابیض	*abyaⱬ*, white.
A	اتباع	*atba'* (pl. of تابع *tabe'*), subjects, followers.
A	اتحاد	*ettehad*, union, alliance.
A	اتحادیه	*ettehadiye*, union, league; اتحادیه کارگران *ettehadiyeye kargaran*, workers' union, trade union.
	آتش	*ateʃ*, fire; آتش زدن *atesh ⱬadan*, to set fire to; آتش گرفتن *ateʃ gereftan*, to catch fire.
	آتش باری	*ateʃbari*, volley (of gunfire).
	آتش بازی	*ateʃbaⱬi*, firework display.
	آتش فشان	*ateʃfeʃan*, volcano.
	آتش کده	*ateʃkade*, fire-temple.
	آتش نشان	*ateʃneʃan*, fireman.
	آتش نشانی	*ateʃneʃani*, fire-fighting service.
A	اتصال	*ettesal*, contiguity, connexion, junction; fusing (of light, etc.).
A	اتفاق	*ettefaq*, happening, event; agreement; alliance; اتفاق افتادن *ettefaq oftadan*, to happen.
A	اتفاقًا	*ettefaqan*, by chance.
A	اتکاء	*etteka*, leaning against; support, reliance.
A	اتمام	*etmam*, completing; باتمام رسیدن *be etmam rasidan*, to be completed, finished.
A	اتهام	*etteham*, imputation, charge.
A	آتی	*ati*, coming, future (adj.).
A	آتیه	*atie*, future (subs.).

A	اثاثیه	*asasiye*, equipment, furniture.
A	آثار	*asar* (pl. of اثر *asar*), effects; signs, memorials, relics; literary remains.
A	اثبات	*esbat*, proof; corroboration, affirmation.
A	اثر	*asar*, sign, trace; effect.
A	اثنا	*asna*, interval (of time); در اثنا(ی) *dar asna(ye)*, in the middle of, during.
A	اجاره	*ejare*, rent, hire.
AP	اجارهنامه	*ejarename*, lease.
A	اجازه	*ejaze*, permission; اجازهنامه *ejazename*, permit, licence.
T	اجاق	*ojaq*, fireplace, hearth.
A	اجباری	*ejbari*, compulsory.
A	اجتماع	*ejtema'*, meeting, gathering; society, social life.
A	اجتماعی	*ejtema'i*, social.
	آجر	*ajor*, (baked) brick.
A	اجراء	*ejra*, execution, putting into effect.
	آجرپز	*ajorpaz*, brick burner.
	آجرپزی	*ajorpazi*, brick burning.
A	اجمالاً	*ejmalan*, briefly.
A	اجناس	*ajnas* (pl. of جنس *jens*), kinds, sorts, species.
	آجیدن	*ajidan*, to stitch, sew.
	آچار	*acar*, screw-driver.
A	احترام	*ehteram*, honouring, revering, respect; احترام (بکسی) گذاشتن *ehteram (be kasi) gozaftan*, to respect (someone).
A	احتکار	*ehtekar*, hoarding, cornering.
A	احتمال	*ehtemal*, probability; احتمال دارد *ehtemal darad*, it is probable.
A	احتیاج	*ehteyaj*, need.
A	احتیاط	*ehteyat*, caution; heed, care.
A	احتیاطی	*ehteyati*, precautionary.
A	احد	*ahad*, one.
A	احداث	*ehdas*, producing, inventing, creation, innovation.
A	احساس	*ehsas*, feeling, perception, sense, emotion.
AP	احساساتی	*ehsasati*, emotional.

6

A احسان *ehsan*, doing good; benefit, favour.

A احشام *ahſam* (pl. of حشم *haſam*), followers, attendants; اغنام و احشام *aɣnam va ahſam*, flocks.

A احمر *ahmar*, red.

A احمق *ahmaq*, stupid, foolish; a fool.

A احیاء *ehya*, revival, resuscitation.

A احیانًا *ahyanan*, perchance.

A اختراع *extera'*, invention.

A اختصاص *extesas*, peculiarity, speciality.

A اختلاط *extelat*, mixture, amalgamation.

A اختلاف *extelaf*, difference, dispute; اختلاف کلمه *extelafe kalame*, discord, disagreement.

آختن *axtan*, to unsheathe, draw (a sword).

A اختیار *exteyar*, control, authority, power; choice, freedom of choice; pleasure, option; باختیار (کسی) گذاشتن *be exteyar(e kasi) goɣaſtan*, to place at the disposal (of someone).

A اختیاری *exteyari*, optional.

A اخذ *axɣ*, taking; اخذ کردن *axɣ k.*, to take.

A آخر *axer*, last, final; finally; آخرین *axerin*, last.

A اخلاف *axlaf* (pl. of خلف *xalaf*), those who come after, posterity.

A اخلاق *axlaq* (pl. of خلق *xolq*), morals, ethics; disposition, character.

اخم *axm*, frown; frowning.

آخوند *axond*, mulla.

A اخوی *axavi*, my brother, brother.

ادا *ada*, grace, beauty; mimicry; coquetry; ادا در آوردن *ada dar avardan*, to mimic (trans.); to act coquettishly.

A ادا *ada*, payment; ادا کردن *ada k.*, to pay; carry out; express.

A آداب *adab* (pl. of ادب *adab*), customs, manners.

A اداره *edare*, managing; office; administration; اداره کردن *edare k.*, to administer; to manage.

A ادامه *edame*, perpetuating, continuation; ادامه پیدا کردن *edame peida k.*, to continue (intrans.); ادامه دادن *edame dadan*, to continue (trans.).

A ادب *adab*, courtesy, politeness; belles lettres; ادب کردن *adab k.*, to chastise, correct; ادب پرور *adab parvar*, literary.

A	ادبیات	*adabiat*, belles lettres.
A	ادراك	*edrak*, comprehending, comprehension.
A	آدم	*adam*, Adam; man, person.
A	ادوار	*advar* (pl. of دوره *doure*), eras, periods.
A	ادویه	*advie* (pl. of دوا *dava*, medicine), spice.
A	ادیب	*adib*, learned; polite; man of letters.
A	اذان	*aẕan*, call to prayer, calling to prayer.
A	اذخار	*eẕẕexar*, storing up.
	آذر	*aẕar*, ninth month of the Persian solar year.
A	اراجیف	*arajif*, rumours.
A	ارادت	*eradat*, devotion, attachment, sincerity.
A	اراده	*erade*, will, desire, inclination.
	آراستن	*arastan*, to adorn.
A	اراضی	*araẕi* (pl. of ارض *arẕ*, the earth), lands.
	آرامش	*arameſ*, quiet.
A	ارباب	*arbab* (pl. of رب *rabb*, lord), master; chief landowner in a village.
	اربابی	*arbabi*, belonging to a large landed proprietor or landlord.
A	ارتباط	*ertebat*, connexion; افسر ارتباط *afsare ertebat*, liaison officer.
A	ارتجاع	*erteja'*, reaction, reactionary tendency.
	ارتش	*arteſ*, army.
A	ارتكاب	*ertekab*, perpetration, commission.
	ارجمند	*arjmand*, exalted, distinguished.
	آرد	*ard*, flour.
	اردك	*ordak*, duck.
	اردو	*ordu*, camp.
	اردوگاه	*ordugah*, camping-place.
	اردی بهشت	*ordi beheſt*, second month of the Persian solar year.
	ارز	*arẕ*, foreign exchange.
	ارزان	*arẕan*, cheap.
	ارزش	*arẕeſ*, value.
	آرزو	*arẕu*, desire.
	ارزیدن	*arẕidan*, to be worth.
A	ارسال	*ersal*, sending, despatching; ارسال داشتن *ersal d.*, to send.
A	ارشاد	*erſad*, guidance.

A   ارض   *arẕ*, earth (the planet).

     ارمنی   *armani*, Armenian; an Armenian.

     اروپا   *orupa*, Europe.

     اروپائی   *orupai*, European; a European.

     اره   *arre*, saw (tool).

     آری   *ari, are*, yes.

     از   *aẕ*, from; of; for; by; by way of; out of; with; belonging to; by means of; than; ازبرای *aẕ baraye*, for; از بهر *aẕ bahr(e)*, for, for the sake of, because; از پشت *aẕ poſt(e)*, behind; از پی *aẕ pei͡(ye)*, after; از رو *aẕ ru*, (to read) at sight; از رو(ی) *aẕ ru(ye)*, (from) off; upon, according to; از سر *aẕ sar*, from the beginning; ازسو(ی) *aẕ su(ye)*, from the direction of; از طرف *aẕ taraf(e)*, on behalf of; from the direction of; از میان *aẕ mian(e)*, from among; از نزد *aẕ naẕd(e)*, from the presence of.

A   ازاء   *eẕa*, lieu; در ازا(ی) *dar eẕa(ye)*, instead (of); in return (for).

     آزاد   *aẕad*, free.

     آزادی   *aẕadi*, freedom, liberty.

     آزادیخواه   *aẕadixah*, liberal.

     آزادیخواهی   *aẕadixahi*, liberalism.

A   ازدحام   *eẕdeham*, crowd; crowding, thronging.

A   ازدواج   *eẕdevaj*, marriage; ازدواج کردن *eẕdevaj k.*, to marry (intrans.).

A   ازدیاد   *eẕdeyad*, increase.

     آزردن   *aẕordan*, to injure, vex, afflict.

A   ازرق   *aẕraq*, blue.

A   ازل   *aẕal*, eternity without beginning.

     آزمایش   *aẕmayeſ*, testing, proving, experiment.

     آزمایشگاه   *aẕmayeſgah*, laboratory.

     آزمودن   *aẕmudan*, to try, prove, experiment.

     اژدر   *eʒdar*, dragon; torpedo.

     اژدرافکن   *eʒdarafkan*, torpedo boat.

     اژدرانداز   *eʒdarandaẕ*, destroyer.

     اژدرشکن   *eʒdarſekan*, cruiser.

A   اساس   *asas*, foundation, basis.

A	اساسًا	*asasan*, fundamentally, basically, in essence.
AP	اساسنامه	*asasname*, charter.
A	اساسى	*asasi*, fundamental, essential.
	آسان	*asan*, easy.
	آسانى	*asani*, being easy, easiness.
	آسايش	*asayeʃ*, ease, comfort.
	آسايشگاه	*asayeʃgah*, sanatorium.
	اسب	*asb*, horse.
A	اسباب	*asbab* (pl. of سبب *sabab*), causes; instruments, belongings, effects; اسباب زحمت شدن *asbabe ẓahmat ʃodan*, to be a nuisance.
	اسبه	*asbe*: دو اسبه *do asbe*, two horse-power.
	اسپانيا	*espania*, Spain.
	استاد	*ostad*, master; professor; master craftsman.
	استان	*ostan*, governorate-general.
	استاندار	*ostandar*, governor-general.
	استاندارى	*ostandari*, offices of a governor-general.
A	استبداد	*estebdad*, despotism, absolute authority.
A	استبدادى	*estebdadi*, despotic, absolute (of government, etc.).
A	استثمار	*estesmar*, exploitation.
A	استثناء	*estesna*, exception; (باستثنا(ى) *be estesna(ye)*, by way of exception, except.
A	استحكام	*estehkam*, firmness, strength.
A	استحكامات	*estehkamat*, fortifications.
A	استخاره	*estexare*, seeking for an augury in the Qorʻan or Hafez.
A	استخدام	*estexdam*, taking into one's service.
	استخوان	*ostoxan*, bone.
	استخوان‌بندى	*ostoxanbandi*, skeleton.
A	استدعا	*estedʻa*, asking, beseeching, supplication.
A	استراحت	*esterahat*, rest, repose.
A	استطاعت	*esteta'at*, being capable (of doing something); having the power (to do something).
A	استعداد	*esteʻdad*, ability.
A	استعفا	*esteʻfa*, resignation (from a post, etc.).
A	استعمار	*esteʻmar*, colonization; imperialism.

A   استعماری   *este'mari*, colonial; imperialistic.

A   استعمال   *este'mal*, use.

A   استغفار   *esteɣfar*, asking pardon, forgiveness.

A   استغفر الله   *astaɣfer ollah*, God forbid (*lit.* I ask pardon of God).

A   استفاده   *estefade*, benefit, advantage; استفاده کردن *estefade k.*, to benefit.

A   استفراغ   *estefraɣ*, vomiting.

A   استقبال   *esteqbal*, going out to meet (someone).

A   استقرار   *esteqrar*, being established.

R   استکان   *estekan*, cup, tea-cup.

A   استمداد   *estemdad*, asking help.

A   استنطاق   *estentaq*, interrogation, judicial examination.

A   استوا   *esteva*: خط استوا *xatti esteva*, equator.

   استوار   *ostovar*, firm, stable; sergeant-major.

   استوارنامه   *ostovarname*, credentials (of an ambassador, etc.).

A   استئصال (استیصال)   *estisal*, extermination.

A   استیضاح   *estiʒah*, interpellation.

A   استیلاء   *estila*, conquest.

A   استئناف (استیناف)   *estinaf*, appeal, appellation; دیوان استئناف *divane estinaf*, court of appeal.

A   اسراف   *esraf*, waste, extravagance, prodigality.

A   اسعار   *as'ar*, prices (rates of exchange, etc.).

F   اسفالته   *asfalte*, asphalted.

   اسفند   *esfand*, rue; twelfth month of the Persian solar year.

F   اسکله   *eskele*, pier, quay, jetty.

F   اسکناس   *eskenas*, bank-note.

A   اسلام   *eslam*, Islam; اسلامی *eslami*, Islamic.

A   اسلوب   *oslub*, style (literary, etc.).

A   اسم   *esm*, name; اسم گذاشتن *esm goʒaʃtan*, to name; اسم بردن *esm bordan*, to mention (by name).

   آسمان   *asman*, sky.

AP   اسم‌نویسی   *esmnevisi*, registration; اسم‌نویسی کردن *esmnevisi k.*, to register.

   آسودن   *asudan*, to rest, be refreshed.

   آسیا   *asia*, Asia; آسیائی *asiai*, Asiatic; an Asiatic.

آسیاب   *asiab*, water-mill.

آسیابان   *asiaban*, miller.

آسیب   *asib*, damage, loss, injury; آسیب دیدن *asib didan*, to suffer loss, damage.

A   اسیر   *asir*, captive, prisoner; اسیر گرفتن (کردن) *asir gereftan* (*k.*), to take captive.

آش   *aʃ*, stew, gruel, pottage.

A   اشارت   *eʃarat*, sign, signal.

A   اشاره   *eʃare*, allusion, hint; sign; اشاره کردن *eʃare k.*, to point; to give a sign.

آشپز   *aʃpaʒ*, cook; آشپزخانه *aʃpaʒxane*, kitchen.

A   اشتباه   *eʃtebah*, mistake; باشتباه *be eʃtebah*, in error.

A   اشتراك   *eʃterak*, partnership; participation; بهای اشتراك *bahaye eʃterak*, cost of subscription.

A   اشتغال   *eʃteɣal*, being occupied (in), occupation.

A   اشتها   *eʃteha*, appetite.

آشتی   *aʃti*, peace.

A   اشجار   *aʃjar* (pl. of شجر *ʃajar*), trees.

A   اشراف   *aʃraf* (pl. of شریف *ʃarif*), nobles.

A   اشرافی   *aʃrafi*, aristocratic.

A   اشغال   *eʃɣal*, occupying, occupation (of a country, etc.).

آشفتگی   *aʃoftegi*, perturbation, agitation, consternation.

آشفتن   *aʃoftan*, to agitate, disturb.

اشکوبه   *oʃkube*, storey.

آشنا   *aʃna*, acquainted; an acquaintance.

آشنائی   *aʃnai*, acquaintance, being acquainted.

A   اصرار   *esrar*, importunity; insistence; اصرار کردن *esrar k.*, to be importunate; to insist.

A   اصطلاح   *estelah*, expression, idiom.

A   اصل   *asl*, foundation, origin; principle.

A   اصلاً   *aslan*, in origin, fundamentally; (with negative verb), not at all, never.

A   اصلاح   *eslah*, reform; correction; اصلاح کردن *eslah k.*, to reform, correct, put right, adjust; to shave, have a haircut.

A   اصلی   *asli*, radical, original, essential, principal; real, true.

A	اصول	*osul* (pl. of اصل *asl*), principles, origins, etc.
A	اضافه	*eẓafe*, addition, adding, joining.
A	اضافی	*eẓafi*, extra.
A	اضطراب	*eẓterab*, agitation, consternation, commotion, anxiety.
T	اطاق	*otaq*, room.
A	اطراف	*atraf* (pl. of طرف *taraf*), sides; در اطراف *dar atraf(e)* concerning.
A	اطلاع	*ettela'*, information.
A	اطمینان	*etminan*, assurance, confidence.
A	اظهار	*eẓhar*, expressing (an opinion, etc.); statement.
A	اعتبار	*e'tebar*, confidence, trust; credit; authority, validity.
AP	اعتبارنامه	*e'tebarname*, credentials (of a deputy of the National Assembly, etc.).
A	اعتدال	*e'tedal*, moderation; temperance; equilibrium.
A	اعتراض	*e'teraẓ*, protest.
A	اعتصاب	*e'tesab*, strike, refusal to work.
A	اعتماد	*e'temad*, trust, reliance.
AP	اعتماد بنفس	*e'temad be nafs*, self-reliance.
A	اعتنا	*e'tena*, taking pains, care, attention.
A	اعلام	*e'lam*, notifying, announcing, notification, announcement.
AP	اعلام خطر	*e'lame xatar*, warning (of danger), alarm.
A	اعلامیه	*e'lamiye*, communiqué; manifesto; announcement.
A	اعلان	*e'lan*, declaration, announcement.
A	اعمال	*e'mal*, causing to act or operate; *a'mal* (pl. of عمل *amal*), actions, deeds.
AP	اعمال نظر	*e'male naẓar*, exerting undue pressure, imposing one's view; showing partiality.
AP	اعمال نفوذ	*e'male nofuẓ*, exerting (undue) influence, bringing (undue) influence to bear.
A	اعنی	*a'ni*, I mean; namely.
A	اعوذ بالله	*a'uẓo bellah*, I take refuge in God, God forbid.
A	اعیان	*a'yan* (pl. of عین *āin*), nobles, great men.
	آغاز	*aɣaẓ*, beginning.
A	اغتشاش	*eɣtefaf*, disturbance, disorder.

A	اغراق	*eɣraq*, exaggeration.
	آغشتن	*aɣeſtan*, to steep in blood.
A	اغلب	*aɣlab*, most, mostly.
A	اغنام	*aɣnam* (pl. of غنم *ɣanam*), flocks; sheep and goats.
A	آفت	*afat*, pest; calamity.
	آفتاب	*aftab*, the sun.
	آفتابه	*aftabe*, water-pot, ewer.
	افتادن	*oftadan*, to fall.
A	افتتاح	*eftetah*, opening, being opened.
A	افتخار	*eftexar*, glory, honour.
A	افتراء	*eftera'*, calumny, unjust imputation.
	افراختن	*afraxtan*, to raise.
A	افراد	*afrad* (pl. of فرد *fard*), individuals.
	افراشتن	*afraſtan*, to raise.
A	افراط	*efrat*, excess, exceeding bounds.
A	افراطی	*efrati*, extreme; an extremist.
	افروختن	*afruxtan*, to kindle, set alight; to blaze.
	آفریدگار	*afaridegar*, the Creator.
	آفریدن	*afaridan*, to create.
	آفرین	*afarin*, applause; bravo.
A	افزار	*afʒar*, tool, implement.
	افزودن	*afʒudan*, to increase (trans. and intrans.).
	افزون	*afʒun*, increasing.
	افسانه	*afsane*, tale, fable.
	افسر	*afsar*, army officer; crown.
	افسردن	*afsordan*, to congeal; to grow dejected; to wither.
	افسوس	*afsus*, ah! alas!; افسوس خوردن *afsus xordan*, to regret.
	افسون	*afsun*, spell.
	افشردن	*afſordan*, to press, squeeze.
A	افطار	*eftar*, breaking the fast (at sunset in Ramazan).
A	افق	*ofoq*, horizon.
A	افکار	*afkar* (pl. of فكر *fekr*), thoughts; افکار عموم *afkare omum*, public opinion.
	افکندن	*afkandan*, to throw (down, away).
T	آقا	*aqa*, sir; master.

A اقامت *eqamat*, sojourn, stay.

A اقتباس *eqtebas*, borrowing, adapting; quotation.

A اقتصاد *eqtesad*, economy, economic affairs.

A اقتصادی *eqtesadi*, economic, pertaining to economic affairs.

Aاقتصادیات *eqtesadiat*, economy, economic affairs.

A اقتضاء *eqteẕa*, demanding, exacting; exigency.

A اقدام *eqdam*, measure, step, action; اقدام کردن *eqdam k.*, to take action.

A اقساط *aqsat* (pl. of قسط), instalments.

A اقسام *aqsam* (pl. of قسم *qesm*), sorts, kinds.

A اقل *aqall*, less, least.

A اقلاً *aqallan*, at least.

A اقلیت *aqalliyat*, minority.

A اقوام *aqvam* (pl. of قوم *qoūm*), peoples; relatives.

A اکابر *akaber* (pl. of کبیر *kabir*), great men; adults who attend classes to acquire literacy.

A اکاذیب *akaẕib*, lies, falsehoods; نشر اکاذیب *naſre akaẕib*, libel, the publication of libel.

A اکبر *akbar*, greatest.

A اکتشاف *ekteſaf*, discovery; reconnaissance.

A اکثریت *aksariyat*, majority.

اکنون *aknun*, now.

A اکید *akid*, strict, severe.

A اکیداً *akidan*, strictly.

آگاه *agah*, aware.

آگاهی *agahi*, awareness; secret police; آگاهی داشتن *agahi d.*, to be aware of, have information of.

اگر *agar*, if; اگرچه *agarce*, although.

آگندن *agandan*, to fill, stuff.

آگهی *agahi*, advertisement.

آل *al*, family, house.

A ال *al*, the (the definite article in Arabic).

A الا *ella*, unless, except; والا *va ella*, and if not, otherwise.

A الآن *alan*, now, immediately.

الاغ *olaɣ*, donkey, ass.

A البته *albatte*, certainly, of course.

A آلت *alat*, instrument, tool; آلت دست *alate dast*, puppet (fig.).

A التفات *eltefat*, favour, kindness; التفات کردن *eltefat k.*, to show kindness (to someone), confer favour (on someone).

A التماس *eltemas*, beseeching, petitioning, prayer, petition.

A الحق *al-haqq*, in truth, truly.

A الساعة *as-saʻe, as-saʻat*, immediately, this minute.

A الغاء *elɣa*, abrogation, cancellation.

A الف *alef*, first letter of Arabic alphabet.

A الفاظ *alfaẓ* (pl. of لفظ *lafẓ*), words.

A الله *allah*, God; ان شاء الله *en ʃa allah*, if God wills; ما شاء الله *ma ʃa allah*, what God wills.

الماس *almas*, diamond.

F آلمان *alman*, Germany.

آلو *alu*, plum.

آلوبالو *alubalu*, morello cherry.

آلودن *aludan*, to stain, defile.

A الهی *elahi*, divine.

A الی *ela*, to, up to, until; الی آخر *ela axer, ad infinitum*.

A اما *amma*, but.

آمادن *amadan*, to prepare.

آمار *amar*, statistics.

A امام *emam*, one who stands before or is followed, especially in religious matters; one of the twelve *imams* of the house of Ali, Mohammad's son-in-law.

A امانت *amanat*, deposit, anything given in trust.

A امت *ommat*, community, people, nation.

A امتناع *emtenaʻ*, refraining, abstaining, refusing.

A امتنان *emtenan*, conferring a favour; obligation (for a favour received).

A امتیاز *emteyaẓ*, concession; distinction, preference.

AP امتیازنامه *emteyaẓname*, agreement or deed for a concession.

A امثال *amsal* (pl. of مثل *masal*), proverbs; likenesses, resemblances.

آمدن   *amadan*, to come.

آمد و شد   *amad o ſod*, coming and going, traffic.

A   امر   *amr*, matter, affair; order; (in grammar) imperative mood.

A   امراض   *amraʒ* (pl. of مرض *maraʒ*), illnesses; امراض داخلی *amraʒe daxeli*, internal diseases; امراض ساریه *amraʒe sarie*, endemic diseases; امراض عصبی *amraʒe asabi*, nervous diseases; امراض مقاربتی *amraʒe moqarebati*, venereal diseases; امراض مناطق حاره *amraʒe manateqe harre*, tropical diseases; امراض نسوان *amraʒe nesvan*, gynaecological diseases.

امروز   *emruʒ*, to-day.

امریکا   *amrika*, America.

امسال   *emsal*, this year.

امشب   *emſab*, to-night.

A   امکان   *emkan*, possibility; امکان داشتن *emkan d.*, to be possible; بقدر امکان *be qadre emkan*, as far as possible.

AP   امکان پذیر   *emkanpaʒir*, possible.

AP   امکان ناپذیر   *emkannapaʒir*, impossible.

A   امنیت   *amniyat*, security.

A   امنیه   *amniye*, gendarmerie.

آموختن   *amuxtan*, to teach; to learn.

A   امور   *omur* (pl. of امر *amr*), matters, affairs; امور خارجه *omure xareje*, foreign affairs; امور داخله *omure daxele*, internal affairs.

آموزش   *amuʒeſ*, teaching; آموزش و پرورش *amuʒeſ va parvareſ*, education.

آموزشگاه   *amuʒeſgah*, school, educational institution.

آموزگار   *amuʒgar*, teacher in a primary school.

آمیختن   *amixtan*, mix.

امید   *omid*, hope.

امیدوار   *omidvar*, hopeful.

آن   *an*, that; it; آنها *anha*, those; they.

انار   *anar*, pomegranate.

انبار   *ambar*, store, warehouse.

انباردار   *ambardar*, store-keeper.

انباشتن   *ambaʃtan*, to fill.

A   انتخاب   *entexab*, choice, selection; انتخاب کردن *entexab k.*, to choose.

A   انتخابات   *entexabat*, election (political, etc.).

A   انتخابی   *entexabi*, chosen by election (government, etc.).

A   انتشار   *enteʃar*, propagation, diffusion, publication.

A   انتظام   *enteʒam*, order, arrangement.

A   انتظامات   *enteʒamat*, (public) order; discipline.

A   انتقاد   *enteqad*, criticism.

A   انتقادی   *enteqadi*, critical, criticizing, appraising.

آنجا   *anja*, there.

انجام   *anjam*, accomplishment, fulfilment; انجام دادن *anjam dadan*, to fulfil, accomplish; انجام یافتن (شدن) *anjam yaftan (ʃ.)*, to be accomplished.

انجمن   *anjoman*, society, council; انجمن شهرداری *anjomane ʃahrdari*, municipal council.

انجیر   *anjir*, fig.

A   انحراف   *enheraf*, turning away, deviation; انحراف ورزیدن *enheraf varʒidan*, to turn away, deviate.

A   انحصار   *enhesar*, monopoly.

A   انحطاط   *enhetat*, decline, decay.

اند   *and*, odd (of numbers over nineteen), e.g. بیست و اند *bist o and*, twenty odd.

انداختن   *andaxtan*, to throw.

اندازه   *andaʒe*, extent; size; dimension.

اندام   *andam*, body, stature; proportion, symmetry.

اندر   *andar*, in (obsolete).

اندرز   *andarʒ*, advice.

اندرون   *andarun*, within, inside; women's quarters (in a house).

اندك   *andak*, little, few, small.

اندکی   *andaki*, a little; short while.

اندوختن   *anduxtan*, to collect, heap up.

اندوخته   *anduxte*, (monetary) reserve; savings.

اندودن   *andudan*, to plaster, smear.

اندیشه   *andiſe*, thought, reflexion, meditation.

A   انس   *ons*, being intimate, familiarity, friendliness; انس گرفتن *ons gereftan*, to become fond of, friendly with (someone).

A   انساب   *ansab* (pl. of نسب *nasab*), genealogies.

A   انسان   *ensan*, man, mankind.

A   انسانیت   *ensaniyat*, humanity.

A   انشاء   *enſa*, composition, writing, style of writing.

A   انضباط   *enʒebat*, order, systematic arrangement.

A   انضمام   *enʒemam*, being annexed, annex.

A   انعام   *en'am*, gratuity, tip.

A   انعدام   *en'edam*, annihilation.

A   انعكاس   *en'ekas*, reflexion, reaction.

A   انفراد   *enferad*, isolation, seclusion.

AP   انفرادی   *enferadi*, solitude, being alone.

A   انقلاب   *enqelab*, revolution (political, etc.).

A   انقلابی   *enqelabi*, revolutionary; a revolutionary.

A   انکار   *enkar*, denial.

A   انکسار   *enkesar*, being broken.

انگاشتن   *engaſtan*, to think, consider, suppose.

انگشت   *angoſt*, finger.

انگشتانه   *angoſtane*, thimble.

انگشت شمار   *angoſtſomar*, able to be counted on the fingers.

انگل   *angal*, parasite.

انگل شناس   *angalſenas*, parasitologist.

انگل شناسی   *angalſenasi*, parasitology.

انگلستان   *englestan*, England.

انگلك   *angolak*, light touch with the finger; انگلك کردن *angolak k.*, to put one's finger in the pie; to stir up trouble on the sly.

انگلیس   *englis*, England.

انگلیسی   *englisi*, English; Englishman.

انگور   *angur*, grape, grapes.

انگیختن   *angixtan*, to stir up, incite.

A   انواع   *anva'* (pl. of نوع *nōu'*), sorts, kinds.

او   *u*, he, she; (obs.) it.

A	اواخر	avaxer (pl. of آخرت axerat), ends; latter part (of month, year, etc.).
	آواز	avaz, voice.
A	اوباش	ōubaſ, hooligans, ruffians.
	آوردن	avardan, avordan, to bring.
A	اوضاع	ōuza' (pl. of وضع vaz'), conditions, states; condition or state of affairs.
A	اوقات	ōuqat (pl. of وقت vaqt), times.
AP	اوقات تلخی	ōuqate talxi, crossness, bad temper.
A	اول	avval, first.
A	اولاً	avvalan, first, in the first place.
A	اولاد	ōulad (pl. of ولد valad), children.
A	اولو	ulu (used as plural of ذو zu), in compounds = lords, masters, possessors of; اولو الامر ulol-amr, those in authority; اولو الالباب ulol-albab, prudent, intelligent.
A	اولی	uli fem. of اولو; ula (fem. of اول avval), first; oula, worthier, fitter.
AP	اولین	avvalin, first.
	آویختن	avixtan, to hang (trans. and intrans.).
	آویزان	avizan, hanging (adj.).
	آه	ah, sigh; آه کشیدن ah kaſidan, to sigh.
A	اهالی	ahali (pl. of اهل ahl), peoples.
A	اهتزاز	ehtezaz, fluttering (subs.); exultation, joy.
A	اهتمام	ehtemam, care, diligence.
	آهختن	ahextan, to unsheathe, draw (a sword, etc.).
	آهسته	aheste, quietly, silently, slowly, by degrees.
	آهك	ahak, lime.
A	اهل	ahl, people; ahl(e), possessed of, e.g. اهل فن ahle fann, an expert, technician; capable of; اهل این کار نیست ahle in kar nist, he is not capable of this, he is not one to do such a thing; اهل اصفهان است ahle esfahan ast, he belongs to (comes from) Isfahan.
A	اهمیت	ahammiyat, importance.
	آهن	ahan, iron.
	آهنگ	ahang, harmony, melody.

آهنگر   *ahangar*, ironsmith.

آهو   *ahu*, gazelle.

آیا   *aya*, particle used to introduce a question; whether; یا ... آیا *aya...ya*, whether...or.

A ائتلاف   *e'telaf*, coalition.

A ایجاد   *ijad*, creating, creation.

A ایراد   *irad*, criticism, complaint, objection; ایراد گرفتن *irad gereftan*, to criticize; نطق ایراد کردن *notq irad k.*, to make a speech.

ایران   *iran*, Persia.

ایرانی   *irani*, Persian (of Persia); a Persian.

ایستادن   *istadan*, to stand, stop (intrans.).

ایستگاه   *istgah*, station.

ایشان   *iʃan*, they.

ایطالیا   *italia*, Italy.

ایطالیائی   *italiai*, Italian; an Italian.

T ایل   *il*, tribe.

T ایلات   *ilat*, tribes.

TP ایلی   *ili*, tribal; tribesman.

A ایمان   *iman*, faith, belief; (به) ایمان آوردن *iman avardan* (*be*), to come to believe (in); (به) ایمان داشتن *iman d.* (*be*), to believe (in).

این   *in*, this.

اینجا   *inja*, here.

آینده   *ayande*, future, coming; the future.

ایوان   *eivan*, porch, balcony.

آئین (آیین)   *ain*, custom, usage; ceremony.

آئین نامه (آیین نامه)   *ainname*, rules of procedure.

ب

با   *ba*, with; با اینکه *ba inke*, notwithstanding, although; با وجودیکه *ba vojudike*, although; باهم *ba ham*, together.

A باب   *bab*, chapter; affair, matter; *dar bab*(*e*), concerning, about.

A بابت   *babat*, item; *babat*(*e*), for, on account of; از بابت *az babat*(*e*), for, on account of; در بابت *dar babat*(*e*), concerning.

T باتلاق   *botlaq, batlaq*, swamp, marsh.

باج   *baj*, tribute, toll.

باجه   *baje*, ticket-office.

T   باجی   *baji*, sister; woman.

باختر   *baxtar*, west; western.

باختن   *baxtan*, to lose (a wager, game, etc.).

باد   *bad*, wind; swelling; باد کردن *bad k.*, to swell (trans. and intrans.).

بادام   *badam*, almond.

بادگیر   *badgir*, cowl of a chimney.

بادنجان   *badenjan*, egg-plant.

بار   *bar*, load; levée; fruit; یك بار *yak bar*, once; دو بار *do bar*, twice; بار آوردن *bar avardan*, to bear fruit; to bring up.

باران   *baran*, rain; باران آمدن *baran amadan*, to rain.

A   بارز   *bareʒ*, clear, evident.

A   بارك الله   *barak allah*, May God bless (you); bravo.

بارکش   *barkaʃ*, carrying loads; freighter.

بارکشی   *barkaʃi*, the carrying of loads; transport.

بارگیری   *bargiri*, haulage capacity; loading (subs.).

بارنامه   *barname*, bill of lading.

بارندگی   *barandegi*, rain.

باروت   *barut*, gunpowder.

باره   *bare*: در باره *dar bare(ye)*, about, concerning.

باری   *bari*: ماشین باری *maʃine bari*, lorry.

باری   *bari*, in short, however.

باریدن   *baridan*, to rain.

باریك   *barik*, narrow; critical (of moment, time, etc.).

باز   *baʒ*, open; again; still; yet; باز آمدن *baʒ amadan*, to come back again, return; باز کردن *baʒ k.*, to open.

بازار   *baʒar*, bazaar, market.

بازارگان   *baʒargan*, merchant.

بازارگانی   *baʒargani*, trade, commerce.

بازبین   *baʒbin*, controller.

بازپرس   *baʒpors*, inspector.

بازپرسی   *baʒporsi*, enquiry; investigation; calling to account.

بازجو   *baʒju*, inspector; one who conducts an enquiry.

بازجوئی *baẓjui*, enquiry, investigation.

بازخواست *baẓxast*, calling to account; judgement; investigation.

بازداشت *baẓdaſt*, arrest, internment.

بازداشتگاه *baẓdaſtgah*, internment camp.

باز داشتن *baẓ daſtan*, to arrest, intern.

بازدید *baẓdid*, control; re-examination (of accounts, etc.); return visit.

بازرس *baẓras*, inspector.

بازرسی *baẓrasi*, inspecting, examining, checking (subs.).

بازرگان *baẓargan*, merchant.

بازرگانی *baẓargani*, trade.

باز نشستگی *baẓneſastegi*, retirement.

باز نشسته *baẓneſaste*, retired; pensioned off.

بازو *baẓu*, forearm.

بازه *baẓe*, wing-spread (of an aeroplane).

بازی *baẓi*, game; toy; بازی کردن بازی درآوردن *baẓi k.*, to play; *baẓi dar avardan*, to 'try on' (see how much will be tolerated).

بازیچه *baẓice*, sport, toy.

باستان *bastan*, ancient.

باستان شناس *bastanſenas*, archaeologist.

باستان شناسی *bastanſenasi*, archaeology.

باستانی *bastani*, ancient.

با سواد *basavad*, literate.   PA

باشگاه *baſgah*, club (social).

با صفا *basafa*, pleasant, agreeable (of a place, etc.).   PA

باطل *batel*, null, void.   A

باطلاق *botlaq, batlaq*, swamp, marsh.   T

باعث *ba'es*, cause.   A

باغ *baɣ*, garden.

باغبان *baɣban*, gardener.

بافت *baft*, weave, texture.

بافندگی *bafandegi*, weaving (subs.).

با فهم *bafahm*, intelligent.   PA

باقلا *baqela*, broad bean.   A

A	باق	*baqi*, remaining, left; remainder; باق ماندن *baqi mandan*, to remain, be left over.
	باك	*bak*, dread, fear.
	بال	*bal*, wing.
	بالا	*bala*, up, upper; above; upper part (of something).
A	بالاخره	*bel-axere*, finally.
A	بالطبع	*bet-tab'*, naturally.
A	بالله	*bellah*, by God.
	بام	*bam*, roof.
	بامداد	*bamdad*, the morrow; in the morning.
	بام غلتان	*bamɣaltan*, kind of stone roller used to roll mud roofs.
F	بانك	*bank*, bank (monetary).
	بانو	*banu*, lady.
	باور	*bavar*, belief; باور كردن *bavar k.*, to credit, believe.
	باید	*bayad*, (impers. verb) must, ought.
	بایستن	*bayestan*, to be necessary (this verb is defective).
	بایگان	*bayagan*, archivist.
	بایگانی	*bayagani*, archives.
	ببر	*babr*, tiger.
	بت	*bot*, idol.
	بتپرست	*botparast*, idolater.
	بچگانه	*baccegane, bacegane*, childish, childishly.
	بچگی	*baccegi, bacegi*, childhood.
	بچه	*bacce, bace*, child.
A	بحث	*bahs*, debate, discussion, argument.
A	بحر	*bahr*, sea; بحر خزر *bahre xaɣar*, the Caspian Sea.
A	بحران	*bohran*, crisis.
A	بخار	*boxar*, steam.
AP	بخاری	*boxari*, chimney; fireplace.
	بخت	*baxt*, luck, fortune.
	بختیار	*baxtyar*, fortunate.
	بخش	*baxʃ*, portion; administrative district smaller than a governorate; squadron (naval).
	بخشدار	*baxʃdar*, official in charge of a *baxʃ* (district).

بخشدارى   *baxʃdari*, offices of a *baxʃdar*.

بخشش   *baxʃeʃ*, gift, present, tip.

بخشنامه   *baxʃname*, official circular.

بخشودگى   *baxʃudegi*, pardon; exemption.

بخشودن   *baxʃudan*, to grant, bestow.

بخشوده   *baxʃude*, excused, exempted.

بخشيدن   *baxʃidan*, to forgive, give, grant; to forgo.

بد   *bad*, bad; (با) بد بودن *bad budan* (*ba*), to be on bad terms (with someone).

A   بدل   *badal*, change, substitution, alteration; substitute.

بدنه   *badane*, body (of an aeroplane, etc.), hull (of a ship).

A   بدوًا   *badvan*, in the beginning.

A   بدون   *bedun(e)*, without (prep.).

بدهكار   *bedehkar*, debtor.

بدهى   *bedehi*, debt (in money).

بدى   *badi*, badness, evil.

A   بديع   *badi'*, wonderful, astonishing, strange; علم بديع *elme badi'*, rhetoric.

A   بذل   *baẕl*, giving, expending (subs.).

بر   *bar*, breast, bosom; fruit, produce; on; up, upon; in, into; at; against; بررو(ى) *bar ru(ye)*, on; بر سر *bar sar(e)*, at; against; بر عليه *bar aleıh(e)*, against; بر آن بودن *bar an b.*, to be determined upon, agreed upon; در بر داشتن *dar bar d.*, to wear, be clothed in; to embrace, include.

برابر   *barabar*, opposite; equal.

برابرى   *barabari*, being opposite; parity.

برات   *barat*, draft, cheque; bill of exchange.

براتكش   *baratkaʃ*, drawer (of a cheque, etc.).

براتگير   *baratgir*, payee (of a cheque, etc.).

برادر   *baradar*, brother.

برادر زاده   *baradarʒade*, nephew, niece (brother's child).

بر آشفتن   *bar aʃoftan*, to agitate; to stir up.

بر افراشتن   *bar afraʃtan*, to raise aloft.

بر آمدن   *bar amadan*, to come out; to swell; از او بر نميايد *aʒ u ba namiayad*, he cannot do it, it is beyond his powers.

بر انداختن   *bar andaxtan*, to overthrow.

بر انگيختن   *bar angixtan*, to incite, stir up.

بر آورد   *baravard*, evaluation, estimate; بر آورد كردن *baravard k.*, to evaluate, make an estimate.

بر آوردن   *bar avardan*, to accomplish.

براى   *baraye*, for, on account of.

برايگان   *berayegan*, free, gratis.

برتر   *bartar*, superior.

برترى   *bartari*, superiority.

A   برج   *borj*, tower; sign of the zodiac.

برجسته   *barjaste*, (adj.) outstanding; projecting.

بر خاستن   *bar xastan*, to rise, get up.

بر خوردار(از)   *bar xordar(az)*, (adj.) possessing; enjoying (something).

بر خوردن   *bar xordan*, to meet, come across; to offend.

برخى   *barxi*, some, a few.

بر داشت   *bardaft*, amount of money, or share, taken by a partner out of the earnings or produce; deduction (in banking, etc.).

بر داشتن   *bar daftan*, to take off, away; to gather (the harvest, etc.).

بردن   *bordan*, to carry off, away; to take; to carry.

بر رسى   *barrasi*, revision; investigation.

برزگر   *barzegar*, agricultural labourer.

برزن   *barzan*, ward (municipal division), district.

برش   *boref*, cutting (subs.); cutting out, cut (in dressmaking); coupon.

برشته   *berefte*, grilled, toasted.

PA   بر عليه   *bar aleih(e)*, against.

برف   *barf*, snow; برف آمدن (باريدن) *barf amadan (baridan)*, to snow.

A   برق   *barq*, lightning; electricity.

PA   بر قرار   *bar qarar*, established, set up.

A   بركت   *barakat*, blessing.

بر كندن   *bar kandan*, to take off (a coat, etc.); to uproot.

برگ   *barg*, leaf; equipment.

بر گزيدن   *bar gozidan*, to choose, select.

برگشت   *bargaft*, return; retrocession, retrogression.

برگشت پذير   *bargaftpazir*, revocable (of a bill, etc.).

برگشتن   *bar gaſtan*, to return.

PA   بر له   *bar lah(e)*, for, in favour of.

بر نامه   *barname*, programme.

برنج   *berenj*, rice; brass.

برنجی   *berenji*, brazen, made of brass.

A   بروز   *boruʒ*, making public or manifest; بروز دادن *boruʒ dadan*, to make public, manifest.

برهنه   *barahne*, bare, naked.

بریدن   *boridan*, to cut.

برین   *barin*, upper.

بز   *boʒ*, goat.

A   بزاز   *baʒʒaʒ*, draper, dealer in cloth.

بزرك   *baʒrak*, linseed.

بزرگ   *boʒorg*, large, big; great.

بزرگمنش   *boʒorgmaneſ*, worthy of, or after the fashion of, a great man.

بزرگوار   *boʒorgvar*, noble, great, illustrious.

بزه   *beʒeh*, sin, crime.

بزهکار   *beʒehkar*, sinful.

بس   *bas*, enough; often; از بس که *aʒ bas ke*, to such a degree that.

A   بساط   *basat*, carpet, anything spread out; paraphernalia.

بست   *bast*, asylum, sanctuary.

بستانکار   *bestankar*, creditor.

بستر   *bestar*, bed.

بستری   *bestari*, confined to bed.

بستن   *bastan*, to bind, tie; to shut.

بستنی   *bastani*, ice-cream.

بسته   *baste*, parcel, package; shut; bound, tied.

A   بسط   *bast*, extent, stretching out; expansion, development.

A   بسم الله   *besmellah*, in the name of God.

بسی   *basi*, much, many a.

بسیار   *besyar*, many; very.

بسیاری   *besyari*, abundance; excessiveness.

بسیج   *basij*, mobilization; بسیج عمومی *basije omumi*, general mobilization.

A	بشاش	*baʃʃaʃ*, cheerful.
A	بشر	*baʃar*, man, human species.
A	بضاعت	*baẓaʿat*, merchandise, goods.
A	بعد	*baʿd*, then (adv.); after, afterwards (adv.); بعد از *baʿd az*, after (prep.); بعد از آنکه *baʿd az anke*, after (conj.).
A	بعدًا	*baʿdan*, afterwards.
AP	بعضى	*baʿẓi*, some.
A	بعيد	*baʿid*, distant, far, remote.
A	بغتةً	*baɣtatan*, suddenly.
A	بقال	*baqqal*, kind of greengrocer.
A	بقيه	*baqiye*, remainder, rest.
A	بكر	*bekr*, virgin; first-fruit; original (adj.).
A	بل	*bal*, but; nay, no, on the contrary.
A	بلا	*bala*, calamity.
A	بلا	*bela*, without (prep.).
A	بلا ترديد	*bela tardid*, without doubt.
A	بلاد	*belad* (pl. of بلد *balad*), countries, regions, cities.
A	بلاشرط	*bela ʃart*, unconditionally.
A	بلاغت	*balaɣat*, eloquence.
A	بلافاصله	*bela fasele*, without interruption, immediately.
	بلبل	*bolbol*, nightingale.
A	بلدان	*boldan* (pl. of بلد *balad*), cities, countries.
AP	بلکه	*balke*, but, nay rather; perhaps.
	بلند	*boland*, high, tall; بلند شدن *boland ʃ.*, to rise, get up; بلند کردن *boland k.*, to lift, raise; (colloq.) to steal.
	بلند قد	*bolandqadd*, tall (of stature).
A	بلور	*bolur*, crystal; cut glass.
AP	بلور شناس	*bolurʃenas*, crystallographer.
AP	بلور شناسى	*bolurʃenasi*, crystallography.
A	بلوط	*balut*, acorn; درخت بلوط *daraxte balut*, oak-tree.
A	بلوغ	*boluɣ*, puberty, maturity.
A	بله	*bale*, yes.
A	بلى	*bali*, yes.
A	بليه	*baliye*, calamity.

F بمب   *bomb*, bomb; بمب افكن *bombafkan*, bomber aeroplane.

بمباران   *bombaran*, bombardment.

A بنا   *bana*, building, edifice; بنا بر *bana bar*, because of, in accordance with; بنا بر اين (آن) *bana bar in (an)*, accordingly; بنا بودن (شدن) (به) *bana b.(ʃ) (be)*, to be decided, resolved (upon); بنا كردن *bana k.*, to build; *bannā*, builder.

بنبست   *bombast*: كوچه بنبست *kuceye bombast*, cul-de-sac.

بند   *band*, tie, band; joint; section, paragraph (of an official document); dam.

بندر   *bandar*, port.

بنده   *bande*, slave; I (used for من *man*, I).

بنفش   *banaʃʃ*, violet-colour.

بنفشه   *banaʃʃe*, violet-colour; pansy.

بنكدار   *bonakdar*, wholesale dealer.

بنگاه   *bongah*, organization, company.

بنه   *bone*, belongings, goods, baggage; basis, foundation.

A بنى   *bani* (oblique pl. of ابن *ebn*), sons (used in compounds such as بنى آدم *bani adam*, the sons of Adam, mankind).

بنياد   *bonyad*, basis, foundation.

A بنيه   *bonye*, constitution, health.

بو   *bu*, smell, odour; بو كردن *bu k.*, to smell (trans.).

بوته   *bote*, plant, bush.

F بودجه   *budje*, budget.

بودن   *budan*, to be, exist.

بوس   *bus*, kiss.

بوسيدن   *busidan*, to kiss.

A بوقلمون   *buqalamun*, turkey; chameleon.

AP بوقلمونى   *buqalamuni*, variegated, of various hues.

بوم   *bum*, country, region.

A بوم   *bum*, owl.

بومى   *bumi*, native.

بوى   *būi*, smell, odour.

به   *be*, to; for; on; by; with; according to.

بها   *baha*, price.

بهار   *bahar*, spring (of the year).

بهبود   *behbud*, recovery; improvement.

بهداری   *behdari*, public health; وزارت بهداری *vezarate behdari*, Ministry of Health.

بهداشت   *behdaſt*, public health, hygiene.

بهر   *bahr*, part, portion; از بهر این *az bahre in*, on this account.

بهره   *bahre*, part, portion.

بهشت   *beheſt*, paradise.

بهل   *behel*, quittance (in banking).

بهمن   *bahman*, eleventh month of the Persian solar year; avalanche.

بی   *bi*, without (prep.).

بیابان   *biaban*, desert.

PA بی اعتنا   *bie'tena*, careless, negligent.

PA بی اعتنائی   *bie'tena'i*, carelessness, negligence; lack of attention.

A بیان   *bayan*, explanation, description; declaration, assertion; معانی بیان *ma'aniye bayan*, rhetoric, theory of literary style.

بی اندازه   *biandaze*, extremely.

بی برگشت   *bibargaſt*, irrevocable (of credit in banking).

A بیت   *beit*, couplet; house.

PA بی تعارف   *bita'arof*, without ceremony.

A بیتوته   *beitute*, passing the night (noun).

بیچاره   *bicare*, without remedy; helpless, destitute.

بیختن   *bixtan*, to sift.

بی خود   *bixod*, unnecessarily; in vain; unwarranted.

بید   *bid*, willow; clothes-moth.

بیدار   *bidar*, awake; بیدار کردن *bidar k.*, to wake (trans.).

بیداری   *bidari*, being awake, wakefulness.

PA بید مجنون   *bide majnun*, weeping willow.

بید مشک   *bidmeſk*, Egyptian willow.

T بیرق   *beiraq*, flag, standard.

بیرون   *birun*, out, outside; بیرون کردن *birun k.*, to turn out, expel.

بیست   *bist*, twenty.

بی سیم   *bisim*, wireless.

بیشتر *biʃtar*, بیش *biʃ*, more.

بی‌شمار *biʃomar*, innumerable.

بیشه *biʃe*, plantation, wood.

PA بی صفا *bisafa*, unpleasant, disagreeable (of a place, etc.).

PA بی فهم *bifahm*, stupid, lacking in intelligence.

بی کس *bikas*, friendless.

بیگانه *bigane*, foreigner.

بیل *bil*, spade; بیل زدن *bil ʒadan*, to dig.

بیم *bim*, fear.

بیمار *bimar*, sick; بیمارستان *bimarestan*, hospital.

بیماری *bimari*, sickness, illness.

بیمه *bime*, insurance.

A بین *bein(e)*, between, among; از بین رفتن *aʒ bein raftan*, to disappear, be destroyed; در بین *dar bein(e)*, between, among.

A بین المللی *bein ol-melali*, international.

بی‌نام *binam*, nameless, anonymous; شرکت بینام *ʃerkate binam*, joint-stock company.

بینوا *binava*, destitute, poor.

PA بی نهایت *binehayat*, extremely.

بینی *bini*, nose.

بیوه *bive*, widow.

بیهوده *bihude*, vain, futile, useless.

بیهوش *bihuʃ*, unconscious; unintelligent, witless.

پ

پا *pa*, foot, leg; پا(ی) *pa(ye)*, at the foot (of).

پاداش *padaʃ*, reward.

پادشاه *padeʃah*, sovereign.

پادشاهی *padeʃahi*, sovereignty.

پادگان *padegan*, garrison.

پادو *padou*, out-runner; jackal (fig.).

پارچه *parce*, cloth, material; piece, segment; also used in counting villages, e.g. سه پارچه ده *se parce deh*, three villages.

پارس   *pars*, bark (of a dog); پارس دادن *pars dadan*, to bark.

پارسا   *parsa*, pure, chaste, devout, pious.

پارسال   *parsal*, last year.

F   پارکه   *parke*, court (legal).

پارو   *paru*, kind of wooden spade; oar; پارو زدن *paru ẕadan*, to row; پارو کردن *paru k.*, to clear away snow (with a wooden spade).

پاس   *pas*, watch (of the day or night); regard, consideration; پاس دادن *pas dadan*, to be on guard, keep watch.

پاسبان   *pasban*, policeman.

پاسدار   *pasdar*, watchman, guard.

پاسگاه   *pasgah*, police post.

پاسیار   *pasyar*, police officer equivalent in rank to an army colonel.

پاشیدن   *paʃidan*, to scatter; to sow.

پاك   *pak*, pure; clean.

پاکار   *pakar*, official who supervises the distribution of water in villages, or is responsible for the protection of the villagers' fields against theft, etc. (the use of the term varies from place to place).

F   پاکت   *pakat*, envelope.

پاکی   *paki*, cleanliness, purity.

پاکیزه   *pakiẕe*, clean; pure; innocent.

F   پالتو   *paltōu*, overcoat.

پالایش   *palayeʃ*, refining.

پالایشگاه   *palayeʃgah*, refinery.

پالودن   *paludan*, to filter, strain.

پانزده   *panẕdah*, fifteen.

پانصد   *pansad*, five hundred.

پایاپای   *payapāi*: قرارداد پایاپای *qarardade payapāi*, barter agreement.

پایان   *payan*, end.

پایمزد   *pāimoẕd*, visiting fee (of a doctor, etc.).

پایه   *paye*, step of a stair; rank, degree; basis, foundation.

پایتخت   *pāitaxt*, capital city.

پائیز   *paiẕ*, autumn.

پائین   *pain*, lower; lower part; down.

پتو   *patu*, blanket.

پختگی   *poxtegi*, being mature; maturity.

پختن   *poxtan*, to cook.

پخته   *poxte*, cooked; mature (of a person).

پخش   *paxʃ*, distribution; diffusion.

پدر   *pedar*, father; پدر زن *pedarʒan*, (husband's) father-in-law.

پدیدار   *padidar*, پدید *padid*, manifest, in sight, visible.

پذیرائی   *paʒirai*, entertaining, welcoming (someone, subs.); پذیرائی کردن (از) *paʒirai k.* (*aʒ*), to entertain (someone).

پذیرفتن   *paʒiroftan*, to accept, receive; to assent to.

پر   *par*, wing; petal; *por*, full!; (used as an adverb), very.

پراکندن   *parakandan*, to disperse, scatter, disband (intrans.).

پرت   *part*: پرت شدن *part ʃ.*, to be off the subject, irrelevant (of a discourse, etc.); پرت کردن *part k.*, to throw; حواس او پرت است *havas(s)e u part ast*, his thoughts are wandering.

پرتقال   *portoqal*, orange (fruit).

پرتگاه   *partgah*, precipice.

پرتو   *partōu*, ray, light.

پرتو شناس   *partōuʃenas*, radiologist; پرتو شناسی *partōuʃenasi*, radiology.

پرتو نگاری   *partōunegari*, radiography.

پرچم   *parcam*, flag, banner, standard.

پرداخت   *pardaxt*, payment.

پرداختن   *pardaxtan*, to pay; to set about, become engaged in.

پرده   *parde*, curtain.

پرده گوش   *pardeye guʃ*, drum of the ear.

پررو   *porru*, barefaced, brazen.

پرستار   *parastar*, nurse.

پرستش   *parasteʃ*, worship.

پرستوك   *parastuk*, swallow (bird).

پرستیدن   *parastidan*, to worship.

پرسش   *porseʃ*, question.

پرسش‌نامه   *porseʃname*, questionnaire.

پرسیدن   *porsidan*, to ask.

پرنده   *parande*, bird.

پروانه   *parvane*, moth, butterfly; permit, pass, licence.

پرورش   *parvareſ*, education; nourishing, rearing, fostering; پرورش دادن *parvareſ dadan*, to educate, bring up; پرورش یافتن *parvareſ yaſtan*, to be educated, brought up.

پرورشگاه یتیمان   *parvareſgahe yatiman*, orphanage.

پرونده   *parvande*, dossier; wrapping, packing sheet.

پرهیختن   *parhixtan*, to abstain from.

پرهیز   *parhiẓ*, abstinence.

پرهیزگاری   *parhiẓgari*, abstinence, sobriety, chastity.

پری   *pari*, fairy.

پریروز   *pariruẓ*, the day before yesterday.

پریشان   *pariſan*, dispersed; distracted; distressed; disturbed.

پریشانی   *pariſani*, dispersion; distraction; distress; being disturbed.

پریشب   *pariſab*, the night before last.

پریوش   *parivaſ*, fairy-like.

پزشك   *peẓeſk*, doctor.

پزشکی   *peẓeſki*, medicine, being a doctor.

پزشکیار   *peẓeſkyar*, doctor's assistant.

پژوهش   *peẓuheſ*, inquiry, examination.

پس   *pas*, behind; then; therefore; consequently; پس از *pas aẓ*, after (prep.); پس از آنکه *pas aẓ anke*, after (conj.).

پس انداز   *pasandaẓ*, savings.

پست   *past,* low, mean, sordid.

F پست   *post*, post.

FP پستخانه   *postxane*, post-office.

پسته   *peste*, pistachio-nut.

پسر   *pesar*, boy, son; پسر عمو *pesarammu*, cousin (i.e. the son of one's paternal uncle).

پسفردا   *pasfarda*, the day after tomorrow.

پسکوچه   *paskuce*, back-street.

پسند   *pasand*, agreeable, pleasant; approved; پسند آمدن *pasana amadan*, to please, be acceptable.

پسندیده   *pasandide*, approved, admired, agreeable.

پسین   *pasin*, afternoon; posterior, last, hindmost.

پشت   *poſt*, back (of the body, etc.); generation, descent; *poſt(e)*, behind; پشت سر *poſte sar(e)*, behind.

پشت بام   *poſte bam*, flat outside surface of a roof.

پشتکار   *poſtekar*, persevering, hardworking; perseverance.

پشتکاری   *poſtekari*, application, perseverance, industry.

پشتگرمی   *poſtgarmi*, enjoying the support (of someone or something).

پشت نویس   *poſtnevis*, endorsed (in banking).

پشت نویسی   *poſtnevisi*, endorsement.

پشتوانه   *poſtevane*, cover (for bank-note issue).

پشت هم انداز   *poſtehamandaȥ*, intriguer.

پشت هم اندازی   *poſtehamandaȥi*, intrigue.

پشتی   *poſti*, prop, support.

پشتیبان   *poſtiban*, supporter.

پشتیبانی   *poſtibani*, support.

پشقاب   *poſqab*, plate.

پشکل   *peſkel*, dung.

پشم   *paſm*, wool.

پشمی   *paſmi*, woollen.

پشمینه   *paſmine*, woollen.

پشیمان   *paſiman*, regretful, sorry, penitent.

پشیمانی   *paſimani*, regret, repentance.

پل   *pol*, bridge; پل شناور *pole ſenavar*, bridge of boats; پل متحرك *pole motaharrek*, drawbridge, swing-bridge.

پلنگ   *palang*, leopard.

پله   *pelle*, step, stair.

پناه   *panah*, asylum, refuge, shelter; پناه بردن *panah bordan*, to take refuge, shelter.

پناهنده   *panahande*, one who takes refuge.

پناهگاه   *panahgah*, shelter, refuge.

پنبه   *pambe*, cotton.

پنج   *panj*, five.

پنجاه   *panjah*, fifty.

پنجره   *panjare*, window.

پنجه   *panje*, fist; claws (of a bird, etc.); prong.

پند   *pand*, advice.

پنداشتن   *pandaſtan*, to consider, think.

پنهان   *panhan*, hidden.

پنیر   *panir*, cheese.

پوچ   *puc*, idle, vain, empty (of words).

پوزش   *puʒeſ*, asking to be excused, apology.

پوست   *pust*, skin.

پوستین   *pustin*, sheepskin coat.

پوسیده   *puside*, rotten.

پوشاك   *puſak*, clothing.

پوشیدن   *puſidan*, to clothe; to wear; to hide (trans.).

پول   *pul*, money.

پولاد   *pulad*, steel.

پولادین   *puladin*, steely, hard as steel.

پهلو   *pahlu*, side; پهلو(ى) *pahlu(ye)*, beside.

پهلوان   *pahlavan*, hero, champion, strong athletic man.

پهن   *pahn*, wide, broad; پهن کردن *pahn k.*, to lay out, spread out.

پهنا   *pahna*, breadth, width.

پهناور   *pahnavar*, broad, wide.

پی   *peī*, foundation (of a building, etc.); trace, track; *peī(ye)*, after, behind; در پی *dar peī(ye)*, after, behind; in search of.

پیاده   *piade*, on foot.

پیاده‌رو   *piaderoū*, pavement.

پیاز   *piaʒ*, onion; bulb; پیازچه *piaʒce*, spring onion.

پیام   *peyam*, message.

پیچ   *pic*, fold; twist; corner (in a road, etc.); screw; پیچ دادن *pic dadan*, to twist, turn (trans.); پیچ خوردن *pic xordan*, to twist, turn (intrans.); پیچ زدن *pic ʒadan*, to gripe (med.).

پیچیدن   *picidan*, to twist, turn (trans. and intrans.); to wrap up (a parcel, etc.).

پیچیده   *picide*, twisted; complicated, involved.

پیدا   *peīda*, apparent, evident; پیدا کردن *peīda k.*, to find; پیدا شدن *peīda ſ.*, to appear.

پیر   *pir*, old person, old (usually of persons); founder or leader of a religious order; پیر مرد *pire mard*, an old man; پیر زن *pire ʒan*, an old woman.

پیرارسال   *pirarsal*, the year before last.

پیراهن   *pirahan*, shirt.

پیسه   *pise*, kind of lichen.

پیش   *piʃ(e)*, before, in front of, with; پیش از before (prep.); پیش از آنکه *piʃ aʒ anke*, before (conj.).

پیش افتادن   *piʃ oftadan*, to take the lead, go to the front.

پیش آمد   *piʃamad*, occurrence, event, happening.

پیش آمدن   *piʃ amadan*, to occur, happen.

پیش آهنگ   *piʃahang*, boy scout, girl guide.

پیش آهنگی   *piʃahangi*, scouting, guiding.

پیش بردن   *piʃ bordan*, to win, succeed (intrans.).

پیش بها   *piʃbaha*, advance (in banking).

پیشبینی   *piʃbini*, foresight, anticipation.

پیش پرداخت   *piʃpardaxt*, advance payment.

پیشخدمت   *piʃxedmat*, head-servant, servant.

پیشرفت   *piʃraft*, advance, progress.

پیشکار   *piʃkar*, official in the Ministry of Finance; steward.

پیشکش   *piʃkaʃ*, present (from an inferior to a superior).

پیش کشیدن   *piʃ kaʃidan*, to bring forward, up.

پیشنماز   *piʃnamaʒ*, prayer-leader.

پیش نویس   *piʃnevis*, minute, draft.

پیشنهاد   *piʃnehad*, proposal.

پیشوا   *piʃva*, leader.

پیشه   *piʃe*, craft, trade, calling, profession; وزارت پیشه و هنر *veʒarate piʃe va honar*, Ministry of Industry.

پیشهور   *piʃevar*, artisan, tradesman, craftsman.

پیغام   *peīɣam*, message.

پیغمبر   *peīɣambar*, prophet.

پیکار   *peıkar*, battle.

پیکر   *peıkar*, face; form, figure, portrait.

پیله   *pile*, silkworm's cocoon.

پیمان   *peīman*, agreement, convention, treaty; measure.

پیمان نامه   *peīmanname*, written undertaking, agreement.

پیمودن   *peīmudan*, to measure, pass over, traverse.

پینه دوز   *pineduʒ*, patcher, botcher.

پیوستگی *peīvastegi*, being joined, continuity, union, junction.

پیوستن *peīvastan*, to join.

پیوسته *peīvaste*, joined; contiguous, continually.

پیوند *peīvand*, ligament, join; پیوند زدن *peīvand ʒadan*, to graft (a tree, etc.).

پیوندی *peīvandi*, grafted (of a tree, etc.).

ت

تا *ta*, up to; until; so that; in order that; by the time that; as long as; as soon as; unless; since; behold, beware; a fold; a (grammatical) particle used in counting.

تاب *tab*, heat, warmth; strength, power; twist; being twisted (of a rope, etc.).

تابان *taban*, shining (of the sun, etc.).

تابستان *tabestan*, summer.

تابش *tabeſ*, shining, brilliance, light (of the sun, etc.).

A   تابع *tabeʿ*, subject, follower.

تابیدن *tabidan*, to shine.

A   تأثیر *taʿsir*, effect; تأثیر بخشیدن *taʿsir baxſidan*, to make an effect, impression.

A   تاجر *tajer*, merchant.

تاجگذاری *tajgoʒari*, coronation.

تاختن *taxtan*, to rush, make an assault; to put to the gallop.

تار و مار *tar o mar*, scattered, topsy-turvy, in confusion

A   تاریخ *tarix*, history; date (day of the month, etc.).

A   تاریخی *tarixi*, historical, historic.

تاریك *tarik*, dark.

تاریکی *tariki*, darkness.

تازه *taʒe*, new, fresh.

تازی *taʒi*, Arabic; saluki dog.

A   تأسف *taʿassof*, regret; تأسف خوردن *taʿassof xordan*, to regret.

A   تاسوعا *tasuʿa*, ninth day of Moharram.

A   تأسیس *taʿsis*, founding, foundation; تأسیس کردن *taʿsis k.*, to found.

38

تافتن   *taftan*, to shine; to twist.

A   تأكيد   *ta'kid*, corroboration; stress, emphasis, insistence.

تالار   *talar*, hall, reception room.

A   تأليف   *ta'lif*, compiling; composition, literary work.

A   تام   *tamm*, complete, entire.

A   تأمل   *ta'ammol*, reflection, careful, consideration.

A   تأمين   *ta'min*, security, securing; provision, providing.

A   تامينيه   *ta'miniye*, security forces, gendarmerie.

F   تانك   *tank*, tank (military).

A   تأنى   *ta'anni*, delay, procrastination.

تاول   *tavel*, blister.

تاوه   *tave*, frying pan.

تب   *tab*, fever; تب و نوبه *tab o noube*, malaria.

تباه   *tabah*, destroyed, spoilt.

A   تبخير   *tabxir*, evaporation.

A   تبديل   *tabdil*, change.

تبر   *tabar*, hatchet.

A   تبرئه   *tabre'e*, exoneration, acquittal, discharge.

تبريزى   *tabrizi*, poplar-tree; native of Tabriz.

A   تبريك   *tabrik*, congratulation; تبريك گفتن *tabrik goftan*, to congratulate.

A   تبسم   *tabassom*, smile.

A   تبصره   *tabsere*, note (to a document, etc.).

A   تبعيت   *tab'iyat*, dependence, subjection; domicile.

A   تبعيد   *tab'id*, exile.

A   تبعيض   *tab'iz*, making exception, discrimination.

A   تبليغ   *tabliɣ*, propaganda.

تبهكار   *tabahkar*, pernicious or destructive person.

تپه   *tappe*, hill.

A   تتبع   *tatabbo'*, investigation, research (into).

A   تجار   *tojjar* (pl. of تاجر *tajer*), merchants.

A   تجارت   *tejarat*, trade.

AP   تجارت خانه   *tejaratxane*, commercial house, trading house.

A   تجارتى   *tejarati*, mercantile.

A   تجاوز   *tajavoz*, aggression.

A تجديد   *tajdid,* renewal; تجديد نظر *tajdide naẓar,* reconsideration; تجديد عهد *tajdide ahd,* renewal of intercourse or friendship.

A تجربه   *tajrebe,* experience.

A تجزيه   *tajʒie,* analysis.

A تجسم   *tajassom,* taking form, embodiment.

A تحت   *taht(e),* under; تحت نظر *tahte naẓar,* under supervision.

A تحديد   *tahdid,* prescribing limits, limitation.

A تحريك   *tahrik,* instigation, incitement.

A تحريم   *tahrim,* prohibiting, prohibition.

A تحسين   *tahsin,* approbation, applause.

A تحصيل   *tahsil,* acquiring, acquisition; study.

A تحفه   *tohfe,* present, gift.

A تحقيق   *tahqiq,* investigation; ascertaining the truth; research.

A تحقيقى   *tahqiqi,* verified, ascertained; critical (of historical method, etc.).

A تحمل   *tahammol,* patience, endurance, long-suffering.

A تحميل   *tahmil,* imposing (a burden or load, fig.).

A تحول   *tahavvol,* development, transformation, change (from one condition to another).

A تحويل   *tahvil,* transfer; consigning; charge; تحويل كردن *tahvil k.,* to hand over; تحويل گرفتن *tahvil gereftan,* to take over.

تخت   *taxt,* throne; seat, sofa; تخت خواب *taxte xab,* bedstead.

تخته   *taxte,* board, plank, table.

تخته نرد   *taxtenard,* back-gammon board.

A تخريب   *taxrib,* devastation, destruction.

تخشائى ارتش   *toxʃaiye arteʃ,* manufacture of armaments.

A تخفيف   *taxfif,* reduction, alleviation, abatement.

A تخلف   *taxallof,* infringement, violation.

A تخليه   *taxlie,* evacuation.

تخم   *toxm,* seed; egg; تخم مرغ *toxme morɣ,* hen's egg.

A تدابير   *tadabir* (pl. of تدبير *tadbir*) plans, arrangements.

A تدبير   *tadbir,* setting in order; policy, deliberation; plan.

A تدريج   *tadrij,* gradation, scale; بتدريج *be tadrij,* by degrees, gradually.

A تدريجى   *tadriji,* gradual.

A تدریس   *tadris*, teaching.

تر   *tar*, wet, moist; fresh.

تراز   *taraẓ*, balance (in banking); تراز کردن *taraẓ k.*, to balance (tr.).

تراز نامه   *taraẓname*, balance sheet.

تراشیدن   *tarafidan*, to shave; to pare; to scrape; to cut.

A تراوش   *taravof*, exudation, oozing, dripping.

تربچه   *torobce*, radish.

A تربیت   *tarbiat*, education.

A ترتیب   *tartib*, arrangement.

A ترجمه   *tarjome* (for *tarjeme*), translation.

A ترجیح   *tarjih*, preferring, giving preference to (subs.).

A تردد   *taraddod*, doubt, hesitation; perplexity.

تردستی   *tardasti*, sleight of hand; dexterity.

A تردید   *tardid*, doubt; تردید داشتن *tardid d.*, to be doubtful.

ترس   *tars*, fear.

ترسناك   *tarsnak*, fearful, frightening.

ترسیدن   *tarsidan*, to fear.

A ترسیم   *tarsim*, tracing, drawing; delineation.

ترش   *torf*, sour, acid.

A ترشح   *taraffoh*, exudation; drizzle.

ترشی   *torfi*, pickles.

A ترقی   *taraqqi*, progress.

A ترك   *tork*, Turk.

A ترك   *tark*, abandoning (subs.).

ترکتازی   *torktaẓi*, plundering excursion.

ترکمان   *torkaman*, Turkoman.

ترکه   *tarke*, switch, twig.

ترکی   *torki*, Turki (language); Turkish (language).

A ترکیب   *tarkib*, compound, mixture; form, shape.

A ترمیم   *tarmim*, reconstruction.

تره   *tare*, *tarre*, leek.

تره بار   *tarebar*, fresh fruit and vegetables.

تریاق   *taryaq*, antidote against poison.

تریاك   *taryak*, opium.

A تزریق   *taẓriq*, injection; transfusion.

A تزلزل *tazalzol*, being shaken; commotion, agitation.

A تزویر *tazvir*, hypocrisy, dissimulation.

A تساوی *tasavi*, equality, being equal.

A تسعه *tes'a*, nine.

A تسلط *tasallot*, dominion, ruling, exercising sway.

A تسلیت *tasliat*, condolence; تسلت گفتن *tasliat goftan*, to condole.

A تسلیم *taslim*, submission; تسلیم کردن *taslim k.*, to surrender (trans.), hand over.

A تستن *tasannon*, being a Sunni; Sunnism.

A تسهیل *tashil*, facilitating, facility.

A تشبیه *taʃbih*, resemblance.

A تشجیع *taʃji'*, encouraging, encouragement.

A تشخیص *taʃxis*, distinguishing, discerning, particularizing (subs.); تشخیص دادن *taʃxis dadan*, to distinguish, discern.

A تشریف *taʃrif*, honouring; تشریف آوردن *taʃrif avardan*, to come; تشریف بردن *taʃrif bordan*, to go; تشریف داشتن *taʃrif d.*, to be present. (These verbs are not used in the 1st person.)

A تشریفات *taʃrifat* (pl. of above), honours, ceremonies; formalities.

A تشکیل *taʃkil*, formation, forming; تشکیل کردن *taʃkil k.*, to form, set up; تشکیل شدن *taʃkil ʃ.*, to be formed; to form a quorum (of a committee, etc.).

A تشنج *taʃannoj*, convulsion, spasm; acute instability.

تشنگی *teʃnegi*, thirst.

تشنه *teʃne*, thirsty.

A تشویش *taʃviʃ*, disquietude, apprehension, unrest; تشویش خاطر *taʃviʃe xater*, anxiety.

A تشویق *taʃviq*, encouragement.

A تشیع *taʃayyo'*, being a Shi'i; Shi'ism.

A تصادف *tasadof*, chance happening; تصادفاً *tasadofan*, by chance.

A تصادم *tasadom*, collision, colliding.

A تصانیف *tasanif* (pl. of تصنیف *tasnif*), literary works; songs.

A تصحیح *tashih*, correction, correcting, editing (a book, etc.).

A تصحیف *tashif*, making an error or change in pronunciation.

A تصدیق *tasdiq*, confirming, corroborating (subs.).

AP تصدیق نامه *tasdiqname*, certificate.

A	تصرف	*tasarrof*, taking possession of.
A	تصرفات	*tasarrofat* (pl. of above), conquests; misappropriations; corruptions (in a text).
A	تصفیه	*tasfie*, purification, purifying, refining.
AP	تصفیه خانه	*tasfiexane*, refinery.
A	تصمیم	*tasmim*, decision; determination; تصمیم داشتن *tasmim d.*, to be determined (upon something); تصمیم گرفتن *tasmim gereftan*, to take a decision, make up one's mind (to do something).
A	تصنیف	*tasnif*, literary composition; song.
A	تصور	*tasavvor*, fancy, imagination, supposition; تصور کردن *tasavvor k.*, to suppose, think.
A	تصویب	*tasvib*, ratification; corroboration; تصویب کردن *tasvib k.*, to ratify; تصویب نامه *tasvibname*, decree, edict.
A	تصویر	*tasvir*, picture, painting, drawing.
A	تطبیق	*tatbiq*, conformity, correspondence; تطبیق کردن (با) *tatbiq k.* (*ba*), to make conformable (with).
A	تظاهر	*tazahor*, making an ostentatious display, demonstration.
A	تعارف	*ta'arof*, compliment; تعارف کردن *ta'arof k.*, to offer (by way of a gift, etc.); to make compliments.
A	تعاون	*ta'avon*, mutual aid; co-operation.
A	تعاونی	*ta'avoni*, co-operative; شرکت تعاونی *ʃerkate ta'avoni*, co-operative society.
A	تعاهد	*ta'ahod*, (mutual) undertaking; covenant.
A	تعبیر	*ta'bir*, interpretation.
A	تعجب	*ta'ajjob*, amazement, surprise; تعجب کردن *ta'ajjob k.*, to be surprised.
A	تعداد	*te'dad*, number, tally.
A	تعدی	*ta'addi*, tyranny, oppression; تعدی کردن *ta'addi k.*, to practice tyranny, oppression.
A	تعدیل	*ta'dil*, adjusting, rectifying, reducing (subs.); moderating, modifying (subs.).
	تعرفه	*ta'refe*, tariff.
A	تعریف	*ta'rif*, making known, explanation; praise.
A	تعصب	*ta'assob*, fanaticism.

A   تعطیل   *ta'til*, suspension; holiday; تعطیل بر دار نبودن *ta'tilbardar nabudan*, not to be capable of suspension.

A   تعلیم   *ta'lim*, teaching.

A   تعمد   *ta'ammod*, doing (something) deliberately or on purpose.

A   تعمیر   *ta'mir*, repairing.

A   تعمیم   *ta'mim*, rendering something universal or general.

A   تعهد   *ta'ahhod*, undertaking; agreement.

AP   تعهد نامه   *ta'ahhodname* (written) undertaking.

A   تغافل   *tayafol*, negligence, carelessness; تغافل ورزیدن *tayafol varzidan*, to show negligence.

A   تغذیه   *tayʒie*, nourishment, nutrition.

A   تغییر   *tayyir*, change, alteration.

AP   تغییر ناپذیر   *tayyirnapaʒir*, unchangeable, unalterable.

A   تفتیش   *taftiʃ*, inspection, examination.

A   تفاوت   *tafavot*, difference.

A   تفرقه   *tafreqe*, deployment, dispersal, dissipation; discord; تفرقه انداختن *tafreqe andaxtan*, to sow discord; تفرقه رفتن *tafreqe raftan*, to deploy.

A   تفریح   *tafrih*, recreation.

A   تفریط   *tafrit*, dissipation; waste; افراط و تفریط *efrat o tafrit*, going to extremes.

A   تفسیر   *tafsir*, commentary; explanation.

A   تفصیل   *tafsil*, detail, particulars.

  تفنگ   *tofang*, rifle, gun.

PT   تفنگچی   *tofangci*, rifleman.

A   تفنن   *tafannon*, diversion, luxury.

A   تقاعد   *taqa'od*, retirement (from work); حقوق تقاعد *hoquqe taqa'od* pension.

A   تقدیر   *taqdir*, predestination.

A   تقدیم   *taqdim*, presenting, offering.

A   تقریباً   *taqriban*, about, approximately.

A   تقسیم   *taqsim*, division, dividing.

A   تقصیر   *taqsir*, shortcoming.

A   تقلب   *taqallob*, deceit, fraud, dishonesty.

A   تقلید   *taqlid*, imitation.

A   تقليل   *taqlil*, diminution, reduction.

A   تقوى   *taqva*, piety.

A   تقويت   *taqviat*, strengthening, supporting, support.

A   تقويم   *taqvim*, calendar, almanac.

   تك   *tak*, single, alone.

A   تكامل   *takamol*, perfection, completion; development.

   تكان   *tekan*, push, jolt; shock; تكان خوردن *tekan xordan*, to shake (intrans.); to be shaken up, startled.

A   تكبر   *takabbor*, pride, arrogance, haughtiness.

A   تكميل   *takmil*, completing, perfecting.

   تگرگ   *tegarg*, hail.

A   تلافى   *talafi*, recompense, retaliation, amends; تلافى كردن *talafi k.*, to make amends, make good, make up.

   تلخ   *talx*, bitter; اوقات فلان كس تلخ شد *ouqate folan kas talx fod*, so-and-so was cross, angry.

A   تلخيص   *talxis*, summarizing; résumé, report.

A   تلف   *talaf*, loss, waste; تلف شدن *talaf f.*, to be destroyed; تلف كردن *talaf k.*, to waste.

A   تلفات   *talafat*, casualties, losses.

A   تلقى   *talaqqi*, meeting, encountering.

A   تلقيح   *talqih*, inoculation.

   تلمبه   *tolombe*, pump.

   تله   *tale*, net, snare.

A   تماشا   *tamafa* (for تماشى *tamafi*), spectacle, sight; entertainment, show.

AT   تماشاچى   *tamafaci*, spectator.

AP   تماشاخانه   *tamafaxane*, theatre.

A   تمام   *tamam*, whole; complete; perfect; all; end; تمام كردن *tamam k.*, to finish (trans.).

A   تماماً   *tamaman*, completely, wholly, *in toto*.

A   تمايل   *tamayol*, inclination; تمايل داشتن *tamayol d.*, to be inclined (to).

F   تمبر   *tambr*, postage stamp.

A   تمدن   *tamaddon*, civilization.

A   تمديد   *tamdid*, prolongation.

A تمرکز   *tamarkoz*, centralization; تمرکز دادن *tamarkoz dadan*, to centralize, concentrate.

A تمرین   *tamrin*, exercise; training.

A تملق   *tamalloq*, flattery.

A تمهید   *tamhid*, spreading out, arrangement.

A تمیز   *tamiz* (for تمییز *tamyiz*), judgement, discernment, separating; clean, neat; دیوان تمیز *divane tamiz*, court of cassation; *tamaiyoz*, discernment, judgement.

تن   *tan*, body, stature; person; تن در دادن *tan dar dadan*, to submit, give in (fig.).

A تناسب   *tanasob*, proportion, being in proportion.

تنبل   *tambal*, lazy.

تنبلی   *tambali*, laziness; تنبلی کردن *tambali k.*, to be lazy.

A تنبیه   *tambih*, punishment; تنبیه کردن *tambih k.*, to punish.

تند   *tond*, swift, rapid, fast; choleric, quarrelsome; bright, gaudy (of a colour); peppery, hot (of food).

تندرست   *tandorost*, healthy (of persons).

تندرستی   *tandorosti*, health (of persons).

تندی   *tondi*, swiftness, rapidity, fastness; being choleric or quarrelsome, irritability; brightness, gaudiness (of colour); being peppery or hot (of food).

A تنزل   *tanazzol*, decline, decrease.

A تنفر   *tanaffor*, hatred, dislike.

A تنفس   *tanaffos*, break, breathing-space; respiration.

A تنقیح   *tanqih*, expurgation.

تنگ   *tang*, narrow, tight; saddle-girth; تنگدستی *tangdasti*, being in narrow straits; تنگنا *tangna*, ravine; تنگه *tange*, straits; mountain pass.

تنور   *tanur*, oven.

تنومند   *tanumand*, strong, powerful.

تنه   *tane*, fusilage (of aeroplane); trunk (of a tree); body.

تنها   *tanha*, alone.

تو   *to*, thou; تو(ی) *tu(ye)*, in.

A توابع   *tavabe'* (pl. of تابع *tabe'*), dependencies; appurtenances.

توانا   *tavana*, powerful; powerful person.

	توانستن	*tavanestan*, to be able.
	توانگر	*tavangar*, powerful, strong; powerful person.
A	توبه	*tŏube*, repentance, penitence.
T	توپ	*tup*, cannon; ball; bale (of cloth).
TP	توپ اندازی	*tupandaƶi*, ballistics.
T	توپچی	*tupci*, artilleryman.
TP	توپخانه	*tupxane*, artillery (branch of army).
TP	توپدار	*tupdar*, gunboat.
	توت	*tut* (white) mulberry; توت فرنگی *tute farangi*, strawberry.
T	توتون	*totun*, tobacco.
	توتی	*tuti* (usually طوطی), parrot.
A	توجه	*tavajjoh*, attention, paying attention.
A	توحش	*tavahhoʃ*, savagery, horror.
	توده	*tude*, heap, mass; توده مردم *tudeye mardom*, the masses.
	تور	*tur*, net.
A	تورم	*tavarrom*, swelling; تورم پول *tavarrome pul*, inflation (econ.).
A	توسط	*tavassot*, mediation; بتوسط *be tavassot(e)*, by the agency of, by means of.
A	توسعه	*tŏuse'e*, amplitude, extension.
A	توسل	*tavassol*, resorting, having recourse (to).
A	توسیع	*tŏusi'*, amplification, extension.
A	توضیح	*tŏuƶih*, making clear; explanation, elucidation.
A	توطئه	*tŏute'e*, plot, conspiracy.
	توفان	*tufan*, storm.
A	توقف	*tavaqqof*, stopping, stop; stoppage; interruption.
A	توقیف	*tŏuqif*, arresting, interning, arrest.
A	توکل	*tavakkol*, depending (upon), reliance (upon), trust.
A	تولد	*tavallod*, birth.
	توله	*tule*, puppy.
A	تولید	*tŏulid*, begetting; production; تولید کردن *tŏulid k.*, to produce.
	تومان	*tuman, toman*, unit of currency equal to ten *rials*.
	توی	*tuye*, see تو above.
A	تهاتری	*tahatori*: قرارداد تهاتری *qarardade tahatori*, barter agreement.
A	تهدید	*tahdid*, threat.

A تهذيب *tahzib*, purifying (subs.); adorning; correcting.

A تهمت *tohmat*, slander, calumny; تهمت زدن *tohmat zadan*, to slander.

تهى *tohi*, empty.

A تهيه *tahiye*, preparing, preparation, making ready or available.

تيپ *tip*, brigade.

تير *tir*, fourth month of the Persian solar year; beam (of wood, etc.); power, strength; shot, bullet; arrow; تير انداختن *tir andaxtan*, to fire (a bullet or an arrow); تير خوردن *tir xordan*, to be hit (by a bullet, etc.).

تيرباران *tirbaran*, execution by a firing squad.

تيره *tire*, clan; obscure, dark; turbid, muddy; sad, sorrowful.

تيز *tiz*, sharp.

تيزرو *tizrou*, fleet (of foot).

تيشه *tiʃe*, adze.

تيغ *tiɣ*, razor; sword; thorn.

تيمارستان *timarestan*, lunatic asylum.

تيمارگاه *timargah*, municipal clinic.

تيمچه *timce*, passage, alley-way.

تيمسار *timsar*, title of respect given to an officer of the rank of major-general or above.

ث

A ثابت *sabet*, firm, fixed; confirmed, certain, proved; fast (of dye).

A ثالث *sales*, third.

A ثالثًا *salesan*, in the third place, thirdly.

A ثانى *sani*, second.

A ثانيًا *sanian*, secondly.

A ثبات *sabat*, stability, firmness, durability.

A ثروت *servat*, *sarvat*, wealth, riches.

AP ثروتمند *servatmand*, *sarvatmand*, wealthy, rich.

A ثقل *seql*, weight, gravity; مركز ثقل *markaze seql*, centre of gravity.

A ثلاثى *solasi*, three-sided, triangular; triple.

A ثلث *sols*, one third.

A ثمر *samar*, fruit, produce; result.

A ثنائى *sonai*, biliteral.

A ثواب *savab*, recompense, reward; good work.

ج

جا *ja*, place; جا(ى) *ja(ye)*, بجا(ى) *beja(ye)*, in place of; بجا آوردن *be ja avardan*, to accomplish, fulfil, perform.

جادو *jadu*, magic; spell, charm.

جادوگر *jadugar*, magician.

A جاده *jadde*, highway, highroad.

A جار *jar*, neighbour.

جار *jar*, proclamation; جار و جنجال *jar o janjal*, commotion, uproar.

جارى *jari*, flowing (adj.); current (month, etc.).

جاشو *jaʃu*
جاشوان *jaʃvan* } crew of a ship.

A جالب *jaleb*, attractive, attracting; جالب توجه *jalebe tavajjoh*, worthy of notice.

جام *jam*, goblet.

A جامد *jamed*, congealed, stagnant; (gramm.), primitive; uninflected.

A جامع *jame'*, comprehensive; مسجد جامع *masjede jame*, Friday mosque.

A جامعه *jame'e*, society, community, association.

جامه *jame*, garment, robe.

جان *jan*, soul; life.

A جانب *janeb*, side; از جانب *az janeb(e)*, on behalf of, on the part of; بجانب *be janeb(e)*, towards.

جانشين *janeʃin*, successor.

جانور *janevar*, animal.

A جانى *jani*, criminal.

جاودانى *javedani*, جاودان *javedan*, immortal, eternal.

جاه *jah*, place, rank, dignity, honour.

PA جاهطلب *jahtalab*, ambitious.

PA جاهطلبى *jahtalabi*, ambition.

A جاهل *jahel*, ignorant.

A جائز *jaez*, lawful, legal, allowable, permitted.

جايگاه *jāigah*, habitation, dwelling; place where anything stands or is contained.

A جبر *jabr*, predestination; algebra.

A جبران *jobran*, compensation, recompense.

A جبرى *jabri*, one who believes in predestination.

A جبل *jabal*, mountain.

A جبلى *jebelli*, natural, inherent, innate.

A جبهه *jebhe, jabhe*, war-front, battle-front.

A جبين *jabin*, forehead, temple.

A جد *jadd*, grandfather; ancestor; *jedd*, effort, labour, exertion.

A جدا *joda*, separate; جدا کردن *joda k.*, to separate (trans.).

AP جداگانه *jodagane*, separate.

A جدى *jeddi*, earnest, serious; energetic, active.

A جديت *jeddiyat*, energy, activity; earnestness.

A جديد *jadid*, new.

A جذب *jazb*, attracting, attraction.

A جرأت *jor'at*, courage, boldness; جرأت داشتن *jor'at d.*, to dare, be bold.

A جراح *jarrah*, surgeon.

A جراحت *jarahat*, wound.

A جراحى *jarrahi*, surgical; جراحى کردن *jarrahi k.*, to perform a surgical operation.

A جر ثقيل *jarre saqil*, crane (mech.).

A جرم *jorm*, sin, crime, fault.

جره *jorre*, measure of water.

A جريان *jarian*, flow, circulation; happening, course of events.

A جريمه *jarime*, fine, mulct.

جز *joz*, besides, except, other, apart; بجز *be joz*, other than.

A جزو *jozv*، جزء *joz'*, part, portion, particle; section (of a book).

A جزا *jaza*, recompense; retribution.

AP جزائى *jazai*, penal; قانون جزائى *qanune jazai*, penal code.

A   جزیره   *jazire*, island.

A   جزئیات   *joz'iat*, details; trifles, particles.

A   جسارت   *jesarat*, boldness, audacity.

    جستجو   *jostoju*, search.

    جستن   *jastan*, to leap; *jostan*, to seek, look for; (colloq.)=to find.

    جست‌وجو   *jostoju*, search.

A   جسم   *jesm*, body; mathematical solid.

A   جسمانی   *jesmani*, corporeal.

    جشن   *jaʃn*, celebration, feast; جشن گرفتن *jaʃn gereftan*, to celebrate (a holiday, etc.).

A   جعل   *ia'l*, counterfeit, forgery.

A   جفا   *jafa*, cruelty, oppression, injustice.

    جفت   *joft*, pair; yoke (of oxen).

    جگر   *jegar*, liver.

A   جلال   *jalal*, grandeur; majesty, splendour.

A   جلب   *jalb*, attracting, attraction.

A   جلد   *jeld*, volume, book; binding (of a book).

    جلگه   *jolge*, plain, level ground.

    جلو   *jelou(e)*, front, in front of.

A   جلوس   *jolus*, sitting (subs.); accession to the throne; جلوس کردن *jolus, k.*, to ascend the throne.

    جلوگیری   *jelougiri*, prevention; جلوگیری کردن (از) *jelougiri k.* (az), to prevent.

A   جلوه   *jelve*, splendour, lustre.

A   جماعت   *jama'at*, crowd; a society; faction, class.

A   جمال   *jamal*, beauty, grace.

A   جمع   *jam'*, collecting, assembling; aggregate, sum total; جمع کردن *jam' k.*, to collect, assemble (trans.); to add.

A   جمعه   *jom'e*, Friday.

A   جمعیت   *jam'iyat*, crowd, multitude; population; society (club).

A   جمله   *jomle*, sum, whole, total; sentence (gramm.); ازآن جمله *az an jomle*, among them; از جمله *az jomle(ye)*, among.

AP   جمله بندی   *jomlebandi*, construction of a sentence.

A   جمهور   *jomhur*, republic.

A	جمهوری	*jomhuri*, republican; republic.
AP	جمهوریخواه	*jomhurixah*, republican, one who supports a republic.
A	جمیع	*jami'*, all, whole.
A	جمیعاً	*jami'an*, altogether.
A	جناب	*janab*, a title of respect.
	جناغ	*janaɣ*, breast-bone of a bird, wishbone; جناغ سینه *janaɣe sine*, breast-bone (of a person).
A	جنایت	*janayat*, crime, iniquity.
AP	جنایتکار	*janayatkar*, a criminal.
	جنبش	*jombeʃ*, movement.
	جنبیدن	*jombidan*, to move.
	جنجال	*janjal*, crowd, multitude; commotion, confusion, brawl.
A	جند	*jond*, army; local troops.
A	جنس	*jens*, kind, sort, species; جنس لطیف *jense latif*, the fair sex.
	جنگ	*jang*, war, battle.
	جنگدیده	*jangdide*, experienced in war.
	جنگل	*jangal*, forest.
	جنگلبان	*jangalban*, forester.
	جنگلبانی	*jangalbani*, forestry.
A	جنوب	*jonub*, south.
A	جنوبی	*jonubi*, southern.
A	جنون	*jonun*, madness.
	جو	*joͧu*, barley, grain of barley; *ju*, stream.
A	جو	*jav*, air, sky, atmosphere.
A	جواب	*javab*, answer; جواب دادن *javab dadan*, to answer; جواب کردن *javab k.*, to dismiss, sack.
	جوال	*javal*, sack, bag.
	جوان	*javan*, young; جوانبخت *javanbaxt*, fortunate.
	جوب	*jub* (for جوی *jui*), stream, small irrigation channel, gutter.
	جوجه	*juje*, chicken.
	جوخه	*juxe*, section, patrol (military and scouting).
	جوخه یار	*juxeyar*, assistant patrol-leader (scouting).
	جور	*jur*, kind, sort.
A	جور	*joͧur*, oppression, tyranny.

جوراب   *jurab*, stocking, sock.

A   جوز   *joūz*, nut.

جوش   *juʃ*, boiling (of water); جوش آمـدن *juʃ amadan*, to come to the boil; جوش خوردن *juʃ xordan*, to boil (intrans.); جوش کردن *juʃ k.*, to become agitated, bothered.

جوشیدن   *juʃidan*, to boil (intrans.); to bubble.

A   جوهر   *joūhar*, jewel; essence, nature; ink.

جوی   *juī*, stream; gutter; small irrigation channel.

A   جهاز   *jahaz*, ship.

جهان   *jahan*, world.

جهاندیده   *jahandide*, experienced.

جهانگرد   *jahangard*, tourist.

جهانگردی   *jahangardi*, touring.

جهانی   *jahani*, belonging to the world, mortal.

A   جهت   *jehat*, side; cause, reason; از جهت *az jehat(e)*, because of; on behalf of.

A   جهل   *jahl*, ignorance.

A   جهول   *jahul*, ignorant, very ignorant.

A   جیب   *jib*, pocket.

جیره   *jire*, ration.

جیره‌بندی   *jirebandi*, rationing.

جیم   *jim*: جیم شدن *jim ʃ.*, to slip away.

چ

چابك   *cabok*, nimble, agile, adroit.

چاپ   *cap*, print.

چاپخانه   *capxane*, printing house, printing office.

چاپلوس   *caplus*, flatterer.

چاپلوسی   *caplusi*, flattery.

چاپی   *capi*, printed.

چاپیدن   *capidan*, to plunder.

چادر   *cador*, tent; veil; چادر زدن *cador zadan*, to pitch a tent; چادر سر کردن *cador sar k.*, to wear a veil.

چادرشب   *cadorʃab*, special kind of veil worn by women in the house.

چادر نشین   *cadornefin*, nomadic; nomad, tent-dweller.

چاروادار   *carvadar*, muleteer.

چارك   *carak*, quarter (of a *man*).

چاره   *care*, remedy, escape.

T   چاق   *caq*, healthy, well; stout; چپق چاق کردن *copoq caq k.*, to prepare a pipe for smoking; کار و بارش چاق است *kar o baref caq ast*, he is doing well, his affairs prosper.

چاقو   *caqu*, penknife.

چال   *cal*, ravine; hollow; pit.

چانه   *cane*, chin, jaw; چانه زدن *cane zadan*, to chatter; to bargain.

چاه   *cah*, well; pit.

چای   *cāi*, tea.

چائیدن   *caidan*, to catch a chill.

چپ   *cap*, left, left side; چپ شدن *cap f.*, to be upset (of a motor, etc.).

T   چپق
T   چپوق   } *copoq*, pipe (for tobacco).

چرا   *cera*, why; yes; چراکه *cera ke*, because.

چراغ   *ceray*, lamp.

چراگاه   *ceragah*, grazing ground.

چرانیدن   *caranidan*, to cause to graze, take to pasture.

چرب   *carb*
چربی   *carbi*   } fat, grease; greasy.

چرخ   *carx*, wheel; cart; sewing machine; (poet.) sky.

چرخه   *carxe*, barrow; axis of a pulley; wheel.

چرخی   *carxi*, carter.

چرك   *cerk*, dirt, pus; dirty.

چرکتاب   *cerktab*, colour which does not show the dirt.

چرك نویس   *cerknevis*, rough copy, draft.

چرکی   *cerki*, dirtiness, filthiness.

چرم   *carm*, leather.

چرند   *carand*, nonsense; چرند و پرند *carand o parand*, nonsense.

چریدن   *caridan*, to graze (intrans.).

چسپیدن   *caspidan*, to stick, adhere.

چشم   *cafm, cefm*, the eye; چشم زدن *cafm zadan*, to cast the evil eye on.

چشم انداز   *caſmanda͡z*, view, prospect.

چشمك   *caſmak*, wink; چشمك زدن *caſmak ͡zadan*, to wink.

چشمه   *caſme*, spring, source; arch of a bridge; vaulted arch.

چشیدن   *caſidan*, to taste.

چطور   *ce t͡our*, how, in what manner.

چغندر (چقندر)   *co͡yondar*, beetroot.

F چك   *cek*, cheque.

چكش   *cako͡ſ*, hammer.

T چكمه   *cakme*, boot.

چكیدن   *cekidan*, to drip, trickle.

چگونه   *cegune*, how, in what way.

چگونگی   *cegunegi*, quality, manner, circumstance.

چلوار   *celvar*, bleached shirting; calico.

چله   *cele*, period of forty days; چله بزرگ *celeye bo͡zorg*, forty days beginning with the winter solstice or the summer solstice; چله کوچك *celeye kucek*, twenty days following the *celeye bo͡zorg*.

چمن   *caman*, meadow.

چمنزار   *caman͡zar*, meadow, meadow-land.

چنار   *cenar*, plane tree.

چنان   *conan*, like that, in that manner, thus; so.

چنانچه   *conance*, as, just as, so that; if, in the event that.

چند   *cand*, how much, how many, how long; some, few.

چندان   *candan*, many, much; so much; چندانکه *candanke*, however much that.

چندی   *candi*, a little while.

چندین   *candin*, so much, so many; how many; several.

چنگ   *cang*, claw of a wild beast; talon of a bird; harp, lute.

چنگال   *cangal*, claw, talon; fork.

چنین   *conin*, like this, in this manner; so.

چوب   *cub*, wood.

چوبی   *cubi*, wooden.

چون   *cun*, because; since; when; چونکه *cunke*, because, since.

چه   *ce*, what; because; how; چه...چه *ce...ce*, whether...or.

چهار   *cahar*, four.

	چهارپا	caharpa, quadruped.
	چهارده	cahardah, fourteen.
	چهل	cehel, forty.
	چیت	cit, calico; printed cotton.
	چیدن	cidan, to collect, gather.
	چیره	cire, brave; strong, powerful; victorious.
	چیز	ciz, thing.
	چین	cin, pleat, fold; China.
	چینی	cini, Chinese; porcelain, china.
	چین دار	cindar, pleated, folded.
	چینه	cine, course of bricks or stone in a wall; stratum.

ح

A	حاتم	hatem, name of a man of the tribe of Teī noted for liberality, hence liberal, generous.
AP	حاتمبخشی	hatembaxſi, liberality.
A	حاجت	hajat, need; حاجت داشتن hajat d., to need.
A	حادثه	hadese, event, happening.
A	حاشیه	haſie, margin, edge, border.
A	حاصل	hasel, produce; crop, harvest; revenue; result.
AP	حاصلخیز	haselxiz, fertile.
A	حاضر	hazer, ready; حاضرکردن hazer k., to make ready, prepare; حاضر شدن hazer ſ., to be ready.
A	حاکم	hakem, governor; judge.
A	حال	hal, state, condition; حال آنکه halanke, now that; بهر حال be har hal, in any case; در عین حال dar eīne hal, at the same time, meanwhile.
A	حالا	hala, now.
A	حالت	halat, state, condition.
A	حائز	haez, possessing (adj.).
A	حائل	hael, intervening, coming in between (adj.); buffer.
A	حب	habb, pill; berry; hobb, love; حب الوطن hobb ol-vatan, patriotism.
A	حبوبات	hobubat (pl. of حب), pulses.

A	حتم	*hatm*, certainty; حتم داشتن *hatm d.*, to be certain.
A	حتمی	*hatmi*, certain, definite.
A	حتی	*hatta*, even (adv.).
A	حتی المقدور	*hattal-maqdur*, as far as possible.
A	حجاب	*hejab*, veiling; veil.
A	حجار	*hajjar*, stone-mason.
A	حد	*hadd*, limit.
A	حدت	*heddat*, vehemence, force, vigour.
A	حدس	*hads*, guess; حدس زدن *hads zadan*, to guess.
A	حدود	*hodud* (pl. of حد *hadd*), limits; در حدود *dar hodud(e)* about.
A	حدیث	*hadis*, tradition (of Muhammad).
A	حذر	*hazar*, avoiding, shunning, prudence, fear; بر حذر (باش) *bar hazar (baʃ)*, beware.
A	حذف	*hazf*, suppressing, cutting off, eliminating (subs.).
A	حراج	*haraj*, public sale, auction.
A	حرارت	*hararat*, heat.
AP	حرامزاده	*haramzade*, bastard.
A	حرص	*hers*, avarice, greed, covetousness.
A	حرف	*harf*, letter of the alphabet; word; حرف زدن *harf zadan*, to speak.
A	حرفه	*herfe*, trade, craft.
A	حرکت	*harakat*, movement, moving; حرکت کردن *harakat k.*, to move; to set out.
A	حروف	*horuf* (pl. of حرف *harf*), letters.
AP	حروفچین	*horufcin*, typesetter.
AP	حروفچینی	*horufcini*, typesetting.
A	حریت	*horriyat*, freedom, liberty.
A	حزب	*hezb*, political party.
A	حس	*hess*, feeling; حس کردن *hess k.*, to feel.
A	حساب	*hesab*, reckoning, account; arithmetic.
AP	حسابدار	*hesabdar*, accountant, bookeeper.
AP	حسابداری	*hesabdari*, accountancy; accountancy department; book-keeping.
A	حساس	*hassas*, sensitive; vital, crucial.

A	حسب	*hasb*: بر حسب. *bar hasb(e)*, in conformity with.
A	حسد	*hasad*, envy, malice; حسد بردن *hasad bordan*, to envy.
A	حسن	*hosn*, comeliness, beauty; goodness; حسن ظن *hosne ʒann*, goodwill.
A	حشرات	*haʃarat*, creeping things, insects.
A	حصار	*hesar*, fort, castle.
A	حصبه	*hasbe*, typhoid.
A	حصول	*hosul*, acquisition; produce; gain, profit.
A	حصير	*hasir*, matting; straw (for a hat, etc.).
A	حضرت	*haʒrat*, presence, dignity, majesty; a title of respect.
A	حضور	*hoʒur*, presence, being present.
A	حفر	*hafr*, digging, cleaning out.
A	حفريات	*hafriyat*, excavations.
A	حفظ	*hefʒ*, preservation; حفظ داشتن *hefʒ d.*, to know by heart; حفظ کردن *hefʒ k.*, to preserve, defend.
A	حق	*haqq*, right; claim, due; truth; reality; در حق *dar haqq(e)*, concerning; الحق *al-haqq*, in truth.
A	حقارت	*heqarat*, scorn, contempt.
A	حق القدم	*haqq ol-qadam*, visiting fee.
AP	حق شناس	*haqqʃenas*, grateful.
AP	حق شناسی	*haqqʃenasi*, gratitude.
AP	حق ناشناس	*haqqnaʃenas*, ungrateful.
AP	حق ناشناسی	*haqqnaʃenasi*, ingratitude.
A	حقوق	*hoquq* (pl. of حق *haqq*), rights; wages; علم حقوق *elme hoquq*, political science.
A	حقه	*hoqqe*, trick.
AP	حقه باز	*hoqqebaʒ*, trickster, impostor.
A	حقیر	*haqir*, base, mean, contemptible.
A	حقیقت	*haqiqat*, truth, reality; حقیقت داشتن *haqiqat d.*, to be true.
AP	حقیقی	*haqiqi*, true.
A	حکایت	*hekayat*, story, tale; relation, narrative.
A	حکم	*hokm*, judgement; order, decree; بحکم آنکه *be hokme anke*, by virtue of the fact that; *hakam*, arbitrator.
A	حکمت	*hekmat*, wisdom; philosophy; medicine.

AP حکمران *hokmran,* ruler, governor.

AP حکمرانی *hokmrani,* rule, ruling, governing.

AP حکمفرما *hokmfarma,* prevailing; dominant, ruling.

A حکمیت *hakamiyat,* arbitration.

A حکومت *hokumat,* rule, government.

A حکیم *hakim,* wise man, philosopher; doctor (of medicine).

A حل *hall,* solution, solving; dissolution.

A حلاج *hallaj,* cotton-dresser.

A حلال *hallal,* being legal, lawful.

A حلقه *halqe,* ring; circle, assembly of friends.

AP حل نشدنی *hall naſodani,* insoluble.

A حلوا *halva,* kind of sweetmeat.

A حلبه *helye,* ornament.

A حمام *hammam,* bath.

A حمد *hamd,* praise; الحمد لله *al-hamdo lellah,* praise be to God.

A حمل *haml,* carrying; حمل و نقل *haml o naql,* transport.

A حمله *hamle,* attack; حمله بردن *hamle bordan,* to make an attack.

A حنا *hanna,* henna.

A حوادث *havades* (pl. of حادثه *hadese*), happenings, occurrences.

A حواله *havale,* transfer; consignment.

A حوصله *hŏusele,* patience; حوصله‌ام سر میرود *hŏuseleam sar miravad,* I am bored.

A حوض *hŏuz,* reservoir of water; basin, tank, pond.

A حوله *hŏule,* towel.

A حومه *hŏume,* environs, surrounding district.

A حیات *hayat,* life.

A حیث *heīs:* از این حیث *az in heīs,* on this account.

A حیثیت *heīsiyat,* repute, reputation; condition, nature.

A حیران *heīran,* astonished, amazed, confused.

A حیف *heīf,* injustice, violence; what a pity; حیف و میل کردن *heīf o meīl k.,* to waste; to appropriate unjustly.

A حیله *hile,* trick, stratagem.

A حیوان *heīvan,* animal.

خ

خار   *xar*, thorn; thistle.

A   خارج   *xarej*, external, outside.

A   خارجه   *xareje*, exterior; abroad; (fem. of خارج), external, foreign.

A   خارجی   *xareji*, foreigner.

خارش   *xareʃ*, sore, itch; scab.

خاره   *xare*, hard stone.

خاستن   *xastan*, to rise, get up.

A   خاص   *xass*, خاصه *xasse*, particular, peculiar, special; noble, excellent.

A   خاطر   *xater*, mind, memory; *xater(e)*, بخاطر *be xater(e)*, for the sake of; بخاطر آمدن *be xater amadan*, to come to mind; بخاطر آوردن *be xater avardan*, to bring to mind; بخاطر داشتن *be xater d.*, to remember.

A   خاطر جمع   *xaterjamʿ*, assured (with one's mind at ease).

خاك   *xak*, dust, earth; territory, country.

خاكستر   *xakestar*, ash, ashes.

خاكی   *xaki*, dusty; khaki (colour).

A   خال   *xal*, mole, freckle.

A   خالص   *xales*, pure; unsullied; net (of prices, etc.).

A   خالصه   *xalese*, Crown Land.

A   خالق   *xaleq*, the Creator.

A   خاله   *xale*, maternal aunt.

A   خالی   *xali*, empty.

خام   *xam*, raw.

خامه   *xame*, pen (for writing); cream.

T   خان   *xan*, title of respect; caravanserai.

خاندان   *xandan*, family.

T   خانم   *xanom*, lady.

خانه   *xane*, house.

خانه بدوش   *xane be duʃ*, nomadic.

خاور   *xavar*, east.

خاور شناس   *xavarʃenas*, orientalist.

A   خائن (خاین)   *xaen (xayen)*, traitor.

A	خباز	*xabbaz*, baker.
AP	خباز خانه	*xabbazxane*, bakery.
A	خبر	*xabar*, news, information; خبر کردن *xabar k.*, to inform (someone of something).
	خبرگزاری	*xabargozari*, news agency.
A	خبره	*xebre*, experienced; connoisseur, expert.
A	خبط	*xabt*, error.
A	ختم	*xatm*, assembly to mourn the dead; kind of funeral ceremony.
	خدا	*xoda*, God; خدای تعالی *xodaye ta'ala*, God most high.
	خدا پرست	*xodaparast*, pious, one who worships God.
PA	خدا حافظ	*xoda hafez*, goodbye (*lit.* God [be your] protector).
PA	خدا حافظی	*xoda hafezi*, saying goodbye; خدا حافظی کردن *xoda hafezi k.*, to say goodbye.
	خداوند	*xodavand*, God; (obs.) lord, master; possessed of.
A	خدم	*xadam* (pl. of خادم *xadem*), retinue; attendants.
A	خدمت	*xedmat*, service; employment; *xedmat(e)* to, with, in the presence of (someone).
AP	خدمتگار	*xedmatgar*, servant.
AP	خدمتگذار	*xedmatgozar*, servant; one ready to serve.
AP	خدمتگذاری	*xedmatgozari*, service, serving.
	خر	*xar*, ass, donkey.
A	خراب	*xarab*, destroyed, ruined, desolate; out of order, broken.
A	خرابه	*xarabe*, ruins.
AP	خرابی	*xarabi*, ruin; desolation, destruction.
A	خراج	*xaraj*, tribute, tax.
	خراشیدن	*xarafidan*, to scratch.
A	خرافات	*xorafat* (pl. of خرافه *xorafe*), superstition.
	خربوزه	*xarbuze*, خربزه *xarboze*, melon.
A	خرج	*xarj*, expenditure, expense; cost; خرج کردن *xarj k.*, to spend (money, etc.).
	خرجین	*xorjin*, saddle-bag.
	خرچنگ	*xarcang*, crab.
	خرد	*xerad*, wisdom.
	خرد	*xord*, small.

خرداد	*xordad*, third month of the Persian solar year.
خردسال	*xordsal*, young; a minor.
خردل	*xardal*, mustard.
خردمند	*xeradmand*, wise.
خرده	*xorde*, small, fine, minute; trifle; خرده گرفتن *xorde gereftan*, to criticize.
خرده مالك	*xordemalek*, peasant proprietor.
خرس	*xers*, bear.
خرگوش	*xarguʃ*, hare.
خرم	*xorram*, happy, glad.
خرما	*xorma*, date (fruit).
خرمن	*xarman*, harvest.
خرمن گاه	*xarmangah*, threshing floor.
A خروج	*xoruj*, exit; going out; rebellion.
خروس	*xorus*, cock.
PA خریت	*xariyat*, stupidity, being an ass.
خریدار	*xaridar*, purchaser, buyer; wishing to buy.
خریداری	*xaridari*, purchase.
خریدن	*xaridan*, to buy.
A خزانه	*xaʒane*, treasury; armoury; magazine (of a gun, etc.), chamber (of a rifle, etc.).
AP خزانه دار	*xaʒanedar*, treasurer; having a magazine or chamber (a gun, rifle, etc.).
خزر	*xaʒar*: بحر خزر *bahre xaʒar*, Caspian Sea.
خزه	*xaʒe*, moss.
A خزینه	*xaʒine*, treasury; magazine; store, treasure.
خس	*xas*, kind of grass.
A خسارت	*xesarat*, loss, damage.
خستگی	*xastegi*, fatigue.
خستگی ناپذیر	*xasteginapaʒir*, tireless.
خسته	*xaste*, tired; خسته شدن *xaste ʃ.*, to be, become tired.
A خسوف	*xosuf*, eclipse of the moon.
خشت	*xeʃt*, sun-baked brick.
خشتمال	*xeʃtmal*, brick-maker; خشتمالی *xeʃtmali*, brick-making.
خشك	*xoʃk*, dry; خشك بار *xoʃke bar*, dried fruits.

	خشك سالى	*xoʃksali*, drought, dry year.
	خشكى	*xoʃki*, dryness; dry land.
A	خشن	*xaʃen*, rough, coarse.
A	خصوص	*xosus*, special, particular; بخصوص *be xosus*, in particular, especially.
A	خصوصاً	*xosusan*, especially.
A	خصوصى	*xosusi*, private; special.
A	خصوصيات	*xosusiyat* (pl. of خصوصيه *xosusiye*), particularities, peculiarities.
A	خصومت	*xosumat*, enmity; altercation; litigation.
A	خط	*xatt*, line; خط راه آهن *xatte rahe ahan*, railroad; خط كشيدن *xatt kaʃidan*, to draw a line; to cross out.
A	خطا	*xata*, fault, error.
A	خطر	*xatar*, danger, alarm; سوت خطر *sute xatar*, danger signal, siren.
A	خطوط	*xotut* (pl. of خط *xatt*), lines.
AP	خطى	*xatti*, in manuscript.
	خفتن	*xoftan*, to sleep.
	خفه	*xafe*, close, oppressive (of atmosphere), stifling; suffocated; خفه كردن *xafe k.*, to suffocate (trans.).
A	خلاص	*xalas*, free, liberated.
A	خلاف	*xelaf, xalaf*, opposing; بر خلاف *bar xelaf(e), bar xalaf(e)*, contrary to; خلاف كردن *xelaf k.*, to do wrong, offend (against the law).
A	خلافت	*xelafat*, caliphate.
	خلبان	*xalaban*, aviator.
AP	خلط مبحث	*xalte mabhas*, confusing the issue (noun).
A	خلع	*xal'*, deposing, removing from office; خلع السلاح *xal' as-selah*, disarming; خلع يد *xal'e yad*, expropriation, dispossession.
A	خلعت	*xel'at*, robe of honour.
A	خليج	*xalij*, gulf, bay.
A	خليفه	*xalife*, caliph.
	خم	*xam*, bent, crooked.
A	خمس	*xoms*, one fifth.

خمیر   *xamir*, leaven; dough.

خندان   *xandan*, laughing (adj.).

خنده   *xande*, laugh.

خندیدن   *xandidan*, to laugh.

خنك   *xonak, xonok*, cool; insipid, flat, dull.

خواب   *xab*, sleep; dream; خواب بودن *xab b.*, to be asleep.

خوابیدن   *xabidan*, to sleep; to stop (intrans., of a watch, etc.).

خواربار   *xarbar*, foodstuffs.

خواستار   *xastar*, desirous, desiring; petitioner.

خواستگاری   *xastgari*, asking in marriage.

خواستن   *xastan*, to want, desire, wish; to be about to.

خواه   *xah*: خواه .... خواه *xah .... xah*, whether .... or.

خواهان   *xahan*, desirous, desiring.

خواهر   *xahar*, sister.

خواهرزاده   *xaharzade*, nephew, niece (sister's child).

خواهش   *xaheʃ*, request, desire.

خوب   *xub*, good; خوب بودن با کسی *xub budan ba kasi*, to be on good terms with someone.

خوبی   *xubi*, goodness.

خود   *xod*, self; بخودی خود *be xodiye xod*, involuntarily, automatically.

خود پسند   *xodpasand*, conceited.

خود پسندی   *xodpasandi*, conceit.

خودداری   *xoddari*, restraint; خوداری کردن (از) *xoddari k. (az)*, to refrain (from)

خودسر   *xodsar*, wilful.

خودسری   *xodsari*, wilfulness.

خودکار   *xodkar*, automatic.

خودکشی   *xodkoʃi*, suicide.

خود مختار PA   *xodmoxtar*, independent, autocratic.

خودنویس   *xodnevis*: قلم خودنویس *qalame xodnevis*, fountain-pen.

خوراك   *xorak*, food.

خوردن   *xordan*, to eat.

خورشت   *xoreʃt*, kind of stew.

خورشید   *xorʃid*, sun.

خوش   *xoʃ*, pleasant, agreeable, cheerful, happy; خـوش آمـدیـد *xoʃ amadid*, welcome (interjection); خـوشـم آمد *xoʃam amad*, I liked it; بمن خوش گذشت *be man xoʃ goʒaʃt*, I enjoyed it.

PA خوش اخلاق   *xoʃaxlaq*, well-behaved, good-natured.

PA خوشحال   *xoʃhal*, happy.

PA خوشحالى   *xoʃhali*, happiness.

خوشنود   *xoʃnud*, happy.

خوشنودى   *xoʃnudi*, happiness.

خوشنویس   *xoʃnevis*, calligraphist; having a good hand.

خوشه   *xuʃe*, ear of corn; cluster or bunch of grapes.

خوشى   *xoʃi*, happiness, cheerfulness.

خوك   *xuk*, pig.

خون   *xun*, blood.

خونخوار   *xunxar*, bloodthirsty, cruel.

خونریزى   *xunriʒi*, bloodshed.

خوى   *xui*, nature, disposition; manner, mode, custom; sweat.

خویش   *xiʃ*, self; relation, relative.

خویشتن   *xiʃtan*, self.

خویشى   *xiʃi*, relationship, consanguinity.

خیابان   *xiaban*, avenue.

خیار   *xiar*, cucumber.

A خیال   *xial*, thought, fancy; خیال داشتن *xial d.*, to think, intend; خیال كردن *xial k.*, to think, suppose.

A خیانت   *xianat*, treachery.

A خیر   *xeir*, welfare; good; charity; goodness; no (opp. of yes).

AP خیر خواه   *xeirxah*, charitable; well-wisher.

AP خیر خواهى   *xeirxahi*, benevolence, kindness.

A خیریه   *xeiriye*, charitable work(s).

خیس   *xis*, drenched, soaked in water.

خیش   *xiʃ*, ploughshare.

خیلى   *xeili*, very.

A خیمه   *xeime*, tent; خیمه زدن *xeime ʒadan*, to pitch a tent.

د

A داخل   *daxel*, interior, internal; who or what enters; داخل شدن *daxel ʃ.*, to enter; داخل بودن *daxel b.*, to 'be in on (something)', have a hand in; داخلی *daxeli*, internal.

داد   *dad*, justice.

داداش   *dadaʃ*, brother (colloq.).

داد خواه   *dadxah*, plaintiff.

داد خواهی   *dadxahi*, demanding justice or redress (subs.).

دادرس   *dadras*, just, administering justice; judge.

دادرسی   *dadrasi*, trial (in a court of law); دیوان دادرسی کشور *divane dadrasiye keʃvar*, High Court of Appeal.

دادستان   *dadsetan*, public prosecutor.

دادسرا   *dadsara*, court (legal, etc.).

دادگاه   *dadgah*, tribunal, law-court; دادگاه استان *dadgahe ostan*, provincial court of appeal; دادگاه جنائی *dadgahe janai*, criminal court.

دادگستری   *dadgostari*, justice; وزارت دادگستری *vezarate dadgostari*, Ministry of Justice.

دادن   *dadan*, to give.

دادنامه   *dadname*, petition (legal).

داد وستد   *dad o setad*, commerce.

دادیار   *dadyar*, prosecutor (legal).

دار   *dar*, gallows; بدار زدن *be dar zadan*, to hang (trans.).

A دار   *dar*, (in compounds) house; country, district; دارالایتام *dar ol-ēitam*, orphanage; دارالتجارة *dar ot-tejarat*, trading-house, commercial house; دار المجانین *dar ol-majanin*, asylum, mad-house; دارالمساکین *dar ol-masakin*, poor-house; دارفنا *dare fana*, the transient world; the realm of destruction.

دارا   *dara*, having, possessing (adj.); rich; دارا بودن *dara b.*, to be rich.

دارائی   *darai*, wealth, possessions; finance; وزارت دارائی *vezarate darai*, Ministry of Finance.

دارچین   *darcin*, cinnamon.

دارو   *daru*, medicine; drug; دارو خانه *daruxane*, pharmacy (shop).

دارو ساز   *darusaz*, dispenser, chemist.

دارو شناس   *daruʃenas*, pharmacologist.

دارو شناسی   *daruʃenasi*, pharmacology.

دارو فروش   *daruforuʃ*, chemist, druggist.

داس   *das*, sickle.

داستان   *dastan*, story, fable.

داشتن   *daʃtan*, to have, possess; to hold; بر آن داشتن *bar an d.*, to agree upon; to cause (someone) to determine (upon a course of action).

داغ   *daɣ*, hot; brand, mark, cautery.

دالان   *dalan*, corridor.

دام   *dam*, snare, trap.

داماد   *damad*, son-in-law, bridegroom.

دامپزشك   *dampeʒeʃk*, veterinary surgeon.

دامپزشکی   *dampeʒeʃki*, veterinary; veterinary surgery.

دامن   *daman*, skirt; foot (of a mountain).

دان   *dan*, grain, berry, seed.

دانا   *dana*, learned; دانائی *danai*, learning, knowledge.

دانستن   *danestan*, to know; to consider, deem.

دانش   *daneʃ*, knowledge, learning.

دانش آموز   *daneʃamuz*, student.

دانش جو   *daneʃju*, student of a higher educational institution.

دانشسرا   *daneʃsara*, teacher's training college.

دانشکده   *daneʃkade*, college of a university.

دانشگاه   *daneʃgah*, university.

دانشمند   *daneʃmand*, learned.

دانگ   *dang*, one sixth of anything (especially real estate).

دانه   *dane*, grain, berry, seed.

داور   *davar*, just; arbitrator.

داوری   *davari*, arbitration.

دائر(دایر)A   *daer, dayer*, in working order, going, open; دائر بر *daer, dayer bar* pertaining to, relative to, concerning; دائر بر اینکه *daer bar inke*, to the effect that.

A   دائره   *daere, dayere*, circle.

A	دائم	*daem, dayem,* permanent, perpetual.
A	دائمًا	*daeman, dayeman,* permanently, perpetually, constantly.
A	دائمی	*daemi, dayemī,* permanent, perpetual.
	دائی	*dai,* maternal uncle.
	دبستان	*dabestan,* primary school.
	دبیر	*dabir,* secondary school teacher; secretary; man of letters.
	دبیرخانه	*dabirxane,* secretariat.
	دبیرستان	*dabirestan,* secondary or middle school.
	دچار	*docar,* meeting with, encountering, facing (adj.).
A	دخالت	*dexalat,* interference.
	دختر	*doxtar,* girl, daughter.
	دختری	*doxtari,* girlhood.
A	دخول	*doxul,* entrance.
A	دخیل	*daxil,* effective, having an effect; having a hand (in an affair); borrowed (of a loan-word).
	دد	*dad,* wild animal, beast of prey.
	در	*dar,* door; in; on; در باب *dar bab(e),* concerning; در باره *dar bare(ye),* concerning; در پس *dar pas(e),* در پشت *dar poſt(e),* behind; در پی *dar pei(ye),* after, following after; در راه *dar rah(e),* for the sake of, in the path of; در زیر *dar ʒir(e),* under; در میان *dar miane(e),* among; در نزد *dar naʒd(e),* with, before, in the presence of.
A	دراج	*dorraj,* kind of partridge.
	دراز	*daraʒ, deraʒ,* long.
	دراز دست	*daraʒdast,* rapacious, oppressive.
	در آمد	*daramad,* income, revenue.
	در آمدن	*dar amadan,* to enter; to come out.
	در آوردن	*dar avardan,* to bring out, produce.
	دربار	*darbar,* court, royal establishment.
	دربان	*darban,* door-keeper.
A	درج	*darj,* including, comprehending (subs.).
A	درجه	*daraje,* degree; rank.
	درخت	*daraxt,* tree.
	درخشان	*daraxſan,* brilliant, shining.
	درخشندگی	*daraxſandegi,* lustre, brilliance.

در خواست   *darxast*, request; demand.

در خور   *darxor*, suitable, becoming, proper.

درد   *dard*, pain; بدرد نمیخورد *be dard namixorad*, it is no use.

دردناك   *dardnak*, painful.

در رسیدن   *dar rasidan*, to arrive; to overtake.

در رفتن   *dar raftan*, to go off (of a gun, etc.); to be dislocated (of a limb); از زیر بار در رفتن *az ʒire bar dar raftan*, to avoid doing (something).

درز   *darʒ*, joint, seam, suture.

A   درس   *dars*, lesson; درس خـوانـدن *dars xandan*, to study, have lessons.

درست   *dorost*, right; safe, sound; entire, complete.

درستی   *dorosti*, rightness; soundness; entireness.

درشت   *doroʃt*, rough, hard, thick; stern.

درشتی   *doroʃti*, roughness, thickness; sternness.

R   درشکه   *doroʃke*, cab.

RT   درشکه‌چی   *doroʃkeci*, cabman.

در کردن   *dar kardan*, to let off (a gun, etc.).

در گذشتن   *dar goʒaʃtan*, to die; to pass over, ignore; to forgive.

در گرفتن   *dar gereftan*, to catch; to 'catch on'; to light (of a fire, intrans.)

درمان   *darman*, cure, remedy.

درمانپذیر   *darmanpaʒir*, curable.

درماندگی   *darmandegi*, want, penury; distress, misery; exhaustion.

در ماندن   *dar mandan*, to be in distress; to be utterly exhausted.

درمانشناس   *darmanʃenas*, therapeutist.

درمانشناسی   *darmanʃenasi*, therapy.

درمانگاه   *darmangah*, clinic.

دروازه   *darvaʒe*, gate.

درود   *dorud*, praise; harvest; timber, plank.

درودگر   *dorudgar*, carpenter.

درودن   *dorudan*, to reap.

دروغ   *doruɣ*, lie, falsehood; دروغ گفتن *doruɣ goftan*, to lie.

درون   *darun*, interior.

درویش   *darviʃ*, poor; content with a simple life; dervish.

دریا   *darya*, sea.

دریابان   *daryaban*, vice-admiral.

دریاچه   *daryace*, lake.

دریادار   *daryadar*, rear-admiral.

دریاسالار   *daryasalar*, admiral.

دریافت   *daryaft*, receipt; perception, understanding; acquisition.

در یافتن   *dar yaftan*, to receive; to understand, comprehend; to acquire.

در یافتی   *daryafti*, receipts; received.

دریغ   *dariɣ*: دریغ داشتن *dariɣ d.*, to withhold, keep back, refuse, spare.

دزد   *doɣd*, thief.

دزدی   *doɣdi*, theft.

دزدیدن   *doɣdidan*, to steal.

دژ   *deʒ*, fortress.

دژبان   *deʒban*, military policeman.

دست   *dast*, hand; دست آخر *daste axer*, the final time or turn; دست بردن *dast bordan*, to prevail, conquer; to excel; to carry off; دست بر داشتن *dast bar d.*, to refrain, desist; دست بر دست نهادن *dast bar dast nehadan*, to sit idle; دست دادن *dast dadan*, to shake hands; to give a hand, assist; to happen; دست دراز کردن *dast daraɣ k.*, to stretch out the hand; to rob; دست بگریبان کسی شدن *dast be geribane kasi f.*, to quarrel, fight with someone; دست شستن *dast fostan*, to wash the hands; to despair; to abandon; دست کشیدن *dast kafidan*, to withhold, desist; دست کم *daste kam*, at least; دست و پاگم کردن *dast o pa gom kardan*, to be perplexed; to be frightened out of one's senses; از دست دادن دست یافتن *dast yaftan*, to master; از دست رفتن *aɣ dast dadan*, to give up, lose; از دست رفتن *aɣ dast raftan*, to be lost, perish; بدست آوردن *be dast avardan*, to acquire; یك دست لباس *yak dast lebas*, a suit of clothes.

دستپاچگی   *dastpacegi*, haste, precipitation; confusion, embarrassment.

دستپاچه   *dastpace*, precipitately; confused, embarrassed.

دست پرورده   *dastparvarde*, protégé.

دستخوش   *dastxoʃ*, sport, toy, victim.

دسترس   *dastras*, within reach, available; در دسترس بودن *dar₁* *dastras b.*, to be within reach, available.

دسترسی   *dastrasi*, access; (به) دسترسی داشتن *dastrasi d.* (*be*), to have access to, the possibility of obtaining (something).

دستفروش   *dastforuʃ*, pedlar, hawker.

دستفروشی   *dastforuʃi*, pedlary, hawking.

دستکش   *dastkaʃ*, glove.

دستگاه   *dastgah*, establishment; workshop, loom; power, wealth; a word used in numbering houses, offices, machinery, etc.

دستگیر   *dastgir*, imprisoned, taken prisoner; one who takes the hand, helper.

دستگیری   *dastgiri*, arrest; help.

دستمال   *dastmal*, handkerchief; napkin.

دستمزد   *dastmoʒd*, wages, recompense.

دست نشانده   *dastneʃande*, puppet (fig.).

دستور   *dastur*, leave, permission; model, rule, basis; custom, mode, manner; grammar book; agenda.

دسته   *daste*, handle; group of people; bundle; troop (military).

دسته بندی   *dastebandi*, factional division.

دستی   *dasti*, hand-made.

دستیار   *dastyar*, assistant.

دستیاری   *dastyari*, assistance, help.

A   دسیسه   *dasise*, plot; stratagem.

دشت   *daʃt*, plain, steppe, open country; field.

دشمن   *doʃman*, enemy.

دشمنی   *doʃmani*, enmity.

دشنام   *doʃnam*, abuse, slander; دشنام دادن *doʃnam dadan*, to abuse, revile.

دشوار   *doʃvar*, difficult.

دشواری   *doʃvari*, difficulty.

A   دعا   *doˁa*, prayer.

A   دعوت   *daˁvat*, invitation; prayer.

A   دعوی   *daˁva*, invocation, prayer; charge, accusation; litigation, plaint; quarrel, dispute.

A	دغل	*daɣal*, falsification, fraud; fraudulent; impostor.
	دفتر	*daftar*, book, record, register; exercise-book; office.
	دفتردار	*daftardar*, keeper of the records.
	دفترداری	*daftardari*, keeping the records (subs.).
A	دفع	*dafʻ*, repelling (subs.).
A	دفعةً	*dafʻatan*, suddenly.
A	دفعه	*dafʻe*, time, turn.
A	دقت	*deqqat*, accuracy; با دقت *ba deqqat*, with care, accurate.
A	دقيق	*daqiq*, subtle, minute, abstruse, accurate.
A	دقيقه	*daqiqe*, minute, moment.
A	دكان	*dokkan*, shop.
AP	دكاندار	*dokkandar*, shopkeeper.
	دكل	*dakal*, mast.
	دگمه	*dogme*, button.
	دل	*del*, heart, stomach.
A	دلاك	*dallak*, barber, bath-attendant.
A	دلال	*dallal*, broker.
A	دلالت	*dalalat*, guidance, direction; indication.
AP	دلالی	*dallali*, brokerage.
	دلاور	*delavar*, bold, warlike, brave.
	دلتنگ	*deltang*, distressed, sad.
	دلتنگی	*deltangi*, distress, sadness.
	دلخور	*delxor*, afflicted, grieved.
	دلداری	*deldari*, comfort, consolation.
	دلربا	*delroba*, ravishing, charming.
	دلگرم	*delgarm*, warm-hearted, friendly.
	دلگرمی	*delgarmi*, friendship, warmth.
	دلگیر	*delgir*, afflicted, sad, melancholy.
A	دلو	*dalv*, bucket.
	دلیر	*dalir*, brave, courageous.
A	دلیل	*dalil*, proof.
	دم	*dam*, breath; moment; blood; *dam(e)*, at; *dom*, tail.
	دماغ	*demaɣ*, brains; *damaɣ*, nose.
	دماغه	*damaɣe*, cape, promontory.

دمبه   *dombe*, sheep's tail; fat of a sheep's tail.

دمل   *domal*, swelling, boil.

دمیدن   *damidan*, to blow, breathe; to blossom.

دنب   *domb*, tail.

دنبال   *dombal(e)*, behind, after.

دنباله   *dombale*, tail; the small of the back; sequel.

دنبه   *dombe*, see دمبه.

دنج   *denj*, cosy (adj.).

دندان   *dandan*, tooth.

دندانه   *dandane*, gear, cog.

دنده   *dande*, rib; gear, cog.

A   دنیا   *donya*, world.

A   دنیوی   *donyavi*, worldly, of this world.

دو   *do*, two.

A   دوا   *dava*, medicine; remedy.

دو آتشه   *do atefe*, well-baked, cooked on both sides (of bread, etc.); ardent, zealous.

دوازده   *davazdah*, twelve.

دوا فروش   *davaforuf*, chemist, druggist.

A   دوام   *davam*, continuance; durability; دوام کردن *davam k.*, to be durable; علی الدوام *alad-davam*, continually, permanently.

دوباره   *dobare*, twice, again.

دوچار   *docar*, meeting with, encountering, facing.

دو چرخه   *docarxe*, bicycle.

دوختن   *duxtan*, to sew; to milk.

دود   *dud*, smoke; دود کشیدن *dud kafidan*, to smoke (a cigarette, etc.); دود کردن *dud k.*, to smoke (of a fire, etc.).

دود کش   *dudkaf*, chimney, flue.

دودمان   *dudman*, tribe, family.

دور   *dur*, far, distant; دور افتادن *dur oftadan*, to be separated, go far apart; دور افکندن *dur afkandan*, to throw away.

A   دور   *dōur*, revolution, period of years; circumference; *dōur(e)*, around, round.

دوربین   *durbin*, far-seeing; long-sighted; telescope; دوربین عکاسی *durbine akkasi*, camera.

دوربینی   *durbini*, far-sightedness.

دوردست   *durdast*, far, distant.

دورو   *doru*, double-faced, hypocritical.

دوروئی   *dorui*, hypocrisy; double-dealing.

A   دوره   *doure*, cycle, period, era; series.

دوری   *duri*, distance, absence; being far; separation; دوری جستن (از)
     duri jostan (*az*), to avoid, to shun.

AP   دوری   *douri*, platter, large flat dish.

دوزخ   *duzax*, hell.

دوست   *dust*, friend; دوست داشتن *dust d.*, to like.

دوستدار   *dustdar*, friend.

دوستی   *dusti*, friendship.

دوش   *duʃ*, shoulder; last night.

دوشاب   *duʃab*, kind of grape syrup.

دو شاخه   *doʃaxe*, bifurcated; having two prongs.

دوشك   *doʃak*, mattress.

دوشیدن   *duʃidan*, to milk.

دوشیزه   *duʃize*, virgin, young unmarried woman; form of address
     used to an unmarried woman.

دوغ   *duɣ*, kind of sour buttermilk.

PA   دو فلزی   *dofelezi*, bi-metallism.

دولا   *dola*, double, having two folds; شتر سواری و دولا دولا *ʃotor
     savari o dola dola*, running with the hare and hunting with
     the hounds.

A   دولت   *doulat*, government; state; felicity; wealth; power, dominion,
     empire.

AP   دولتمند   *doulatmand*, rich, wealthy.

A   دولتی   *doulati*, belonging to the state.

A   دون   *dun*, base, mean, despicable.

دویدن   *davidan*, to run.

دویست   *devist*, two hundred.

ده   *dah*, ten; *deh*, village.

دهات   *dehat*, country (as opposed to town); villages.

دهاتی   *dehati*, countryman, peasant.

دهدار   *dehdar*, headman of a village.

دهستان   *dehestan*, group of villages or a village forming an administrative division (smaller than a *baxʃ*).

دهقان   *dehqan*, husbandman, peasant; farmer.

دهکده   *dehkade*, village.

دهن   *dahan*, mouth.

دهنه   *dahane*, orifice; lid; bit of a bridle; mouth (of a river).

دی   *deī*, tenth month of the Persian solar year.

A   دیار   *deyar* (pl. of دار *dar*), region.

دیبا   *diba*, brocade.

دیباچه   *dibace*, introduction, preface.

دیدار   *didar*, sight, vision; visiting, visit.

دیداری   *didari*, payable on sight.

دیدن   *didan*, to see.

دید و بازدید   *did o baẓdid*, call and return call; visiting and returning a visit.

دیده   *dide*, seen; eye.

دیر   *dir*, late; دیرکردن *dir k.*, to be late.

دیروز   *diruẓ*, yesterday.

دیری   *diri*, lateness.

دیرین   *dirin*, دیرینه *dirine*, old, ancient.

دیشب   *diʃab*, last night.

دیگ   *dig*, pot, saucepan, cauldron.

دیگر   *digar*, other; again, further; next.

A   دیم   *deīm*, dry farming.

A   دیمی   *deīmi*, cultivated by dry farming.

A   دین   *din*, religion, faith; *deīn*, debt.

A   دینار   *dinar*, unit of currency, now $\frac{1}{100}$th part of one *rial*.

AP   دیندار   *dindar*, pious, religious.

دیو   *div*, devil, demon, evil spirit.

دیوار   *divar*, wall.

A   دیوان   *divan*, tribunal of justice; royal court; muster-roll; collection of poems in the alphabetical order of the final letters of the various end-rhymes.

دیوانه   *divane*, mad, insane; madman.

دیوانه وار   *divanevar*, like a madman.

ذ

A	ذات	*ẕat*, soul, essence; person, self.
A	ذات الریه	*ẕat or-rie*, pneumonia.
A	ذخیره	*ẕaxire*, treasure, hoard.
A	ذرت	*ẕorrat*, millet; maize.
A	ذرع	*ẕar'*, a unit of length equal to 41 in. or 104 cm.
A	ذره	*ẕarre*, atom, particle; ذرہبین *ẕarrebin*, magnifying glass.
A	ذ کر	*ẕekr*, remembrance; mention; ذ کر کردن *ẕekr, k.*, to mention; to commemorate.
A	ذلت	*ẕellat*, abjectness.
A	ذو	*ẕu*, possessed of; ذو حیاتین *ẕu hayatein*, amphibious.
A	ذوق	*ẕoūq*, taste; pleasure, joy.
A	ذو الحجه	*ẕol-hejje*, the twelfth month of the Mohammadan lunar year.
A	ذو القعده	*ẕol-qa'de*, the eleventh month of the Mohammadan lunar year.
A	ذهن	*ẕehn*, understanding, memory.
A	ذی	*ẕi*, possessed of; ذی روح *ẕiruh*, spiritual, spirited; animate; ذی نفع *ẕinaf'*, interested (financially or materially).
A	ذی حجه	*ẕihejje*, see ذو الحجه.
A	ذی قعده	*ẕiqa'de*, see ذو القعده.
A	ذیل	*ẕeil*, continuation; postscript, appendix; بطریق ذیل *be tariqe ẕeil*, as follows.

ر

A	رابط	*rabet*, link, ligature; liaison officer.
A	رابطه	*rabete*, conjunction; link, ligature; liaison; connexion.
A	راجع	*raje'*, returning, retrograde; referring; راجع به *raje' be*, with reference to.
	راز	*raẕ*, secret; mystery.
A	رأس	*ra's*, head; cape, promontory.
	راست	*rast*, straight; true; direct; راست نمودن *rast namudan*, to put on.
	راستگو	*rastgu*, truthful; truthful person.
	راستگوئی	*rastgui*, truthfulness.

راستی   *rasti*, truth; straightness; directness; really, in truth.

A   راضی   *raẓi*, satisfied, content, pleased; راضی کردن *raẓi k.*, to satisfy, content.

ران   *ran*, thigh.

راندن   *randan*, to drive.

رانندگی   *ranandegi*, driving.

راه   *rah*, road, way, path, passage; راه افتادن *rah oftadan*, to set out; راه رفتن *rah raftan*, to walk along, about; براه انداختن *be rah andaxtan*, to mobilize (capital, etc.); to set in operation.

راه آهن   *rahe ahan*, railroad, railway.

راهنما   *rahnama*, guide; leader.

A   رأی   *ra'i, rāi*, judgement; counsel; act of seeing.

A   رائج (رایج)   *ra'ej (rayej)*, current; circulating freely.

رایزن   *rāizan*, counsellor (of an embassy, etc.).

رایزنی   *rāizani*, consultation, deliberation.

A   رب   *rabb*, God.

A   رباعی   *roba'i*, quatrain.

A   ربح   *rebh*, usury.

A   ربط   *rabt*, connexion; ربط داشتن *rabt d.*, to be connected (with), to concern.

A   ربع   *rob'*, quarter, one fourth.

ربودن   *robudan*, to seize, snatch.

A   رتبه   *rotbe*, rank, degree.

A   رجال   *rejal* (pl. of رجل *rajol*), men; distinguished men.

A   رجل   *rajol*, a man.

A   رجوع   *roju'*, reference; رجوع کردن *roju' k.*, to refer.

A   رحمت   *rahmat*, mercy; رحمت کردن *rahmat k.*, to have mercy.

A   رحمن   *rahman*, merciful, compassionate (of God).

A   رحیل   *rahil*, journey, departure.

A   رحیم   *rahim*, merciful, compassionate.

رخ   *rox*, cheek, face; رخ دادن *rox dadan*, to occur.

رخت   *raxt*, wearing apparel; goods and chattels; رخت بستن *raxt bastan*, to pack one's belongings; to die.

رخت خواب   *raxte xab*, bed-clothes.

A	رد	*radd*, refutation; rejection; repulse; sending back; رد و بدل *radd o badal*, exchange (of words, etc.).
A	ردیف	*radif*, row; order, arrangement; از این ردیف *az in radif*, in this order, of this kind.
	رزم	*razm*, war; battle.
	رزمجو	*razmju*, eager for battle.
	رزمناو	*razmnav*, cruiser.
	رژه	*reze*, march-past.
A	رساله	*resale*, letter, treatise; mission; prophetic office.
	رستائی	*rostai*, see روستائی.
	رستن	*rastan*, to escape; *rostan*, to grow.
	رسد	*rasad*, troop; رسد پیش‌آهنگی *rasade pišahangi*, scout troop; سر رسد *sarrasad*, scout-master; رسد یار *rasadyar*, assistant scout master.
	رسدبان	*rasadban*, police officer whose rank is equivalent to that of a lieutenant in the army.
A	رسم	*rasm*, custom; drawing, marking out; rule, regulation.
	رسمی	*rasmi*, official.
	رسن	*rasan*, rope; halter.
A	رسول	*rasul*, prophet (especially used of Mohammad).
	رسید	*rasid*, receipt; arrival.
	رسیدگی	*rasidegi*, arrival; maturity, ripeness; investigation; رسیدگی کردن *rasidegi k.*, to look into, investigate; see to.
	رسیدن	*rasidan*, to arrive, reach; to be ripe, ripen.
	رشتن	*reštan*, to spin, twist.
	رشته	*rešte*, thread, line, rope; series; subject; kind of macaroni or paste put in stews.
A	رشد	*rošd*, maturity, age of discretion.
A	رشوه	*rešve*, bribe; رشوه خوردن *rešve xordan*, to take bribes.
AP	رشوه خوری	*rešvexori*, taking bribes (subs.).
A	رضایت	*rezayat*, satisfaction, contentment.
AP	رضایت بخش	*rezayatbaxš*, satisfactory.
A	رضی	*razia*: رضی الله عنه *razia 'llah anhu*, May God be pleased with him.

A رعايت   *re'ayat*, observation, observance.

A رعد   *ra'd*, thunder.

A رعيت   *ra'iyat, raiyat*, husbandman, peasant; subject, vassal.

A رغبت   *reɣbat*, desire.

رفتار   *raftar*, conduct.

رفتگر   *roftegar*, dustman.

رفتن   *raftan*, to go; *roftan*, to sweep.

رفت و روب   *roft o rub*, sweeping (subs.).

رفته رفته   *rafte rafte*, gradually.

A رفع   *raf*, removal; lifting, raising; abolishing; رفع حجاب *raf'e hejab*, unveiling, abolishing the veil (subs.).

A رفيق   *rafiq*, comrade, friend.

A رقابت   *raqabat*, rivalry.

A رقاص   *raqqas*, dancer.

A رقت   *reqqat*, compassion, sympathy, tenderness.

AP رقت بار   *reqqatbar*, deplorable, miserable.

AP رقت انگيز   *reqqatangiz*, exciting pity or commiseration (adj.).

A رقص   *raqs*, dance, dancing.

A رقيق   *raqiq*, thin; delicate, tender.

رك   *rok*, frank, straightforward, open; ركگو *rokgu*, outspoken.

A ركن   *rokn*, pillar, prop, support; ركن ستاد *rokne setad*, department or bureau of the military general staff.

A ركيك   *rakik*, coarse, vulgar.

رگ   *rag*, vein; lineage, race, stock.

رگشناس   *ragſenas*, angiologist.

رگشناسی   *ragſenasi*, angiology.

A رمال   *rammal*, geomancer.

F رمان   *roman*, novel (book).

A رمز   *ramz*, riddle, enigma; cypher.

رميدن   *ramidan*, to shy (of a horse, etc.).

رنج   *ranj*, trouble, vexation; affliction; pain; رنج بردن *ranj bordan*, to suffer distress.

رنجور   *ranjur*, sick, infirm; afflicted, grieved.

رنگ   *rang*, colour.

رنگرز   *rangraz*, dyer.

رنگرزی   *rangraẓi*, dyeing (subs.).

رو   *ru*, face; (ی)رو *ru(ye)*, on, upon; رو برو *ru be ru*, opposite, face to face; از این رو *aẓ in ru*, for this reason.

روا   *rava*, lawful, permissible, right; روا بودن *rava b.*, to be lawful, permissible; روا داشتن *rava d.*, to consider or hold lawful or permissible.

A   روابط   *ravabet* (pl. of رابطه *rabete*), relations.

A   رواج   *ravaj*, currency, circulation; current, circulating freely, in great demand, vendible; رواج یافتن *ravaj yaftan*, to become current.

روادید   *ravadid*, visa.

روان   *ravan*, flowing, fluent.

روانامه   *ravaname*, exequatur.

روانه   *ravane*: روانه کردن *ravane k.*, to despatch; روانه شدن *ravane ʃ.*, to set out.

A   روایت   *revayat*, narration, narrative; tradition.

روباه   *rubah*, fox.

A   روح   *ruh*, soul.

A   روحانی   *ruhani*, *rōuhani*, spiritual.

A   روحیه   *ruhiye*, morale.

رود   *rud*, river.

رودبار   *rudbar*, place watered by many streams.

رودخانه   *rudxane*, river; river-bed.

روده   *rude*, intestine, gut, casing.

روده درازی   *rudedaraẓi*, garrulity, being long-winded.

روز   *ruẓ*, day.

روز افزون   *ruẓafẓun*, increasing daily, increasing.

روزگار   *ruẓgar*, time (= indefinite portion of history); providence.

روزنامه   *ruẓname*, newspaper.

A   رؤسا   *ro'asa* (pl. of رئیس *ra'is*), heads, chiefs, leaders.

روستا   *rusta*, village, inhabited place.

روستائی   *rustai*, villager, husbandman.

روسیه   *rusiye*, Russia.

روش   *raveʃ*, conduct; custom, way, mode.

روشن   *rōuʃan*, light, bright; روشنائی *rōuʃanai*, light; brightness.

	روغن	*rouγan*, clarified butter; grease.
	رو نوشت	*runeveſt*, copy (of a document, etc.).
	رو نویس	*runevis*, copy (of a document, etc.).
	روی	*rūi*, face; روی دادن *rūi dadan*, to occur.
	رویان	*ruyan*, embryo.
	رویان شناس	*ruyanſenas*, embryologist.
	رویان شناسی	*ruyanſenasi*, embryology.
	روی هم رفته	*ruye ham rafte*, altogether, on the whole.
	رهبر	*rahbar*, leader.
	رهبری	*rahbari*, leadership; رهبری کردن *rahbari k.*, to lead.
A	رهن	*rahn*, pledge, pawn.
	رهنمونی	*rahnamuni*, leadership, guiding.
A	ریاست	*riasat*, leadership; being head (of a department, etc.).
	ریال	*rial*, unit of currency approximately $1\frac{1}{2}d$.
	ریخت	*rixt*, shape, figure, form, appearance.
	ریختن	*rixtan*, to pour, spill; to cast away.
	ریخته گر	*rixtegar*, founder.
	ریخته گری	*rixtegari*, founding.
	ریز	*riz*, small, minute.
	ریزبین	*rizbin*, microscope.
PA	ریزحساب	*rizhesab*, cash account.
	ریزه	*rize*, small, minute; crumb.
	ریستن	*ristan*, to spin, twist.
	ریسمان	*risman*, thread, string, cord.
	ریش	*riſ*, wound; beard.
	ریشتن	*riſtan*, to spin, twist.
	ریگ	*rig*, sand, gravel, dust.
	ریواس	*rivas*, rhubarb.
A	ریه (رئه)	*rie*, lung.
A	رئیس	*ra'is*, head, chief, director, manager.

ز

	ز	‏ze‏, poetical for ‏از‏ ‏az‏.
	زار	‏zar‏, groan, plaint, lamentation; weeping.
	زارى	‏zari‏, lamentation, weeping.
A	زارع	‏zare'‏, peasant, husbandman.
	زاغ	‏zaɣ‏, magpie; crow, raven, rook.
	زانو	‏zanu‏, knee; ‏چهار زانو نشستن‏ cahar ‏zanu nefastan‏, to sit cross-legged; ‏دو زانو نشستن‏ do ‏zanu nefastan‏, to kneel sitting on one's heels.
A	زاویه	‏zavie‏, corner, angle.
	زائیدن	‏zaidan‏, to give birth (to).
	زبان	‏zaban‏, tongue; language.
	زبان گنجشك	‏zabangonjefk‏, ash (tree).
	زبر	‏zabar‏, above, high, upon; the term for the short vowel a or fathe (because it is placed over the letter); ‏zebr‏, rough, harsh, coarse.
	زبردست	‏zabardast‏, tyrannical; skilful; (in rank), superior.
A	زحمت	‏zahmat‏, trouble; ‏زحمت كشیدن‏ ‏zahmat kafidan‏, to take trouble.
AP	زحمتكش	‏zahmatkaf‏, one who takes trouble; toiler.
	زخم	‏zaxm‏, wound.
	زخمى	‏zaxmi‏, wounded; wounded person.
	زدن	‏zadan‏, to strike, beat; to play (an instrument).
	زد و خورد	‏zad o xord‏, struggle, fighting.
	زدودن	‏zadudan‏, to polish, clean.
	زر	‏zar‏, gold.
A	زراعت	‏zera'at‏, agriculture.
AP	زراعتى	‏zera'ati‏, agricultural.
	زرد	‏zard‏, yellow.
	زردآلو	‏zardalu‏, apricot.
	زردچوبه	‏zardcube‏, turmeric.
	زردك	‏zardak‏, kind of carrot.
	زردى	‏zardi‏, yellowness; jaundice.
	زرشك	‏zerefk‏, barberry.

زرگر   *zargar*, goldsmith.

زره‌پوش   *zerepuʃ* } ironclad, armoured (vehicle).
زره‌دار   *zeredar* }

زرین   *zarrin*, golden.

زشت   *zeʃt*, ugly.

زغال   *zoɤal*, coal; زغال چوب *zoɤale cub*, charcoal; زغال سنگ *zoɤale sang*, coal.

A   زکام   *zokam*, catarrh, cold.

A   زلزله   *zelzele*, earthquake.

زلف   *zolf*, curl, ringlet.

A   زمام   *zemam*, rein, bridle.

AP   زمامدار   *zemamdar*, ruler.

A   زمان   *zaman*, time, season.

زمستان   *zamestan*, winter.

زمین   *zamin*, earth, ground; زمین خوردن *zamin xordan*, to fall down.

زمین شناس   *zaminʃenas*, geologist.

زمین شناسی   *zaminʃenasi*, geology.

زمینه   *zamine*, ground, background, groundwork.

زن   *zan*, a woman; wife.

زناشوئی   *zanaʃui*, matrimony, wedlock.

زنبق   *zambaq*, iris (flower).

زنبور   *zambur*, bee, wasp.

زنبیل   *zambil*, basket.

زنجیر   *zanjir*, chain.

زندان   *zendan*, prison, jail.

زندانبان   *zendanban*, gaoler.

زندانی   *zendani*, prisoner, convict.

زندگی   *zendegi*, life.

زنده   *zende*, alive.

زنگ   *zaŋg*, bell; rust.

زننده   *zanande*, striking; offensive; one who strikes, hits.

زنهار   *zenhar*, beware.

A   زوج   *zōuj*, pair, couple; spouse.

زود   *zud*, early; quickly; soon.

زور   *ʒur*, force, strength, power, violence; زور گفتن *ʒur goftan*, to throw one's weight about, use violence.

A   زورق   *ʒouraq*, skiff, yawl.

زورگوئی   *ʒurgui*, using violence.

زه   *ʒeh*, bow-string; زه کشیدن *ʒeh kaʃidan*, to drain (land).

زهر   *ʒahr*, poison, venom; anger, indignation.

زهرابه   *ʒahrabe*, toxin.

زهرشناسی   *ʒahrʃenasi*, toxicology.

زه کشی   *ʒehkaʃi*, drainage (of land).

A   زیاد   *ʒiad*, much, many; too, too much; (with negative verb) very; زیاد کردن *ʒiad k.*, to increase (trs.).

A   زیادت   *ʒiadat*, increase.

AP   زیادی   *ʒiadi*, increase.

A   زیارت   *ʒiarat*, pilgrimage; visit; زیارت رفتن *ʒiarat raftan*, to go on a pilgrimage; زیارت کردن *ʒiarat k.*, to visit (trans.).

زیان   *ʒian*, damage, loss, injury.

زیبا   *ʒiba*, comely, beautiful.

زیتون   *ʒeitun*, olive (fruit).

زیر   *ʒir*, under, below, beneath.

زیرا   *ʒira*, زیراکه *ʒirake*, because.

زیر پیراهن   *ʒirpirahan*, vest.

زیر دریائی   *ʒirdaryai*, submarine.

زیر دست   *ʒir dast*, inferior (in rank or position).

زیر زمین   *ʒirʒamin*, cellar.

زیر زمینی   *ʒirʒamini*, subterranean; cellar.

زیر شلواری   *ʒirʃalvari*, under-pants, drawers.

زیست   *ʒist*, life, existence.

زیستن   *ʒistan*, to live.

زین   *ʒin*, saddle; زین کردن *ʒin k.*, to saddle (a horse, etc.).

زینت   *ʒinat*, decoration, ornament.

زیور   *ʒivar*, ornament.

ژ

ژرف   *ʒarf*, deep.

س

A	سابق	*sabeq*, former.
A	سابقًا	*sabeqan*, formerly.
A	سابقه	*sabeqe*, the past; past acquaintance; past experience; precedent.
A	ساحل	*sahel*, shore, beach, coast.
	ساخت	*saxt*, make, manufacture; construction, build.
	ساختگی	*saxtegi*, machination; 'frame-up'.
	ساختمان	*saxteman*, construction, building.

ساختن   *saxtan*, to make; ساختن (باكسی) *(ba kasi) saxtan*, to come to an arrangement (with someone); ساختن (بكسی) *(be kasi) saxtan*, (of the climate) to suit (someone).

	ساخته	*saxte*, made; false, counterfeit, 'framed'.
	ساده	*sade*, simple, plain; open, sincere, artless.
	سار	*sar*, starling.
	ساروج	*saruj*, plaster, mortar.
	سازش	*sazeʃ*, arrangement, combination, collusion.
	سازگار	*sazgar*, adaptable (a person); salubrious.
	سازمان	*sazman*, organization.
	ساز وبرگ	*saz o barg*, equipment.
	ساس	*sas*, bug.
A	ساعت	*sa'at*, hour; clock, watch.
A	ساق	*saq*, leg from the ankle to the knee, shank; stem of a tree; stalk of a plant.
A	ساقی	*saqi*, cup-bearer.
A	ساكت	*saket*, silent, quiet.
	سال	*sal*, year.
	سالك	*salak*, Baghdad boil.
	سالمند	*salmand*, adult (person).
	سامان	*saman*, side, quarter.
	سان	*san*, military parade.
A	سائر (سایر)	*sa'er (sayer)*, other, the rest.
	سایه	*saye*, shade, shadow.
A	سبب	*sabab*, cause, reason; ازاین سبب *az in sabab*, باین سبب *be in sabab*, for this reason.

سبد   *sabad*, basket.

سبز   *sabʐ*, green.

سبزی   *sabʐi*, greenness; potherbs.

A   سبقت   *sebqat*, precedence; سبقت جستن *sebqat jostan*, to take the lead, go to the front.

A   سبك   *sabk*, style, method.

سبك   *sabok*, light (not heavy).

سبو   *sabu*, measure of water.

سبوس   *sabus*, bran.

سپارنده   *separande*, depositor.

سپاسگزار   *sepasgoʐar*, grateful.

سپاسگزاری   *sepasgoʐari*, gratitude.

سپاه   *sepah*, army.

سپاهی   *sepahi*, soldier.

سپردن   *sepordan*, to entrust, consign, make over, deposit.

سپرده   *seporde*, deposit.

سپری   *separi*, completed, finished; سپری شدن *separi ʃ.*, to be finished, come to an end, pass away.

سپس   *sepas*, then, afterwards.

T   سپور   *sopur*, dustman.

سپه   *sepah*, army.

سپهبد   *sepahbod*, field-marshal.

سپهسالار   *sepahsalar*, army commander.

ستاد   *setad*, staff; ستاد کل ارتش *setade kolle arteʃ*, general staff (of an army).

ستادن   *setadan*, to take.

ستاره   *setare*, star.

ستم   *setam*, oppression, tyranny.

ستمکار   *setamkar*, oppressor.

ستمکش   *setamkaʃ*, one suffering oppression.

ستوان   *setvan*, lieutenant.

ستودن   *sotudan, setudan*, to praise.

ستون   *sotun*, column; pillar; mast.

ستوه   *sotuh*, distress, affliction.

ستیزه   *setiʐe*, broil, dispute, quarrel.

A   سجل   *sejell*, register; سجل احوال *sejelle ahval*, identity card.

A   سحر   *sahar*, period from midnight to dawn, and especially the period before dawn.

A   سخاوت   *saxavat*, generosity, liberality.

سخت   *saxt*, hard, firm; severe, stern; very.

سختی   *saxti*, hardness, firmness; severity, sternness.

سخن   *soxan*, word; speech, discourse; سخن راندن *soxan randan*, to speak.

سخنچین   *soxancin*, gossip (person); سخنچینی *soxancini*, gossip.

سخنران   *soxanran*, orator.

سخنرانی   *soxanrani*, speech; oration; broadcast talk.

سخنسنج   *soxansanj*, weigher of words; poet.

سخنور   *soxanvar*, eloquent; speaker, orator.

سخنوری   *soxanvari*, making a speech (subs.)

A   سد   *sadd*, obstruction, wall, rampart; dam.

AP   سدبندی   *saddbandi*, damming, building a dam.

سر   *sar*, head, top, summit; cover (of a dish, etc.); *sar(e)*, at; over; سر بالا *sar bala*, up; سر آمدن *sar amadan*, to fall due; boil over; سر بسر گذاشتن *sar be sar gozaſtan*, to tease; سر کشیدن *sar kaſidan*, to drink up, drink to the dregs; to revolt, turn aside; سر و کله زدن *sar o kalle ʒadan*, to argue, dispute; بسر آمدن *be sar amadan*, to fall due.

A   سر   *serr*, secret, mystery.

سزاپا   *sarapa*, from head to foot.

سرازیر   *saraʒir*, downhill.

سرازیری   *saraʒiri* ⎱
سراشیب   *saraſib* ⎰ descent, descending, declivity.

سرافراز   *sarafraʒ*, honoured, exalted.

A   سرایت   *sarayat*, penetrating, infecting; contagion, infection; passing from one thing to another (subs.).

سرب   *sorb*, lead (mineral).

سرباز   *sarbaʒ*, private soldier; سر باز یکم *sarbaʒ yakom*, lance-corporal; سربازخانه *sarbaʒxane*, barracks.

سربالا   *sarbala*, uphill.

سربهر   *sarbahr*, police officer equal in rank to an army captain.

سرپاس   *sarpas*, police officer equal in rank to an army brigadier.

سرپاسبان   *sarpasban*, police officer equal in rank to an army sergeant.

سرتیپ   *sartip*, brigadier; major-general.

سرجوخه   *sarjuxe*, patrol-leader; corporal.

PA   سرحد   *sarhadd*, frontier.

سرخ   *sorx*, red.

سرخك   *sorxak*, measles; kind of bug.

سرد   *sard*, cold.

سرداب   *sardab*, kind of cellar or basement.

سردار   *sardar*, leader, chief; general.

سردرد   *sardard*, headache.

سر رسید   *sarrasid*, falling due, expiration; maturity (of a bill).

سر رسید نامه   *sarrasidname*, bill-book.

سر زمین   *sarzamin*, region, area.

سر سره   *sorsore*, slipway.

سرشار   *sarſar*, brim-full; enormous, large.

سرشتن   *sereſtan*, to mix, knead.

سر شیر   *sarſir*, cream.

A   سرطان   *saratan*, cancer.

PA   سر عمله   *saramale*, foreman.

سرفه   *sorfe*, cough.

سرکار   *sarkar*, title of respect used in place of شما *ſoma*, 'you'.

سرکش   *sarkaſ*, refractory, obstinate; rebellious; hard-mouthed (of a horse).

سرکه   *serke*, vinegar.

سرگذشت   *sargozaſt*, recollection or relation of the past.

سرگرد   *sargord*, major (military officer).

سر لشکر   *sarlaſkar*, divisional commander; lieutenant-general.

سرما   *sarma*, cold (noun); سرما خوردن *sarma xordan*, to catch cold.

سرماخوردگی   *sarmaxordegi*, chill, catching a chill.

سرمایه   *sarmaye*, capital (money, stock, etc.).

سرمایه دار   *sarmayedar*, capitalist.

سرمایه‌داری   *sarmayedari*, capitalism.

سرمشق   *sarmaſq*, example.

سرمه   *sorme*, collyrium.

سرناوی   *sarnavi*, able seaman.

سرنگون   *sarnegun*, upside down; overturned.

سرنوشت   *sarneveſt*, fate, destiny.

سرنیزه   *sarnēīze*, spear-head; (fig.) armed force.

سرو   *sarv*, cypress-tree; سرو آزاد *sarve aȝad*, cedar.

سروان   *sarvan*, captain (military).

سرود   *sorud*, song; سرود ملی *sorude melli*, national anthem.

سرودن   *sorudan*, to sing.

سره   *sare*, pure; undiluted.

سرهنگ   *sarhang*: سرهنگ یکم *sarhang yakom*, colonel; سرهنگ دوم *sarhang dovvom*, lieutenant-colonel.

A   سری   *serri*, secret (adj.).

سریشم   *seriſom*, glue.

سزا   *saȝa*, worthy, deserving of; suitable, proper; بسزا *be saȝa*, fitting.

سست   *sost*, weak, feeble; soft, languid.

سستی   *sosti*, weakness, feebleness; softness, languidness.

A   سطح   *sath*, spreading out (subs.); surface of anything.

A   سطل   *satl*, pail, bucket.

A   سعادت   *sa'adat*, felicity, happiness, good fortune.

A   سعایت   *sa'ayat*, slander; evil-speaking; intrigue.

A   سعی   *sāī*, endeavour, exertion; سعی کردن *sāī k.*, to try.

A   سفارت   *sefarat*, embassy, mission; legation; سفارت کبری *sefarate kobra*, embassy.

سفارش   *sefareſ*, recommendation; order (for goods, etc.); سفارش دادن *sefareſ dadan*, to order (goods etc.); سفارش کردن *sefareſ k.*, to make a recommendation (on someone's behalf).

سفارشی   *sefareſi*, registered (of a letter etc.); specially ordered (of goods, etc.).

سفت   *seft*, firm, solid, set; stiff; hard.

سفتن   *softan*, to bore, pierce, drill.

سفته   *softe*, letter of credit.

سفته باز   *softebaȝ*, speculator.

سفته بازی   *softebaȝi*, speculation.

A   سفر   *safar*, journey.

A   سفرا   *sofara* (pl. of سفیر *safir*), ambassadors, ministers pleni-potentiary; envoys.

A   سفره   *sofre*, table-cloth; سفره انداختن *sofre andaxtan*, to spread out the table-cloth, lay the table.

سفید   *sefid*, white.

سفید آب   *sefidab*, white lead.

PA   سفیده صبح   *sefideye sobh*, period immediately preceding the dawn.

A   سفیر   *safir*, envoy; minister plenipotentiary; سفیر کبیر *safire kabir*, ambassador.

A   سقف   *saqf*, roof.

A   سقوط   *soqut*, fall, falling.

A   سکران   *sokran*, intoxicated, drunk.

A   سکوت   *sokut*, silence.

A   سکه   *sekke*, coin.

سگ   *sag*, dog; سگ تازی *sage tazi*, saluki (dog).

سگماهی   *sagmahi*, sturgeon; seal; shark.

A   سل   *sell*, consumption, tuberculosis.

A   سلاح   *selah*, arms, weapons.

A   سلاطین   *salatin* (pl. of سلطان *soltan*), sultans, rulers.

A   سلام   *salam*, greeting; saluting; levée; سلام علیکم *salam aleıkom*, peace (be) upon thee (form of greeting).

A   سلامت   *salamat* ⎫
AP   سلامتی   *salamati* ⎭ health, well-being; salvation.

A   سلب   *salb*, depriving, deprivation; spoiling, seizing; سلب مصونیت *salbe masuniyat*, deprivation of immunity.

A   سلسله   *selsele*, chain; series; dynasty.

A   سلطان   *soltan*, ruler, sultan; police officer whose rank is equivalent to that of an army captain.

A   سلطه   *salte*, power.

A   سلطنت   *saltanat*, rule, reign; power, dominion.

AP   سلمانی   *salmani*, barber.

A   سلیقه   *saliqe*, taste, good taste.

سم   *som*, hoof.

A   سم   *samm*, poison.

A   سماجت   *semajat*, obstinacy.

A سماق *somaq*, sumach.

A سماوی *samavi*, heavenly.

A سمت *samt*, side, direction; *samt(e)*, بسمت *be samt(e)*, towards.

A سمج *semej*, obstinate.

سمسار *semsar*, dealer in secondhand goods.

A سن *senn*, year, age; tooth; kind of locust.

سنباده *sombade*, emery.

A سنبل *sombol*, hyacinth.

A سنبله *sombole*, ear of grain.

سنج *sanj*, weight, measure.

سنجاب *sanjab*, ermine.

T سنجاق *sanjaq*, pin.

سنجد *sanjed*, jujube tree.

سنجیدن *sanjidan*, to weigh.

A سنخ *senx*, root, origin; class, kind, group.

A سند *sanad*, document; written authority.

سنگ *sang*, stone; a measure of weight.

سنگتراش *sangtaraʃ*, stone-mason.

سنگتراشی *sangtaraʃi*, stone-cutting.

سنگدل *sangdel*, stony-hearted.

سنگسار *sangsar*, stony place; سنگسار کردن *sangsar k.*, to stone (a person).

سنگشناس *sangʃenas*, petrologist.

سنگشناسی *sangʃenasi*, petrology.

سنگفرش *sangfarʃ*, paved with stones.

سنگك *sangak*, kind of bread baked on pebbles.

سنگلاخ *sanglax*, stony place.

سنگواره *sangvare*, fossil.

سنگین *sangin*, heavy; dignified.

سو *su*, side, direction; سو(ی) *su(ye)*, towards; بسو(ی) *be su(ye)*, towards.

A سوء *suʿ*, evil, badness.

AP سوا *seva*: سوا(ی) *seva(ye)*, except.

A سوابق *savabeq* (pl. of سابقه *sabeqe*), past events, past career, record.

A	سواد	*savad*, blackness; literacy.
	سوار	*savar*, riding, mounted; horseman.
	سواری	*savari*, riding (noun).
AP	سوء استفاده	*su'e estefade*, misuse; misappropriation.
A	سؤال	*so'al*, question.
	سوت	*sut*, whistle.
	سوخت	*suxt*, fuel.
	سوختن	*suxtan*, to burn (intrans.); to be out (in a game).
	سود	*sud*, benefit, profit; سود ناویژه *sude navize*, gross profit; سود ویژه *sude vize*, net profit.
	سور	*sur*, banquet, feast.
A	سوره	*sure*, chapter of the Qor'an.
	سوزاك	*suzak*, gonorrhœa.
	سوزش	*suzeʃ*, burn, burning.
	سوسك	*susk*, beetle.
	سوسن	*susan*, lily.
AP	سوء ظن	*su'e ʒann*, suspicion.
AP	سوق الجیشی	*souq ol-jeiʃi*, strategic.
AP	سوء قصد	*su'e qasd*, attempt on someone's life.
	سوگند	*sougand*, oath; سوگند خوردن *sougand xordan*, to take oath; سوگند دادن *sougand dadan*, to administer an oath (to someone).
	سوگواری	*sougvari*, mourning.
	سوهان	*souhan*, file, whetstone.
	سه	*se*, three.
A	سهل	*sahl*, easy.
A	سهم	*sahm*, share, portion; dread, terror.
AP	سهمگین	*sahmgin*, dreadful, terrifying.
A	سهو	*sahv*, omission, blunder, error; oversight.
A	سهولت	*sohulat*, ease, facility.
	سی	*si*, thirty.
A	سیاحت	*siahat*, travel.
A	سیاست	*siasat*, politics; policy.
AP	سیاستمدار	*siasatmadar*, statesman.
A	سیاسی	*siasi*, political; diplomatic.

	سیاه	*siah*, black.
	سیاه سرفه	*siahsorfe*, whooping-cough.
	سیاهی	*siahi*, blackness.
	سیب	*sib*, apple.
	سیب زمینی	*sibe ẓamini*, potato.
	سیخ	*six*, roasting spit; skewer.
A	سید	*seīyed*, descendant of Mohammad.
	سیر	*sir*, full, satiated; garlic; one fortieth of a *man*.
A	سیر	*seīr*, walking; travel.
	سیرابی	*sirabi*, tripe (food).
A	سیرت	*sirat*, disposition, temperament, nature.
	سیزده	*siẓdah*, thirteen.
A	سیل	*seīl*, torrent, flood, flux.
AP	سیلاب	*seīlab*, flood, inundation, torrent.
	سیلی	*sili*, blow or slap in the face.
	سیم	*sim*, wire; silver; سیم خاردار *sime xardar*, barbed wire.
	سیماب	*simab*, quicksilver, mercury.
F	سیمان	*siman*, cement.
	سیمرغ	*simorɣ*, fabulous bird.
	سینه	*sine*, bosom, breast.
	سینه پهلو	*sinepahlu*, pneumonia.
	سینی	*sini*, tray.
	سیه روز	*siahruẓ*, afflicted, unfortunate.

ش

	شاخ	*ʃax*, branch; horn, antler.
	شاخه	*ʃaxe*, branch.
	شاد	*ʃad*, cheerful; glad; exulting.
	شادباش	*ʃadbaʃ*: شادباش گفتن *ʃadbaʃ goftan*, to offer congratulations.
	شادمان	*ʃadman*, happy, cheerful.
	شادی	*ʃadi*, gladness, joy; festivity.
	شاش	*ʃaʃ*, urine.
	شاشیدن	*ʃaʃidan*, to pass water.
A	شاعر	*ʃa'er*, poet.

AP	شاعرانه	ʃaʻerane, poetical.
	شاگرد	ʃagerd, pupil; apprentice; boy, odd-job man.
	شالوده	ʃalude, draft, outline, plan; شالوده ریختن ʃalude rixtan, to draw up a plan; to lay the foundations.
	شام	ʃam, evening; supper.
A	شام	ʃam, Syria; Damascus.
A	شامخ	ʃamex, high, lofty.
A	شامل	ʃamel, including, containing (adj.).
A	شأن	ʃaʻn, dignity; کسر شأن kasre ʃaʻn, derogation of one's dignity or position.
	شانزده	ʃanzdah, sixteen.
	شانه	ʃane, comb; shoulder; شانه خالی کردن ʃane xali k., to make an excuse (in order not to do something), to divest oneself of responsibility (for).
	شاه	ʃah, king, sovereign.
PA	شاهبلوط	ʃahbalut, sweet chestnut.
	شاهتوت	ʃahtut, mulberry.
A	شاهد	ʃahed, witness.
	شاهراه	ʃahrah, main road.
	شاهزاده	ʃahzade, prince.
	شاهوار	ʃahvar, fit for a king.
	شاهی	ʃahi, royal; kingship.
	شایان	ʃayan, brilliant; fitting, suitable.
	شاید	ʃayad, perhaps.
	شایستگی	ʃayestegi, fitness, suitability.
	شایستن	ʃayestan (defective), to be fitting; to suit, befit.
	شایسته	ʃayeste, fitting, worthy.
A	شایع	ʃayeʻ, published, divulged; notorious; widespread.
	شب	ʃab, night, eve.
A	شباب	ʃabab, youth.
	شبان	ʃaban, shepherd.
	شبانه	ʃabane, by night, at night; شبانه روز ʃabane ruz, day and night; twenty-four hours.
A	شباهت	ʃabahat, likeness, resemblance; شباهت داشتن ʃabahat d., to be like, resemble.

شبدر   *ʃabdar*, clover.

شب نشینی   *ʃabneʃini*, evening party, reception; sitting up all night (subs.).

شب نم   *ʃabnam*, dew.

A   شبهه   *ʃobhe*, doubt, ambiguity; suspicion.

A   شبیه   *ʃabih*, resembling, like.

شپره   *ʃappare*, bat (zoolog.).

شپش   *ʃepeʃ*, louse.

شپشه   *ʃepeʃe*, weevil.

شتاب   *ʃetab*, haste, speed.

شتابزدگی   *ʃetabʒadegi*, speed, precipitancy; over-hastiness.

شتابنما   *ʃetabnama*, speedometer.

شتافتن   *ʃetaftan*, to hurry.

شتر   *ʃotor*, camel; شتربان *ʃotorban*, camel-driver.

شترمرغ   *ʃotormorɣ*, ostrich.

A   شجاع   *ʃoja'*, brave, courageous.

AP   شجره نامه   *ʃajarename*, genealogical tree.

A   **شخص**   *ʃaxs*, person; شخصی *ʃaxsi*, someone, anyone; a certain person; شخصاً *ʃaxsan*, personally.

A   شدت   *ʃeddat*, severity, violence; hardship, adversity.

شدن   *ʃodan*, to become; (obs.) to go.

A   شدید   *ʃadid*, strong, violent, severe.

A   شر   *ʃarr*, evil, wickedness.

A   شراب   *ʃarab*, wine.

A   شرافت   *ʃarafat*, nobility, honour.

A   شربت   *ʃarbat*, syrup, sherbet; medicinal draught.

A   شرح   *ʃarh*, explaining, expounding, explanation.

A   شرط   *ʃart*, condition, stipulation; wager, bet; شرط کردن *ʃart k.*, to lay down a condition; شرط بستن *ʃart bastan*, to wager; بشرط اینکه *be ʃarte inke*, on condition that.

A   شرطی   *ʃarti*, conditional.

A   شرع   *ʃar'*, Mohammadan law.

A   شرف   *ʃaraf*, nobility, dignity, honour; در شرف *dar ʃorof(e)*, on the point of, on the verge of; overlooking.

AP   شرفیاب   *ʃarafyab*, having the honour of meeting someone (adj.).

A   شرقی   *ʃarqi*, eastern.

A شرك *ʃerk*, polytheism.

A شركا *ʃoraka* (pl. of شريك *ʃarik*), partners, associates.

A شركت *ʃerkat*, company (commercial, etc.); partnership; شركت جستن *ʃerkat jostan*, to participate (in).

شرم *ʃarm*, shame.

شرمسار *ʃarmsar* ⎫
شرمگين *ʃarmgin* ⎭ ashamed.

A شروع *ʃoruʿ*, beginning, commencement; شروع كردن *ʃoruʿ k.*, to begin.

A شريان *ʃarian*, artery.

A شرير *ʃarir*, wicked, malignant, perverse.

A شريعت *ʃariʿat*, Mohammadan law.

A شريف *ʃarif*, noble, eminent, illustrious.

A شريك *ʃarik*, partner, associate; accomplice.

شست *ʃast*, the thumb.

شستن *ʃostan*, to wash.

شست و شو *ʃost o ʃu*, washing.

شش *ʃeʃ*, six; *ʃoʃ*, lung.

شصت *ʃast*, sixty.

A شط *ʃatt*, bank of a river; large river.

A شعار *ʃeʿar*, motto; sign, mark.

A شعاع *ʃoʿaʿ*, light, splendour, lustre; تحت الشعاع قرار گرفتن (دادن) *taht oʃ-ʃoʿa qarar gereftan (dadan)*, to over-shadow.

A شعب *ʃoʿab* (pl. of شعبه *ʃoʿbe*), branches, sub-divisions.

A شعبان *ʃaʿban*, eighth month of the Mohammadan lunar year.

A شعبه *ʃoʿbe*, branch.

A شعر *ʃeʿr*, poetry; verse; شعرگفتن *ʃeʿr goftan*, to compose poetry.

A شعرا *ʃoʿara* (pl. of شاعر *ʃaʿer*), poets.

A شعله *ʃoʿle*, blaze, flash, flame; شعله زدن *ʃoʿle zadan*, to blaze, flame.

AP شعله‌ور *ʃoʿlevar*, blazing.

شغال *ʃaɣal*, jackal.

A شغل *ʃoɣl*, business, occupation.

A شفا *ʃefa*, remedy, cure.

AP شفاخانه *ʃefaxane*, hospital; school clinic.

A شفاعت *ʃefaʿat*, intercession; mediation.

A شفاهى *ʃefahi*, oral.

A شفقت *ʃafaqat*, compassion; mercy; commiseration.

A شك *ʃakk*, doubt, suspicion.

شكار *ʃekar*, prey, game; the chase, hunting.

PT شكارچى *ʃekarci*, huntsman, shooter.

شكارى *ʃekari*, pertaining to hunting or shooting (dogs, horses, etc.); pertaining to game or prey.

شكاف *ʃekaf*, split, tear; fissure.

شكافتن *ʃekaftan*, to split (trans. and intrans.).

A شكايت *ʃekayat*, complaint.

A شكر *ʃokr*, praise, thanksgiving, gratitude.

شكر *ʃekar, ʃakar*, castor sugar.

شكست *ʃekast*, defeat; شكست خوردن *ʃekast xordan*, to be defeated, suffer defeat; شكست دادن *ʃekast dadan*, to defeat.

شكستگى *ʃekastegi*, fracture.

شكستن *ʃekastan*, to break.

شكسته *ʃekaste*, broken; broken in health, infirm (from age, etc.); kind of cursive handwriting.

شكسته بند *ʃekasteband*, bone-setter.

PA شكسته نفس *ʃekastenafs*, humble.

PA شكسته نفسى *ʃekastenafsi*, humility.

A شكل *ʃekl*, form, shape, figure; appearance.

شكوفه *ʃekufe*, blossom.

شگفت *ʃegeft*, wonder, astonishment.

A شل *ʃall*, crippled, lame.

شل *ʃol*, loose, lax; flabby, soft.

A شلاق *ʃallaq*, whip; شلاق زدن *ʃallaq ɀadan*, to whip.

شلتوك *ʃaltuk*, rice in the husk.

شلتوك كارى *ʃaltukkari*, rice cultivation.

شلخته *ʃalaxte*, sloven; slovenly, slipshod.

شلغم *ʃalɣam*, turnip.

شلوار *ʃalvar*, trousers.

شلوق *ʃoluq*, tumult; disorder, confusion.

شليك *ʃelik*, volley, discharge (of a gun, etc.).

شليل *ʃalil*, nectarine.

شما	*ʃoma,* you.	
شمار	*ʃomar,* reckoning; بشمار رفتن *be ʃomar raftan,* to be reckoned (as).	
شماره	*ʃomare,* number.	
A شمال	*ʃamal, ʃomal,* north.	
A شمالى	*ʃamali, ʃomali,* northern.	
شمردن	*ʃomordan,* to count, reckon.	
A شمس	*ʃams,* the sun.	
A شمسى	*ʃamsi,* solar.	
شمش	*ʃemʃ,* ingot of gold.	
شمشاد	*ʃemʃad,* box-tree.	
شمشير	*ʃamʃir,* sword.	
A شمع	*ʃam',* candle.	
AP شمع دان	*ʃam'dan,* candlestick.	
A شمه	*ʃeme,* little (noun).	
شنا	*ʃena,* swimming.	
شناختن	*ʃenaxtan,* to know, recognize.	
شناسائى	*ʃenasai,* acquaintanceship.	
شناسنامه	*ʃenasname,* identity card.	
شنبه	*ʃambe,* Saturday; يك شنبه *yak ʃambe,* Sunday; دو شنبه *do ʃambe,* Monday; سه شنبه *se ʃambe,* Tuesday; چهار شنبه *cahar ʃambe,* Wednesday; پنج شنبه *panj ʃambe,* Thursday.	
شنفتن	*ʃenoftan,* to hear.	
شنو	*ʃenōu,* swimming.	
شنوا	*ʃenava,* sharp (of the ear); ready to listen, attentive.	
شنونده	*ʃenavande,* hearer, listener.	
شنيدن	*ʃenidan,* to listen, hear.	
شوخ	*ʃux,* mirthful, jovial.	
شوخى	*ʃuxi,* joke, jollity, mirth.	
شور	*ʃur,* salt, brackish.	
شورش	*ʃureʃ,* rebellion, insurrection; disturbance; saltiness, brackishness.	
شوروا	*ʃurva,* broth, gruel.	
A شوروى	*ʃōuravi,* U.S.S.R.; Soviet.	
شورهزار	*ʃureʒar,* salt marsh.	

F   شوسه   *ʃose*, metalled (of a road).

A   شوق   *ʃouq*, desire, yearning.

     شوم   *ʃum*, unlucky, inauspicious, ill-omened.

     شوهر   *ʃouhar*, husband.

A   شهادت   *ʃahadat*, bearing witness (subs.); martyrdom; attestation of faith (especially the Mohammadan).

     شهر   *ʃahr*, town, city.

     شهربانی   *ʃahrbani*, police; police-station.

A   شهرت   *ʃohrat*, fame, repute; publicity; rumour; شهرت داشتن *ʃohrat d.*, to be rumoured, reported; to be famous.

     شهردار   *ʃahrdar*, mayor (of a town).

     شهرداری   *ʃahrdari*, municipality.

     شهرستان   *ʃahrestan*, administrative division (smaller than a province).

     شهرنشین   *ʃahrneʃin*, townsman.

     شهری   *ʃahri*, urban; townsman.

     شهریور   *ʃahrivar*, eighth month of the Persian solar year.

A   شهید   *ʃahid*, martyr.

A   شیء   *ʃeiʼ*, thing.

A   شیاد   *ʃaiyad*, impostor; hypocrite.

     شیب   *ʃib*, descent, declivity.

     شیپور   *ʃeipur*, bugle.

     شیپور زن   *ʃeipurʒan*, bugler.

A   شیخ   *ʃeix*, old man, elder; sheikh.

     شیر   *ʃir*, lion; milk; water-tap.

     شیرخوار   *ʃirxar*, suckling.

     شیرخوارگاه   *ʃirxargah*, orphanage (for babies).

     شیره   *ʃire*, syrup made of grape-juice or other fruit.

     شیری   *ʃiri*, milkman.

     شیرین   *ʃirin*, sweet.

     شیرینی   *ʃirini*, sweetness; sweetmeat.

     شیشه   *ʃiʃe*, sheet of glass, glass; carafe, bottle.

     شیشه بر   *ʃiʃebor*, glass-cutter, glazier.

     شیشه ساز   *ʃiʃesaʒ*, glass-blower.

A   شیطان   *ʃeitan*, Satan; the devil; naughty.

A   شیطانی   *ʃeitani*, mischievousness; mischievous.

A شیطنت   *ſeïtanat*, naughtiness, mischievousness.

A شیعه   *ſi'e*, party, sect (applied particularly to the partisans of Ali, i.e. the Shi'i sect).

A شیعی   *ſi'i*, belonging to the Shi'i sect.

F شیمی   *ſimi*, chemistry.

F شیمیائی   *ſimiai*, chemical.

شیوا   *ſiva*, eloquent; fluent.

شیوه   *ſive*, style; method, manner.

شیهه   *ſeïhe*, neigh, neighing.

ص

F صابون   *sabun*, soap.

A صاحب   *saheb*, possessed of, endowed with; master, owner; صاحب خانه *sahebxane*, landlord, owner of the house; صاحب مال *sahebmal*, rich; صاحب نظر *sahebnaʒar*, clear-sighted, lucid, high-minded.

AP صاحب منصب   *sahebmansab*, military officer.

A صادر   *sader*, issuing, originating, proceeding, emanating (adj.); صادر کردن *sader k.*, to issue; to export.

A صادرات   *saderat*, exports.

A صاف   *saf*, pure, clear; candid.

صافکن   *safkon*, strainer; filter.

A صالح   *saleh*, good, just, honest.

A صبح   *sobh*, morning.

AP صبحانه   *sobhane*, breakfast.

A صبر   *sabr*, patience, waiting patiently; صبر کردن *sabr k.*, to wait.

A صبور   *sabur*, patient, very patient.

A صحبت   *sohbat*, conversation, associating together; صحبت کردن *sohbat k.*, to speak.

A صحت   *sehhat*, soundness, integrity.

A صحرا   *sahra*, plain, desert, open country.

A صحن   *sahn*, court, court-yard (especially of a shrine).

A صحیفه   *sahife*, book, volume (especially a religious book).

صد   *sad*, one hundred.

A   صدا   *sada*, voice, noise; صدا زدن *sada zadan*, to call; با صدای بلند *ba sadaye boland*, with a loud voice.

A   صداق   *sadaq*, marriage portion settled on wife.

A   صداقت   *sadaqat*, sincerity; loyalty; friendship.

A   صدد   *sadad*: در صدد بر آمدن (بودن) *dar sadad bar amadan (budan)*, to intend (to do something); to be about (to do something).

A   صدف   *sadaf*, pearl, shell.

A   صدق   *sadq*, truthful, honest, upright, sincere; *sedq*, truth, veracity; *sodq*, *sodoq* (pl. of *sadq*), speakers of truth, true friends; صدق پیدا کردن *sedq peida k.*, to be established as true.

A   صدمه   *sadame*, injury, loss; صدمه دیدن *sadame didan*, to suffer loss or injury.

A   صدور   *sodur*, issuing, proceeding (noun); exit.

A   صدیق   *sadiq*, true, faithful, sincere; sincere friend; *seddiq*, very sincere, very true.

A   صراحت   *sarahat*, candidness, frankness; صراحت لهجه *sarahate lahje*, frank or plain speaking.

A   صراف   *sarraf*, money-changer.

A   صرف   *sarf*, spending, using, employing; grammar, accidence; agio, premium; صرف کردن *sarf k.*, to spend, consume; صرف نظر کردن *sarfe nazar k.*, to abstain, refrain; *serf*, pure, unmixed; merely.

A   صرفه   *sarfe*, gain, profit; expense; صرفه داشتن *sarfe d.*, to be profitable, advantageous.

AP   صرفه جو   *sarfeju*, economical.

AP   صرفه جوئی   *sarfejui*, being economical, economy, saving.

A   صریح   *sarih*, clear, evident.

A   صعب   *sa'b*, difficult.

A   صغیر   *sayir*, small; minor, not of age.

A   صف   *saff*, line, row; drawing up in battle array; صف کشیدن *saff kasidan*, to draw up in line.

A   صفا   *safa*, purity; being pleasant, agreeable.

A   صفت   *sefat*, quality, attribute.

A	صفحه	*safhe*, page; side; expanse, surface; tract, region; record (of a gramophone).
A	صفر	*sefr*, zero, nought.
A	صلاح	*salah*, rectitude, integrity; propriety, fitness; welfare.
A	صلاحیت	*salahiyat*, competence.
A	صلح	*solh*, peace.
A	صلوات	*salavat*, form of praise consisting in the words صل علی *sall ala* (for *salla ala*) محد و آل محد *mohammad va ale mohammad*, (O God) bless Mohammad and his family.
A	صلیب	*salib*, cross, gibbet.
AP	صمیمی	*samimi*, sincere, cordial.
AP	صمیمیت	*samimiyat*, sincerity, cordiality.
	صنار	*sannar*, ten *dinars* (formerly 100 *dinars*).
A	صناعت	*sana'at*, industry.
A	صناعی	*sana'i*, industrial.
A	صنایع	*sanaye'* (pl. of صنعت *san'at*), industries.
	صندلی	*sandali*, chair.
A	صندوق	*sanduq*, chest, casket, box; till; safe, strong-box.
AP	صندوقدار	*sanduqdar*, cashier.
A	صنعت	*san'at*, industry; art, craft; صنعتی *san'ati*, industrial.
A	صنف	*senf*, kind, category; guild; trade, craft.
	صنوبر	*sanoubar*, fir-tree; cone-bearing tree.
A	صورت	*surat*, face; image, form, figure; بهر صورت *be har surat*, in any case; در این صورت *dar in surat*, in this case; در صورتیکه *dar suratike*, whereas, provided that.
AP	صورت جلسه	*surate jalse*, minutes of a meeting.
AP	صورت حساب	*surate hesab*, bill, account.
AP	صورتی	*surati*, pink (adj.).
AP	صوری	*suri*, external, formal.
A	صوفی	*sufi*, Sufi, mystic.
A	صیاد	*saiyad*, hunter, huntsman.
A	صید	*sēid*, hunting, the chase; prey, game.
A	صیغه	*siɣe*, temporary marriage; temporary wife.
A	صیف	*sēif*, summer (May and June).
A	صیفی	*sēifi*, belonging to the summer; summer crop.

AP	صیفی کاری	*seifikari*, cultivation of summer crops (such as melons, marrows, cucumbers, etc.).
A	صیقل	*seiqal*, polish, lustre; صیقل زدن *seiqal zadan*, to polish.

ض

A	ضابط	*zabet*, assessor; bailiff.
A	ضامن	*zamen*, guarantor; surety.
A	ضایع	*zaye'*, lost, perished, wasted, spoilt.
A	ضبط	*zabt*, confiscation, taking possession of; administering, control.
A	ضخیم	*zaxim*, thick.
A	ضد	*zedd*, opposite; contrary; بر ضد *bar zedd(e)*, against.
AP	ضد عفونی	*zedde ofuni*, disinfectant.
AP	ضد هوائی	*zedde havai*, anti-aircraft.
AP	ضرابخانه	*zarrabxane*, mint (coinage).
A	ضرر	*zarar*, injury, harm, hurt; ضرر ندارد *zarar nadarad*, it does not matter, there is no harm in it.
A	ضرورت	*zarurat*, necessity.
A	ضروری	*zaruri*, necessary.
A	ضعف	*za'f*, weakness.
A	ضعیف	*za'if*, weak.
A	ضمانت	*zamanat*, surety, bond.
A	ضمن	*zemn*, cover, fold; *zemn(e)*, in the course of, while; در این ضمن *dar in zemn*, meanwhile.
A	ضمناً	*zemnan*, meanwhile.

ط

A	طاس	*tas*, die, dice.
A	طاعون	*ta'un*, plague, pestilence.
A	طاق	*taq*, arch; cupola; measure of water.
A	طاقت	*taqat*, power, force, strength, endurance.
AP	طاقتفرسا	*taqatfarsa*, exhausting.
AP	طاقچه	*taqce*, window-sill, niche.

A	طالب	*taleb*, one who asks, demands, requests; searcher, student.
AP	طالبی	*talebi*, kind of melon.
A	طالع	*tale'*, who or what arises, appears; horoscope, fortune, fate.
A	طاٴوس	*taus*, peacock.
A	طائفه (طایفه)	*ta'efe (tayefe)*, people, nation, tribe, family.
A	طب	*tebb*, medicine.
A	طبابت	*tababat*, art or practice of medicine.
A	طبع	*tab'*, nature, disposition; printing.
A	طبق	*tebq(e)*, according to, in accordance with; بر طبق *bar tebq(e)*, according to, in accordance with.
A	طبقه	*tabaqe*, class (social); storey.
AP	طبقه بندی	*tabaqebandi*, division into classes.
A	طبل	*tabl*, drum.
A	طبیب	*tabib*, doctor, physician; طبیب مجاز *tabibe mojaz*, a practising doctor (not qualified by examination).
A	طبیعت	*tabi'at*, nature, disposition.
AP	طبیعی	*tabi'i*, natural, physical.
	طپانچه	*tapance*, pistol.
A	طراوت	*taravat*, freshness, moisture.
A	طرح	*tarh*, foundation, plan, draft.
A	طرز	*tarz*, form, manner, mode.
A	طرف	*taraf*, side, quarter, end; defendant, adversary; از طرف *az taraf(e)*, from the side, direction of; on behalf of; بطرف *be taraf(e)*, towards.
AP	طرفدار	*tarafdar*, supporter, partisan, follower.
AP	طرفداری	*tarafdari*, supporting, support; partiality.
A	طریق	*tariq*, way, road; بر این طریق *bar in tariq*, in this way.
A	طریقه	*tariqe*, road, way; manner, way, fashion; rite, observance; darvish order.
	طشت	*tast*, large basin, ewer, bowl.
A	طعنه	*ta'ne*, irony, sarcasm, gibe, insult; طعنه زدن *ta'ne zadan*, to make insulting insinuations.
A	طغیان	*toyian*, rebellion, breaking bounds.

A طفره   *tafre*, evasion, eluding; (زدن) طفره رفتن *tafre raftan* (*zadan*), to evade, dodge.

A طفل   *tefl*, child.

A طفیل   *tofeil*, parasite; uninivited guest.

A طلا   *tala*, gold.

AP طلائی   *talai*, golden.

A طلب   *talab*, demand, request, claim.

AP طلبکار   *talabkar*, creditor.

A طلسم   *telesm*, talisman.

A طلوع   *tolu'*, rising (of the sun, etc.); طلوع کردن *tolu' k.*, to rise (of the sun, etc.).

A طمع   *tama'*, coveting (subs.); desire, greed, covetousness; طمع داشتن *tama' d.*, to be covetous, greedy.

A طور   *tour*, way, manner; چطور *cetour*, how.

طوطی   *tuti*, parrot.

A طول   *tul*, length; طول کشیدن *tul kafidan*, to last, take time.

A طولانی   *tulani*, long.

A طویله   *tavile*, stable (subs.).

A طی   *tei*, going or travelling through (subs.); fixing, settling (the price of anything); *tei(ye)*, در طی *dar tei(ye)*, throughout the course (of).

A طیاره   *taiyare*, aeroplane.

A طیب   *tib*, *teib*, being good; being favourable; بطیب خاطر *be tibe xater*, willingly, with willing heart; out of goodness of heart.

A طین   *tin*, clay, loam.

ظ

A ظالم   *zalem*, tyrant, oppressor; tyrannical, oppressive.

A ظاهر   *zaher*, external, outer; clear, manifest; ظاهر کردن *zaher k.*, to develop (a film).

A ظاهراً   *zaheran*, apparently.

A ظرف   *zarf*, vessel, pot; در ظرف *dar zarf(e)*, meanwhile, in the meantime; during (= within the period of).

A ظرفیت *ẓarfiyat*, capacity; tonnage (of a ship, etc.).

A ظریف *ẓarif*, witty, subtle; fine, elegant.

A ظفر *ẓafar*, victory.

A ظلم *ẓolm*, oppression, tyranny.

A ظلمت *ẓolmat*, darkness.

A ظن *ẓann*, thinking.

A ظنین *ẓanin*, suspicious.

A ظهر *ẓohr*, midday.

A ظهور *ẓohur*, appearance, emergence; ظهور کردن *ẓohur k.*, to appear, emerge (of a person).

ع

A عاج *aj*, ivory.

A عاجز *ajeẓ*, weak, impotent.

A عادت *adat*, custom, habit.

A عادل *adel*, just.

A عادی *adi*, usual, customary.

A عارض *areẓ*, happening, occurring (adj.).

A عاری *ari*, devoid (of), free (from).

A عاریه *ariye*, anything borrowed or lent.

A عازم *aẓem*, setting out (on a journey, adj.); intent upon (doing something); determined, resolute.

A عاشق *aʃeq*, lover; amorous.

A عاشورا *aʃura*, 10th day of Moharram, on which the Imam Hosein was killed.

A عاطفه *atefe*, affection, sympathy.

A عاقبت *aqebat*, end, conclusion, issue; the future life; عاقبت الامر *aqebat ol-amr*, in the end, finally.

A عاقل *aqel*, wise, intelligent.

A عالم *alam*, the world; *alem*, learned.

A عالی *ali*, high, sublime, eminent.

A عام *amm*, common, universal; the common people.

A عامل *amel*, tax-collector (obs.); agent, official.

A عامه *amme*, the common people.

A عائد (عايد) *aed* (*ayed*), what returns or reverts; accruing, returning.

A عايدات *ayedat*, revenue.

A عبا *aba*, kind of cloak.

A عبادت *ebadat*, adoration, divine worship.

A عبارت *ebarat*, sentence, phrase, word; explanation, interpretation; عبارت از *ebarat aʒ*, consisting in, of.

AP عبارتپردازی *ebaratpardaʒi*, high-flown style (of writing).

A عبد *abd*, slave.

A عبرت *ebrat*, example, warning.

A عبری *ebri*, Hebrew.

A عبور *obur*, crossing, traversing (subs.); عبور کردن *obur k.*, to cross, traverse; to pass through; عبور و مرور *obur o morur*, circulation, traffic.

A عتیق *atiq*, old, ancient.

A عتیقه *atiqe*, antique (subs.).

A عثمانی *osmani*, Ottoman.

A عجب *ajab*, strange, marvellous, wonderful (usu. interj.).

A عجز *ajʒ*, being weak, infirm (subs.).

A عجله *ajale*, haste; عجله داشتن *ajale d.*, to be in a hurry; عجله کردن *ajale k.*, to hasten (intrans.).

A عجوز *ajuʒ*, عجوزه *ajuʒe*, old woman.

A عجیب *ajib*, wonderful, strange.

A عجیبه *ajibe*, wonder, marvel.

A عدالت *adalat*, justice, equity.

A عدد *adad*, number.

A عدس *adas*, lentil.

A عدل *adl*, equity, justice; bale (of cotton, etc.).

A عدلیه *adliye*, Ministry or Department of Justice.

A عدم *adam*, non-existence; absence, lack.

A عدو *adu*, enemy.

A عده *edde*, number (of persons).

A عذاب *aʒab*, torment, torture; pain; punishment.

A عذر *oʒr*, excuse, apology; عذر خواستن *oʒr xastan*, to apologize, ask pardon.

A	عراده	*arrade*, gun-carriage; small ballista; word used in counting cannons, etc.
A	عرب	*arab*, Arab.
A	عربى	*arabi*, Arabic; Arabian.
A	عرض	*arẓ*, representing, petitioning; petition; عرض کردن *arẓ k.*, to petition; (in 1st pers. only) to say (in polite speech).
A	عرفان	*erfan*, knowledge (especially spiritual); mysticism.
A	عرفى	*orfi*, customary (of law, etc.), according to common use and wont.
A	عرق	*araq*, sweat; anything oozing out from pores; essence; arrack, spirits.
A	عرق النسا	*erq on-nesa*, the sciatic nerve; sciatica.
A	عروس	*arus*, bride; daughter-in-law.
AP	عروسك	*arusak*, doll.
AP	عروسى	*arusi*, wedding.
A	عز	*eẓẓ*, power; خدای عز و جل *xodaye aẓẓa va jalla*, God, who is powerful and glorious.
A	عزت	*eẓẓat*, grandeur, glory; esteem.
A	عزم	*aẓm*, purpose, resolution, undertaking.
A	عزيز	*aẓiẓ*, dear, precious.
A	عزيمت	*aẓimat*, starting (subs.); undertaking; resolution.
A	عسل	*asal*, honey.
A	عشاير (عشائر)	*aſaer* (pl. of عشيره *aſire*), tribes.
A	عشر	*oſr*, one tenth.
A	عشرت	*eſrat*, pleasure; conversation, society.
A	عشق	*eſq*, love.
A	عصا	*asa*, staff, stave.
A	عصب	*asab*, tendon, nerve.
A	عصبانى	*asabani*, irritable.
A	عصر	*asr*, afternoon, evening; period (of time).
AP	عصرانه	*asrane*, afternoon tea.
A	عضله	*aẓole*, muscle.
A	عضو	*oẓv*, limb; member.
A	عضويت	*oẓviyat*, membership.
A	عطا	*ata*, grant, bestowal; gift.

A عطار *attar*, dealer in perfumes, drugs, spices or groceries.

A عطر *atr*, perfume.

A عطسه *atse*, sneeze.

A عظمت *aẕamat*, greatness.

A عظيم *aẕim*, huge.

A عفت *effat*, chastity.

A عفو *afv*, pardon, forgiveness; عـفـو عمومى *afve omumi*, general amnesty.

A عفيف *afif*, chaste.

A عقاب *oqab*, eagle.

A عقايد *aqayed* (pl. of عقيده *aqide*), beliefs; opinions.

A عقب *aqab*, rear, hinder part; slow (of a watch); *aqab(e)*, behind; after; عقب نشستن *aqab nefastan*, to retreat.

A عقد *aqd*, contract (especially a marriage contract); covenant, engagement, treaty; عقد بستن *aqd bastan*, to make a marriage contract.

A عقدى *aqdi*, wife married by an *aqd* or contract of unlimited period.

A عقرب *aqrab*, scorpion.

A عقل *aql*, reason, intellect.

A عقيده *aqide*, belief; opinion.

A عقيم *aqim*, barren, sterile.

A عكاس *akkas*, photographer.

AP عكاسخانه *akkasxane*, photographic establishment, studio.

AP عكاسى *akkasi*, photography.

A عكس *aks*, reflexion; photograph; reverse, contrary; عكس انداختن *aks andaxtan*, to take a photograph; بر عكس *bar aks*, on the contrary.

A عكس العمل *aks ol-amal*, reaction.

A علاج *elaj, alaj*, cure, treatment.

A علاف *allaf*, purveyor of provender, chandler.

A علاقه *alaqe*, inclination, interest; friendship, affection, attachment.

AP علاقهمند *alaqemand*, attached, interested.

A علامت *alamat*, mark, sign, signal.

A	علاوه	*alave*, excess; besides, moreover, in addition; علاوه بر این *alave bar in*, in addition to this; بعلاوه *be alave*, in addition.
A	علت	*ellat*, cause, reason.
A	علف	*alaf*, fodder, forage.
A	علم	*alam*, standard, flag; *elm*, knowledge; science; theory.
AP	علمدار	*alamdar*, standard-bearer; (fig.) leader.
A	علمی	*elmi*, scientific.
A	علوم	*olum* (pl. of علم *elm*), sciences.
A	علی	*ala*, against; according to; in; with; by; على الخصوص *alal-xosus*, in particular; على الدوام *alad-davam*, continually; على رغم *ala raɣm(e)*, contrary to.
A	علیا	*olya* (fem. of اعلى *a'la*), more or most high; علیا حضرت *olya haɣrat*, her majesty.
A	علیه	*aleih*, upon him; against him; against; بر علیه *bar aleih*, against him, against.
A	عمارت	*emarat*, building, edifice.
A	عمامه	*emame, amame*, turban.
A	عمدًا	*amdan*, on purpose.
A	عمده	*omde*, principal, chief; عمده مالك *omdemalek*, large land-owner.
A	عمر	*omr*, life.
A	عمران	*omran*, cultivation, bringing land into cultivation.
A	عمق	*omq*, depth.
A	عمل	*amal*, practice; doing; putting into practice; operation (surgical); عمل کردن *amal k.*, to practise, put into practice; to operate (med.); بعمل آمدن *be amal amadan*, to be produced, to grow (intrans.); بعمل آوردن *be amal avardan*, to produce, grow (trans.); اطاق عمل *otaqe amal*, operating theatre.
A	عمله	*amale*, workman, labourer.
A	عملی	*amali*, practical.
A	عمو	*ammu* (usually pronounced *amu*), paternal uncle; پسر عمو *pesarammu*, cousin (son of a paternal uncle); دختر عمو *doxtarammu*, cousin (daughter of a paternal uncle).

A	عموم	*omum*, the public, the community.
A	عمومًا	*omuman*, generally.
A	عمومی	*omumi*, common, general, universal.
A	عمومیت	*omumiyat*, generality, universality.
A	عمه	*amme*, paternal aunt; پسر عمه *pesaramme*, cousin (son of a paternal aunt); دختر عمه *doxtaramme*, cousin (daughter of a paternal aunt).
A	عنان	*enan*, rein, bridle.
A	عنصر	*onsor*, element.
A	عنقریب	*an qarib*, shortly, soon.
A	عنکبوت	*ankabut*, spider.
A	عنوان	*envan*, title; superscription; address; way, manner; بعنوان *be envan(e)*, as, by way of.
A	عوارض	*avarez* (pl. of عارضت *arezat*), dues, tolls.
A	عوام	*avamm* (usually pronounced *avam*), common people, populace.
AP	عوامانه	*avamane*, popular, pertaining to the common people.
AP	عوام فریب	*avamfarib*, demagogue.
AP	عوام فریبی	*avamfaribi*, demagogy.
A	عوامل	*avamel* (pl. of عامل *amel*), factors, causes.
A	عوض	*avaz*, equivalent, compensation; *avaz(e)*, instead of, in place of.
A	عهد	*ahd*, age, reign; oath; treaty, covenant; agreement; عهد بستن *ahd bastan*, to conclude an agreement.
AP	عهدنامه	*ahdname*, treaty of agreement.
A	عهده	*ohde*, obligation; charge, trust, responsibility; از عهده بیرون آمدن *az ohde birun amadan*, to fulfil (an obligation), carry out (a task, etc.); بر عهده گرفتن *bar ohde gereftan*, to undertake (responsibility for).
AP	عهدهدار	*ohdedar*, entrusted (with an affair), responsible, charged (with).
A	عیاش	*aiyaʃ*, pleasure-seeker; debauchee, rake.
AP	عیاشی	*aiyaʃi*, luxury, addiction to pleasure; debauchery.
A	عیال	*aiyal*, wife, family.
AP	عیال بار	*aiyalbar*, having a large family.

A عیب *eib*, fault, blemish; عیب گرفتن *eib gereftan*, to find fault; عیب ندارد *eib nadarad*, it does not matter.

A عید *id, eid*, feast, holiday.

A عیسی *isa*, Jesus.

A عیسوی *isavi*, Christian.

A عیش *eiʃ*, luxury.

A عین *ein*, eye; substance, essence; fountain, source.

A عیناً *einan*, exactly like.

AP عینک *einak*, spectacles.

غ

A غار *ɣar*, cave.

A غارت *ɣarat*, plunder, pillage; غارت کردن *ɣarat k.*, to plunder; بغارت بردن *be ɣarat bordan*, to carry off as booty.

غاز *ɣaᷱ*, goose.

A غافل *ɣafel*, negligent; careless; incautious.

AP غافلگیر *ɣafelgir*: غافلگیر کردن *ɣafelgir k.*, to take unawares, catch by surprise.

A غالب *ɣaleb*, prevailing, predominant; triumphant, victorious; غالب آمدن *ɣaleb amadan*, to be victorious.

A غالباً *ɣaleban*, generally.

A غامض *ɣameᷱ*, obscure, abstruse.

A غائب (غایب) *ɣaʼeb (ɣayeb)*, absent, concealed.

A غائله *ɣaʼele*, misfortune, evil, calamity; fuss, ado.

A غبار *ɣobar*, dust; vapour, fog.

A غدیر *ɣadir*: عید غدیر *ide ɣadir*, the anniversary of the day when Ali was designated as Mohammad's successor, 18th Zo'l-Hejje.

A غرامت *ɣaramat*, indemnity.

A غربی *ɣarbi*, western.

A غرس *ɣars*, planting (trees).

A غرض *ɣaraᷱ*, rancour, spite, malignity; ulterior motive; aim, object.

A غرغر *ɣorɣor*, murmuring, muttering, grumbling.

A	غرغره	ɣarɣare, gargling.
A	غرق	ɣarq, sinking, submersion, drowning.
A	غروب	ɣorub, setting (of the sun, etc.).
A	غره	ɣorre, blaze on the forehead of a horse.
A	غريب	ɣarib, strange; stranger, foreigner.
A	غزل	ɣaʒal, ode.
A	غش	ɣaʃ, fainting, swooning (subs.).
A	غصه	ɣosse, grief, sorrow; غصه خوردن ɣosse xordan, to be grieved, sad.
A	غفران	ɣofran, pardon, remission.
A	غفلت	ɣeflat, negligence, carelessness.
A	غلا	ɣala, being dear or high-priced; scarcity.
A	غلام	ɣolam, slave; servant.
A	غلط	ɣalat, error, mistake.
AP	غلط گیری	ɣalatgiri, correcting (especially printer's proofs, subs.)
AP	غلط نامه	ɣalatname, corrigenda, errata.
A	غله	ɣalle, grain, corn.
A	غليظ	ɣaliʒ, thick; coarse.
A	غم	ɣam, grief, sadness; anxiety.
AP	غمگین	ɣamgin, sad.
	غنچه	ɣonce, bud.
A	غنی	ɣani, rich, wealthy.
A	غنیمت	ɣanimat, booty.
	غوره	ɣure, unripe grapes; unripe dates.
A	غوص	ɣōus: غوص شناور ɣōuse ʃenavar, floating dock.
A	غوطه	ɣute, dive, diving, dipping.
A	غوغا	ɣōuɣa, tumult, uproar.
A	غیب	ɣēib, being absent, hidden.
A	غیبت	ɣēibat, concealment, absence; speaking evil of someone behind his or her back.
A	غیر	ɣēir, other; different; alien; ɣēir(e) un-, non-; غیر از ɣēir aʒ, other than; و غیره va ɣēire, etc.
AP	غیر رسمی	ɣēire rasmi, unofficial.
AP	غیر قابل تحمل	ɣēire qabele tahammol, intolerable.

ف

A	فاتح	*fateh*, conqueror; victorious.
A	فاتحه	*fatehe*, opening chapter of the *Qor'an*, which is recited especially as a prayer for the dead.
A	فاحش	*faheʃ*, manifest, notorious; obscene.
A	فاحشه	*faheʃe*, whore.
AP	فاحشه خانه	*faheʃexane*, brothel.
	فاخته	*faxte*, ring-dove.
	فارسى	*farsi*, Persian (language).
A	فارغ	*fareɣ*, free, ceasing from labour, having just finished some work.
A	فارغ التحصيل	*fareɣ ot-tahsil*, graduate of a college or university.
A	فاسد	*fased*, vicious, corrupt.
	فاش	*faʃ*, divulged; public, spread abroad; clear, manifest.
A	فاصله	*fasele*, interval, space, intermediate distance.
A	فاضل	*fazel*, excellent; learned.
A	فاقد	*faqed*, devoid of, wanting.
	فال	*fal*, omen; فال گرفتن *fal gereftan*, to take an omen.
F	فاميل	*famil*, family.
A	فانوس	*fanus*, storm-lantern.
A	فانى	*fani*, transitory.
A	فائده (فايده)	*faede* (*fayede*), benefit, profit, gain.
A	فائق (فايق)	*faeq* (*fayeq*), superior, paramount; great, high.
A	فتح	*fath*, victory, conquest.
A	فتحه	*fathe*, the vowel *a*.
A	فترت	*fetrat*, interregnum.
A	فتنه	*fetne*, sedition, rebellion.
A	فتوت	*fotovvat*, generosity, chivalry.
A	فتوح	*fotuh* (pl. of فتح *fath*), victories, conquests; conquest.
A	فتوى	*fatva*, judicial decree.
A	فتيله	*fatile*, wick.
A	فجيع	*faji'*, tragic; calamitous, disastrous; atrocious.
A	فحاش	*fahhaʃ*, abusive; obscene, lewd.
AP	فحاشى	*fahhaʃi*, abuse; obscenity, lewdness.

A	فحش	*fohʃ*, abuse.
A	فحوی	*fahva*, import, drift; sense, meaning; contents.
A	فدا	*fada*, ransom, sacrifice.
AP	فداکاری	*fadakari*, self-sacrifice, devotion.
	فرا	*fara*, up, upon; above; again; behind, back; فرا آوردن *fara avardan*, to bring back or up; to attract.
	فراخور	*faraxor*, worthy, fit, proper, suitable.
	فراز	*faraᵹ*, up, upon, above; again; under; behind, back; top; high, exalted.
A	فراش	*farraʃ*, house or office servant.
AT	فراش باشی	*farraʃbaʃi*, head-servant.
A	فراغت	*faraɣat*, leisure; freedom from work or care.
	فراموش	*faramuʃ*, forgotten; فراموش کردن *faramuʃ k.*, to forget.
F	فرانسوی	*feransavi*, French; Frenchman.
F	فرانسه	*feranse*, France.
	فراوان	*faravan*, abundant, copious, plentiful.
	فراوانی	*faravani*, abundance, plenty.
	فراهم	*faraham*, available, prepared, ready, assembled; فراهم ساختن *faraham saxtan*, to make available.
	فربه	*farbeh*, fat (adj.).
A	فرح	*farah*, gladness, joy.
A	فرد	*fard*, individual (subs.).
	فردا	*farda*, tomorrow.
	فرز	*ferᵹ*, quick, quickly.
	فرزند	*farᵹand*, child.
	فرستادن	*ferestadan*, to send.
	فرسخ	*farsax*, measure of length about three and a half miles.
	فرسودگی	*farsudegi*, being worn out.
A	فرش	*farʃ*, floor-covering, carpet; فرش کردن *farʃ k.*, to carpet.
	فرشته	*fereʃte*, angel.
A	فرصت	*forsat*, opportunity.
A	فرض	*farᵹ*, supposition; fancy; indispensable duty; بالفرض *bel-farᵹ*, supposing that.
A	فرضیه	*farᵹiye*, indispensable precept.
A	فرع	*far'*, branch, subdivision.

A	فرعی	*far'i*, derivative; secondary.
A	فرق	*farq*, difference; separation, distinction.
A	فرقه	*ferqe*, sect; group.
	فرمان	*farman*, order, command; decree.
	فرمانبردار	*farmanbardar*, obedient.
	فرماندار	*farmandar*, governor.
	فرمانداری	*farmandari*, being a governor; offices of a governor.
	فرمانده	*farmandeh*, commander (of an army, etc.).
	فرماندهی	*farmandehi*, command (of an army, etc.).
	فرمانروا	*farmanrava*, monarch, sovereign.
	فرمانروائی	*farmanravai*, sovereignty.
	فرمایش	*farmayeʃ*, order, command.
	فرمودن	*farmudan*, to order, command; (in 2nd and 3rd persons only) to say, do, etc. (in polite speech).
	فرنگ	*farang* ⎫
	فرنگستان	*farangestan* ⎬ Europe.
	فرنگی	*farangi*, European.
PA	فرنگی مآب	*farangima'ab*, westernized.
	فرو	*foru*, down, below; low; فرو بردن *foru bordan*, to swallow; to submerge; فرو رفتن *foru raftan*, to go under, sink, sink in; فرو شدن *foru ʃ.*, to sink, go down; فرو نشستن *foru neʃastan*, to sit down; to subside.
	فروتنی	*forutani*, humility.
	فروختن	*foruxtan*, to sell.
	فرود	*forud*, below, under, down; فرود آمدن *forud amadan*, to come down, descend.
	فروردین	*farvardin*, first month of the Persian solar year.
A	فروع	*foru'* (pl. of فرع *far'*), branches, subdivisions.
	فروند	*farvand*, tiller (of a ship); word used in counting ships.
	فرهنگ	*farhang*, culture; dictionary; وزارت فرهنگ *veʒarate farhang*, Ministry of Education.
	فرهنگستان	*farhangestan*, academy.
	فرهنگی	*farhangi*, cultural, educational.
	فریاد	*faryad*, lamentation, cry.
	فریفتن	*fariftan*, to deceive.

فزونى   *fozuni*, surplus (subs.).

A   فساد   *fesad*, corruption.

A   فسخ   *fasx*, breaking (an agreement); annulling, cancelling; اختيار فسخ *exteyare fasx*, option of terminating (an agreement).

فشار   *fešar*, pressure.

فشردن   *fešordan*, to squeeze, press.

فشنگ   *fešang*, cartridge.

A   فصاحت   *fasahat*, eloquence.

A   فصل   *fasl*, section; season (of the year).

A   فصيح   *fasih*, eloquent; classical (of a language).

A   فضل   *fazl*, excellence; learning; virtue; grace, favour.

A   فضول   *fozul*, meddling, officious.

AP   فضولى   *fozuli*, meddling, officiousness; impertinent interference.

A   فضيلت   *fazilat*, excellence; learning; virtue.

A   فطر   *fetr*: عيد فطر *ide fetr*, the festival of breaking the fast of Ramazan, 1st Shavval.

A   فعال   *fa'al*, active, energetic; *fa"al*, very active, very energetic.

A   فعاليت   *fa'aliyat*, activity, energy.

A   فعل   *fe'l*, action; فعلاً *fe'lan*, actually, at present; in practice.

فغان   *feɣan*, complaint, lamentation.

A   فقر   *faqr*, poverty.

A   فقره   *faqare*, vertebra.

A   فقط   *faqat*, only, merely.

A   فقير   *faqir*, poor.

A   فكر   *fekr*, thought, thinking; فكر كردن *fekr k.*, to think.

A   فلاحت   *falahat*, agriculture.

A   فلاحتى   *falahati*, agricultural.

A   فلاكت   *falakat*, poverty, distress.

A   فلان   *folan*, such a one, a certain.

AP   فلانى   *folani*, so-and-so.

A   فالج   *falaj*, paralyzed.

A   فلز   *felezz*, ore, metal.

A   فلزى   *felezzi*, metallic, mineral (adj.).

A   فلسفه   *falsafe*, philosophy.

A   فلفل   *felfel*, pepper.

A   فن   *fann*, science, art; technique.

A   فنا   *fana*, annihilation, non-existence.

فنجان   *fenjan*, cup.

فندق   *fondoq*, hazel-nut.

A   فنون   *fonun* (pl. of فن *fann*), arts, sciences.

A   فنى   *fanni*, technical.

A   فواره   *favvare*, fountain; jet of water.

A   فوت   *fout*, death.

A   فوج   *fouj*, body of men, company, troop, squadron.

A   فورا   *fouran*, immediately.

A   فوریت   *fouriyat*, urgency.

A   فوق   *fouq*, above; top, upper part; فوق الذكر *fouq oz-zekr*, above-mentioned.

فهرست   *fehrest*, index, table of contents.

A   فهم   *fahm*, understanding, intelligence.

AP   فهمیدن   *fahmidan*, to understand.

A   فى   *fi*, in; فى ما بین *fi ma bein*, between.

A   فى الجمله   *fel-jomle*, in short.

A   فى الفور   *fel-four*, immediately.

فیروزه   *firuze*, turquoise.

A   فیض   *feiz*, grace, bounty, excellence.

فیل   *fil*, elephant.

A   فیلسوف   *filsuf*, philosopher.

ق

T   قاب   *qab*, frame; vessel, case.

A   قابل   *qabel*, worthy; able; *qabel(e)*, capable of, liable to, susceptible of.

T   قابلمه   *qablame*, cooking-vessel.

T   قاتى   *qati*, mixed.

T   قاچ   *qac*, slice.

T   قاچاق   *qacaq*, smuggling; smuggled; قاچاقچى *qacaqci*, smuggler.

T   قارچ   *qarc*, fungus, mushroom.

A   قاره   *qare*, continent.

T	قاشق	*qaʃoq*, spoon; قاشق چای خوری *qaʃoqe caïxori*, teaspoon.
A	قاضی	*qaẕi*, judge.
T	قاطر	*qater*, mule.
A	قاعده	*qaʿede*, rule, custom, principle.
A	قافله	*qafele*, caravan, body of travellers.
A	قافیه	*qafie*, rhyme.
A	قالب	*qaleb*, mould; form.
	قالی	*qali*, carpet.
	قالیباف	*qalibaf*, carpet-weaver.
	قالیبافی	*qalibafi*, carpet-weaving.
	قالیچه	*qaliche*, small carpet.
A	قانع	*qaneʿ*, contented; convinced, persuaded.
A	قانون	*qanun*, law; rule, custom.
AP	قانونگذاری	*qanungoʒari*, legislating, legislation.
T	قایق	*qayeq*, boat.
A (قایل) A	قائل	*qael (qayel)*, maintaining (an opinion), agreeing, accepting.
A (قایم)	قائم	*qaem (qayem)*, erect; firm, fixed, durable; guardian; hidden.
A	قباحت	*qabahat*, foul, shameful or abominable act.
A	قباله	*qabale*, title-deed, bill of sale.
A	قبر	*qabr*, grave.
AP	قبرستان	*qabrestan*, graveyard, cemetery.
A	قبض	*qabẕ*, receipt, voucher.
A	قبضه	*qabʒe*, hilt (of a sword), handle; word used in counting swords, rifles, etc.
A	قبل	*qabl*, before; قبل از *qabl aʒ*, before.
A	قبلاً	*qablan*, beforehand, previously.
A	قبله	*qeble*, point towards which prayers are directed (i.e. the Ka'ba in Mecca).
A	قبول	*qabul*, consenting, accepting, receiving (noun).
A	قبیح	*qabih*, shameful, foul, abominable.
A	قبیل	*qabil*, sort, kind; از این قبیل *aʒ in qabil*, of this kind.
T	قپان	*qappan*, large pair of scales.
TP	قپاندار	*qappandar*, weigher.
TP	قپانداری	*qappandari*, weighing; weighing charges.
A	قتال	*qetal*, conflict, battle.

A   قتل   *qatl*, killing, slaying; murder.

AP   قحطى   *qahti*, scarcity, dearth, famine.

A   قد   *qadd*, stature.

A   قدر   *qadr*, value, worth; power; dignity; size, measure; amount; آنقدرکه *an qadr ke*, as much as; بقدریکه *be qadrike*, as much as; چقدر *ce qadr*, how much; *qadar*, fate; whatever is fixed or ordained by God; قدرى *qadri*, little (subs.).

A   قدرت   *qodrat*, power, strength.

AP   قدردانى   *qadrdani*, just appreciation of merit, appreciation.

T   قدغن   *qadaɣan*, forbidden.

A   قدم   *qadam*, foot; step, pace; قدم بر داشتن *qadam bar d.*, to take a step forward, advance.

A   قدوس   *qodus*, holy; *qoddus*, very holy.

A   قديم   *qadim*, old, ancient.

A   قرار   *qarar*, firmness, stability; legal finding; قرار دادن *qarar dadan*, to fix, establish; قرار شدن (بودن) *qarar ſ. (b).*, to be decided, resolved, settled; قرار گرفتن *qarar gereftan*, to be fixed, firm; to become quiet, still steady; to be calmed, appeased; مورد مذاکره قرار گرفتن *mōured-e moɀakere qarar gereftan*, to become the subject of discussion; از این قرار *aɀ qarar(e)*, according to; at the rate of; باین قرار *in qarar*, as follows; of this nature; بقرار *be qarar(e)*, according to; بر قرار *bar qarar*, firm, fixed, established.

AP   قرارداد   *qarardad*, contract, agreement; قرارداد بستن *qarardad bastan*, to make an agreement.

A   قرآن   *qor'an*, the Qor'an.

A   قربان   *qorban*, sacrifice; sacrificial victim.

AP   قربانى   *qorbani*, sacrifice; sacrificed; قربانى کردن *qorbani k.*, to sacrifice.

A   قرص   *qors*, firm, strong; tough.

A   قرعه   *qor'e*, lottery; قرعه کشى *qor'ekaſi*, drawing lots (subs.).

A   قرقره   *qerqere*, spool, reel, bobbin.

   قرمز   *qermeɀ*, red, crimson.

A   قرن   *qarn*, century.

F   قرنتين (قرنطينه)   *qarantin (qarantine)*, quarantine.

A   قريب   *qarib*, near; relation, kinsman.

A   قريحه   *qarihe*, nature, genius; innate disposition.

A   قريه   *qarie*, village.

T   قزل آلا   *qezelala*, trout.

A   قس على هذا   *qes ala haza*, and so on, in proportion (*lit.* take measurement from this).

A   قسط   *qest*, instalment.

A   قسم   *qesm*, kind, sort.

A   قسمت   *qesmat*, part, portion, share; fate, destiny; قسمت کردن *qesmat k.*, to divide, share out.

A   قشر   *qefr*, bark (of a tree), peel, rind; crust, shell.

T   قشلاق   *qeflaq*, winter-quarters.

     قشنگ   *qafang*, beautiful.

     قشنگی   *qafangi*, beauty.

T   قشون   *qofun*, army.

A   قصاب   *qassab*, butcher.

AP   قصابخانه   *qassabxane*, butcher's shop.

A   قصبه   *qasabe*, large village, small town.

A   قصد   *qasd*, intention, design, determination, resolution.

A   قصر   *qasr*, palace.

A   قصص   *qesas* (pl. of قصه *qesse*), stories, tales.

A   قصه   *qesse*, tale, story.

A   قصیده   *qaside*, poem or ode (longer than a غزل *yazal*).

A   قضا   *qaza*, fate, predestination.

A   قضاوت   *qazavat*, judgement.

A   قضائی   *qazai*, judicial, juridical.

A   قطار   *qetar*, series, row; railway-train; word used in numbering camels.

A   قطب   *qotb*, pole; axis, pivot.

AP   قطبنما   *qotbnama*, compass.

A   قطره   *qatre*, drop (small quantity).

A   قطع   *qat'*, cutting off, breaking off, interrupting; terminating, concluding; قطع نظر از *qat'e nazar az*, apart from.

A   قطعاً   *qat'an*, definitely.

A   قطعه   *qet'e*, segment; portion; word used in numbering miscellaneous articles.

A	قعود	*qoʿud*, sitting down (noun).
A	قفا	*qafa*, nape of the neck; در قفا *dar qafa*, in secret.
A	قفس	*qafas*, cage.
A	قفسه	*qafase*, shelf, cupboard, cabinet.
A	قفل	*qofl*, lock, bolt.
A	قفیز	*qafiẕ*, measure of ground, one-tenth *jarib*.
A	قلاب	*qolab*, hook.
A	قلابی	*qallabi*, counterfeit, false; coiner of false money; cheat.
A	قلب	*qalb*, heart; transmutation, permutation; counterfeit.
A	قلع	*qalʿ*, putting down, suppressing; tin.
A	قلعه	*qalʿe*, fortress.
A	قلم	*qalam*, pen (for writing); قلم شدن *qalam ʃ.*, to be badly fractured (a bone, etc.).
AP	قلمداد	*qalamdad*, declared, counted, enumerated.
AP	قلمدان	*qalamdan*, pencase.
AP	قلمرو	*qalamroū*, jurisdiction, sovereignty.
AP	قلمكار	*qalamkar*, kind of printed calico.
A	قلمه	*qalame*, cutting (botan., subs.).
A	قله	*qolle*, summit of a mountain.
	قلیان	*qalian*, water-pipe, hubble-bubble; قلیان كشیدن *qalian kaʃidan*, to smoke a hubble-bubble.
A	قلیل	*qalil*, little small; قلیلاً *qalilan*, little, a little (adv.).
A	قمار	*qomar*, playing at dice, or any game of hazard; gambling, any game of hazard.
AP	قماربازی	*qomarbaẕi*, gambling (at cards).
A	قماش	*qomaʃ*, cotton piece goods.
A	قمری	*qamari*, lunar.
A	قمع	*qamʿ*, putting down, suppressing (subs.).
A	قنات	*qanat*, subterranean canal.
A	قناد	*qannad* ⎫
AP	قنادی	*qannadi* ⎬ maker of sugar candy, confectioner.
A	قناعت	*qanaʿat*, contentment, ability to do without something; قناعت كردن *qanaʿat k.*, to be content (with a little), to make do.
	قند	*qand*, lump sugar.

T   قنداق   *qondaq*, swaddling clothes.

قنددان   *qanddan*, sugar-bowl.

قنسل (قنسول)   *qonsol* (*qonsul*), consul; قنسلى (قنسولى) *qonsoli* (*qonsuli*), consular; قنسلگرى (قنسولگرى) *qonsolgari* (*qonsulgari*), consulate.

A   قوا   *qova* (pl. of قوت *qovvat*), forces; قواى تأمينيه *qovaye ta'miniye*, security forces.

A   قوانين   *qavanin* (pl. of قانون *qanun*), laws.

A   قوت   *qovvat*, strength, power, force.

قوچ   *quc*, buck, ram.

T   قورباغه   *qorbaɣe*, frog.

TP   قورخانه   *qurxane*, arsenal.

قورى   *quri*, tea-pot.

قوز   *quẕ*, hump; قوز پشت *quẕpoſt*, hunchback.

A   قوس   *qôus*, arc (of a circle); قوس قزح *qôuse qaẕah*, rainbow.

T   قوش   *quſ*, kind of falcon or hawk.

T   قوطى   *quti*, small tin or box.

A   قول   *qôul*, word, saying; قول دادن *qôul dadan*, to promise.

A   قوم   *qôum*, people, nation; tribe, family, kindred.

A   قوه   *qovve*, power; قوه برق *qovveye barq*, electric power.

A   قوى   *qavi*, strong; stout (in build).

قهرمان   *qahraman*, champion, hero.

A   قهرى   *qahri*, inevitable, compulsory.

A   قهوه   *qahve*, coffee.

A   قى   *qei*, vomiting.

A   قياس   *qias*, analogy; conjecture.

A   قيافه   *qiafe*, facial appearance.

A   قيام   *qiam*, standing up, rising up; insurrection; قيام كردن *qiam k.*, to undertake, set about (doing something).

A   قيامت   *qiamat*, resurrection; tumult.

A   قيد   *qeid*, confinement, restriction; bondage; با قيد احتياط *ba qeide ehteyat*, with reserve (an expression used to indicate that an item of news reported has not been confirmed).

A   قير   *qir*, pitch, tar.

T   قيصى   *qeisi*, kind of apricot.

A	قیم	*qeīyem*, guardian.
A	قیمت	*qeīmat*, value, price.
A	قیمومیت	*qeīmumiyat*, mandate, protectorate.

ك

A	کاتب	*kateb*, scribe, writer.
	کاج	*kaj*, fir-tree; pine-tree; cedar.
	کاخ	*kax*, palace.
	کار	*kar*, work; action, thing, affair; business, occupation; بکار بردن *be kar bordan*, to use.
	کار آگاه	*karagah*, detective, informer.
	کار آموز	*karamuʒ*, probationer.
	کار آموزی	*karamuʒi*, probation.
	کار پرداز	*karpardaʒ*, quartermaster; manager, agent.
	کار پردازی	*karpardaʒi*, stores department.
	کار خانه	*karxane*, factory; workshop.
	کارد	*kard*, knife.
	کاردار	*kardar*, chargé d'affaires.
	کارزار	*karʒar*, battle; field of battle.
	کارشناس	*karʃenas*, expert (subs.).
	کارشناسی	*karʃenasi*, expert knowledge.
	کارفرما	*karfarma*, employer.
	کارکنان	*karkonan*, personnel.
	کار گزار	*kargoʒar*, official, functionary; correspondent (of a bank).
	کار گزاری	*kargoʒari*, agency (polit. and com.).
	کار گزین	*kargoʒin*, head of a personnel department.
	کار گزینی	*kargoʒini*, personnel department.
	کار مزد	*karmoʒd*, commission, factorage.
	کارمند	*karmand*, employee.
	کاروان	*karvan*, caravan, large company of travellers.
	کاروانسرا	*karvansara*, caravanserai.
	کاستن	*kastan*, to diminish, lessen (trans.).
	کاسه	*kase*, bowl; کاسه از آش گرمتر *kase aʒ aʃ garmtar*, one who is "more Catholic than the Pope".

كاش   *kaʃ*, would that.

كاشتن   *kaʃtan*, to sow; to cultivate.

A   كاشف   *kaʃef*, discoverer, revealer.

كاشكى   *kaʃki*, would that.

كاشى   *kaʃi*, painted or glazed tiles.

كاشىكارى   *kaʃikari*, painted or glazed tile work.

كاغذ   *kayaʒ*, paper; letter (epistle).

A   كافر   *kafer*, unbeliever, heathen.

كافور   *kafur*, camphor.

A   كافى   *kafi*, sufficient.

كال   *kal*, unripe.

كالا   *kala*, goods.

كالبد   *kalbod*, body; mould, form, figure.

كالبدشكافى   *kalbodʃekafi*, dissection.

كالبدشناسى   *kalbodʃenasi*, anatomy.

كالبدگشائى   *kalbodgoʃai*, autopsy.

كام   *kam*, desire, wish.

كامران   *kamran*, successful, fortunate.

A   كامل   *kamel*, perfect; complete.

كامياب   *kamyab*, successful; one who obtains what he desires.

كاميابى   *kamyabi*, success; achieving one's desire.

كان   *kan*, mine; mineral deposit.

كانشناس   *kanʃenas*, mineralogist.

كانشناسى   *kanʃenasi*, mineralogy.

كانون   *kanun*, club (social); hotbed (fig.).

كاه   *kah*, straw.

كاهگل   *kahgel*, mixture of mud and straw used for plaster in building.

A   كاهل   *kahel*, indolent, idle.

AP   كاهلى   *kaheli*, sloth, indolence.

كاهو   *kahu*, lettuce.

A   كباب   *kabab*, meat roasted on a spit or skewer.

A   كبريت   *kebrit*, match (for lighting).

كبك   *kabk*, partridge.

كبوتر   *kabutar*, pigeon, dove.

كبود   *kabud*, blue; black and blue, bruised.

	كبوده	*kabude*, kind of poplar.
A	كبير	*kabir*, great; large.
A	كبيسه	*kabise*, intercalary; سال كبيسه *sale kabise*, leap-year.
A	كتاب	*ketab*, book.
AP	كتابچه	*ketabce*, notebook.
AP	كتابخانه	*ketabxane*, library.
AP	كتابدار	*ketabdar*, librarian.
AP	كتابفروش	*ketabforuʃ*, bookseller.
A	كتان	*kattan, katan*, linen, flax.
A	كتب	*kotob* (pl. of كتاب *ketab*), books.
	كترى	*ketri*, kettle.
	كتك	*kotak*, blow (with a stick, etc.); كتك زدن *kotak ʒadan*, to strike, hit; كتك خوردن *kotak xordan*, to be struck, beaten.
	كتل	*kotal*, mountain pass.
	كتيرا	*ketira*, gum tragacanth.
A	كثافت	*kesafat*, filth.
A	كثرت	*kesrat*, being numerous; superfluity, excess.
A	كثيف	*kasif*, dirty.
	كج	*kaj*, crooked, curved, bent.
	كجا	*koja*, where.
	كجدم	*kajdom*, scorpion.
	كچل	*kacal*, scald-head.
A	كحال	*kahhal*, oculist.
A	كحل	*kohl*, collyrium, antimony.
	كدام	*kodam*, which (of two or more).
	كدخدا	*kadxoda*, village headman.
	كدو	*kadu*, marrow (plant).
A	كذا	*kaʒa*, like this, such, such like; such and such.
A	كرايه	*keraye*, hire, rent, fare.
	كرباس	*kerbas*, kind of coarse linen.
	كرجى	*karaji*, rowing-boat.
	كردار	*kerdar*, action, conduct.
	كردن	*kardan*, to do, make.
	كرسى	*korsi*, seat; throne; bench; kind of table covered by a quilt and placed over a brazier to serve as a heating apparatus.

کرفس *karafs*, celery.

T   کرک *kork*, woollen; down, soft wool.

  کرکس *kargas*, vulture.

  کرم *kerm*, worm.

A   کرم *karam*, bounty, generosity.

  کره *kare*, butter; *korre*, foal.

A   کره *korre*, sphere, globe.

A   کریم *karim*, generous, liberal; merciful; gracious.

  کس *kas*, person; کسی *kasi*, anyone.

A   کساد *kasad*, dullness of market; decline of trade.

A   کسالت *kesalat*, indisposition.

A   کسب *kasb*, gaining, acquiring (subs.); trade.

A   کسر *kasr*, loss; deficit; کسر الشأن *kasr of-ʃaʿn*, loss of dignity, something derogatory to one's position.

A   کسل *kesel*, indisposed; out of sorts.

A   کسوف *kosuf*, eclipse (of the sun).

  کش *keʃ*, elasticity; elastic (noun).

  کشاورز *keʃavarʒ*, husbandman, cultivator.

  کشاورزی *keʃavarʒi*, agriculture.

  کشت *keʃt*, cultivation; sown field.

  کشتن *keʃtan*, to sow, till; *koʃtan*, to kill.

  کشتی *kaʃti*, ship; با کشتی *ba kaʃti*, by boat; by sea; *koʃti*, wrestling; کشتی گرفتن *koʃti gereftan*, to wrestle, struggle,

A   کشف *kaʃf*, revealing, discovering, discovery; کشف حجاب *kaʃfe hejab*, prohibition of the veil.

  کشک *kaʃk*, dried butter-milk; آش کشک *aʃe kaʃk*, kind of pottage.

  کشمش *keʃmeʃ*, raisin, sultana; raisins, sultanas.

  کشمکش *keʃmakeʃ*, struggle.

  کشور *keʃvar*, country; وزارت کشور *veʒarate keʃvar*, Ministry of the Interior.

  کشیدن *kaʃidan*, to draw, pull; to attract; to extend, protract; to delineate, paint; to lead (to), reach, result in; خجالت کشیدن *xejalat kaʃidan*, to be ashamed; (از) دست کشیدن *dast kaʃidan (aʒ)*, to abandon, give up; زحمت کشیدن *ʒahmat kaʃidan*, to take pains, or trouble.

كشيش   *kaʃiʃ*, priest (Christian).

T   كشيك   *kaʃik*, guard, sentry; كشيك بودن (داشتن) *kaʃik budan (d.)*, to be on guard, on duty.

كف   *kaf*, froth, foam.

A   كف   *kaff*, the palm of the hand.

A   كفاش   *kaffaʃ*, shoemaker.

A   كفايت   *kefayat*, sufficiency; ability, capacity.

كفتار   *kaftar*, hyena.

كفتر   *kaftar*, pigeon.

كفترباز   *kaftarbaʒ*, pigeon-fancier.

كفتربازى   *kaftarbaʒi*, pigeon-fancying; rearing pigeons.

A   كفر   *kofr*, unbelief; كفر نعمت *kofre neʿmat*, ingratitude.

A   كفش   *kaff*, shoe; كفش راحتى *kaffe rahati*, slipper.

كفگير   *kafgir*, skimmer.

A   كفن   *kafan*, winding-sheet, shroud.

A   كفه   *kaffe*, tray of a pair of scales.

A   كفيل   *kafil*, security, surety (person); one who acts for another.

كل   *kal*, stag; any male animal.

A   كل   *koll*, all, universal; the whole.

كلاغ   *kalaɣ*, crow, rook, raven.

كلافه   *kalafe*, reel, spindle; skein, hank.

A   كلام   *kalam*, speech, discourse; علم كلام *elme kalam*, scholastic theology.

كلانتر   *kalantar*, headman; سركلانتر *sarkalantar*, police official in charge of a police-station.

كلانترى   *kalantari*, police station; area under the jurisdiction of a police-station.

كلاه   *kolah*, hat; كلاه بر داشتن *kolah bar d.*, to take off the hat; كلاه سركسى گذاشتن، كلاه كسى بر داشتن *kolahe kasi bar d.*, *kolah sare kasi goɣaʃtan*, to swindle, cheat someone.

كلفت   *koloft*, thick.

كلك   *kalak*: كلك كسى (چيزى) را كندن *kalake kasi (ciʒi) ra kandan*, to get rid of someone; (put an end to an affair).

كلم   *kalam*, cabbage.

A   كلمه   *kaleme*, word; saying, discourse.

كلنگ   *kolang*, pick-axe.

كلوخ   *kolux*, clod of earth.

كله   *kalle*, head; top, summit; cone; سر و كله زدن *sar o kalle ʒadan*, to wear out, exhaust oneself (in trying to convince someone of something).

كله پاچه   *kallepace*, head and trotters (of sheep, etc.).

A   كلى   *kolli*, all, every, universal; total; بكلى *be kolli*, altogether, in general.

G   كليد   *kalid*, key.

G   كليسا   *kalisa*, church.

A   كليه   *kolie*, kidney; *kolliye*, all; universality, totality; the whole.

كم   *kam*, few, little; كم كردن *kam k.*, to decrease (trans.); *kam kam*, little by little; كمى *kami*, little (subs.).

A   كمال   *kamal*, perfection, excellence.

كمان   *kaman*, bow.

PA   كم بضاعت   *kambaʒaʿat*, poor; possessed of little capital.

كم بود   *kambud*, deficiency, deficit.

كمر   *kamar*, waist; loins; كمر بستن *kamar bastan*, to gird up one's loins.

كمرو   *kamru*, timid, diffident.

كمزور   *kamʒur*, weak.

كمك   *komak*, help.

كمند   *kamand*, lasso.

كمياب   *kamyab*, rare, scarce.

كميابى   *kamyabi*, rarity, scarcity.

كنار   *kenar*, side; shore, coast; edge; كنار آمدن (با) *kenar amadan (ba)*, to come to terms (with); بر كنار *bar kenar*, aside; بر كنار رفتن *bar kenar raftan*, to withdraw, go aside, retire.

كناره گيرى   *kenaregiri*, retirement, going into retirement, withdrawing.

كنج   *konj*, corner, nook.

كنجد   *konjed*, rape (plant).

كنجكاوى   *konjkavi*, research; investigation, digging into the depths of something; curiosity, "nosiness".

كند   *kond*, dull, slow-witted; blunt.

کندن *kandan*, to dig; to root out, tear up; to raze to the ground.

کنسل *konsol*, consul; سرکنسل *sarkonsol*, consul-general.

کنسلگری *konsolgari*, consulate.

کنسلیار *konsolyar*, vice-consul.

کنش *koneʃ*, action, operation.

کنشت *keneʃt*, synagogue.

کنگر *kangar*, kind of artichoke.

کنون *konun*, now; the present; کنونی *konuni* (adj.), present, actual.

کوبیدن *kubidan*, to pound, beat, bruise; to knock.

کوت *kut*, manure.

کوتاه *kutah*, short; کوتاهقد *kutahqadd*, short of stature.

کوتوله *kutule*, dwarf (person).

کوچ *kuc*, migration; striking camp, marching.

کوچك *kucek*, small, little.

کوچه *kuce*, street.

کود *kud*, manure.

کودك *kudak*, small child, infant.

کودکستان *kudakestan*, kindergarten.

کور *kur*, blind.

کوره *kure*, furnace, forge; brick-kiln; lime-kiln.

کوری *kuri*, blindness.

کوزه *kuʒe*, earthen jug.

کوشش *kuʃeʃ*, effort, endeavour, striving.

کوشیدن *kuʃidan*, to strive, try.

کوفتن *kuftan*, to bruise, pound; to knock.

کوفته *kufte*, balls of pounded meat cooked in stew or soup; wearied, stiff.

کوك *kuk*, wound-up (of a watch, etc.); tuned; کوك کردن *kuk k.*, to wind (a watch, etc.); to tune (an instrument).

کول *kul*, the shoulder, back; کول کردن (گرفتن) *kul k.* (*gereftan*), to carry on the back.

کوله‌بار *kulebar*, haversack, rucksack.

کولی *kouli*, gipsy.

کوه *kuh*, mountain.

کویر *kavir*, salt and sour ground; salt desert.

کُه   *ke*, who, which; that; so that, **in** order that; because; when; than; = saying.

کهر   *kahar*, bay (colour).

کهربا   *kahroba*, magnet.

کهنه   *kohne*, old, ancient (of things).

کی   *ki*, who (interrog.); *keī*, when (interrog.).

کیسه   *kise*, bag; sack; purse.

کیف   *kif*, purse; bag.

A   کیف   *keīf*, pleasure, intoxication, enjoyment; کیف کردن *keīf k.*, to be intoxicated, exhilarated.

کیفر   *keīfar*, retribution, reward.

A   کیفیت   *keīfiyat*, state of affairs, circumstances, particulars, condition.

کین   *kin*, کینه *kine*, hatred, enmity, rancour, malevolence, malice; revenge, vengeance.

گ

گاری   *gari*, cart.

گاریچی   *garici*, carter.

گاز   *gaʒ*, biting, bite; گاز گرفتن *gaʒ gereftan*, to bite.

گاز انبر   *gaʒambor*, tongs; pincers.

گازر   *gaʒor*, bleacher, fuller.

گام   *gam*, step, pace; cubit.

گامیش   *gamiʃ*, buffalo.

گاو   *gav*, ox; cow.

گاوچران   *gavcaran*, cowherd.

گاومیش   *gavmiʃ*, buffalo.

گاه   *gah*, time; place (in compounds); گاه بگاه *gah be gah*, sometimes. from time to time; گاهی *gahi*, sometimes.

گبر   *gabr*, Zoroastrian.

گپ   *gap*, idle report; gossip.

گچ   *gac*, lime; plaster; gypsum.

گدا   *gada*, beggar.

گداختن   *godaxtan*, to smelt; to melt (trans.).

گداز   *godaz*, fusion, melting.

گذاشتن   *gozaftan*, to place, put; to allow, let, permit; to leave.

گذر   *gozar*, way, passage; ferry, ford.

گذرنامه   *gozarname*, passport.

گذشتن   *gozaftan*, to pass, proceed, go on; در گذشتن *dar gozaftan*, **to** pass over, forgive; to die; کار گذشته بود *kar gozafte bud*, there was nothing for it.

گذشتگی   *gozaftegi*: از خود گذشتگی *az xod gozaftegi*, self-sacrifice, devotion.

گذشته   *gozafte*, past; هفته گذشته *hafteye gozafte*, last week; گذشته از *gozafte az*, apart from; in addition to.

گر   *gar*, scab, mange; see also اگر *agar*.

گراز   *goraz*, hog, boar.

گران   *geran*, dear, expensive; heavy.

گرانبها   *geranbaha*, valuable, costly, precious.

گرانی   *gerani*, heaviness; dearness; scarcity; gravity.

گربه   *gorbe*, cat.

گرد   *gard*, dust; powder; *gerd*, round; *gerd(e)*, around; گرد آمدن *gerd amadan*, to gather round.

گرداب   *gerdab*, whirlpool.

گردان   *gardan*, turning, revolving (adj.); *gordan*, battalion.

گردش   *gardef*, revolution, turn; stroll; circulation.

گردگیری   *gardgiri*, dusting (subs.).

گردن   *gardan*, neck; گردن بند *gardanband*, necklace.

گردنکش   *gardankaf*, stubborn, obstinate, refractory; arrogant.

گردن بند   *gardanband*, necklace.

گردنکش   *gardankaf*, stubborn, obstinate, refractory; arrogant.

گردنکلفت   *gardankoloft*, ruffian, bully.

گردنه   *gardane*, mountain pass; neck of land.

گردو   *gerdu*, walnut.

گردون   *gardun*, wheel; heavens, sky; chance, fortune; windlass.

گرده   *garde*, pollen.

گردیدن   *gardidan*, to become; to revolve, go round.

گرز   *gorz*, mace, club.

گرسنگی   *gorosnegi*, hunger.

گرسنه   *gorosne*, hungry.

گرفتار   *gereftar*, imprisoned, captured, caught; *gereftar(e)* afflicted by

گرفتاری   *gereftari*, bondage; embarrassment, entanglement, difficulty.

گرفتن   *gereftan*, to take, seize; to take hold of; to make prisoner; to catch (of a fire, etc.); to 'catch on'.

گرگ   *gorg*, wolf.

گرم   *garm*, warm, hot; ardent.

گرما   *garma*, heat, warmth.

گرمابه   *garmabe*, kind of Turkish bath.

گرمسیر   *garmsir*, winter habitation in lowlands; place with a hot or warm climate.

گرمسیری   *garmsiri*, belonging to a place with a hot or warm climate.

گرمی   *garmi*, warmth, heat; briskness (of market, etc.).

گرو   *gerōu*, pledge, pawn, deposit.

گروگان   *gerōugan*, hostage.

گروه   *goruh*, troop, squadron; company, band of people.

گروهان   *goruhan*, company (military).

گروهبان   *goruhban*, sergeant.

گرویدن   *geravidan*, to believe (in); to turn (towards).

گره   *gere*, knot; one-sixteenth of a χar'.

گریبان   *gariban*, collar; neck.

گریختن   *gorixtan*, to flee.

گریز   *gorĭ* χ, flight, flying; abhorrence, aversion; escape.

گریستن   *geristan*, to weep.

گریه   *gerie*, weeping; plaint, lamentation.

گز   *ga* χ, tamarisk-tree; cubit.

گزارش   *go* χ *are* $\int$, report, statement.

گزیدن   *ga* χ *idan*, to bite; to sting; *go* χ *idan*, to choose, select.

گس   *gas*, astringent (adj.).

گستاخ   *gostax*, arrogant, audacious, impudent.

گسستن
گسیختن   *gosestan*
gosixtan } to break off, snap asunder.

گشاد   *go* $\int$ *ad*, wide, broad, open; گشادبازی *go* $\int$ *adba* χ *i*, extravagance.

گشادن   *go* $\int$ *adan*, to open.

گشایش   *go* $\int$ *aye* $\int$, opening; expansion (fig.).

گشت   *ga* $\int$ *t*, patrol, patrolling.

گشتن   *ga* $\int$ *tan*, to become; to turn; to walk about.

گشودن   *gofudan*, to open.

گفتار   *goftar*, speech, conversation.

گفتگو   *goftogu, goftegu*, conversation.

گفتن   *goftan*, to speak, say.

گفت‌وگو   *goftogu*, conversation.

گل   *gel*, mud; clay; گل رس *gele ros*, clay; *gol*, flower; گل سرخ *gole sorx*, red rose.

گلاب   *golab*, rose-water.

گلابی   *golabi*, pear.

گلزار   *golzar*, flower-bed.

گلستان   *golestan*, flower-garden, rose-garden.

گلشن   *golfan*, rose-bed.

گل کلم   *gole kalam*, cauliflower.

گلو   *galu*, throat.

گلو درد   *galudard*, sore throat.

گلوله   *golule*, bullet.

گله   *galle, gale*, flock, herd; *gele*, complaint.

گله‌دار   *galledar*, herdsman.

گله‌داری   *galledari*, keeping flocks; being a herdsman.

گلیم   *gelim*, coarse kind of carpet or rug.

گم   *gom*, lost.

گماشتن   *gomaftan*, to appoint, set over.

گماشته   *gomafte*, factor, agent.

گمان   *gaman*, fancy, surmise; گمان بردن (کردن) *gaman bordan* (*k.*), to fancy, suppose, think.

گمراه   *gomrah*, having lost one's way, astray.

گمراهی   *gomrahi*, deviation, aberration.

T گمرك   *gomrok*, customs duties.

TP گمرك خانه   *gomrokxane*, customs-house.

گمنام   *gomnam*, nameless, anonymous, inglorious.

گناه   *gonah*, sin.

گناهکار   *gonahkar*, sinner.

گنبد   *gombad*, dome.

گنج   *ganj*, treasure, hoard, store.

گنجه   *ganje*, cupboard.

گنجیدن *gonjidan*, to be contained or held, go (into).

گند *gand*, anything fetid.

گندزدا *gandẕada*, disinfectant.

گندزدائی *gandẕada'i*, disinfecting (subs.).

گندم *gandom*, wheat.

گنده *gonde*, big, bulky.

گنه‌گنه *ganegane*, quinine.

گوار *gavar*, گوارا *gavara*, digestible, agreeable; sweet (of water).

گواه *gavah*, witness.

گواهی *gavahi*, evidence, testimony, proof.

گواهی‌نامه *gavahiname*, certificate.

گوجه *gouje*, plum; گوجه فرنگی *goujeye farangi*, tomato.

گود *goud*, deep; excavated.

گودی *goudi*, depth; excavated place.

گور *gur*, grave; گور خر *gure xar*, wild ass.

گوساله *gusale*, calf.

گوسفند *gusfand*, sheep, sheep and goats.

گوش *guʃ*, ear; گوش کردن (دادن) *guʃ k. (dadan)*, to listen.

گوشت *guʃt*, flesh, meat.

گوشزد *guʃẕad*: گوشزد کردن *guʃẕad k.*, to notify, report, let (a thing) be known.

گوشواره *guʃvare*, ear-ring.

گوشه *guʃe*, corner; گوشه زدن *guʃe ẕadan*, to hint (at something); to make allusions (to).

گوگرد *gugerd*, sulphur.

گول *gul*, fraud, deceit; گول زدن *gul ẕadan*, to deceive; گول خوردن *gul xordan*, to be deceived.

گوناگون *gunagun*, of different kinds.

گونه *gune*, kind, sort; آنگونه *angune*, in that way, thus; اینگونه *ingune*, in this way, thus.

گوهر *gouhar*, gem, jewel.

گویا *guya*, it seems, perhaps; as it were; talkative, eloquent.

گهواره *gahvare*, cradle.

گیاه *giah*, weed; grass.

گیاهشناس *giahʃenas*, botanist.

گیاهشناسی   *giahſenasi*, botany.

گیتی   *giti*, the world.

گیج   *gij*, giddy, dizzy, dazed.

گیجی   *giji*, giddiness, vertigo; perplexity.

گیر   *gir*, hold; seizing, taking; گیرم آمد *giram amad*, it came into my possession; گیر آوردن *gir avardan*, to acquire, obtain; گیر کردن *gir k.*, to get or be stuck, be in a fix.

گیرودار   *gir o dar*, struggle, conflict.

گیس   *gis*, گیسو *gisu*, hair, locks; ringlet of hair.

گیلاس   *gilas*, cherry.

گیوه   *give*, kind of shoe with a cotton upper.

ل

لا   *la*, fold; دولا *do la*, two-fold; two-ply; سهلا *se la*, three-fold; three-ply; (ی)لا *la(ye)*, in, in between.

A   لا   *la*, no, not.

A   لا ابالی   *la obali* (*lit.* I don't care), nonchalant; careless; reckless.

A   لا اقل   *la aqall*, at least.

A   لابد   *la bodd*, necessarily, unavoidably; of course.

لات   *lat*, vagabond.

A   لاجرم   *la jaram*, necessarily, unavoidably; of course.

لاجورد   *lajvard*, azure, lapis lazuli.

لاجوردی   *lajvardi*, azure; made of lapis lazuli.

لاروب   *larub*, dredger.

لاروبی   *larubi*, dredging; clearing silt, etc., from irrigation channels.

A   لازم   *lazem*, necessary; لازم داشتن *lazem d.*, to need.

لاش   *laſ*, corpse, carcase.

لاشخور   *laſxor*, feeding on carrion; vulture.

لاغر   *laγer*, thin.

لاف   *laf*, boast, bragging; لاف زدن *laf ẕadan*, to boast.

لال   *lal*, dumb.

لاله   *lale*, tulip, anemone.

لای   *lāi*, sediment; silt; clay.

A   لایحه   *layehe*, (parliamentary) bill.

A لائق (لایق) *laeq* (*layeq*), worthy; capable.

A لا ينقطع *la yanqat'*, unceasingly, without interruption.

لب *lab*, lip; edge; shore, bank, coast.

A لباس *lebas*, garment, apparel.

لبریز *labriz*, overflowing (adj.).

لبو *labu*, (cooked) beetroot.

لپه *lappe*, split peas.

A لثه *lase*, gums (of the teeth).

لج *lajj*, obstinate.

A لجاجت *lejajat*, obstinacy; quarrelling, disputing (subs.).

AP لجباز *lajbaz*, obstinate.

لجن *lajan*, ooze, slime.

A لجوج *lajuj*, obstinate.

A لحاظ *lehaz*: از لحاظ *az lehaz(e)*, in respect of.

A لحاف *lehaf*, kind of quilt.

A لحظه *lahze*, look, glance; moment; twinkling of an eye.

A لحن *lahn*, tone, tune; way of speaking, intonation.

A لحیم *lahim*, solder.

لخت *loxt*, naked; لخت کردن *loxt k.*, to strip; to rob.

لختی *loxti*, nakedness.

A لذت *lezzat*, pleasure, delight, enjoyment; لذت بردن *lezzat bordan*, to enjoy, delight in.

لرزه *larze*, shivering, trembling (subs.); tremor.

لرزیدن *larzidan*, to shake, shiver, tremble.

A لزوم *lozum*, necessity, need.

لشتن *leftan*, to lick.

لشکر *lafkar*, army; division (of an army).

A لطافت *letafat*, grace, elegance; *bon mot*.

A لطف *lotf*, favour, kindness.

A لطمه *latme*, loss, injury; لطمه زدن *latme zadan*, to cause injury or loss.

A لطیف *latif*, graceful, delicate, elegant; witty.

A لعابی *la'abi*, enamel (adj.).

لعل *la'l*, ruby.

A لعنت *la'nat*, curse, imprecation.

A	لغت	*loɣat*, word, language, dialect, speech, idiom; dictionary.
	لغزش	*laɣʒeʃ*, slip, slide.
	لغزیدن	*laɣʒidan*, to slip.
A	لغو	*laɣv*, revocation, cancellation.
A	لغوی	*loɣavi*, verbal, literal.
A	لفّا	*laffan*, enclosed, as an enclosure (in a letter, parcel, etc.).
A	لفاف	*lefaf*, wrapper.
A	لفافه	*lefafe*, cover, envelope, wrapping.
A	لفظ	*lafz*, word.
A	لفظی	*lafzi*, literal, verbal; تحت اللفظی *taht ol-lafzi*, literal.
A	لقاء	*leqa*, meeting, encountering (subs.).
A	لقب	*laqab*, title (of honour).
A	لقلق	*laqlaq*, stork.
	لك	*lak*, spot, stain.
A	لكن	*laken*, but, still, nevertheless.
	لكه	*lake*, spot, stain; لكه‌دار *lakedar*, stained, spotted.
	لگام	*legam*, bridle.
	لگد	*lagad*, kick; لگد زدن *lagad zadan*, to kick.
	لگدمال	*lagadmal*, kicked, trodden upon; لگدمال کردن *lagadmal k.*, to trample upon.
	لگن	*lagan*, basin.
A	لم یزرع	*lam yazraʻ*, barren (of land).
	لند	*lond*: لند لند کردن *lond lond k.*, to mutter, grumble.
	لنگ	*lang*, lame; لنگ زدن *lang zadan*, to limp; *long*, loin-cloth.
	لنگر	*langar*, anchor; لنگر انداختن *langar andaxtan*, to cast anchor.
	لنگرگاه	*langargah*, anchorage.
	لنگه	*lenge*, half a load, one of two packs placed on a beast of burden; match, doublet.
	لنگیدن	*langidan*, to limp.
A	لو	*lou*: و لو *va lou*, even if.
A	لوازم	*lavazem* (pl. of لازم *lazem*), necessities.
	لوبیا	*lubia*, kidney bean.
	لور	*lur*, new milk; whey.
A	لوزتین	*louzatein*, tonsils.
	لوس	*lus*, spoilt (of a child); namby-pamby.

لوله   *lule*, pipe, pipe-line; tube; barrel (of a gun).

لوله‌کشی   *lulekaſi*, canalization, piping of water.

له   *leh*, bruised (of fruit, etc.), squashed.

A   لهجه   *lahje*, accent; tongue; dialect.

A   لهذا   *lehaʒa*, therefore.

A   لیاقت   *liaqat*, worthiness, merit.

لیز   *liʒ*, slippery (of ground).

لیسیدن   *lisidan*, to lick.

لیمو   *limu*, lemon.

لیوان   *livan*, glass, tumbler.

م

ما   *ma*, we.

A   ما   *ma*, what; مابعد *ma ba'd*, what (is) after, what follows; ماشاء الله *ma ſa allah*, what God wills.

A   ماباقی   *ma baqi*, remainder, rest (what is remaining).

A   مابین   *ma bēin(e)*, between, among (what is between).

مات   *mat*, amazed, astonished.

AP   ماجراجو   *ma jara ju*, adventurer, mischief-maker.

ماچ   *mac*, kiss.

A   مآخذ   *ma'axeʒ*, (pl. of مأخذ), sources, origins.

A   مأخذ   *ma'xaʒ*, source, origin.

A   مادام   *ma dam*: مادامیکه *ma damike*, as long as, whilst, during.

مادر   *madar*, mother.

مادر زن   *madarʒan*, mother-in-law (of husband).

ماده   *made*, female, she-.

A   ماده   *madde*, matter (as opposed to spirit), substance; article (of a law, etc.)

A   مادی   *maddi*, material (as opposed to spiritual).

مادیان   *madian*, mare.

مار   *mar*, snake, serpent.

مارپیچ   *marpic*, serpentine, spiral.

مارچوبه   *marcube*, asparagus.

A   مازاد   *ma ʒad*, surplus, what is over.

مازوت   *mazut*, heavy oil, diesel oil.

ماست   *mast*, kind of curd.

ماسه   *mase*, fine sand; black earth.

ماش   *maʃ*, pease, pulse.

FA   ماشین آلات   *maʃinalat*, machinery; machine-tools.

FP ماشین سوارکن   *maʃinsavarkon*, fitter, erector or mounter of machines.

A   مافوق   *ma foūq*, beyond, above.

A   مال   *mal*, riches, wealth, property, possessions; mount, beast for riding; *mal(e)*, belonging to.

AP   مآل اندیش   *maʿalandiʃ*, provident, circumspect.

مالش   *maleʃ*, rubbing, stroking, pat; reproving, reproof.

A   مالك   *malek*, owner, possessor, proprietor.

A   مالکیت   *malekiyat*, possession, ownership.

ماله   *male*, kind of harrow.

A   مالی   *mali*, financial.

A   مالیات   *maliyat*, taxes, revenue.

مالیدن   *malidan*, to rub.

ماما   *mama*, midwife.

مامائی   *mamai*, midwifery.

A   مأمور   *maʿmur*, ordered, commanded; an official, anyone to whom authority is delegated.

A   مأموریت   *maʿmuriyat*, command, order, commission, charge.

ماندن   *mandan*, to remain.

مانستن   *manestan*, to resemble (obs. except in 3rd pers. sing. present).

A   مانع   *maneʿ*, one who refuses, prohibits; impediment, obstacle.

مانند   *manand(e)*, like, resembling.

A   مأنوس   *maʿnus*, familiar, intimate.

A   ماوراء   *ma vara*, that which is behind or beyond; ماوراء الطبعیة *ma vara ot-tabʿiyat*, supernatural; ماوراء النهر *ma vara on-nahr*, Transoxiana.

ماه   *mah*, moon; month.

ماهانه   *mahane*, monthly.

ماهتاب   *mahtab*, moonlight.

A   ماهر   *maher*, skilful.

ماهوت	*mahut*, broadcloth.	
ماهوت پاك‌كن	*mahutpakkon*, clothes-brush.	
ماهور	*mahur*, ridge in undulating ground.	
ماهوش	*mahvaſ*, moonlike.	
ماهى	*mahi*, monthly; fish.	
ماهيانه	*mahiane*, monthly.	
ماهيچه	*mahice*, muscle.	
ماهيچه شناس	*mahiceſenas*, myologist.	
ماهيچه شناسى	*mahiceſenasi*, myology.	
مايحتاج	A	*ma yahtaj*, necessities.
مايل (مائل)	A	*mayel (mael)*, inclined, partial (to); مايل بودن *mayel b.*, to be inclined (to), want (to), be partial (to).
مأيوس	A	*ma'yus*, disappointed, despairing, without hope.
مايه		*maye*, capital; stock; essence, substance; ferment, leaven; vaccine; مايه ضعف *mayeye ʒa'f*, cause of weakness.
مايه زنى		*mayeʒani*, vaccination.
مايه كوبى		*mayekubi*, innoculation.
مباح	A	*mobah*, allowed, lawful.
مبادا		*mabada*, lest; let it not be; روز مبادا *ruʒe mabada*, day of judgement; rainy day (fig.).
مبادرت	A	*mobaderat*, start, commencement (of a task), precipitation.
مبادله	A	*mobadele*, exchange; recompense.
مبارز	A	*mobareʒ*, combatant, fighter.
مبارك	A	*mobarak*, blessed; fortunate.
مباشر	A	*mobaſer*, overseer, supervisor; agent, bailiff.
مبالغه	A	*mobaleүe*, exaggeration.
مبانى	A	*mabani*, edifices, buildings; foundations.
مبتدى	A	*mobtadi*, beginner.
مبتكر	A	*mobtaker*, initiator.
مبتلا	A	*mobtala*, afflicted.
مبحث	A	*mabhas*, dissertation, investigation, debate.
مبدأ	A	*mabda'*, origin, source.
مبدل	A	*mobaddal*, changed, altered.
مبذول	A	*mabʒul*, bestowed, lavished.
مبرا	A	*mobarra*, exempted, free, absolved.

A   مبعث   *mab'as*: عيد مبعث *ide mab'as*, 27th Rajab, the anniversary of the day Mohammad began his prophetic mission.

A   مبلغ   *mablaɣ*, sum (of money); *moballeɣ*, propagandist.

A   مبنى   *mabna, mabni*, built (upon), founded (upon).

A   مبهم   *mobham*, doubtful, obscure.

A   مبهوت   *mabhut*, stupified, confounded, astonished.

A   متاثر   *mota'asser*, touched, affected; impressed.

A   متاخرين   *mota'axxerin*, the moderns (as opposed to the ancients).

A   متاسف   *mota'assef*, regretful, sorry.

AP   متاسفانه   *mota'assefane*, with regret, regretfully.

A   متانت   *matanat*, dignity.

A   متبوع   *matbu'*: دولت متبوع *doulate matbu'*, sovereign government, that government to which one is subject.

A   متجاوز   *motajaveᴢ*, aggressive, transgressing; aggressor, transgressor; exceeding (adj.).

A   متحد   *mottahed*, united.

A   متحرك   *motaharrek*, moved, moving, mobile.

A   متحير   *motahāɩyer*, amazed, astonished; stupefied.

A   متخصص   *motaxasses*, expert, specialist.

A   مترجم   *motarjem*, translator.

A   مترق   *motaraqqi*, progressive.

A   متروك   *matruk*, abolished, obsolete; fallen into disuse.

A   متزلزل   *motaᴢalᴢel*, shaken, convulsed (by an earthquake); shaking, unsteady.

A   متشتت   *motaʃattet*, divergent (of opinions, etc.).

A   متشكر   *motaʃakker*, grateful, thankful.

A   متشنج   *motaʃannej*, convulsed, violently agitated.

A   متصدى   *motasaddi*, in charge (of), charged (with).

A   متصرف   *motasarraf*, whatever is in one's possession or power; *motasarref*, possessor, occupant.

A   متصل   *mottasel*, continual; adjoining, contiguous.

A   متضاد   *motaᴢadd*, mutually opposed, contrary.

A   متعاهد   *mota'ahed*, confederate; contracting party; covenanted.

A   متعلق   *mota'alleq*, belonging (to), connected (with); attached (to).

A متعلقات   *mota'alleqat*, appurtenances.

A متفاوت   *motafavet*, distinct, separate, different.

A متفرق   *motafarreq*, dispersed, scattered.

A متفق   *mottafeq*, united; ally, confederate; ملل متفق *melale mottafeq*, the United Nations.

A متفقين   *mottafeqin*, Allied Powers.

A متقابل   *motaqabel*, opposite; counter-.

A متقاعد   *motaqa'ed*, retired; pensioned.

A متقدم   *motaqaddem*, preceding, anterior.

A متقلب   *motaqalleb*, unreliable, deceitful.

A متكبر   *motakabber*, proud, haughty.

A متمايل   *motamayel*, inclining, inclined (towards), disposed (to).

A متمدن   *motamadden*, civilized.

A متمكن   *motamakken*, powerful, possessed of authority or riches; firmly established.

A متمنى   *motamanni*, one who asks, wishes or hopes; requesting, asking earnestly (adj.).

A متن   *matn*, text (of a document, etc.).

A متناسب   *motanaseb*, suitable, fitting; proportionate.

A متوجه   *motavajjeh*, turned, inclined (towards); inclined, attentive.

A متوحش   *motavahheʃ*, scared, terrified.

A متوسط   *motavasset*, middling, moderate, mediocre.

A متوسل   *motavassel*, having recourse (to; adj.); mediator, intercessor; متوسل شدن *motavassel ʃ.*, to have recourse (to).

A متولد   *motavalled*, born.

A متولى   *motavalli*, superintendent of a mosque; administrator of a charitable foundation.

A متهم   *mottahem*, suspected, accused.

A متين   *matin*, dignified, staid.

A مثبت   *mosbat*, confirmed, established, proved; positive, affirmative.

A مثقال   *mesqal*, one-sixteenth of a *sir*.

A مثل   *masal*, proverb; instance, case in point; *mesl*, similitude *mesl(e)*, like, resembling; مثلا *masalan*, for example.

A مثلث   *mosallas*, triangle; made into three or a third.

A مثنوی *masnavi*, poetry composed of distichs corresponding in measure, each consisting of a pair of rhymes; title of several works of this kind, especially one by Jalal od-Din Rumi.

A مثنی *mosanna*, doubled, two-fold.

A مجاز *mojaz*, permitted, allowed, lawful.

A مجازات *mojazat*, penalty, requital; punishment.

A مجاور *mojaver*, adjacent.

A مجتهد *mojtahed*, person competent to practice religious jurisprudence (according to the Shi'i sect).

A مجددا *mojaddadan*, newly, anew, again.

A مجرد *mojarrad*: بمجرد اینکه *be mojarrade inke*, as soon as.

A مجروح *majruh*, wounded.

A مجری *majra*, place where anything flows; *mojri*, one who executes an order; *mojra*, executed.

A مجسم *mojassam*, rendered corporeal; in relief; personified.

A مجسمه *mojassame*, statue.

A مجلس *majles*, assembly; مجلس شورای ملی *majlese ſouraye melli*, National Consultative Assembly.

A مجله *majalle*, periodical, magazine.

A مجمع *majma'*, assembly, concourse.

A مجموع *majmu'*, sum, totality.

A مجموعه *majmu'e*, collection, compendium.

A مجهز *mojahhaz*, equipped, prepared; armed.

مچ *moc*, wrist; مچ پا *moce pa*, ankle.

مچپیچ *mocpic*, puttees.

A محاسبات *mohasebat*, accounts, computations.

A محاضرات *mohazerat* conversations, colloquies (of great men).

A محاضره *mohazere*, pleading before a judge; conversation.

A محافظ *mohafez*, defender, protector.

A محافظه *mohafeze*, preservation, protection.

AP محافظه کار *mohafezekar*, conservative.

AP محافظه کاری *mohafezekari*, conservatism.

A محاکمه *mohakame*, citing before a judge; trial.

A محال *mohal*, impossible.

A	محبت	*mohabbat*, love, affection.
A	محبس	*mahbas*, prison.
A	محبوب	*mahbub*, beloved; محبوب القلوب *mahbub ol-qolub*, popular.
A	محبوبيت	*mahbubiyat*, being beloved, liked or popular.
A	محتاج	*mohtaj*, needy.
A	محترم	*mohtaram*, respected, honoured, venerable.
A	محتكر	*mohtaker*, hoarder.
A	محتمل	*mohtamel*, probable.
A	محراب	*mehrab*, place in a mosque where the prayer-leader leads the prayers with his face towards Mecca.
A	محرم	*mahram*, unlawful, forbidden; intimate friend, confidant.
AP	محرمانه	*mahramane*, secret, secretly; confidential, private.
A	محروم	*mahrum*, deprived, debarred; محروم ماندن *mahrum mandan*, to be deprived.
A	محسن	*mohsen*, one who does good; benefactor.
A	محسوب	*mahsub*, reckoned, computed; محسوب شدن *mahsub ſ.*, to be reckoned.
A	محصل	*mohassel*, student.
A	محصول	*mahsul*, harvest, crop; revenue; produce or sum of anything.
A	محض	*mahz*, pure, unmixed; mere, simple; *mahz(e)*, for, for the sake of; بمحض اینکه *be mahze inke*, as soon as.
A	محضر	*mahzar*, public notary's office.
A	محظوظ	*mahzuz*, pleased, delighted.
A	محفوظ	*mahfuz*, preserved, protected, kept safe.
A	محقر	*mohaqqar*, despised.
A	محقق	*mohaqqaq*, confirmed, authenticated; *mohaqqeq*, verifier, confirmer, investigator.
A	محك	*mehakk*, touchstone, test.
A	محكم	*mohkam*, strong, stable; firm; fortified.
A	محكمه	*mahkame*, tribunal, court of justice, law-court.
A	محكوم	*mahkum*, condemned, convicted, sentenced.
A	محل	*mahall*, place, station; provision (budgetary).

A	محله	*mahalle*, quarter (of a city, etc.).
A	محلی	*mahalli*, local.
A	محنت	*mehnat*, toil, affliction.
A	محو	*mahv*, obliterating, annihilating (subs.).
A	محور	*mehvar*, axis.
A	محول	*mohavval*, transformed, changed; transferred.
A	محیط	*mohit*, circumference; environment.
A	مخابره	*moxabere*, message, dispatch; مخابره کردن *moxabere k.*, to telegraph.
A	مخارج	*maxarej*, expenses.
A	مخاطره	*moxatere*, danger, peril.
A	مخالف	*moxalef*, opposed, hostile; enemy; contrary, opposite.
A	مخبر	*moxber*, correspondent (of a newspaper, etc.).
A	مختار	*moxtar*, invested with power, authority or choice.
A	مخترع	*moxtare'*, inventor.
A	مختص	*moxtass*, special, peculiar, private.
A	مختصر	*moxtasar*, abbreviated, abridged.
A	مختصراً	*moxtasaran*, briefly.
A	مختل	*moxtall*, confused, disturbed, out of order.
A	مختلط	*moxtalet*, mixed; confused.
A	مختلف	*moxtalef*, different, diverse.
A	مخصوص	*maxsus*, peculiar, special, specific, particular.
A	مخفف	*moxaffaf*, contracted (of word, etc.); alleviated, made light; despised.
A	مخلص	*moxles*, sincere; pure; loyal.
A	مخلوق	*maxluq*, created.
A	مخلوقات	*maxluqat*, created beings.
A	مداخل	*madaxel* (pl. of مدخل *madxal*), entrances; income; perquisites.
A	مداخله	*modaxele*, interference, meddling.
A	مداد	*medad*, pencil.
A	مدارا	*modara*, civility, moderation.
A	مداوا	*modava*, curing a disease, medical treatment.
A	مداومت	*modavamat*, *modavemat*, persistence, continuance, perpetuity.

A مدبر *modabber*, administrator; skilful manager; prudent, skilful, efficient.

A مدت *moddat*, period (of time).

A مدخليت *madxaliyat*, derivation; having influence, being concerned (in something; subs.).

A مدد *madad*, help, succour.

A مدرسه *madrase, madrese*, school.

A مدرك *madrak*, documentary evidence.

A مدعا *modda'a*, claim, argument.

A مدعى *modda'i*, claimant, accuser; مدعى عليه *modda'a aleīh*, defendant (law); مدعى العموم *modda'i ol-omum*, Public Prosecutor.

A مدنى *madani*, civil, secular; urban.

A مديد *madid*, long (of time).

A مدير *modir*, director; مدير كل *modire koll*, director-general.

A مديون *madyun*, indebted.

A مذاكره *mozakere*, discussion, conversation.

A مذكر *mozakkar*, masculine.

A مذكور *mazkur*, mentioned.

A مذلت *mazallat*, baseness, meanness; misery.

A مذهب *mazhab*, religion, doctrine, sect.

A مراتب *marateb* (pl. of مرتبه *martabe*), steps, grades, degrees; بمراتب *be marateb*, appreciably, markedly, to a considerable degree.

A مراتع *marate'* (pl. of مرتع *marta'*), pastures.

A مراجعت *moraja'at*, return, returning.

A مراعات *mora'at*, showing regard or respect to (something), taking care of; observation, consideration.

A مرافعه *morafe'e*, dispute, carrying on a law-suit.

A مراقب *moraqeb*, looking after, watching over (adj.).

A مراقبت *moraqebat*, guarding, looking after, watching over, attention, care.

A مرام *maram*, ideology; doctrine, creed; aim, object; desire.

A مرامى *marami*, ideological, doctrinal.

A مربا *morabba*, jam, conserve.

A مربع *morabba'*, squared; quadrilateral.

A	مربوط	*marbut*, connected, related.
A	مربی	*morabbi*, teacher.
A	مرتب	*morattab*, in order, arranged, orderly.
A	مرتبه	*martabe*, time, occasion.
A	مرتجع	*mortaje'*, reactionary.
A	مرتع	*marta'*, meadow, pasture.
A	مرتكب	*mortakeb*, committing a crime (adj.).
	مرجان	*marjan*, coral.
A	مرحله	*marhale*, stage (of a journey, etc.); phase.
A	مرحمت	*marhamat*, mercy; pity; favour.
A	مرحوم	*marhum*, deceased.
A	مرخص	*moraxxas*, permitted to leave.
AP	مرخصی	*moraxxasi*, leave, furlough; permission to leave.
	مرد	*mard*, man.
	مرداب	*mordab*, creek, lagoon; stagnant water.
	مرداد	*mordad*, fifth month of the Persian solar year.
	مردار	*mordar*, carrion.
	مردانگی	*mardanegi*, manliness, generosity.
	مردانه	*mardane*, brave, manly; for men.
A	مردد	*moraddad*, doubtful, perplexed, irresolute, hesitating.
	مردم	*mardom*, people.
	مردمان	*mardoman*, people.
	مردمشناسی	*mardomſenasi*, anthropology.
	مردن	*mordan*, to die; (obs.) to go out, be extinguished.
	مردی	*mardi*, manliness, valour.
	مرز	*marz*, frontier.
	مرزدار	*marzdar*, frontier guard.
	مرزداری	*marzdari*, guarding the frontier.
A	مرسلين	*morsalin* (oblique sound masc. pl. of مرسل *morsal*), prophets, apostles.
A	مرسوم	*marsum*, customary.
A	مرشد	*morſed*, spiritual guide or adviser; head of a religious order.
A	مرض	*maraz*, disease, sickness.
A	مرطوب	*martub*, moist, damp.
A	مرعوب	*mar'ub*, terrified, frightened.

	مرغ	*marɣ*, kind of grass; meadow; *morɣ*, bird, fowl.
	مرغابی	*morɣabi*, water-fowl.
	مرغزار	*marɣɀar*, water-meadow, meadow; pasture.
A	مرغوب	*marɣub*, desired, coveted.
A	مرقوم	*marqum*, written.
A	مرکب	*markab*, mount, horse; *morakkab*, compound, compounded, composed; ink.
A	مرکز	*markaɀ*, centre; capital city.
A	مرکزی	*markaɀi*, central.
	مرگ	*marg*, death.
	مرمر	*marmar*, marble.
A	مرموز	*marmuɀ*, obscure; occult.
A	مروارید	*morvarid*, pearl.
A	مروت	*morovvat*, generosity, chivalry.
A	مرور	*morur*, passing by, through, over or across; بمرور زمان *be morure ɀaman*, with the passing of time.
A	مریض	*mariɀ*, sick, ill; sick person.
A	مزاج	*meɀaj*, temperament, constitution.
A	مزاحم	*moɀahem*, inconvenient, troublesome; causing inconvenience, troubling (adj.).
A	مزایده	*moɀayede*, putting up to tender (subs.).
A	مزبور	*maɀbur*, above-mentioned, aforesaid.
	مزخرف	*moɀaxraf*, nonsensical.
A	مزخرفات	*moɀaxrafat*, nonsense.
	مزد	*moɀd*, reward, hire, wages.
	مزدور	*moɀdur*, mercenary, hired labourer; hireling.
A	مزرعه	*maɀra'e*, hamlet and the cultivated land round it.
A	مزمن	*moɀmen*, chronic.
	مزه	*maɀe*, taste, flavour.
A	مزیت	*maɀiyat*, excess, superabundance.
A	مزید	*maɀid*, increase, augmentation; increased, augmented.
	مژده	*moʒde*, good news.
	مس	*mes*, copper.
A	مسابقه	*mosabeqe*, contest, match, race.
A	مساعدت	*mosa'edat*, help, assistance.

A مساعده   *mosa'ede*, advance (loan).

A مسافات   *masafat* (pl. of مسافت *masafat*), distances; regions.

A مسافت   *masafat*, distance.

A مسافر   *mosafer*, traveller.

A مسافرت   *mosaferat*, travelling, journey; مسافرت کردن *mosaferat k.*, to travel.

A مسامحه   *mosamahe*, negligence; connivance.

A مساوی   *mosavi*, equal.

A مسائل   *masael* (pl. of مسئله *mas'ale*), problems, questions.

   مست   *mast*, drunk, intoxicated; in rut.

A مستأصل   *mosta'sal*, extirpated.

A مستبد   *mostabedd*, despotic, arbitrary; despot.

A مستحق   *mostahaqq*, worthy, deserving.

A مستخدم   *mostaxdam* (usually pronounced *mostaxdem*), employee.

A مستدعی   *mostad'i*, imploring, supplicating (adj.).

A مستراح   *mostarah*, place for easing nature, lavatory.

A مسترد   *mostaradd*, restored, returned.

A مستشار   *mostaʃar*, advisor.

A مستظرفه   *mostaʒrafe*: صنایع مستظرفه *sanaye'e mostaʒrafe*, fine arts.

A مستعد   *mosta'edd*, able, capable, fit, apt.

A مستعمل   *mosta'mal*, used, current, employed; second-hand.

A مستفید   *mostafid*, obtaining advantage (adj.).

A مستفیض   *mostafiʒ*, receiving favour, grace, benefit (adj.).

A مستقبل   *mostaqbel*, future (subs.); one who advances to meet someone.

A مستقل   *mostaqell*, independent.

A مستقیم   *mostaqim*, direct, straight.

A مستقیماً   *mostaqiman*, straight, straight on; directly

A مستنطق   *mostanteq*, inspector, interrogator.

A مستولی   *mostouli*, predominant, paramount, powerful.

A مسجد   *masjed*, mosque.

A مسخره   *masxare*, ridiculing, deriding (subs.); pleasantry.

A مسدود   *masdud*, shut, closed; obstructed, blocked.

A مسرت   *masarrat*, joy, happiness.

A مسرور   *masrur*, happy, glad.

A مسرى   *mosri*, contagious.

A مسكرات   *moskerat*, intoxicating drinks.

A مسكين   *meskin*, poor, wretched; pauper.

AP مسكين خانه   *meskinxane*, poor-house.

    مسگر   *mesgar*, coppersmith.

A مسلح   *mosallah*, armed.

A مسلسل   *mosalsal*, linked, successive, consecutive; machine-gun.

A مسلك   *maslak*, doctrine, ideology.

A مسلم   *moslem*, Moslem; *mosallam*, safe, sound; certain, sure.

A مسلمان   *mosalman*, Moslem.

A مسلول   *maslul*, consumptive.

A مسموم   *masmum*, poisoned.

A مسن   *mosenn*, aged, old (of persons).

A مسواك   *mesvak*, toothbrush.

A مسهل   *moshel*, purgative.

A مسيح   *masih*, Messiah; حضرت مسيح *hazrate masih*, Jesus Christ.

A مسير   *masir*, journey, course; line, direction.

A مسئله   *mas'ale*, problem, question.

A مسئول   *mas'ul*, responsible (for).

A مسئوليت   *mas'uliyat*, responsibility.

A مشار اليه   *mosaron eleih*, the afore-mentioned.

A مشاوره   *mosavere*, consultation, asking advice.

A مشاهده   *mosahede*, observing, witnessing, observation.

    مشت   *most*, fist; handful; مشت زدن *most zadan*, to strike with the fist; to box.

A مشترك   *mostarak*, shared, common; *mostarek*, associate; common, joint.

    مشتزنى   *mostzani*, boxing, fisticuffs.

A مشتق   *mostaqq*, derivative, derived; inflected.

    مشتمال   *mostmal*, مشتمالى *mostmali*, massage.

    مشتمال   *mostmali*, مشتمالى *mostmali*, blow with the fist.

A مشتمل   *mostamel*, comprehending, comprising, containing (adj.).

A مشخص   *mosaxxas*, distinguished, defined, specified.

A مشربه   *mesrabe*, *masrabe*, copper bowl used in the *hammam*.

A مشرف   *mosarraf*, honoured, exalted; *mosref*, imminent, impending; overhanging, overlooking (adj.); examiner, inspector.

A	مشرق	*ma∫req*, east (subs.).
A	مشرك	*mo∫rek*, polytheist.
A	مشروب	*ma∫rub*, drinkable; watered, irrigated; drink.
A	مشروط	*ma∫rut*, stipulated, conditional; مشروط به *ma∫rut be*, conditional upon.
A	مشروطيت	*ma∫rutiyat*, constitution, constitutional government.
A	مشروع	*ma∫ru'*, legal, legitimate.
A	مشعل	*ma∫'al*, torch.
A	مشعوف	*ma∫'uf*, pleased, satisfied.
A	مشغول	*ma∫γul*, occupied.
A	مشق	*ma∫q*, copy, model; exercise, practice; drill.
	مشك	*ma∫k*, skin (for carrying water, etc.); *me∫k, mo∫k*, musk.
A	مشكل	*mo∫kel*, difficult.
A	مشكوك	*ma∫kuk*, dubious, doubtful; uncertain.
	مشكى	*me∫ki*, black.
A	مشمول	*ma∫mul*, included, contained, comprehended; covered (by), falling (under); liable to military service.
A	مشورت	*ma∫varat*, counsel, advice; مشورت كردن (دادن) *ma∫varat k. (dadan)*, to advise, counsel.
۱	مشهور	*ma∫hur*, famous, well-known.
۱	مصالح	*masaleh* (pl. of مصلحت *maslahat*), interests; affairs; materials.
A	مصداق	*mesdaq*, touchstone; meaning.
A	مصدر	*masdar*, batman; infinitive; source, origin.
A	مصر	*mesr*, Egypt.
A	مصرف	*masraf*, consumption, use.
A	مصرى	*mesri*, Egyptian.
A	مصطفى	*mostafa*, chosen.
A	مصلحت	*maslahat*, welfare; what is advisable or prudent; مصلحت ديدن *maslahat didan*, to consider advisable.
A	مصمم	*mosammam*, determined (to); resolved (upon).
A	مصنوع	*masnu'*, manufactured, made; مصنوعى *masnu'i*, artificial.
A	مصون	*masun*, immune.
A	مصونيت	*masuniyat*, immunity.
A	مصيبت	*mosibat*, misfortune, disaster, calamity.

A مضاف *moẓaf*, annexed, added.

A مضافات *moẓafat*, annexes, appendages, appurtenances.

A مضامين *maẓamin* (pl. of مضمون *maẓmun*), contents.

A مضايقه *moẓayeqe*, reducing to straits; withholding, sparing (subs.).

A مضبوط *maẓbut*, possessed, occupied; confiscated, seized; managed, controlled.

A مضحك *moẓhek*, ridiculous, droll.

A مضرت *maẓarrat*, detriment, damage, hurt, harm.

A مضطرب *moẓtareb*, agitated, anxious; disturbed.

A مضمون *maẓmun*, content, contents; sense, meaning.

A مضيقه *maẓiqe*, straitened circumstances.

A مطابق *motabeq*, equal (to), according (to).

A مطالب *mataleb* (pl. of مطلب *matlab*), matters, subjects.

A مطالعه *motale'e*, reading, study.

A مطب *matabb*, surgery.

A مطبخ *matbax*, kitchen.

A مطبعه *matba'e*, printing house; printing press.

A مطبوعات *matbu'at*, the Press.

A مطرب *motreb*, singer, musician.

A مطرح *matrah*, discussed, debated; propounded, exposed to discussion.

A مطلب *matlab*, matter, subject.

A مطلع *mottale'*, informed.

A مطلق *motlaq*, absolute, independent; unconditional.

A مطلوب *matlub*, desired; demanded.

A مطمئن *motma'enn*, quiet, secure, content; assured, certain.

A مطيع *moti'*, obedient.

A مظلوم *maẓlum*, oppressed; diffident, modest.

A مع *ma'a*, with; معذلك *ma'a ẓalek*, معذا *ma'a haẓa*, notwithstanding, nevertheless.

A معادل *mo'adel*, equal, equivalent.

A معارف *ma'aref* (pl. of معرفت *ma'refat*): وزارت معارف *veẓarate ma'aref*, Ministry of Education.

A معاش *ma'aʃ*, livelihood, means of subsistence.

A معاشرت *mo'aʃerat, mo'aʃarat*, social intercourse.

A   معاصر   *mo'aser*, contemporary.

A   معاف   *mo'af*, absolved, excused, exempted.

AP   معافی   *mo'afi*, immunity, exemption.

A   معامله   *mo'amele*, business transaction; business dealing.

A   معانی   *ma'ani* (pl. of معنی *ma'na*), meanings; rhetoric, theory of literary style.

A   معاون   *mo'aven*, assistant, deputy; under-secretary (polit.).

A   معاونت   *mo'avenat*, assistance, aid; function of an assistant.

A   معبر   *ma'bar*, ford, ferry.

A   معتاد   *mo'tad*, accustomed, addicted (to).

A   معتبر   *mo'tabar*, authentic; esteemed; reputable.

A   معتدل   *mo'tadel*, moderate, temperate.

A   معترض   *mo'tarez*, hindering, objecting (to; adj.); parenthetic.

A   معترف   *mo'taref*, avowing, declaring, acknowledging (adj.).

A   معتقد   *mo'taqed*, believing (in); believer.

A   معتمد   *mo'tamad*, trustworthy.

A   معجزه   *mo'jeze*, miracle.

A   معدل   *mo'addel*, average.

A   معدن   *ma'dan*, mine, quarry; mineral deposit.

A   معدنی   *ma'dani*, mineral (adj.).

A   معدود   *ma'dud*, numbered; limited.

A   معده   *me'de*, stomach.

A   معذرت   *ma'zarat*, pardon, excuse; معذرت خواستن *ma'zarat xastan*, to ask pardon.

A   معذور   *ma'zur*, excused, exempted.

A   معرض   *ma'raz*, place of exposure (to view, etc.).

A   معرفت   *ma'refat*, knowledge, divine knowledge, science, learning.

A   معرفی   *mo'arrefi*, introducing, presenting (subs.).

A   معرکه   *ma'reke*, arena; battle; turmoil, hubbub; anything which is outstanding, whether in a good or a bad sense.

A   معروض   *ma'ruz*, submitted, requested; representation, petition.

A   معروف   *ma'ruf*, known.

A   معروفیت   *ma'rufiyat*, fame, being known; معروفیت داشتن *ma'rufiyat d.*, to have a name; to be famous (for).

A   معزول   *ma'zul*, dismissed, removed, displaced.

A معطر *mo'attar*, perfumed, scented.

A معطل *mo'attal*, delayed, kept waiting.

AP معطلى *mo'attali*, delay.

A معقول *ma'qul*, rational, reasonable; sensible.

A معكوس *ma'kus*, inverted, turned upside down.

A معلم *mo'allem*, teacher.

AP معلمى *mo'allemi*, teaching (subs.).

A معلوم *ma'lum*, known; evident.

A معما *mo'amma*, riddle.

A معمار *me'mar*, architect.

AP معمارى *me'mari*, being an architect; architecture.

A معمول *ma'mul*, usual, customary.

A معمولاً *ma'mulan*, generally.

A معنوى *ma'navi*, spiritual.

A معنى *ma'ni, ma'na*, meaning.

A معين *mo'ayyan*, fixed, determined, settled.

F مغازه *maɣaze*, shop, store.

A مغرب *maɣreb*, west (subs.).

مغز *maɣz*, brain; marrow; kernel.

A مغلوب *maɣlub*, conquered, overcome; مغلوب کردن *maɣlub k.*, to conquer.

مغول *moɣul*, Mongol.

A مفاد *mofad*, sense, purport; contents.

مفت *moft*, free, gratis.

A مفتاح *meftah*, key.

A مفتخر *moftaxer*, honoured, proud, glorying (in).

مفتخوار *moftxar*, مفتخور *moftxor*, parasite (fig.).

A مفتش *mofattef*, inspector.

A مفتوح *maftuh*, opened; conquered; مفتوح شدن *maftuh f.*, to be conquered.

A مفرد *mofrad*, single, simple; singular (gramm.).

A مفرط *mofret*, excessive.

A مفسد *mofsed*, mischievous, destructive, depraved; disturber of the peace; seditious person.

A مفسر *mofasser*, commentator.

A	مفصل	*mafsel*, joint (of a limb); *mofassal*, detailed, fully described.
A	مفصلاً	*mofassalan*, in detail, fully.
A	مفقود	*mafqud*, lost, missing.
A	مفلس	*mofles*, poor, destitute.
A	مفهوم	*mafhum*, understood; meaning, sense.
A	مفيد	*mofid*, beneficial, useful.
A	مقابل	*moqabel*, opposite; در مقابل *dar moqabel(e)*, opposite, in opposition to; in return.
A	مقابله	*moqabele*, collating, comparing (subs.).
A	مقارن	*moqaren*, associated, connected, related; near; nearly.
A	مقاصد	*maqased* (pl. of مقصد *maqsad*), designs, aims.
A	مقاطعه	*moqate'e*, contract (for work or for taxes, etc.).
AP	مقاطعه‌کار	*moqate'ekar*, contractor.
A	مقاله	*maqale*, essay, article.
A	مقام	*maqam*, post, position, office; place.
A	مقامات	*maqamat* (pl. of مقامه *maqame*), authorities.
A	مقاومت	*moqavamat*, resistance.
A	مقایسه	*moqayese*, comparing, comparison.
A	مقبره	*maqbare*, grave, mausoleum; graveyard.
A	مقتدر	*moqtader*, powerful.
A	مقتصر	*moqtasar*, abbreviated, abridged.
A	مقتضا	*moqtaza*, مقتضی *moqtazi*, exacted, required; exigency.
A	مقدار	*meqdar*, quantity, amount.
A	مقدر	*moqaddar*, predestined, predetermined.
A	مقدرات	*moqaddarat*, divine decrees, destinies.
A	مقدس	*moqaddas*, sanctified, holy.
A	مقدم	*moqaddam*, antecedent, preceding; placed before.
A	مقدمه	*moqaddame*, preface, preamble.
A	مقراض	*meqraz*, shears.
A	مقرر	*moqarrar*, established, confirmed; agreed upon, fixed, settled.
A	مقررات	*moqarrarat*, regulations, provisions, stipulations.
A	مقرون	*maqrun*, conjoined; connected, related.
A	مقصد	*maqsad*, destination; design, aim, end.
A	مقصر	*moqasser*, guilty; one who falls short or fails in his duty.
A	مقصود.	*maqsud*, object, purpose, desire.

A مقنن *moqannan*, legal, ordered by law; *moqannen*, legislative; legislator.

A مقننه *moqannene*: قوه مقننه *qovveye moqannene*, legislature.

A مقياس *meqyas*, measure.

A مقيد *moqaiyad*, bound, fixed; registered; stipulated.

A مقيم *moqim*, dweller, resident.

A مكاتب *mokateb*, correspondent.

A مكاتبه *mokatebe*, correspondence, corresponding (by letter).

A مكارى *mokari*, carrier, muleteer.

A مكافات *mokafat*, recompense, compensation; retaliation.

A مكان *makan*, place; habitation; situation.

A مكتب *maktab* }
AP مكتب خانه *maktabxane* } old-fashioned type of school.

A مكتوب *maktub*, written; letter (epistle).

A مكرر *mokarrar*, repeated, reiterated.

A مكلف *mokallaf*, charged with a duty.

مكيدن *makidan*, to suck.

A مكيده *makide*, trick, stratagem.

مگر *magar*, but, unless, except; perhaps, by chance, haply.

مگس *magas*, fly.

A ملاح *mallah*, seaman.

A ملاحظه *molaheze*, looking attentively, considering, contemplating (subs.); having one's eye upon; consideration, regard; circumspection; observation.

A ملاذ *malaz*, asylum, refuge.

A ملازم *molazem*, attendant, servant.

A ملاطفت *molatefat*, courtesy, politeness, favour.

A ملافه *malafe* (for ملحفه *malhafe*), sheet (bedding).

A ملاقات *molaqat*, meeting, encounter.

A ملامت *malamat*, blaming, reproving (subs.); rebuke, censure.

A ملائم (ملايم) *molaem* (*molayem*), **mild, gentle; conformable** (with).

A ملت *mellat*, people, nation.

A ملتفت *moltafet*, paying attention to, understanding (adj.); ملتفت شدن *moltafet ʃ.*, to understand.

A ملحق *molhaq*, joined, annexed; contiguous; adherent, belonging (to).

A   ملحوظ   *malhuz*, considered, regarded, observed, taken into account.

   ملخ   *malax*, locust.

A   ملعون   *mal'un*, cursed, accursed.

A   ملغى   *molya*, abolished, abrogated, revoked.

A   ملك   *malak*, angel; *malek*, king; *melk*, property, real estate; *molk*, kingship; dominion; kingdom.

A   ملكه   *malake*, quality, faculty.

A   ملكه   *maleke* (fem. of ملك *malek*), queen.

   ململ   *malmal*, muslin.

   ملوان   *malavan, malvan*, sailor.

A   ملوك الطوائف   *moluk ot-tavaef*, feudal barons, petty local rulers.

A   ملوك الطوائفى   *moluk ot-tavaefi*, feudal.

A   ملى   *melli*, national, popular; privately-owned (of a school); حكومت ملى *hokumate melli*, representative government; ملى كردن *melli k.*, to nationalise.

   مليون   *meliun*, million.

A   ممالك   *mamalek* (pl. of مملكت *mamlakat*), countries.

A   ممانعت   *momane'at*, prevention, obstruction.

A   ممتاز   *momtaz*, choice, select.

A   ممتحن   *momtahen*, examiner.

A   ممتد   *momtadd*, extended, prolonged.

A   ممتنع   *momtane'*, prohibited; impossible; inaccessible.

A   ممدوح   *mamduh*, praised.

A   ممسك   *momsek*, avaricious, parsimonious, stingy.

A   ممكن   *momken*, possible.

A   مملكت   *mamlakat*, country, state.

A   مملو   *mamlovv*, full, filled.

A   ممنوع   *mamnu'*, forbidden.

A   ممنون   *mamnun*, grateful.

A   مميز   *momaiyez*, discriminating, discerning (adj.); examiner, discerner; auditor.

A   مميزه   *momaiyeze*, discernment, judgement; common-sense.

   من   *man*, I; measure of 40 *sir*.

A   من   *man*, who, whoever; *men*, from, out of; من جمله *men jomle-(ye)*, from among, among; منها *menha*, from it, minus.

A منادی   *manadi*, proclamations; *monada*, proclaimed; proclamation; *monadi*, herald, crier.

A منار   *menar*, minaret.

A مناسب   *monaseb*, suitable, fitting, comfortable; proportionate.

A مناسبات   *monasebat*, pl. of مناسبت *monasebat*.

A مناسبت   *monasebat*, suitability, aptness; propriety; relation, connexion, intercourse.

A منافات   *monafat*, opposition, incompatibility.

A مناقشه   *monaqeſe*, dispute, quarrel, contention.

A منافع   *manafe'* (pl. of منفعت *manfa'at*), benefits; advantages; gains; profits; interests.

A مناقصه   *monaqese*, putting up to tender.

A منبر   *membar*, pulpit.

A منبع   *mamba'*, source, spring, origin.

A منت   *mennat*, obligation, favour; منت داشتن *mennat d.*, to consider oneself or hold oneself indebted for a favour; منت گذاشتن *mennat goʒaſtan*, to place or hold someone under an obligation.

A منتخب   *montaxab*, chosen, selected; selection.

A منتشر   *montaſer*, published, diffused, spread.

A منتظر   *montaʒer*, awaiting, expecting (adj.).

A منتقل   *montaqel*, transferred.

A منتهی   *montaha*, end, conclusion; utmost extent; finally; *montahi*, terminating.

A منشور   *mansur*, scattered; in prose.

A منجر   *monjer*, terminating (in), leading to, resulting (in; adj.).

A منجم   *monajjem*, astronomer, astrologer.

A منجمد   *monjamed*, congealed.

A منحرف   *monharef*, turning aside (adj.); منحرف ساختن *monharef saxtan*, to dissuade.

A منحصر   *monhaser*, limited (to); confined; surrounded, besieged.

A منحل   *monhall*, dissolved, disbanded.

A مندرج   *mondarej*, included, contained, inserted.

A منزل   *manʒel*, house; home; stage (in a journey); منزل کردن *manʒel k.*, to stay, dwell.

A	منزله	*manẓele*, station, rank; بمنزله *be manẓele(ye)*, as, by way of, with the rank of.
A	منشاء	*manſa'*, origin, source, spring, beginning.
A	منشور	*manſur*, charter, diploma, decree.
A	منشی	*monſi*, secretary, clerk.
AP	منشیگری	*monſigari*, being a clerk.
A	منصب	*mansab*, office, post.
A	منصرف	*monsaref*, abandoning (a project, etc.; adj.); turning back; declinable; غیر منصرف *ɣeire monsaref* (gramm.), indeclinable, imperfectly declined.
A	منصف	*monsef*, arbitrator; just, equitable.
A	منطق	*manteq*, logic.
A	منظره	*manẓare*, view, landscape; scene; appearance.
A	منظم	*monaẓẓam*, arranged, in order, orderly.
A	منظور	*manẓur*, object, aim; seen; considered; provided for, foreseen; بمنظور *be manẓur(e)*, with the intention of.
A	منظوم	*manẓum*, arranged in a series, row or line; in verse.
A	منع	*man'*, preventing, prevention; hindering, hindrance.
A	منعقد	*mon'aqed*, agreed upon, concluded.
A	منعکس	*mon'akis*, reflected.
A	منفذ	*manfaẓ*, pass, passage.
A	منفرد	*monfared*, alone, single.
A	منفعت	*manfa'at*, benefit, gain.
A	منفی	*manfi*, negative.
AP	منفی باف	*manfibaf*, negative; one who makes negative criticism.
AP	منفی بافی	*manfibafi*, negative criticism.
A	منقار	*menqar*, beak (of a bird).
A	منقرض	*monqareẓ*, elapsed (of time); extinct.
A	منقسم	*monqasem*, divided.
A	منقل	*manqal*, brazier.
A	منقلب	*monqaleb*, changeable; overturned, upset.
A	منکر	*monker*, one who denies or rejects.
A	منکسر	*monkaser*, broken.
A	منکوب	*mankub*, vanquished; منکوب کردن *mankub k.*, to vanquish.

A   منور   *monavvar*, illuminated, enlightened; منور الفكر *monavvar ol-fekr*, enlightened, intellectual.

A   منوط   *manut*, dependent (upon).

A   منهدم   *monhadem*, destroyed, demolished.

A   منيع   *mani'*, inaccessible, impregnable.

   مو   *mu*, hair.

A   موات   *mavat*, waste-land, dead lands.

A   مواجب   *mavajeb*, wages.

A   مواجه   *movajeh*, confronting, meeting face to face (adj.).

A   مواد   *mavadd* (pl. of ماده *madde*), matters, materials; articles; مواد اوليه *mavadde avvaliye*, raw materials.

A   موازين   *mavazin* (pl. of ميزان *mizan*), measures; metres.

A   موافق   *movafeq*, conformable, agreeable, consenting, agreeing.

A   موافقت   *movafeqat*, agreement, conformity, consent.

A   موانع   *mavane'* (pl. of مانع *mane'*), obstacles, hindrances.

A   مؤثر   *mo'asser*, effective.

A   موج   *mouj*, wave.

A   موجب   *mujeb*, cause, reason.

A   مؤجر   *mujer*, lessor, one who hires out.

A   موجود   *moujud*, present, existing; ready at hand, available.

A   موحش   *movahhef*, terrible, dreadful.

A   مؤخر   *mo'axxar*, posterior; delayed; *mo'axxer*, one who delays.

A   مؤدب   *mo'addab*, polite, civil.

A   مودت   *mavaddat*, friendship, love.

   مورچه   *murce*, ant.

A   مورخ   *movarrax*, dated; *movarrex*, historian.

A   مورد   *moured*, place of arrival; cause; instance, case.

A   موروثى   *mourusi*, hereditary.

A   موز   *mouz*, banana.

F   موزه   *muze*, museum.

F   موزيك   *muzik*, music; military band.

A   مؤسس   *mo'asses*, founder.

A   مؤسسه   *mo'assese* (for *mo'assase*), institution, foundation, establishment.

F   موسقى ,موسيقى   *museqi*, *musiqi*, music.

A	موسم	*mōusem*, time, season.
	موش	*muʃ*, mouse; موش صحرا *muʃe sahra*, field-mouse; rat.
	موشك	*muʃak*, squib, rocket.
	موشكاف	*muʃekaf*, hair-splitting (adj.); addicted to subtle reasoning.
A	موضوع	*mōuʒu'*, subject, topic; object; matter, case, proposition.
A	موظف	*movaʒʒaf*, charged with a duty.
A	موعد	*mōu'ed*, promise, agreement; stipulated period, term, specified day (when a bill, etc., falls due).
A	موفق	*movaffaq*, successful.
A	موفقيت	*movaffaqiyat*, success.
A	موقع	*mōuqe'*, time or place where anything happens; situation; occasion, time; موقعيكه *mōuqe'ike*, when; چ از موقعيكه *mōuqe'ike*, since (from the time that).
A	موقعيت	*mōuqe'iyat*, situation; site, position.
A	موقوف	*mōuquf*, suspended, stopped, put off, postponed.
A	موقوفات	*mōuqufat*, pious bequests, endowments.
A	مؤكد	*mo'akkad*, confirmed, corroborated.
A	مولانا	*mōulana*, our lord; title given to Jalal od-Din Rumi.
A	مؤلف	*mo'allaf*, composed, published; *mo'allef*, author.
A	مولود	*mōulud*, born; birthday.
	موم	*mum*, wax.
A	مؤمن	*mo'men*, believer.
	مومى	*mumi*, waxen.
	موميا	*mumia*, mummy.
	موميا كارى	*mumiakari*, mummification.
A	مؤنث	*mo'annas*, feminine.
A	موهوم	*mōuhum*, imagined, imaginary.
A	موهومات	*mōuhumat*, superstitions, imaginary things.
A	مؤيد	*mo'ayyad*, confirmed, fortified, assisted; *mo'ayyed*, corroborative, one who confirms.
	مويز	*maviʒ*, dried grapes, raisins.
	مه	*meh*, fog, mist.
A	مهاجر	*mohajer*, refugee, fugitive, emigrant.
A	مهاجرت	*mohajerat*, emigration; fleeing from one's country.
A	مهاجم	*mohajem*, attacker.

A   مهار   *mahar*, bridle, halter; word used in counting camels; joystick of an aeroplane.

مهتاب   *mahtab*, مهتابى *mahtabi*, moonlight.

مهتر   *mehtar*, groom; greater, elder.

A   مهجور   *mahjur*, separated.

مهر   *mehr*, love, friendship; sun; seventh month of the Persian solar year; *mohr*, seal.

A   مهر   *mahr*, marriage portion settled on the wife before marriage.

مهربان   *mehraban*, kind, benevolent, beneficent.

مهربانى   *mehrabani*, kindness.

مهره   *mohre*, small shell; vertebra; bead.

A   مهلت   *mohlat*, delay, respite.

A   مهلك   *mohlek*, destructive, fatal, deadly.

A   مهم   *mohemm*, important.

A   مهمات   *mohemmat*, important affairs.

مهمان   *mehman*, guest.

مهمانخانه   *mehmanxane*, hotel.

مهماننواز   *mehmannavaz*, hospitable.

مهماننوازى   *mehmannavazi*, hospitality.

مهمانى   *mehmani*, entertainment, reception.

A   مهمل   *mohmal*, nonsensical.

A   مهملات   *mohmalat*, nonsense.

مهميز   *mehmiz*, spur, goad.

مهناوى   *mehnavi*, petty officer (naval).

A   مهندس   *mohandes*, engineer.

AP   مهندسى   *mohandesi*, engineering.

A   مهيا   *mohaiya*, prepared, ready.

A   مهيب   *mohib*, formidable, dreadful.

A   مهيج   *mohaiyej*, exciting, stimulating.

ميان   *mian*, middle; *mian(e)*, among, between; در ميان نهادن *dar mian nehadan*, to discuss, bring up (for discussion); يك روز در ميان *yak ruz dar mian*, on alternate days.

PT   ميانجى   *mianji*, mediator; go-between.

PT   ميانجيگرى   *mianjigari*, mediation.

میانه   *miane*, middle.

A   میت   *meïyet*, dead (person).

میخ   *mix*, nail, stake.

میخك   *mixak*, carnation; clove.

میخی   *mixi*, cuneiform.

A   میدان   *meïdan*, open field, arena, parade-ground; square (of a town); میدان جنگ *meïdane jang*, battle-field.

میراب   *mirab*, official in charge of the distribution of water.

A   میراث   *miras*, heritage, succession, patrimony.

AP   میر غضب   *mirɣaӡab*, executioner.

میز   *miӡ*, table; سر میز *sare miӡ*, at table.

A   میزان   *miӡan*, pair of scales, balance; measure; metre; میزان کردن *miӡan k.*, to weigh.

میزبان   *miӡban*, host, master of the house.

A   میسر   *moyassar*, facilitated, rendered easy; ready, prepared.

میش   *miʃ*, ewe.

F   میکرب   *mikrob*, microbe.

FP   میکربشناس   *mikrobʃenas*, bacteriologist.

FP   میکربشناسی   *mikrobʃenasi*, bacteriology.

A   میل   *meïl*, inclination, tendency.

میل   *mil*, mile; obelisk; bodkin; axle-tree.

A   میلاد   *milad*, birth; عید میلاد *ide milad*, Christmas.

A   میلادی   *miladi*, of the Christian era.

میله   *mile*, filament, fibre; piston-rod, axle.

میمون   *meïmun*, monkey, ape.

F   مین   *min*, mine.

FP   مینروب   *minrub*, mine-sweeper.

میوه   *mive*, fruit.

میهن   *mihan*, fatherland, motherland.

میهنپرست   *mihanparast*, patriot.

میهنپرستی   *mihanparasti*, patriotism.

میهندوست   *mihandust*, patriot.

میهندوستی   *mihandusti*, patriotism.

A   مئه   *mi'a*, one hundred.

ن

PA   نا اهل   *naahl,* unfit, incapable, unworthy.

A   نابغه   *nabeɣe,* genius.

نابكار   *nabekar,* useless, unserviceable; worthless fellow, idler.

نابود   *nabud,* annihilated.

نابينائى   *nabinai,* blindness.

ناپسند   *napasand,* displeasing.

ناترس   *natars,* fearless.

نا تمام   *natamam,* incomplete.

ناتوان   *natavan,* weak.

ناتوانى   *natavani,* weakness.

PA   نا جنس   *najens,* ignoble, uncivil.

ناجور   *najur,* ill-sorted, ill-matched.

ناچار   *nacar,* forced by necessity, constrained; indispensable.

ناچيز   *naciʒ,* worthless, insignificant; trifle.

A   ناحيه   *nahie,* neighbourhood, district.

ناخدا   *naxoda,* captain (naval); ناخدا سوم *naxoda sevvom,* lieutenant-commander (naval).

ناخن   *naxon,* nail, talon, claw.

ناخوانده   *naxande,* uninvited.

ناخوش   *naxoʃ,* ill, indisposed.

ناخوشى   *naxoʃi,* illness, indisposition.

نادان   *nadan,* ignorant.

نادانى   *nadani,* ignorance.

A   نادر   *nader,* rare.

نادرست   *nadorost,* imperfect; out of order; not right or true.

A   نادره   *nadere,* rarity (something rare).

نارس   *naras,* unripe.

نارگيل   *nargil,* coconut.

نارنجك   *naranjak,* hand-grenade.

نارنگ   *narang,* bitter orange.

نارنگى   *narangi,* mandarine, tangerine.

نارو   *narōu,* unreliable, treacherous; نارو زدن *narōu ʒadan,* to
'play a dirty game'.

	ناروا	*narava*, unlawful, prohibited.
	نارون	*narvan*, kind of elm tree.
	ناز	*naᴣ*, blandishment, fondling; coquetry; feigned disdain.
	نازبالش	*naᴣbaleſ*, pillow, bolster, cushion.
	نازك	*naᴣok*, thin, slender, delicate, fragile.
	ناساز	*nasaᴣ*, discordant, dissonant.
	ناسپاس	*nasepas*, ungrateful.
	ناسزا	*nasaᴣa*, unseemly, improper, unworthy.
	ناشتائى	*naſtai*, breakfast.
A	ناشر	*naſer*, publisher; one who divulges, diffuses.
PA	ناشكر	*naſokr*, ungrateful.
	ناشناس	*naſenas*, unknown.
A	ناشى	*naſi*, inexpert.
PA	ناصواب	*nasavab*, not right, bad, sinful.
A	ناطق	*nateq*, speaker; speaking (adj.).
A	ناظر	*naᴣer*, overseer; bailiff.
	ناف	*naf*, navel.
A	نافذ	*nafeᴣ*, piercing, penetrating (adj.).
A	نافع	*nafe'*, useful, profitable.
A	ناقص	*naqes*, deficient, defective.
	ناكس	*nakas*, base, ignoble, mean.
	ناگاه	*nagah*, suddenly.
	ناگزير	*nagoᴣir*, indispensable, inevitable; forced by necessity.
	ناگوار	*nagavar*, distasteful; indigestible.
	ناله	*nale*, lamentation, complaint.
	نام	*nam*, name; reputation, renown.
	نامبرده	*namborde*, mentioned, aforesaid.
	نامرد	*namard*, unmanly, base, ignoble, mean; coward.
	نامزد	*namᴣad*, nominated; affianced, engaged.
	نامور	*namvar*, celebrated, renowned.
A	ناموس	*namus*, reputation, good name; chastity, modesty.
	نامه	*name*, letter, epistle.
	نامه‌بر	*namebar*, letter-carrier.
	ناميدن	*namidan*, to name.
	نان	*nan*, bread.

نانوا   *nanva*, baker.

نانواخانه   *nanvaxane*, bakery.

نانوائی   *nanvai*, baking; bakery.

ناو   *nav*, warship; vessel.

ناو استوار   *navostavar*, chief petty officer (naval).

ناوبان   *navban*, second lieutenant (naval).

ناوبر   *navbar*, navigator.

ناوبری   *navbari*, navigation.

ناوبر هوائی   *navbare havai*, aero-navigation.

ناوچه   *navce*, sloop.

ناوسروان   *navsarvan*, first lieutenant (naval).

ناوشکن   *navʃekan*, torpedo-boat, destroyer.

ناوگان   *navgan*, fleet (of ships).

ناوگروه   *navgoruh*, flotilla.

ناوی   *navi*, ordinary seaman, sailor.

ناهار   *nahar*, lunch.

ناهموار   *nahamvar*, uneven, rough.

A   نائب   *naeb*, deputy, substitute, assistant; secretary (in the diplomatic service).

AP   نائب سرهنگ   *naebsarhang*, lieutenant-colonel.

A   نائل (نایل)   *nael (nayel)*, arriving, obtaining, acquiring; attaining (adj.).

A   نبات   *nabat*, plant.

A   نباتی   *nabati*, vegetable (adj.).

نبرد   *nabard*, battle, engagement.

نبردناو   *nabardnav*, battle cruiser.

A   نبض   *nabʐ*, pulse; نبض (کسیرا) گرفتن *nabʐe (kasira) gereftan*, to take (someone's) pulse.

A   نبوغ   *nobuɣ*, genius (abstr.).

A   نبی   *nabi*, prophet.

نبیره   *nabire*, great-grandchild.

A   نتایج   *natayej*, pl. of نتیجه.

A   نتیجه   *natije*, result, consequence; offspring.

A   نثر   *nasr*, scattering (subs.); prose.

A   نجات   *nejat*, liberation, rescue; نجات دادن *nejat dadan*, to rescue, liberate; نجات یافتن *nejat yaftan*, to be saved.

A	نجار	*najjar*, carpenter.
AP	نجارى	*najjari*, carpentry, being a carpenter.
A	نجاست	*nejasat*, filth, dirt.
A	نجس	*nejes*, unclean, especially ceremonially unclean.
A	نجوم	*nojum* (pl. of *najm*), stars; علم نجوم *elme nojum*, astronomy, astrology.
A	نجيب	*najib*, noble, generous, excellent; well-bred.
A	نحس	*nahs*, ill-omened, inauspicious, unlucky.
A	نحو	*nahv*, way, manner; syntax.
	نخ	*nax*, thread, cotton.
A	نخبه	*noxbe*, choice part of anything.
	نخست	*naxost*, first.
PA	نخست وزير	*naxostvazir*, prime minister.
	نخستين	*naxostin*, first.
A	نخل	*naxl*, palm-tree.
	نخود	*noxod*, pea.
	نخودچى	*noxodci*, chick-pea.
	نخى	*naxi*, cotton (adj.).
PA	نخير	*naxeir*, no.
A	ندامت	*nedamat*, repentance, contrition, regret.
A	نديم	*nadim*, boon companion, intimate friend.
A	نذر	*nazr*, vow, promise made to God.
	نر	*nar*, male, masculine.
	نرخ	*nerx*, price, tariff, rate (of exchange, etc.).
	نرد	*nard*, backgammon.
	نردبان	*nardeban*, ladder.
	نرگس	*narges*, narcissus.
	نرم	*narm*, soft; mild, gentle.
A	نزاع	*neza'*, dispute, contention, controversy, litigation.
	نزاكت	*nezakat*, politeness, courtesy.
	نزد	*nazd(e)*, near, beside; with, before (of place).
	نزديك	*nazdik*, near.
	نزديكى	*nazdiki*, nearness.
A	نزول	*nozul*, descending, alighting (subs.); descent.
	نژاد	*nezad*, race, descent, extraction.

A نساج nassaj, weaver.

A نسب nasab, race, lineage, stock; genealogy.

A نسبت nesbat, affinity, connexion; proportion; attribute; نسبت دادن nesbat dadan, to attribute; نسبت داشتن nesbat d., to be related, connected; نسبت به nesbat be, with relation to.

A نسبة nesbatan, relatively.

A نسج nasj, tissue, texture; weaving.

A نسخ nasx, annulling, cancelling (subs.); abrogation, cancellation; a certain style of handwriting.

A نسخه nosxe, copy (of a book, etc.); prescription.

A نسق nasaq, order, series; arrangement; style, mode.

A نسيم nasim, zephyr, gentle breeze.

A نسيه nesie, on credit (of purchase).

A نشاط nefat, cheerfulness, gladness.

نشان nefan, sign, signal, mark; order, medal; target; نشان دادن nefan dadan, to show.

نشانى nefani, sign; address.

نشخوار nefxar, chewing the cud, ruminating (adj.).

A نشر nafr, diffusing, publishing (subs.).

نشستن nefastan, to sit, sit down.

A نصب nasb, erecting, fixing (subs.).

A نصب العين nasb ol-ain, example, model.

A نصرانى nasrani, Christian.

A نصرانيت nasraniyat, Christianity.

A نصف nesf, half; نصف شب nesfe fab, midnight.

A نصيب nasib, part, portion; destiny, fate.

A نصيحت nasihat, advice, exhortation.

A نظافت nezafat, cleanliness, neatness.

A نطق notq, speech, oration.

A نظارت nezarat, inspection, supervision.

A نظام nezam, order, arrangement; military affairs; army.

AP نظام نامه nezamname, regulations, standing orders; articles of association, constitution.

AP نظام وظيفه nezamvazife, military service.

A نظامى nezami, military.

A	نظر	*naẓar*, looking at, seeing; sight, vision; look, glance; بنظر من *be naẓare man*, in my opinion.
A	نظری	*naẓari*, speculative, theoretical.
A	نظم	*naẓm*, order, arrangement; verse.
A	نظمیه	*naẓmiye*, police, police-station.
A	نظیر	*naẓir*, like, alike, resembling, equal (to).
A	نعل	*na'l*, horse-shoe; piece of metal put on the heel of a shoe.
AP	نعلبند	*na'lband*, farrier.
A	نعمت	*ne'mat*, bounty, beneficence; favour.
A	نغمه	*nayme*, melody, tone.
A	نفاق	*nefaq*, hypocrisy; discord; quarrel, dispute.
	نفت	*naft*, petrol.
	نفت کش	*naftkaʃ*, tanker.
	نفر	*nafar*, person, individual.
A	نفرت	*nefrat*, aversion, hatred; نفرت داشتن *nefrat d.*, to hate.
A	نفس	*nafas*, breath, respiration; نفس کشیدن *nafas kaʃidan*, to breathe heavily, blow; *nafs*, soul, spirit.
A	نفوذ	*nofuẓ*, influence; نفوذ کردن *nofuẓ k.*, to influence; to penetrate.
A	نفوس	*nofus* (pl. of نفس *nafs*), souls; persons, individuals.
AP	نقاره‌خانه	*naqarexane*, band of music; the place where drums are beaten at stated intervals for royalty.
A	نقاره	*naqare*, kettle-drum.
A	نقاش	*naqqaʃ*, painter.
AP	نقاشی	*naqqaʃi*, art of painting.
A	نقاط	*noqat* (pl. of نقطه *noqte*), points, regions.
A	نقد	*naqd*, cash, ready money; نقد کردن *naqd k.*, to cash.
A	نقداً	*naqdan*, for the present, at present.
A	نقره	*noqre*, silver.
A	نقش	*naqʃ*, painting; imprint, picture; role.
A	نقشه	*naqʃe*, map; plan; نقشه کشیدن *naqʃe kaʃidan*, to make a plan.
A	نقص	*naqs*, defect, deficiency; detriment.
A	نقصان	*noqsan*, loss.
A	نقطه	*noqte*, point.
A	نقل	*naql*, quoting; transporting (subs.).
A	نقلیه	*naqliye*, transport.

A نكات (pl. of نكته *nokte*), points, subtleties.

A نكته *nokte*, point, subtlety.

نگارش *negareʃ*, painting, drawing; writing.

نگاشتن *negaʃtan*, to paint, draw, write.

نگاه *negah*, look, glance; نگاه كردن *negah k.*, to look; نگاه داشتن *negah d.*, to hold, keep.

نگاهبانى *negahbani*, keeping watch (subs.).

نگران *negaran*, anxious, apprehensive.

نگرانى *negarani*, anxiety.

نگرستن *negarestan*, to look.

نگهبان *negahban*, guard, custodian, watch.

نگهبانى *negahbani*, keeping guard, custody.

نگين *negin*, ring (ornament).

نم *nam*, dew, moisture; dampness.

نماز *namaʐ*, prayers; نماز خواندن *namaʐ xandan*, to say prayers.

نمايان *namayan*, apparent, appearing, clear.

نمايش *namayeʃ*, apparition, appearance; play, show.

نمايندگى *namayandegi*, representative (noun); being a representative.

نماينده *namayande*, representative (noun).

نمد *namad*, felt.

نمره *nomre*, number.

نمك *namak*, salt.

نمودار *namudar*, appearing; visible; graphic, graphically; exemplar, proof.

نمودن *namudan*, to show, appear; to seem; to do.

نمونه *namune*, example, sample.

ننگ *nang*, disgrace, infamy.

نو *nou*, new.

نواخت *navaxt*, tone; manner.

نواختن *navaxtan*, to soothe, caress; to play (an instrument).

نوار *navar*, ribbon, roll of braid or edging.

نوار چسب *navarcasb*, roll of sticking paper.

A نواقص *navaqes* (pl. of نقص), shortcomings, defects, deficiencies.

نو آموز *nouamuʐ*, beginner, learner, novitiate, novice.

نوان خانه *navanxane*, poor-house.

A	نوبت	*noubat*, turn, time; نوبت دادن *noubat d.*, to keep watch, sentry-go.
	نوبر	*noubar*, fresh fruits newly ripe; first fruits.
	نود	*navad*, ninety.
A	نور	*nur*, light; نور چشمی *nure calmi*, light of my eye(s).
	نور افکن	*nurafkan*, searchlight.
	نورس	*nouras*, fresh, young, tender.
	نوروز	*nouruz*, New Year.
	نوزده	*nuzdah*, nineteen.
	نوشابه	*nulabe*, draught, drink.
	نوشتن	*nevestan*, to write.
	نوشیدن	*nulidan*, to drink.
A	نوع	*nou'*, kind, species, sort, manner.
	نوك	*nuk*, beak, tip, point, end.
	نوکر	*noukar*, servant.
	نوکری	*noukari*, being a servant, service.
	نومید	*noumid (naomid)*, hopeless, despairing.
	نومیدی	*noumidi (naomidi)*, hopelessness, despair.
	نوه	*nave*, grandchild.
	نوید	*novid, navid*, good news.
	نه	*na*, no; نه...نه *na...na*, neither...nor; *noh*, nine.
	نهادن	*nehadan*, to place, put.
	نهال	*nehal*, sapling, young plant, shoot.
	نهان	*nehan*, hidden.
	نهانی	*nehani*, secret (adj. and noun); secretly.
A	نهایت	*nehayat*, extremity; very much, extremely.
A	نهر	*nahr*, river, stream, canal.
A	نهضت	*nahzat, nehzat*, movement (fig.).
	نهنگ	*nahang*, whale.
A	نهی	*nahi*, prohibition, prohibiting.
	نی	*nei*, pipe, flute; reed.
	نیا	*nia*, ancestor, forefather.
	نیاز	*niaz*, need, indigence; نیاز داشتن *niaz d.*, to need.
	نیازمند	*niazmand*, needy.
A	نیران	*niran* (pl. of نار *nar*), fires; (pl. of نور *nur*), flames, lights.

نيرو   *niru*, force, strength; نيروى دريائى *niruye daryai*, navy; نيروى هوائى *niruye havai*, air force.

نيز   *niẓ*, also.

نيزه   *nēize*, spear.

نيست   *nist*: نيست و نابود كردن *nist o nabud k.*, to annihilate.

نيش   *niʃ*, sting.

نيك   *nik*, good; (obs.) very good.

نيكو   *niku*, good.

نيكى   *niki*, goodness.

نيل   *nil*, indigo.

نيلوفر   *nilufar*, waterlily.

نيم   *nim*, half.

نيم تنه   *nimtane*, short jacket.

نيمكت   *nimkat*, bench, form; sofa.

نيمه   *nime*, half.

و

A   و   *va*, and.

و   *o*, and.

وابسته   *vabaste*, attaché; attached to.

A   واثق   *vaseq*, firm, solid.

A   واجب   *vajeb*, necessary, obligatory.

A   واحد   *vahed*, unit; one; single, unique.

وادار   *vadar*, compelled, obliged; وادار كردن *vadar k.*, to compel; to restrain, hold back.

وا داشتن   *va daʃtan*, to compel; to restrain, hold back.

A   وارث   *vares*, heir.

A   وارد   *vared*, arriving (adj.); وارد بودن *vared b.*, to be appropriate; to be *au courant*; وارد شدن *vared ʃ.*, to enter; وارد كردن *vared k.*, to import.

A   واردات   *varedat*, imports.

وا رسى   *varasi*, investigation; control.

وارونه   *varune*, inverted, upside down.

وا زدن   *va ẓadan*, to refuse, reject.

واژگون   va3gun, inverted.

واژه   va3e, word.

A   واسط   vaset, middle (adj.); mediator.

A   واسطه   vasete, mediator; بـواسطه be vasete(ye), by means of; because of.

A   واضح   va3eh, clear, evident.

A   واعظ   va'e3, preacher.

A   واقع   vaqe', happening, occurrence; happening, occurring; واقع شـدن vaqe' ʃ., to happen; سورد نـوازش واقع شدن mourede nava3eʃ vaqe' ʃodan, to become the object of favour; در واقع dar vaqe', in reality; واقعًا vaqe'an, in reality, really.

واکردن   va kardan, to open.

واکنش   vakoneʃ, reaction.

واگذار   vago3ar, transferred, handed over, made over.

واگذاری   vago3ari, transfer, handing over, making over; transferred.

واگذاشتن   va go3aʃtan, to hand over, transfer, make over.

واگیر   vagir, infectious (of disease).

A   والد   valed, parent; father.

A   والله   vallahe, by God!

A   والی   vali, governor.

وام   vam, debt, loan.

A   وبا   vaba, cholera, plague.

A   وجاهت   vajahat, beauty, presence.

A   وجدان   vejdan, conscience.

A   وجدانی   vejdani, conscientious, pertaining to the conscience.

A   وجود   vojud, existence; person, presence; بـوجـود آوردن be vojud avardan, to create; با وجود ba vojud(e), in spite (of).

A   وجوه   vojuh (pl. of وجه vajh), sums (of money).

A   وجه   vajh, face; appearance; mode, manner.

A   وجهه   vejhe, prestige.

A   وحدت   vahdat, unity.

A   وحشت   vahʃat, terror, dread.

AP   وحشتناك   vahʃatnak, frightening, terrifying (adj.).

A	وحشی	*vahſi*, wild, savage.
AP	وحشیگری	*vahſigari*, savagery, barbarity.
A	وحوش	*vohuſ* (pl. of وحش *vahſ*), wild beasts.
A	وخیم	*vaxim*, critical, perilous.
	ور آمدن	*var amadan*, to rise; to swell.
	ور داشتن	*var daſtan*, to take away, up, off.
	ور رفتن	*var raftan*, to fidget.
	ورزش	*varʒeſ*, exercise, exertion.
	ورزیدن	*varʒidan*, to exercise.
	ورزیده	*varʒide*, trained, in training.
	ور شکست	*varſekast*, bankrupt.
	ور شکستگی	*varſekastegi*, bankruptcy.
A	ورق	*varaq*, leaf, sheet (of paper).
A	ورم	*varam*, swelling (subs.).
A	ورود	*vorud*, entrance.
A	وزارت	*veʒarat*, ministry (political).
AP	وزارت امور خارجه	*veʒarate omure xareje*, Ministry of Foreign Affairs.
AP	وزارت بازرگانی	*veʒarate baʒargani*, Ministry of Trade.
AP	وزارت بهداری	*veʒarate behdari*, Ministry of Health.
AP	وزارت پیشه و هنر	*veʒarate piſe o honar*, Ministry of Industry.
AP	وزارت خواربار	*veʒarate xarbar*, Ministry of Food.
AP	وزارت دادگستری	*veʒarate dadgostari*, Ministry of Justice.
AP	وزارت دارائی	*veʒarate darai*, Ministry of Finance.
AP	وزارت راه	*veʒarate rah*, Ministry of Roads.
AP	وزارت فرهنگ	*veʒarate farhang*, Ministry of Education.
AP	وزارت کشور	*veʒarate keſvar*, Ministry of the Interior.
A	وزن	*vaʒn*, weight; metre.
A	وزیر	*veʒir*, minister (political).
AP	وسائط نقلیه	*vasa'ete naqliye*, means of transport.
A	وسایل (وسائل)	*vasayel* (*vasa'el*) (pl. of وسیله *vasile*), means.
A	وسط	*vasat*, middle (subs.).
A	وسعت	*vos'at*, extent, spaciousness.
A	وسیع	*vasi'*, wide, spacious, extensive.
A	وسیله	*vasile*, means; بوسیله *be vasile(ye)*, by means of; با این وسیله
		be in vasile, in this way, by this means.

A	وصف	*vasf*, describing, description.
A	وصول	*vosul*, arrival; collection (of taxes, etc.).
A	وصی	*vasi*, executor (law).
A	وصیت	*vasiyat*, last will, testament; وصیت کردن *vasiyat k.*, to make a will.
A	وضع	*vaz'*, position, situation, state.
A	وضو	*vozu'*, ablution, ceremonial cleaning (before prayer).
A	وطن	*vatan*, native country, home.
AP	وطنپرست	*vatanparast*, patriotic; patriot.
AP	وطنپرستی	*vatanparasti*, patriotism.
AP	وطنفروش	*vatanforush*, traitor (to one's country).
AP	وطنفروشی	*vatanforushi*, betraying one's country (subs.).
A	وطنی	*vatani*, native, belonging to the homeland.
A	وظیفه	*vazife*, duty.
A	وعده	*va'de*, promise; وعده دادن (کردن) *va'de dadan (k.)*, to promise.
A	وعظ	*va'z*, sermon; preaching.
A	وفات	*vafat*, death.
A	وفق	*vefq*, accordance, conformity; وفق دادن *vefq dadan*, to adapt, co-ordinate; to be conformable with; بر وفق *bar vefq(e)*, in accordance with.
A	وفور	*vofur*, abundance.
A	وقار	*veqar*, dignity, gravity, majesty.
A	وقت	*vaqt*, time; سر وقت *sare vaqt*, punctually; وقتیکه *vaqtike*, when.
A	وقف	*vaqf*, endowment, religious bequest.
A	وکالت	*vekalat*, acting as or being a substitute, deputy, representative or agent; the office of a deputy, etc.
AP	وکالت نامه	*vekalatname*, letter of attorney.
A	وکیل	*vakil*, agent, deputy, representative, substitute, attorney; lawyer; (obs.) sergeant.
	ول	*vel*: ول کردن *vel k.*, to leave alone, let go.
A	ولایت	*velayat*, province.
PA	ولخرج	*velxarj*, extravagant, prodigal.
PA	ولخرجی	*velxarji*, extravagance, prodigality.

A   ولی   *vali*, but, yet, however; *valēi*, friend; guardian.

A   ولیعهد   *valiahd*, heir-apparent.

A   وهله   *vahle*, time, turn; moment.

A   وهم   *vahm*, fear, anxiety, apprehension; imagining; conceiving a false idea.

   وی   *vēi*, he.

   ویران   *vēiran*, laid waste; desolate; ruined, depopulated.

   ویژه   *viʒe*, pure, unmixed, mere; special; بویژه *be viʒe*, especially.

ه

A   هادی   *hadi*, guide.

   هار   *har*, mad, rabid.

A   هجره   *hejre*, Mohammadan era.

A   هجری   *hejri*, appertaining to the Mohammedan era.

A   هجوم   *hojum*, attacking, attack.

A   هدایا   *hadaya* (pl. of هدیه *hadiye*), presents.

A   هدر   *hadar*, anything unprofitable or vain; useless effort; بهدر رفتن *be hadar raftan*, to be in vain, to come to naught.

A   هدف   *hadaf*, target; aim, object.

A   هدیه   *hadiye*, present, offering.

   هر   *har*, every, all; each, any; هر جا *har ja*, everywhere; هرچندکه *har cand ke*, although, however much; هرچه *har ce*, whatever (subs.); هر دو *har do*, both; هرسه *har se*, all three; هرکدام *har kodam*, each, whoever (of two or more); هرکس *har kas*, whoever; هرکه *har ke*, whoever; whenever; هرگاه *hargah*, whenever.

   هراس   *haras*, terror, fear, dread; alarm, warning.

   هراسان   *harasan*, frightened, fearing.

   هر آینه (آئینه)   *har ayene* (*aine*), in any case.

   هرج و مرج   *harj o marj*, anarchy.

   هرگز   *hargez*, ever; (with negative verb) never.

   هرزه   *harʒe*, vain, futile, frivolous; nonsense.

   هزار   *haʒar*, one thousand.

   هزینه   *haʒine*, expenditure; cost; هزینه زندگی *haʒineye ʒendegi*, cost of living.

هستى	*hasti*, existence.
هشت	*haſt*, eight.
هشتاد	*haſtad*, eighty.
هشتن	*heſtan*, to leave, let go.
هشیار	*hoſyar*, intelligent, prudent.
A هضم	*haẓm*, digestion.
هفت	*haft*, seven.
هفتاد	*haftad*, seventy.
هفته	*hafte*, week.
هفده	*hefde*, seventeen.
هل	*hel*, cardamom.
A هلاك	*halak*, perishing; destruction, ruin; هلاك کردن *halak k.*, to destroy.
A هلال	*helal*, new moon.
هلو	*holu*, peach.
هم	*ham*, also, likewise; هم...هم *ham...ham*, both...and; بهم خوردن *be ham xordan*, to break up (intrans.), be disordered; بهم زدن *be ham ẓadan*, to break up (trans.), to mix up, put in disorder; to shut (a book, etc.); بهم رسیدن *be ham rasidan*, to meet.
همان	*haman*, that same, that very.
هماهنگ	*hamahang*, harmonious.
همایون	*homayun*
همایونى	*homayuni* } august, royal, blessed.
A همت	*hemmat*, inclination, desire, resolution; ambition, aspiration.
همچنان	*hamconan*, همچنین *hamconin*, thus, in like manner, similarly.
همدردى	*hamdardi*, sympathy.
هم دیگر	*ham digar*, each other.
همراه	*hamrah*, with, together with; fellow-traveller.
همراهى	*hamrahi*, being in the company (of); help, co-operation.
همسایه	*hamsaye*, neighbour.
همشهرى	*hamſahri*, fellow-townsman.
همشیره	*hamſire*, sister.
PA همعقیده	*hamaqide*, of the same opinion; co-believer.
همکار	*hamkar*, fellow-workman; همکارى *hamkari*, co-operation.

همگان   *hamegan*, all.

همیهنان   *hammihanan*, fellow-countrymen.

هموار   *hamvar*, level, even.

همواره   *hamvare*, always.

همه   *hame*, all; the whole.

A   همهمه   *hamhame*, murmur, murmuring.

همیشه   *hamiſe*, always.

همین   *hamin*, this very, this same; همینکه *haminke*, as soon as.

هند   *hend*, India.

A   هندسه   *hendese*, geometry.

هندو   *hendu*, Hindu, Indian (subs.).

هندوانه   *hendavane*, water-melon.

هندوستان   *hendustan*, India.

هندی   *hendi*, Indian.

هنر   *honar*, skill, art; virtue.

هنرپیشه   *honarpiſe*, actor, artist.

هنرستان   *honarestan*, technical school.

هنگ   *häng*, regiment.

هنگام   *hengam*, time, hour, season; هنگامیکه *hengamike*, when.

هنگامه   *hengame*, tumult, commotion, riot.

هنوز   *hanuẓ*, still, yet.

هو   *hōu*: هوکردن *hōu k.*, to ridicule; to heckle.

A   هوا   *hava*, air, atmosphere, weather; desire; lust; هوا(ی چیزی) *hava(ye ciẓi) k.*, to long for, desire (something).

AP   هواپیما   *havapēima*, aeroplane; کشتی هواپیمابر *kaſliye havapēimabar*, aircraft carrier.

AP هوانورد   *havanavard*, aeroplane pilot.

AP   هوا نوردی   *havanavardi*, aero-navigation.

AP   هوائی   *havai*, aerial (adj.).

هوبره   *hubare*, bustard.

هوچی   *hōuci*, demagogue, heckler.

هوچیگری   *hōucigari*, demagogy, heckling.

هوس   *havas*, desire, lust.

هوش   *huſ*, intellect, mind.

هوشیار   *huſyar*, intelligent; prudent.

A   هول   *hōul*, fright, terror.

AP   هولناك   *hōulnak*, dreadful, frightening.

A   هويت   *hoviyat*: ورقه هويت *varaqeye hoviyat*, identity card.

هويج   *havij*, carrot.

هيا هو   *haiyahu*, hullabaloo, uproar.

هيجده   *hijdah*, eighteen.

هيچ   *hic*, any; ever; (with negative verb) none; never; هيچ كس *hic kas*, anyone; (with negative verb) no one; هيچ كدام *hic kodam*, any (of two or more); (with negative verb) none (of two or more); هيچ گونه *hic gune*, in any way; (with negative verb) in no way; هيچ وقت *hic vaqt*, ever, at any time; (with negative verb) never.

هيزم   *hizom*, firewood.

هيكل   *heikal*, figure, form, stature.

A   هيئت   *hei'at*, committee, commission, delegation; هيئت مديره *hei'ate modire*, executive committee.

ى

يا   *ya*, or; O!; يا...يا *ya...ya*, either...or.

يابو   *yabu*, cob, pack-horse.

ياد   *yad*, remembrance, recollection; memory; ياد آمدن (افتادن) *yad amadan (oftadan)*, to come to mind; ياد آوردن *yad avardan*, to remember, recall; to remind; ياد داشتن *yad d.*, to remember.

ياد آورى   *yadavari*, reminder.

ياد بود   *yadbud*, memorial, anything given in remembrance.

ياد داشت   *yaddaft*, note; memorandum; aide-mémoire; ياد داشت پرداخت *yaddafte pardaxt*, debit note; ياد داشت در يافت *yaddafte daryaft*, credit note; ياد داشت كردن *yaddaft k.*, to note.

يادگار   *yadgar*, souvenir, keepsake.

يار   *yar*, friend, helper.

يارستن   *yarastan*, to be able (obs.).

يارو   *yaru*, fellow (subs.).

یاری   *yari*, help; friendship.

یازده   *yaχdah*, eleven.

یاس   *yas*, jasmine.

A   یأس   *ya's*, despair.

یاسمن   *yasaman*, jasmine.

یاغی   *yaɣi*, rebel, outlaw.

یاغیگری   *yaɣigari*, rebellion, outlawry.

یافتن   *yaftan*, to find.

A   یاقوت   *yaqut*, ruby, cornelian.

یال   *yal*, neck; mane (of an animal).

یاور   *yavar*, assistant; police officer equal in rank to an army major; (obs.) major (mil.).

یاوری   *yavari*, assistance, help.

یاوه‌گو   *yavegu*, one who talks vainly, foolishly.

A   یتیم   *yatim*, orphan.

یخ   *yax*, ice; یخ بستن *yax bastan*, to freeze (intrans.).

یخچال   *yaxcal*, ice pit; place where ice is kept.

یدک   *yadak*, led horse; spare, reserve.

یدک‌کش   *yadakkaʃ*, tug-boat, tow-boat.

یدکی   *yadaki*, spare; اسباب یدکی *asbabe yadaki*, spare parts.

T   یراق   *yaraq*, arms, accoutrements.

یزدان   *yaχdan*, God.

A   یعنی   *ya'ni*, that is to say, namely, to wit.

یغما   *yaɣma*, plunder, booty, pillage.

یقه   *yaqe* (usually pronounced *yaxe*), collar.

A   یقین   *yaqin*, certainty, assurance; certain, sure; یقین داشتن *yaqin d.*, to be certain (of something).

یک   *yak, yek*, one; یکچندی *yak (yek) candi*, a little while; یک دیگر *yak (yek) digar*, one another; یکی *yaki, yeki*, one, someone, a certain one.

یکسان   *yaksan*, equal, the same.

یکسر   *yaksar*, without interruption; directly; entirely, from beginning to end; non-stop.

یکنواخت   *yaknavaxt*, monotonous.

یگانگی   *yaganegi*, unity; singularity.

	یگانه	*yagane*, unique; single, sole.
A	یمن	*yomn*, prosperity, felicity.
T	یواش	*yavaſ*, gently, slowly.
T	یورتمه	*yortme*, trot, trotting.
T	یورقه	*yorqe*, ambling (noun, of a horse).
	یوز	*yuχ*, cheetah.
	یوز پلنگ	*yuχ palang*, panther.
	یوغ	*yuɣ*, yoke.
A	یوم	*yōum*, day.
	یونان	*yunan*, Greece.
	یونانی	*yunani*, Greek, Grecian.
A	یهودی	*yahudi*, Jew, Jewish.
T	ییلاق	*yeīlaq*, summer quarters.

ENGLISH—PERSIAN

VOCABULARY

A

Abandon, to, ترك كردن *tark k.*

Abandoned, متروك *matruk.*

Abandonment, ترك *tark.*

Abate, to (intrans., of a storm, etc.), ساكت شدن *saket ʃ.*

Abbreviate, to, خلاصه كردن *xolase k.*, مختصر كردن *moxtasar k.*

Abbreviation, خلاصه *xolase*, اختصار *extesar.*

Abdicate, to, استعفا دادن *esteʿfa dadan.*

Abdication, استعفا *esteʿfa.*

Abeyance, وقفه *vaqfe*, سكوت *sokut*; to fall in abeyance, از اعتبار افتادن *az eʿtebar oftadan.*

Abhor, to, (از) تنفر داشتن *tanaffor d. (az).*

Abhorrence, تنفر *tanaffor.*

Ability, استعداد *esteʿdad.*

Able, با استعداد *baesteʿdad*; to be able (to do something), توانستن *tavanestan.*

Abolish, to, منسوخ كردن *mansux k.*; ملغى كردن *molya k.*

Abolition, الغا *elya.*

Abortion, سقط جنين *seqte janin.*

Abound, to, فراوان بودن *faravan b.*

About (=concerning), در باره *dar bare(ye)*, در باب *dar bab(e)*, در بابت *dar babat(e)*, در اطراف *dar atraf(e)*, در خصوص *dar xosus(e)*, راجع به *rajeʿ be*; (=around), در اطراف *dar atraf(e)*; (=nearly), تقريبًا *taqriban*, در حدود *dar hodud(e)*; he was about to go, ميخواست برود *mixast beravad.*

Above, (ی)بالا *bala(ye)*; (=what is above), ما فوق *ma fouq.*

Abroad (=a foreign country), خارجه *xareje*; (=outside), بيرون *birun.*

Abrogate, to, see Abolish.

Absence, غيبت *yeibat.*

Absent, غائب *yaʿeb*; to be absent, غائب بودن *yaʿeb b.*, حاضر نبودن *hazer nabudan.*

Absent-minded, پریشان فکر *parifanfekr.*

Absolute, مطلق *motlaq.*

Absolutely, مطلقاً *motlaqan,* کاملاً *kamelan.*

Absolve, to, see Pardon and Exempt.

Absorb, to, جذب کردن *jazb k.*

Absorbent, جاذب *jazeb.*

Absorption, جذب *jazb.*

Abstain, to, پرهیز کردن *parhiz k.*; (=to refrain), احتراز کردن *ehteraz k.,* امتناع کردن *emtena' k.*

Abstemious, پرهیزکار *parhizkar.*

Abstention, پرهیزکاری *parhizkari*; (=refraining), احتراز *ehteraz,* متناع *emtena'.*

Abstinence, پرهیزکاری *parhizkari.*

Abstract (opp. concrete), مطلق *motlaq.*

Abstruse, مبهم *mobham.*

Absurd, بیهوده *xandeavar,* مسخره *masxare*; مزخرف *mozaxraf*; خنده آور *bihude.*

Absurdity, مسخرگی *masxaregi,* بیهودگی *bihudegi.*

Abundance, فراوانی *faravani,* وفور *vofur.*

Abundant, فراوان *faravan,* وافر *vafer.*

Abuse, فحش *fohf,* هتاکی *hattaki*; to abuse (someone), فحش دادن *fohf dadan*; (a privilege, etc.), سوء استفاده کردن (از) *su'e estefade k. (az).*

Abusive, فحاش *fahhaf.*

Abusiveness, فحاشی *fahhafi.*

Academy, فرهنگستان *farhangestan.*

Accelerate, to (trans.) تسریع کردن *tasri' k.*

Acceleration, تسریع *tasri'.*

Accent, see Pronunciation and Stress.

Accept, to, قبول کردن *qabul k.,* پذیرفتن *paziroftan*; (=admit), قائل بودن *qa'el b.*

Acceptable, مطبوع *matbu'.*

Acceptance, قبول *qabul.*

Access, دسترس *dastras*; (=entrance), مدخل *madxal.*

Accessible, to be, در دسترس بودن *dar dastras b.*

Accession (to throne), جلوس *jolus*; see also Increase.

Accessory, see Accomplice.

Accidence, صرف sarf.

Accident, حادثه hadese, اتفاق ettefaq; (=mistake), خطا xata.

Accidentally (=by chance), اتـفاقًا ettefaqan; (=by mistake), اشتباهًا eftebahan.

Accommodation, to have, جا داشتن ja d.

Accompany, to, همراه رفتن hamrah raftan.

Accomplice, شریك farik, همدست hamdast.

Accomplish, to, (دادن) انجام کردن anjam k. (dadan).

Accomplished (=cultured), باهنر bahonar, فاضل fazel.

Accomplishment (=bringing to completion), اتمام etmam; (=skill, etc.), هنر honar, فضل fazl.

Accord, موافقت movafeqat, توافق tavafoq.

Accordance: in accordance with, see According to.

According to, بر طبق bar tebq(e), مطابق motabeq(e), بر حسب bar hasb(e), بنابر bana bar, از قرار az qarar(e), بقرار be qarar(e).

Accordingly, بنا بر این bana bar in.

Account (=reckoning), حساب hesab, صورت حساب surate hesab; (=description), شرح farh, بیان bayan; on account of (=because of), از جهت az jehat(e), نظر به nazar be, از بابت az babat(e); on no account, بهیچ وجه be hic vajh.

Accountancy, حسابداری hesabdari; محاسبات mohasebat.

Accountant, حسابدار hesabdar; محاسب mohaseb.

Account-book, دفتر حساب daftare hesab.

Accoutrements, ساز و برگ saz o barg, یراق yaraq.

Accrue, to, عاید گردیدن ayed gardidan.

Accumulate, to (trans.), جمع کردن jam' k.

Accuracy, دقت deqqat.

Accurate, دقیق daqiq.

Accursed, ملعون mal'un.

Accusation, اتهام etteham; false accusation, تهمت tohmat, افتراء eftera.

Accuse, to, متهم کردن mottaham k.; (falsely) تهمت زدن (به) tohmat zadan (be).

Accused, متهم mottaham.

Accustom: to get accustomed to, عادت کردن (به) adat k. (be).

Ace, آس *as*.

Achieve, to (=finish), انجام کردن (دادن) *anjam k. (dadan)*.

Acid (adj.), ترش *torf*.

Acknowledge, to, (به) اقرار کردن (به) اعتراف کردن *e'teraf k. (be)*, اقرار کردن (به) *eqrar k. (be)*; تصدیق کردن (به) *tasdiq k. (be)*.

Acknowledgement, اعتراف اقرار *e'teraf, eqrar*.

Acorn, بلوط *balut*.

Acquaintance (abstr.), آشنائی *afnai*; (person) آشنا *afna*.

Acquainted, آشنا *afna*; to be acquainted with, آشنا بودن با *afna b. ba*.

Acquire, to, حاصل کردن بدست آوردن *hasel k.*, تحصیل کردن *tahsil k.*, *be dast avardan*.

Acquisition, تحصیل *tahsil*.

Acquit, to, تبرئه کردن *tabre'e k.*

Acquittal, تبرئه *tabre'e*.

Across: he went across the plain, از دشت عبور کرد *az daft obur kard*.

Act, to, کردن *kardan*, عمل کردن *amal k.*; to act (for someone), کفالت کردن *kefalat k.*; (in a play), بازی کردن *bazi k.*

Acting (doing duty for someone, adj.), کفیل *kafil*.

Action, عمل *amal*; (legal), مرافعه *morafe'e*; (military), جنگ *jang*, نبرد *nabard*; to take action, اقدام کردن *eqdam k.*

Active, فعال *fa'al*; very active, فعال *fa"al*.

Activity, فعالیت *fa'aliyat*.

Actor, بازیگر *bazigar*, هنرپیشه *honarpife*.

Actual (=present), فعلی *fe'li*; (=true), واقعی *vaqe'i*, حقیقی *haqiqi*.

Actually, فعلاً *fe'lan*, فی الواقع *fel-vaqe'*.

Acute, تیز *tiz*, زیرك *zirak*; acute angle, زاویه حاده *zavieye hadde*.

Adapt, to, منطبق ساختن *montabeq saxtan*, وفق دادن *vefq dadan*.

Add, to, جمع کردن *jam' k.*; (=to increase), اضافه کردن *ezafe k.*, افزودن *afzudan*, علاوه کردن *alave k.*

Addendum, ضمیمه *zamime*.

Addicted, معتاد *mo'tadd*.

Addition, جمع *jam'*; (=increase), اضافه افزایش *ezafe, afzayef*, ازدیاد *ezdeyad*; in addition, باضافه *be ezafe*, بعلاوه *be alave*.

Additional, اضافی *ezafi*.

Address, نشانی *nefani*, آدرس *adres*.

Adhere, to (fig.), ملحق شدن molhaq ʃ.

Adherent, طرفدار tarafdar.

Adjacent, مجاور mojaver, پهلو pahlu.

Adjective, صفت sefat.

Adjourn, to (a meeting, etc.), ختم جلسه کردن xatme jalse k.

Adjournment (of a meeting, etc.), ختم جلسه xatme jalse.

Adjust, to (= to modify), تعدیل کردن taʿdil k.; (= to arrange) تنظیم کردن tanʒim k.

Adjustment, تعدیل taʿdil, تنظیم tanʒim.

Adjutant, آجودان ajudan.

Administer, to, اداره کردن edare k.

Administration, اداره edare; (=government), حکومت hokumat, دولت doulat.

Administrative, اداری edari.

Admirable, قابل تحسین qabele tahsin.

Admiral, دریابان daryaban; admiral of the fleet, دریا سالار daryasalar.

Admiralty, وزارت دریاداری veʒarate daryadari.

Admission, ورود vorud; (= acknowledgement), اعتراف eʿteraf.

Admit, to, وارد کردن vared k.; (= to acknowledge), اعتراف کردن eʿteraf k.

Admonish, to, نصیحت کردن nasihat k.

Adopt, to (a policy, etc.), قبول کردن qabul k., اختیار کردن exteyar k., اتخاذ کردن ettexaʒ k.

Adoration, see Worship.

Adorn, to, آراستن arastan, زینت دادن ʒinat dadan.

Adroit, زرنگ ʒarang.

Adroitness, زرنگی ʒarangi.

Adult, کبیر kabir, بالغ baleɣ; adults, سالمندان salmandan.

Adulterer, زناکار ʒenakar.

Adultery, زنا ʒena.

Advance (of money, etc.), مساعده mosaʿede; to buy in advance, پیش خرید پیشخرید کردن piʃxarid k., سلف خریدن salaf xaridan; (= progress), پیشرفت piʃraft, ترق کردن piʃraft k., پیشروی piʃravi; to advance, پیشرفت کردن taraqqi k.; (of an army) جلو رفتن jelou raftan.

Advantage, فائده faʿede, نفع nafʿ, منفعت manfaʿat, سود sud.

Advantageous, مفید *mofid*, نافع *nafe'*.

Adventure, سرگذشت *sargoẕaſt*.

Adventurer (in a bad sense), ماجراجو *majaraju*.

Adversary, see Enemy.

Adverse, مخالف *moxalef*, ناموافق *namovafeq*.

Adversity, بدبختی *badbaxti*, نکبت *nekbat*, مشقت *maſaqqat*.

Advertise, to, آگهی دادن *agahi dadan*, اعلان کردن *e'lan k*.

Advertisement, آگهی *agahi*, اعلان *e'lan*.

Advertiser, آگهی دهنده *agahi dehande*, اعلان کننده *e'lan konande*.

Advice, نصیحت *nasihat*, پند *pand*; to seek advice from someone, مشاوره کردن (با) *moſavere k. (ba)*.

Advisable, صلاح *salah*; to consider advisable, مصلحت دیدن *maslahat didan*.

Advocate, وکیل *vakil*.

Adze, تیشه *tiſe*.

Aerial (adj.), هوائی *havai*.

Aeronautics, هوانوردی *havanavardi*.

Affair, امر *amr*.

Affect, to, تأثیر کردن (در) *ta'sir k. (dar)*, اثر کردن (بر) *asar k. (bar)*.

Affection, علاقه *alaqe*, عاطفه *atefe*, مهر *mehr*.

Affectionate, با عاطفه *baatefe*, مهربان *mehraban*.

Affianced, نامزد *namẕad*.

Affidavit, شهادت نامه *ſahadatname*.

Affinity, قرابت *qarabat*, بستگی *bastegi*.

Affirm, to, تصدیق کردن *tasdiq k*.

Affirmation, تصدیق *tasdiq*, اثبات *esbat*.

Affirmative, مثبت *mosbat*.

Afflicted, مبتلا *mobtala*.

Afforestation, احداث جنگل *ehdase jangal*.

Aforesaid, فوق الذکر *fōuq oẕ-ẕekr*, مزبور *maẕbur*.

After (prep.), پس از *pas aẕ*, بعد از *ba'd aẕ*; (conj.), پس از آنکه *pas aẕ anke*, بعد از آنکه *ba'd aẕ anke*; (in search of), عقب *aqab(e)*, پی *pei(e)*, در پی *dar pei(e)*.

Afternoon, بعد (پس) از ظهر *ba'd (pas) aẕ ẕohr*, عصر *asr*.

Afterwards, بعد *ba'd*, پس از آن *pas aẕ an*, پس *pas*, بعد از آن *bə'd aẕ an*, پس از آن *pas aẕ an*.

Again, دوباره *dobare*, بار دیگر *bare digar*, باز *baʒ*.

Against, خلاف *xelaf(e)*; بر خلاف *bar xelaf(e)*, ضد *ʒedd(e)*, بر ضد *bar ʒedd(e)*, مخالف *moxalef(e)*; judgement was given against him, بر علیه او حکم دادند *bar aleihe u hokm dadand*.

Age, سن *senn*; (=epoch) عصر *asr*.

Agency, کارگزاری *kargoʒari*, نمایندگی *namayandegi*.

Agenda, دستور *dastur*.

Agent, کارگزار *kargoʒar* نماینده *namayande*; عامل *amel*.

Aggregate, مجموع *majmu'*, جمع *jam'*.

Aggress, to, تجاوز کردن *tajavoʒ k*.

Aggression, تجاوز *tajavoʒ*.

Aggressive, متجاوز *motajaveʒ*.

Aggressor, متجاوز *motajaveʒ*, تجاوز کننده *tajavoʒ konande*.

Agile, چابك *cabok*, چالاك *calak*.

Agility, چابکی *caboki*, چالاکی *calaki*.

Agitation, تشویش *taʃviʃ*, اضطراب *eʒterab*, آشفتگی *aʃoftegi*.

Agitator, تحریك کننده *tahrik konande*, محرك *moharrek*.

Agree, to, موافقت کردن *movafeqat k*.

Agreeable, پسندیده *pasandide*, دلپذیر *delpaʒir*.

Agreement, موافقت *movafeqat*; (=treaty), قرارداد *qarardad*, پیمان *peiman*, عهدنامه *ahdname*; (=settlement), قرار *qarar*.

Agricultural, کشاورزی *keʃavarʒi*, فلاحتی *falahati*.

Agriculture, کشاورزی *keʃavarʒi*, فلاحت *falahat*.

Ague, تب و لرز *tab o larʒ*.

Aim, نشانه‌گیری کردن مقصود *maqsud*, هدف *hadaf*; to aim (a gun, etc.), نشانه‌گیری کردن *neʃanegiri k*.

Air, هوا *hava*; air force, نیروی هوائی *niruye havai*; by air (=by aeroplane), با هواپیما *ba havapeima*.

Air bombardment, بمباران هوائی *bombarane havai*.

Aircraft, هواپیما *havapeima*, طیاره *taiyare*.

Aircraft-carrier, کشتی هواپیمابر *kaʃtiye havapeimabar*.

Airman, خلبان *xalaban*, هوانورد *havanavard*.

Alarm, هراس *haras*, ترس *tars*, وحشت *vahʃat*; (=danger siren), سوت خطر *sute xatar*.

Alas, دریغ *dariɣ*, حیف *heif*, وای *vai*.

Albumen, سفیده تخم مرغ ‌ *sefideye toxme morɣ.*

Algebra, جبر ‌ *jabr.*

Alienate, to, دلگیر کردن ‌ *delgir k.*

Alight, to, پائین آمدن ‌ *pain amadan*, نزول کردن ‌ *nozul k.,* پیاده شدن ‌ *piade ʃ.*

Alike, شبیه بهم ‌ *ʃabih be ham;* (=equal), برابر ‌ *barabar,* یکسان ‌ *yaksan.*

Alive, زنده ‌ *ʒende.*

All, همه ‌ *hame*, کل ‌ *koll,* جمیع ‌ *jamiʻ,* جمله ‌ *jomle,* تمام ‌ *tamam.*

Allay, to, تسکین دادن ‌ *taskin dadan.*

Alleviation, تخفیف ‌ *taxfif.*

Alleviate, to, تخفیف کردن ‌ *taxfif k.*

Alley, کوی ‌ *kūi.*

Alliance, اتحاد ‌ *ettehad.*

Allied, متحد ‌ *mottahed,* متفق ‌ *mottafeq.*

Allow, to, اجازه دادن ‌ *ejaʒe dadan,* گذاشتن ‌ *goʒaʃtan.*

Allowable, مجاز ‌ *mojaz,* روا ‌ *rava.*

Allowance (of money, etc.), کمک خرج ‌ *komake xarj.*

Allude, to, اشاره کردن ‌ کنایه زدن ‌ *kenaye ʒadan,* گوشه زدن ‌ *guʃe ʒadan,* اشاره کردن ‌ *eʃare k.*

Allusion, کنایه ‌ *kenaye,* اشاره ‌ *eʃare.*

Ally, متحد ‌ *mottahed,* متفق ‌ *mottafeq;* the Allies, متفقین ‌ *mottafeqin.*

Almanac, تقویم ‌ *taqvim.*

Almond, بادام ‌ *badam.*

Aloft, بالا ‌ *bala,* فراز ‌ *faraz.*

Alone, تنها ‌ *tanha.*

Along: along with, همراه ‌ *hamrah(e).*

Alphabet, الف با ‌ *alef ba.*

Also, هم ‌ *ham,* نیز ‌ *niz.*

Altar (for sacrifice), قربانگاه ‌ *qorbangah,* مذبح ‌ *mazbah.*

Alter, to, تغییر دادن ‌ *taɣyir dadan.*

Alteration, تغییر ‌ *taɣyir.*

Alternate, یك در میان ‌ *yak dar mian.*

Although, اگرچه ‌ *agarce,* هرچندکه ‌ *har cand ke,* با وجودیکه ‌ *ba vojudike.*

Altogether, جمعًا ‌ *jamʻan;* (=taking everything into consideration), روی هم رفته ‌ *ruye ham rafte.*

Always, همیشه hamiʃe, همواره hamvare.

Amazed, to be, تعجب کردن taʿajjob k., حیرت نمودن heirat n., مبهوت شدن mabhut ʃ., مات شدن mat ʃ.

Amazement, تعجب taʿajjob, حیرت heirat.

Ambassador, سفیر کبیر safire kabir.

Ambiguity, ابهام ebham, ایهام iham.

Ambiguous, مبهم mobham, مشکوک maʃkuk.

Ambition, جاه طلبی jahtalabi; (=aspiration), همت hemmat.

Ambitious, جاه طلب jahtalab.

Amble, to, یورقه رفتن yorqe raftan.

Ambulance, امبولانس ambulans.

Ambush, کمینگاه kamingah.

Amelioration (=improvement), بهبودی behbudi; (=reform), اصلاح eslah.

America, امریکا amrika.

American, امریکائی amrikai.

Amnesty, عفو afv; general amnesty, عفو عمومی afve omumi.

Among, میان mian(e), در میان dar mian(e), بین bein(e), ما بین ma bein(e), از جمله aʒ jomle(ye).

Amount, مقدار meqdar.

Amphibious, ذو حیاتین ʒu hayatein.

Amplification, بسط bast, توسعه touseʿe.

Amusement (=recreation), تفریح tafrih, سرگرمی sargarmi.

Anaemia, کم خونی kamxuni.

Analogy, قیاس qias.

Analyse, to, تجزیه کردن tajʒie k.

Analysis, تجزیه tajʒie.

Anarchy, هرج و مرج harj o marj.

Anatomy, کالبدشناسی kalbodʃenasi.

Ancestor, نیا nia, جد jadd.

Anchor, لنگر langar; to cast anchor, لنگر انداختن langar andaxtan.

Anchorage, لنگرگاه langargah.

Ancient, قدیم qadim.

And, و va, o.

Anemone, لاله lale.

Angel, فرشته fereʃte, ملك malak.

Anger, غضب ɣaӡab, خشم xeʃm.

Angiology, معرفت العروق maʿrefat ol-oruq.

Angle, زاویه ӡavie.

Angry, غضبناك ɣaӡabnak, خشمناك xeʃmnak.

Animal, حیوان heivan; (=living being), جانور janevar; (adj.), حیوانی heivani.

Animate, جاندار jandar, زنده ӡende.

Ankle, مچ پا moce pa.

Annex (to a document, etc.), ضمیمه ӡamime, الحاق elhaq.

Annihilate, to, نیست و نابود کردن nist o nabud k., استیصال کردن estisal k.

Annihilation, استیصال estisal.

Announce, to, اعلام کردن eʿlam k., ابلاغ کردن eblaɣ k.

Announcement, اعلام eʿlam, ابلاغ eblaɣ, آگاهی agahi.

Annoy, to, اذیت کردن aӡiyat k.; he will be annoyed, اوقاتش تلخ میشود ōuqataʃ talx miʃavad.

Annoyance, اوقات تلخی ōuqate talxi.

Annual, سالیانه saliane.

Annul, to, لغو کردن laɣv k.

Annulment, لغو laɣv.

Anonymous, مجهول majhul, گمنام gomnam.

Another (adj.), دیگر digar; (pronoun), دیگری digari.

Answer, جواب javab; to answer, جواب دادن javab dadan.

Ant, مورچه murce.

Anterior, پیشین piʃin, سابق sabeq, مقدم moqaddam.

Anthem: national anthem, سرود ملی sorude melli.

Anthropologist, مردمشناس mardomʃenas.

Anthropology, مردمشناسی mardomʃenasi.

Anti-aircraft gun, توپ ضد هوائی tupe ӡedde havai.

Anticipate, to (=to foresee), پیش بینی کردن piʃbini k.; (=to forestall), پیشدستی کردن piʃdasti k.

Anticipation (=foresight), پیش بینی piʃbini; (=forestalling), پیشدستی piʃdasti.

Antidote, تریاق taryaq.

Antimony, کحل kohl.

Antique (noun), عتیقه atiqe; (adj.), عتیق atiq.

Antler, شاخ *ʃax*.

Anxiety, نگرانی *negarani*, تشویش *taʃviʃ*.

Anxious, نگران *negaran*, مشوش *moʃavvaʃ*, پریشان خاطر *pariʃanxater*.

Any, هیچ *hic*, هر *har*.

Anyhow, بهر نوع *be har noŭ*ʾ; (=in any case), در هر صورت *dar har surat*.

Anyone, کس *hic kas*, هر کس *har kas*.

Anything, هیچ چیز *hic ciɤ*, هر چیز *har ciɤ*.

Apart, سوا *seva*; جدا *joda*; apart from, گذشته از *goɤaʃte aɤ*.

Ape, میمون *meĭmun*.

Apogee, اوج *ōuj*.

Apologize, to, معذرت خواستن *maʿɤarat xastan*, عذر خواستن *oɤr xastan*, پوزش نمودن *puɤeʃ n*.

Apology, معذرت *maʿɤarat*, عذر *oɤr*, پوزش *puɤeʃ*.

Apoplexy, سکته *sakte*; to have apoplexy, سکته کردن *sakte k*.

Apostasy, ارتداد *ertedad*.

Apostate, مرتد *mortadd*.

Apostle (of Christ), حواری *havari*.

Apparent, ظاهر *ɤaher*, پدید *padid*, هویدا *hoveĭda*, پیدا *peĭda*, آشکار *aʃkar*.

Apparently, ظاهراً *ɤaheran*.

Appeal, to (to a court of appeal), باستیناف رفتن (بردن) *be estinaf raftan* (*bordan*).

Appear, to (=to become visible), ظاهر شدن *ɤaher ʃ.*, پدید آمدن *padia amadan*; (=to be evident), معلوم شدن *maʿlum ʃ.*

Appearance, پیدایش *peĭdayeʃ*, ظهور *ɤohur*; (bodily appearance), هیکل *heĭkal*, ریخت *rixt*; (facial appearance), صورت *surat*.

Appendix, ذیل *ɤeĭl*, ضمیمه *ɤamime*.

Appetite, اشتها *eʃteha*.

Applaud, to, تحسین گفتن *tahsin k.*, آفرین گفتن *afarin goftan*.

Applause, تحسین *tahsin*, آفرین *afarin*.

Apple, سیب *sib*.

Applicable, to be, مورد داشتن *mōured d.*, وارد بودن *vared b.*

Applicant, داوطلب *davtalab*, در خواست کننده *darxast konande*.

Application, در خواست *darxast*; (=perseverance), پشتکار *poʃtekar*.

Apply, to, در خواست کردن *darxast k.*; this does not apply to you, این شامل حال شما نیست *in ʃamele hale ʃoma nist*.

Appoint, to, تعیین کردن ta'yin kardan; (=to take into service), استخدام کردن estexdam k.; (=to nominate), نام‌زد کردن namẕad k.

Appointment (=appointed time), موعد mou'ed, قرار ملاقات qarare molaqat; (=post), کار kar.

Appraise, قیمت کردن qeimat k., قضاوت کردن qaẕavat k., تقویم کردن taqvim k.

Appraisement, قضاوت qaẕavat; تقویم taqvim.

Apprehension (=fear), نگرانی negarani; see also Comprehension.

Apprehensive, نگران negaran.

Apprentice, شاگرد ſagerd.

Apprenticeship, شاگردی ſagerdi.

Approach, to, نزدیك شدن naẕdik ſ.

Appropriate, مناسب monaseb; to appropriate, ضبط کردن ẕabt k.

Approval, تحسین tahsin, تصویب tasvib.

Approve, to, تحسین کردن tahsin k., تصویب کردن tasvib k.

Approximate, تقریبی taqribi.

Approximately, تقریباً taqriban, در حدود dar hodud(e).

Appurtenances, متعلقات mota'alleqat.

Apricot, قیسی qeisi, زرد آلو ẕardalu.

Apt, زرنگ ẕarang, زیرك ẕirak, مستعد mosta'edd; (=suitable), مناسب monaseb, وارد vared.

Aptitude, زرنگی ẕarangi; (=talent), استعداد este'dad.

Aquatic, آبی abi.

Arab, عرب arab.

Arabia, عربستان arabestan.

Arabian, عربی arabi, تازی taẕi; (=an Arab), عرب arab.

Arabic, عربی arabi.

Arbitrary, مطلق motlaq, خود مختار xodmoxtar, مستبد mostabedd.

Arbitrate, to, حکمیت کردن hakamiyat k.; میانجیگری کردن mianjigari k.

Arbitration, حکمیت hakamiyat, داوری davari; میانجیگری mianjigari.

Arbitrator, حکم hakam, داور davar; میانجی mianji, منصف monsef.

Arc, قوس qous.

Arch, طاق taq; (of a bridge), چشمه caſme.

Archaeologist, باستان‌شناس bastanſenas.

Archaeology, باستان‌شناسی bastanſenasi.

Archer, تیرزن tirʒan, تیرانداز tirandaʒ.

Architect, معمار me‘mar.

Architecture, معماری me‘mari.

Archives, بایگانی bayagani.

Archivist, بایگان bayagan.

Ardent, باغیرت baɣeirat.

Ardour, غیرت ɣeirat.

Arduous, پر زحمت porʒahmat.

Area (=superficial extent), فضا faʒa, مساحت masahat, عرصه arse.

Argue, to, مناظره کردن monaʒere k., بحث کردن bahs k.

Argument, مناظره monaʒere, مباحثه mobahese.

Aristocracy, طبقه اشراف tabaqeye aʃraf.

Aristocratic, اشرافی aʃrafi.

Arithmetic, علم حساب elme hesab.

Arm, بازو baʒu; to arm, مسلح کردن mosallah k.

Armed, مسلح mosallah.

Armenia, ارمنستان armanestan.

Armenian, ارمنی armani.

Armoured, زره پوش ʒerepuʃ, زره دار ʒeredar.

Arms, اسلحه aslehe.

Army, ارتش arteʃ, قشون qoʃun, جیش jeiʃ, سپاه sepah.

Around, پیرامون piramun(e), دور dour(e), گرد gerd(e).

Arrange, to, تنظیم کردن tanʒim k., ترتیب دادن tartib dadan.

Arrangement, تنظیم tanʒim, ترتیب tartib.

Arrest, توقیف touqif, دستگیری dastgiri; to arrest, توقیف کردن touqif k., دستگیر کردن dastgir k.

Arrival, ورود vorud.

Arrive, to, وارد شدن vared ʃ., (نه) رسیدن rasidan (be).

Arrogance, تکبر takabbor, گستاخی gostaxi, نخوت nexvat.

Arrogant, متکبر motakabber, گستاخ gostax, بانخوت banexvat.

Arrow, تیر tir.

Arsenal, قورخانه qurxane.

Art, فن fann, هنر honar, حرفه herfe, صنعت san‘at; fine arts, فنون مستظرفه fonune mostaʒrafe.

Artery, شریان ʃarian.

Arthrologist, بندشناس *bandʃenas*.

Arthrology, بندشناسی *bandʃenasi*.

Article (literary), مقاله *maqale*; articles of association, نظام نامه *neẓam-name*.

Artificial, مصنوعی *masnuʿi*.

Artillery, توپخانه *tupxane*.

Artilleryman, توپچی *tupci*.

Artisan, پیشهور *piʃevar*.

Artist (=a master at one's work), استاد *ostad*; see also Painter.

As: as he said, بطوریکه گفت *be tourike goft*; he went as the head of the delegation, بعنوان رئیس هیئت رفت *be envane raʾise heiʾat raft*; as slowly as possible, هرچه یواشتر *har ce yavaʃtar*; as long as, تا ، تا اینکه *ta*, *ta inke*, مادامیکه *madamike*; as soon as, همینکه *haminke*, بمجرد اینکه *be mojarrade inke*; as much as, بقدریکه *be qadrike*; so much as, آنقدر...که *anqadr... ke*; twice as much, دو برابر *do barabar*; as far as possible, حتی المقدور *hattal-maqdur*; as follows, بقرار ذیل *be qarare ẓeil*; (=like), مثل *mesl(e)*, مانند *manand(e)*, همچو *hamcu*, چون *cun*.

Ascend, to, بالا رفتن *bala raftan*; (=to mount), سوار شدن *savar ʃ.*

Ascendancy, غلبه *ɣalabe*, تفوق *tafavvoq*, تسلط *tasallot*.

Ascendant (astrol.), طالع *taleʿ*.

Ascension, معراج *meʿraj*, صعود *soʿud*.

Ascent, معرج *meʿraj*, صعود *soʿud*; (=slope), سرابالائی *sarabalai*.

Ascertain, to, تحقیق کردن *tahqiq k.*

Ascetic, زاهد *ẓahed*.

Asceticism, ریاضت *riaẓat*, زهد *ẓohd*.

Ash (tree), زبان گنجشك *ẓabangonjaʃk*.

Ashamed, شرمسار *ʃarmsar*, شرمنده *ʃarmande*, خجل *xejel*; to be ashamed, خجالت کشیدن *xejalat kaʃidan*.

Ashes, خاکستر *xakestar*.

Asia, آسیا *asia*.

Asiatic, آسیائی *asiai*.

Aside: to put aside, کنار گذاشتن *kenar goẓaʃtan*.

Ask, to, (از) پرسیدن *porsidan* (aẓ), (از) سؤال کردن *soʾal k.* (aẓ), (از) استفسار کردن *estefsar k.* (aẓ); (=to demand), (از) خواستن *xastan* (aẓ); (=to request), (از) خواهش کردن *xaheʃ k.* (aẓ).

Asleep, خوابیده *xabide*; to be asleep, خواب بودن *xab b.*

Asparagus, مارچوبه *marcube*.

Aspiration, آرزو *arezu, arzu*, همّت *hemmat*.

Aspire, to, آرزو داشتن *arezu d.*, همّت کردن *hemmat k.*

Ass, خر *xar*, الاغ *olay*.

Assassin, see Murderer.

Assassinate, to, see Kill.

Assemble, to, جمع شدن *jam' f.*; (a machine), سوار کردن *savar k.*

Assembly, اجتماع *ejtema'*; (=place of assembly, meeting together), مجلس *majles*.

Assent, قبول *qabul*, موافقت *movafeqat*.

Assert, to, ادعا کردن *edde'a k.*, اقرار کردن *eqrar k.*, اظهار کردن *ezhar k.*

Assertion, ادعا *edde'a*, اقرار *eqrar*, اظهار *ezhar*.

Assess, to, تقویم کردن *taqvim k.*, قیمت کردن *qeïmat k.*; (taxes), مالیات بستن *maliat bastan.*

Assessment, بر آورد *baravard*, تقویم *taqvim*; (of taxes) مالیات بندی *maliat-bandi.*

Assessor, خبره *xebre*.

Assets, موجودی *moüjudi*, دارائی *darai*.

Assign, to (hand over), واگذار کردن *vagozar k.*, انتقال دادن *enteqal dadan.*

Assignation (=handing over), انتقال *enteqal*; (=meeting), میعاد *mi'ad*, موعد *moü'ed.*

Assignment, انتقال *enteqal*.

Assimilate, to, تحلیل بردن *tahlil bordan.*

Assimilation, تحلیل *tahlil.*

Assist, to, کمک کردن *komak k.*, مساعدت کردن *mosa'edat k.*

Assistance, کمک *komak*, مساعدت *mosa'edat*, یاری *yari.*

Assistant, معاون *mo'aven*, نائب *naeb*; (=helper), یار *yar.*

Associate, شریك *farik*; to associate (with), معاشرت کردن *mo'aferat k.*

Association (=intercourse), معاشرت *mo'aferat*; (=public company), شرکت *ferkat*; (=society), انجمن *anjoman.*

Assume, to, تصور کردن *tasavvor k.*; فرض کردن *farz k.*

Assumption, تصور *tasavvor*; فرض *farz.*

Assurance, اطمینان *etminan.*

Assure, to, اطمینان دادن *etminan dadan.*

Astringent (adj.), گس gas.

Astrolabe, اصطرلاب ostorlab.

Astrologer, منجم monajjem.

Astrology, علم نجوم elme nojum.

Astronomer, منجم monajjem, رصاد rassad, ستاره شناس setarefenas.

Astronomical table, زیج ʒij.

Astronomy, علم نجوم elme nojum, علم هیئت elme heï'at.

Asylum, پناه‌گاه panahgah, ملجاء malja, بست bast; lunatic asylum, دار المجانین dar ol-majanin.

At, در dar, به be, دم dam(e); at the house, در منزل dar manʒel; at the door, دم در dame dar; at all events, بهر صورت be har surat; not at all, هیچ hic (+ neg. verb).

Athlete, پهلوان pahlavan.

Atmosphere, جو jav, هوا hava.

Atom, ذره ʒarre.

Atone, to, کفاره دادن kaffare dadan.

Atonement, کفاره kaffare.

Atrocious, فجیع faji'.

Atrocity, فاجعه faje'e.

Attaché, وابسته vabaste.

Attachment (abstr.), انس ons, دلبستگی delbastegi.

Attack, حمله hamle, هجوم hojum; to attack, حمله کردن (به) hamle k. (be), هجوم آوردن (بر) hojum avardan (bar).

Attempt, سعی saï, کوشش kufef, تلاش talaf, قصد qasd; an attempt on the life of someone, سوء قصد su'e qasd; to attempt, سعی کردن saï k., کوشش kufef k., کوشیدن kufidan, تلاش کردن talaf k., قصد کردن qasd k.

Attend, to (= to listen), گوش دادن (کردن) guf dadan (k.), توجه کردن tavajjoh k., التفات کردن eltefat k.; (= to be present), حاضر شدن haʒer f.; (= to wait upon), خدمت کردن xedmat k.

Attendants (retinue), ملازمان molaʒeman, خدم و حشم xadam va hafam.

Attention, توجه tavajjoh; to pay attention, توجه کردن tavajjoh k., التفات کردن eltefat k.

Attest, to, شهادت دادن fahadat dadan.

Attestation, شهادت fahadat, گواهی gavahi.

Attorney, وکیل vakil; power of attorney, وکالت نامه vekalatname.

Attract, to, جلب کردن jalb k., جذب کردن jaẕb k.

Attraction, جلب jalb, جذب jaẕb, جاذبه jaẕebe, کشش kaʃeʃ; جاذبیت jaẕebiyat.

Attractive, جاذب jaẕeb; (=beautiful), دلربا delroba.

Attribute, صفت sefat, وصف vasf; to attribute to, نسبت دادن به nesbat dadan be.

Auction, حراج harraj.

Audacious, see Bold.

Audit, ممیزی momaɪyeẕi.

Auditor, ممیز momaɪyeẕ.

Augur, فالگو falgu.

Augury, فال fal.

Aunt (paternal), عمه amme; (maternal), خاله xale.

Auspices: under the auspices of, درتحت توجهات dar tahte tavajjohat(e).

Auspicious, همایون homayun, خجسته xojaste, مبارک mobarak, بختیار baxtyar, نیك اختر nikaxtar.

Authentic, صحیح sahih, حقیقی haqiqi.

Authenticity, صحت sehhat, حقیقت haqiqat.

Author, نویسنده nevisande, مؤلف mo'allef, مصنف mosannef.

Authority, see Power and Permission; (to quote) on the authority of, بقول be qōul(e).

Authorize, to, see Allow.

Autocracy, استبداد estebdad.

Autocrat, مستبد mostabedd.

Automatic, خودکار xodkar.

Automatically, خود بخود xod be xod.

Autopsy, کالبدگشائی kalbodgoʃai.

Autumn, پائیز paiẕ.

Auxiliary: auxiliary forces, واحدهای کمکی vahedhaye komaki.

Available, فراهم faraham.

Avalanche, بهمن bahman.

Avarice, حرص hers, بخل boxl, امساك emsak.

Avaricious, بخیل baxil, ممسك momsek, حریص haris, خسیس xasis.

Avenge, to, انتقام کشیدن enteqam kaʃidan.

Avenue, خیابان xiaban.

Average, معدل mo'addel; (adj.) متوسط motavasset, معمولی ma'muli, عادی adi.

Avoid, to, اجتناب کردن (از) ejtenab k. (az), احتراز کردن (از) ehteraz k. (az).

Awake, بیدار bidar.

Aware, مطلع mottale', آگاه agah.

Away, see Absent and Far.

Awful, هولناك houlnak, مهیب mohib.

Axe, تبر tabar.

Axis, محور mehvar.

Axle, میل mil, میله mile.

Azure, لاجوردی lajvardi.

B

Back (subs.), پشت poʃt; to come back, بر گشتن bar gaʃtan; to give back, پس دادن pas dadan; at the back (of), در پشت dar poʃt(e).

Backbone, ستون فقرات sotune faqarat, مهره پشت mohreye poʃt.

Backgammon, نرد nard; backgammon board, تخته نرد taxte nard.

Background, زمینه zamine.

Backward, عقب aqab; (=dull), كند kond.

Backwater, مرداب mordab.

Bacteriologist, میکربشناس mikrobʃenas.

Bacteriology, میکربشناسی mikrobʃenasi.

Bad, بد bad, فاسد fased.

Badness, بدی badi, فساد fesad.

Bag, كیف kif, كیسه kise.

Baggage, اسباب asbab, اثاثیه asasiye.

Bailiff, ناظر nazer, مباشر mobaʃer.

Bake, to, see Cook.

Baked, برشته bereʃte.

Baker, نانوا nanva, خباز xabbaz.

Bakery, نانوائی nanvai, خبازخانه xabbazxane.

Balance, قپان میزان mizan, موازنه movazene; (=scales), ترازو tarazu, qappan.

Balance-sheet, صورت خرج و دخل surate xarj o daxl, تراز نامه tarazname.

Balcony, بالاخانه balaxane.

Bale (of cloth, etc.), توپ *tup*, عدل *adl*.

Ball, توپ *tup*.

Balloon, بالون *balun*.

Ballot-box, صندوق رای *sanduqe ra'i*.

Banana, موز *mōuz*.

Band, بند *band*, پیوند *peivand*; (=group), گروه *goruh*, دسته *daste*; (music), موزیك *muzik*.

Bank (monetary), بانك *bank*; (of a river), کنار *kenar*; (=a dam), بند *band*.

Banker, بانكدار *bankdar*.

Banknote, اسكناس *eskenas*.

Bankrupt, ورشکست *varʃekast*.

Bankruptcy, ورشکستگی *varʃekastegi*.

Banner, پرچم *parcam*, بیرق *beiraq*, علم *alam*.

Banquet, بزم *bazm*, ضیافت *ziafat*, ولیمه *valime*, سور *sur*.

Baptism, تعمید *ta'mid*.

Barbarian, وحشی *vahʃi*.

Barbarity, وحشیگری *vahʃigari*.

Barber, دلاك *dallak*, سلمانی *salmani*.

Barberry, زرشك *zereʃk*.

Bare, برهنه *barahne*, لخت *loxt*.

Barefoot, پا برهنه *pabarahne*.

Bare-headed, سر برهنه *sarbarahne*.

Bareness, برهنگی *barahnegi*, لختی *loxti*.

Bargain, to, چانه زدن *cane zadan*.

Bark (of a tree), پوست *pust*, قشر *qeʃr*; (of a dog), وق وق *vaq vaq*, پارس *pars*.

Barley, جو *jōu*.

Barracks, سربازخانه *sarbazxane*.

Barrel, خمره *xomre*; (of a gun), لوله *lule*.

Barren (of land), لم یزرع *lam yazra'*; (of a woman), عقیم *aqim*; (of a tree), بی ثمر *bisamar*.

Barrister, وكیل *vakil*.

Barrow, چرخ دستی *carxe dasti*, چرخه *carxe*.

Barter, معاوضه *mo'aveze*, مبادله *mobadele*; barter agreement, قرارداد پایاپای *qarardade payapāi*.

Base (=vile), دون *dun,* فرومایه *forumaye,* پست *past;* (=foundation), پایه *paye,* اساس *asas.*

Bashful, خجالت‌کش *xejalatkaʃ.*

Basic, اساسی *asasi.*

Basically, اساسًا *asasan.*

Basin, لگن *lagan,* طشت *taʃt.*

Basis, see Base.

Basket, سبد *sabad,* زنبیل *ʒambil.*

Bastard, حرامزاده *haramʒade.*

Bat (animal), شپره *ʃappare,* خفاش *xaffaʃ.*

Bath, حمام *hammam.*

Bath-attendant, دلاك *dallak.*

Bathe, to (for pleasure), آبتنی کردن *abtani k.*

Bath-keeper, حمامی *hammami.*

Baton, عصا *asa,* چوب *cub,* تعلیمی *ta'limi.*

Battalion, گردان *gordan.*

Battle, پیکار *nabard,* نبرد‌ *jang,* جنگ *raʒm,* رزم *harb,* حرب‌ محاربه *moharabe,* پیکار‌ *peikar.*

Battle-array, صف آرائی *saffarai.*

Battle-field, کارزار *karʒar,* میدان جنگ *meidane jang.*

Battle-front, جبهه *jebhe, jabhe.*

Bay (colour), کهر *kahar.*

Bayonet, سر نیزه *sarneiʒe.*

Bazaar, بازار *baʒar.*

Be, to, بودن *budan;* (=to become), شدن *ʃodan.*

Beach, ساحل *sahel;* (=sea shore), لب دریا *labe darya.*

Bead, مهره *mohre,* دانه *dane.*

Beak, منقار *menqar,* نوك *nuk.*

Beam, پرتو *partou,* شعاع *ʃo'a';* (of wood), تیر *tir.*

Bean: broad bean, باقلا *baqela;* kidney bean لوبیا *lubia.*

Bear, خرس *xers;* to bear (=to carry), بردن *bordan;* (=to suffer), تحمل کردن *tahammol k.;* (=to give birth to), زائیدن *ʒaidan.*

Beard, ریش *riʃ.*

Bearded, ریشدار *riʃdar.*

Beardless, بیریش *biriʃ.*

Beast, بهیمه bahime, حیوان heivan, جانور janevar.

Beat, to (=to strike), زدن zadan; (at a game), بردن (از کسی) (az kasi) bordan; see also Defeat.

Beautiful, قشنگ qafang, خوشگل xofgel, زیبا ziba.

Beauty, قشنگی qafangi, خوشگلی xofgeli, جمال jamal, زیبائی zibai.

Because, اینجهت از zira (ke), از اینکه az in ke, چونکه cun ke; از اینکه (که) az in jehat ke, از جهت اینکه az jehate in ke.

Become, to, شدن fodan, گشتن gaftan, گردیدن gardidan; (=to suit), آمدن (به) amadan (be) (3rd. pers. sing. only).

Becoming (=fitting), سزاوار sazavar, در خور darxor, مناسب monaseb.

Bed, تخت خواب taxte xab; to be confined to bed, بستری بودن bestari b.; to go to bed, خوابیدن xabidan.

Bedclothes, رخت خواب raxte xab.

Bedroom, اطاق خواب otaqe xab, خوابگاه xabgah.

Bee, زنبور عسل zambure asal.

Beef, گوشت گاو gufte gav.

Bee-hive, کندو kandu.

Beer, آبجو abe jou.

Beetle, سوسک susk.

Beetroot, چقندر coqondar, چغندر coyondar.

Before (of time) (adv.), پیش pif, پیشتر piftar; (prep.), پیش pif(e), پیش از pif az, قبل از qabl az; (conj.), پیش از اینکه pif az inke, قبل از اینکه qabl az inke; (=sooner), زودتر zudtar, جلوتر jeloutar; (of place), پیش pif(e), جلو jelou(e).

Beg, to, گدائی کردن gadai k.; (=to beseech), استدعا کردن ested'a k.

Beggar, گدا gada.

Begging, گدائی gadai.

Begin, to, شروع کردن foru' k., آغاز کردن ayaz k.

Beginning, آغاز ayaz, ابتدا ebteda; in the beginning, در بدو امر dar badve amr, اولاً avvalan.

Beguile, to, فریب دادن farib dadan, اغفال کردن eyfal k., فریفتن fariftan.

Behalf: on behalf of, از طرف az taraf(e).

Behaviour, رفتار raftar, حرکت harakat.

Behead, to, سر بریدن sar boridan.

Behind (adv. and prep.), پس *pas(e)*, در پس *dar pas(e)*, عقب *aqab(e)*, در عقب *dar aqab(e)*, پشت *poſt(e)*, در پشت *dar poſt(e)*, دنبال *dombal(e)*, پشت سر *poſte sar(e)*.

Behold, اينك *inak*.

Being (= creature), مخلوق *maxluq*; (= existence), هستی *hasti*, وجود *vojud*.

Beings (= creatures), مخلوقات *maxluqat*, موجودات *moujudat*.

Belief, عقیده *aqide*, اعتقاد *e'teqad*.

Believe, to, عقیده داشتن باور کردن *bavar k.*, گرویدن *geravidan*; to believe in, ایمان آوردن (به) *iman avardan (be)*, (به) اعتقاد داشتن (به) *e'teqad d. (be)*, (به) *aqide d. (be)*.

Believer, مؤمن *mo'men*.

Bell, زنگ *ʒang*.

Belles-lettres, ادبیات *adabiyat*; علم ادب *elme adab*.

Belong, to: it belongs to him, مال اوست *male ust*, متعلق اوست *mota'alleqe ust*.

Belongings, اسباب *asbab*, اثاثیه *asasiye*.

Beloved, محبوب *mahbub*.

Below, زیر *ʒir(e)*, در زیر *dar ʒir(e)*, پائین *pain(e)*, تحت *taht(e)*.

Belt (= girdle), کربند *kamarband*.

Bench, نیمکت *nimkat*.

Bend, پیچ *pic*; to bend (trans.), خم کردن *xam k.*; (trs. and intrans.), پیچیدن *picidan*.

Beneath, see Below.

Benefactor, منعم *mon'em*, ولینعمت *valeine'mat*.

Beneficial, مفید *mofid*, سودمند *sudmand*, نافع *nafe'*.

Benefit, فائده *fa'ede*, سود *sud*, نفع *naf'*, منفعت *manfa'at*; to benefit, فائده بردن *fa'ede bordan*, سود بردن *sud bordan*.

Bent, کج *kaj*, خم شده *xam ſode*, خمیده *xamide*.

Bequest, وصیت *vasiyat*; (= endowment), وقف *vaqf*, موقوفه *mouqufe*.

Bereaved, to be, محروم شدن *mahrum ſ.*

Bereavement, محرومیت *mahrumiyat*.

Berry, دانه *dane*.

Beseech, to, استدعا کردن *ested'a k.*

Beside, جنب *janeb(e)*, پهلو(ی) *pahlu(ye)*, در پهلو(ی) *dar pahlu(ye)*, جامب *jamb(e)*, در جنب *dar jamb(e)*; (= on the edge of), لب *lab(e)*, کنار *kenar(e)*

Besides, بر این علاوه *alave bar in*, بعلاوه *be alave*.

Best, بهترین *behtarin*; it is best that you should go, بهتر است که بروید *behtar ast ke beravid*.

Bestow, to, بخشیدن *baxʃidan*, عطا کردن *ata k.*, ارزانی داشتن *arʒani d.*

Bet, شرط *ʃart*; to bet, شرط بستن *ʃart bastan*.

Betrothe, to, نامزد کردن *namʒad k.*

Better, بهتر *behtar*, به *beh*.

Between, میان *mian(e)*, در میان *dar mian(e)*, بین *beīn(e)*, در بین *dar beīn(e)*, مابین *ma beīn(e)*.

Bevel, هنجار *hanjar*.

Beware, to, بر حذر بودن *bar haʒar b.*

Beyond, آنطرف *an taraf(e)*, آنسو(ی) *an su(ye)*, آنور *an var(e)*.

Bible, کتاب مقدس *ketabe moqaddas*.

Bibliographer, کتابشناس *ketabʃenas*.

Bicycle, دو چرخه *docarxe*.

Bicyclist, دو چرخه سوار *docarxesavar*.

Bid, to, see Command; (at cards), اعلام کردن *e'lam k.*; (at an auction), پیش‌نهاد دادن *piʃnehad dadan*.

Bifurcation, دوشاخه *doʃaxe*.

Big, بزرگ *boʒorg*.

Bigness, بزرگی *boʒorgi*.

Bile, صفرا *safra*, زهره *ʒahre*.

Biliteral, مثنی *mosanna*.

Bill, see Account; (=bill of exchange), برات *barat*; (parliamentary), لایحه *layehe*; bill of lading, بار نامه *barname*.

Bimetallism, دو فلزی *dofeleʒi*.

Bind, to, بستن *bastan*; (a book), جلد کردن *jeld k.*

Binding (of a book), جلد *jeld*; (of a garment), طراز *taraʒ*; legally binding, معتبر *mo'tabar*.

Binoculars, دوربین *durbin*.

Bird, پرنده *parande*; to kill two birds with one stone, با یک تیر دو نشان زدن *ba yak tir do neʃan ʒadan*; a bird in the hand is worth two in the bush, سیلی نقد به از حلوای نسیه *siliye naqd beh aʒ halvaye nesie*.

Birth, تولد *tavallod*; to give birth to, زائیدن *ʒaidan*.

Birthday, روز تولد *ruʒe tavallod*.

Bishop, اسقف osqof.

Bit (of bridle), دهنه dahane; (= piece), پاره pare, ریزه riʒe, تکه tekke.

Bitch, لاس las.

Bite, لقمه loqme; to bite, گزیدن gaʒidan, گاز گرفتن gaʒ gereftan; (= to sting, of a mosquito, etc.), زدن ʒadan.

Bitter, تلخ talx.

Bitterness, تلخی talxi.

Bitumen, قیر qir.

Black, سیاه siah, مشکی meʃki; black and blue, کبود kabud.

Blackness, سیاهی siahi.

Blacksmith, نعلبند na'lband.

Bladder (anat.), مثانه masane.

Blamable, مقصر moqasser.

Blame (= censure), ملامت malamat, سرزنش sarʒaneʃ.

Blandishment, ناز naʒ, نوازش navaʒeʃ.

Blanket, پتو patu.

Blaspheme, to, کفر گفتن kofr goftan.

Blasphemy, کفر kofr.

Blaze (on a horse's forehead), غره ɣorre.

Bleach, to, سفید کردن sefid k.

Bleacher, گازر gaʒor.

Bleed, to (intrans.), خون آمدن xun amadan.

Blemish, عیب eib.

Bless, to, درود گفتن dorud goftan, برکت دادن barakat dadan.

Blessed, مبارك mobarak.

Blessing, برکت barakat, درود dorud.

Blight (on trees, etc.), زنگ ʒang, شته ʃete.

Blind, کور kur, نابینا nabina.

Blindness, کوری kuri, نابینائی nabinai.

Blister, طاول tavel; to blister (intrans.), طاول زدن tavel ʒadan; (trans.) داغ کردن daɣ k.

Block, to, مسدود کردن masdud k.

Blood, خون xun; (= breed), رگ rag, رگه rage, نژاد neʒad.

Bloodmoney, خونبها xunbaha, دیه die.

Bloodshed, خونریزی xunriʒi.

Bloodthirstiness, خونخواری *xunxari*.

Bloodthirsty, خونخوار *xunxar*.

Bloodvessel, رگ *rag*, عرق *erq*.

Bloody, خونین *xunin*, خونآلود *xunalud*.

Blossom, شکوفه *fekufe*; to blossom, شکوفه زدن *fekufe zadan*.

Blotting-paper, کاغذ خشک کن *kayaze xofkkon*.

Blouse, پیراهن زنانه *pirahane zanane*, بلیز *boliz*.

Blow, ضرب *zarb*, ضربت *zarbat*; to blow (of a breeze, etc.), دمیدن *damidan*, وزیدن *vazidan*; to blow (with the breath), فوت کردن *fut k.*; (=to pant), نفس کشیدن *nafas kafidan*.

Blue, آبی *abi*; dark blue, نیلی *nili*, سرمهٔ *sormei*.

Blunder, خطا *xata*, غلط *yalat*.

Blunt (=not sharp), کند *kond*; (=outspoken), رکگو *rokgu*.

Blush, to, قرمز شدن *qermez f.*

Boar, گراز *goraz*, خوک وحشی *xuke vahfi*.

Board, تخته *taxte*; to take on board, سوار کردن *savar k.*

Boarding school, مدرسه شبانه روزی *madraseye fabaneruzi*.

Boast, لاف *laf*; to boast, لاف زدن *laf zadan*.

Boasting, گزاف گوئی *gazafgui*.

Boat, قایق *qayaq*.

Bodily (appertaining to the body), جسمانی *jesmani*.

Bodkin (for sewing up sacks), سوزن جوال دوز *suzane javalduz*.

Body (human), جسم *jesm*, تن *tan*, بدن *badan*; (corpse of an animal), لاشه *lafe*, لاش *laf*; (corpse of a human being) نعش *na'f*; (of a car, etc.), بدنه *badane*.

Bogy, ابو الهول *abol houl*.

Boil, دمل *domal*, کورک *kurak*; Baghdad boil, سالک *salak*; to boil (trans.), جوشاندن *jufandan*, جوشانیدن *jufanidan*; (intrans.), جوشیدن *jufidan*, جوش خوردن *juf xordan*; (to cook by boiling), آبپز کردن *abpaz k.*; to boil over, سر رفتن *sar raftan*.

Boiler, دیگ *dig*.

Bold, بیباک *bibak*, دلیر *dalir*, شجاع *foja'*, با جرأت *bajor'at*; (in a bad sense), گستاخ *gostax*.

Boldness, بیباکی *bibaki*, شجاعت *foja'at*, جرأت *jor'at*, دلیری *daliri*; (in a bad sense), گستاخی *gostaxi*.

Bolster, بالش *baleʃ*.

Bolt (=bar), چفت *ceft*; to bolt, چفت کردن *ceft k.*

Bomb, بمب *bomb*.

Bombardment, بمباران *bombaran*.

Bomber, هواپیمای بمب افکن *havapeïmaye bombaʃkan*.

Bond (=contract), سند *sanad*; (=tie), بند *band*; قید *qeïd*.

Bondage, اسارت *asarat*, عبودیت *obudiyat*.

Bone, استخوان *ostoxan*; (=made of bone), استخوانی *ostoxani*.

Bone-setter, شکسته بند *ʃekasteband*.

Book, کتاب *ketab*.

Bookkeeper, حسابدار *hesabdar*.

Bookkeeping, حسابداری *hesabdari*.

Bookseller, کتابفروش *ketabforuʃ*.

Bookshop, کتابفروشی *ketabforuʃi*.

Boom (of a ship), تیر *tir*.

Boot, چکمه *cakme*.

Bootblack, واکسی *vaksi*.

Booty, see Plunder.

Border (=boundary), سرحد *sarhadd*; (=margin), حاشیه *haʃie*; to border on (adjoin), مجاور بودن (با) *mojaver b. (ba)*.

Bore, to (=to pierce), سفتن *softan*, سنبیدن *sombidan*; (=to tire), خسته کردن *xaste k.*; he was bored, حوصله‌اش سر رفت *hōuseleaʃ sar raft*.

Boring, خسته کننده *xaste konande*, خنك *xonak*.

Born: to be born, متولد شدن *motavalled ʃ.*, تولد یافتن *tavallod yaftan*.

Borrow, to, قرض کردن *qarz k.*

Bosom, آغوش *aɣuʃ*, بر *bar*, سینه *sine*.

Botanist, گیاهشناس *giahʃenas*.

Botany, گیاهشناسی *giahʃenasi*.

Botcher, پینه‌دوز *pineduz*.

Both, هر دو *har do*, both...and, هم....هم *ham...ham*.

Bother, زحمت *zahmat*; I do not wish to bother you, نمیخواهم برای شما زحمت فراهم کنم *namixaham baraye ʃoma zahmat faraham konam*, نمیخواهم بشما زحمت برسانم (بدهم) *namixaham be ʃoma zahmat berasanam (bedeham)*.

Bottle, شیشه *ʃiʃe*, بتری *botri*.

Bottom, ته *tah*, پائین *pain*; (of the sea), قعر *qaʿr*.

Bound, to, جستن *jastan*; to be bound (compelled), مجبور شدن *majbur ʃ.,*
ناچار بودن *nacar b.*

Boundless, بیحد *bihadd,* بیپایان *bipayan,* بی انتها *bienteha,* بیکران *bikaran.*

Boundary, سرحد *sarhadd,* مرز *marʒ.*

Bounty, نعمت *neʿmat;* see also Generosity.

Bow, کمان *kaman;* (=an arc), قوس *qôus;* (of a violin), آرشه *arʃe;*
(of worship), سجده *sejde;* (of respect), تعظیم *taʿʒim.*

Bowstring, زه *ʒeh.*

Bowl, کاسه *kase.*

Box, صندوق *sanduq,* جعبه *jaʿbe;* (a tree), شمشاد *ʃemʃad;* a box on the ear,
گوشمال *guʃmal;* to box (with the fists), مشت زنی کردن *moʃtʒani k.*

Boxing, مشتزنی *moʃtʒani.*

Boy, پسر *pesar.*

Brace, see Pair.

Bracelet, دست بند *dastband,* النگو *alangu.*

Braces, بند شلوار *bande ʃalvar.*

Brackish, شور *ʃur.*

Brackishness, شوری *ʃuri.*

Brain, مغز *maɣʒ,* دماغ *demaɣ.*

Brake, ترمز *tormoʒ;* to put the brake on, ترمز کردن *tormoʒ k.*

Bran, سبوس *sabus.*

Branch, شاخه *ʃaxe;* (=sub-division), شعبه *ʃoʿbe.*

Brand (=cautery), داغ *daɣ;* to brand, داغ کردن *daɣ k.*

Brass, برنج *berenj.*

Brassière, پستان بند *pestanband.*

Brave, see Bold.

Bravo, آفرین *afarin,* بارك الله *barak allah.*

Brawl, عربده *arbade.*

Brawling, عربده بازی *arbadebaʒi.*

Brazen (=made of brass), برنجی *berenji;* (=impudent), پر رو *porru.*

Brazier, منقل *manqal.*

Breach, شکاف *ʃekaf,* رخنه *rexne;* to breach, رخنه کردن *rexne k.,* شکافتن
ʃekaftan.

Bread, نان *nan.*

Breadth, پهنا *pahna,* عرض *arʒ.*

Break, to, شکستن *ʃekastan*; to break in pieces, خرد کردن *xord k.*; to break in (a horse), رام کردن *ram k.*; to break up (bring to an end), بهم زدن *be ham ʒadan*; to break up (of an assembly, etc., intrans.), بهم خوردن *be ham xordan*; we broke with each other, میانه ما بهم خورد *mianeye ma be ham xord*; to break off relations, قطع رابطه کردن *qat'e rabete k.*

Breakfast, ناشتائی *naʃtai*, صبحانه *sobhane*.

Breast, سینه *sine*, بر *bar*; (of a woman), پستان *pestan*.

Breastbone, جناغ *janaɣ*.

Breath, نفس *nafas*, دم *dam*; shortness of breath, تنگه نفس *tangeye nafas*.

Breathe, to, نفس کشیدن *nafas kaʃidan*.

Breeches, شلوار سواری *ʃalvare savari*.

Bribe, رشوه *reʃve*; to bribe, رشوه دادن *reʃve dadan*; to take bribes, رشوه گرفتن (خوردن) *reʃve gereftan (xordan)*.

Bribery, رشوه *reʃve*.

Brick (unburnt), خشت *xeʃt*; (burnt), آجر *ajor*.

Brick-burner, آجر پز *ajorpaʒ*.

Brick-burning, آجر پزی *ajorpaʒi*.

Brick-kiln, کوره *kure*, کوره آجرپزی *kureye ajorpaʒi*.

Bricklayer, بنا *banna*.

Brickmaker, خشت‌مال *xeʃtmal*, خشت‌زن *xeʃtʒan*.

Brickmaking, خشت‌مالی *xeʃtmali*, خشت‌زنی *xeʃtʒani*.

Bride, عروس *arus*.

Bridegroom, داماد *damad*.

Bridge, پل *pol*.

Bridle, دهنه *dahane*.

Brief, مختصر *moxtasar*.

Briefly, مختصراً *moxtasaran*, اجمالاً *ejmalan*.

Brigade, تیپ *tip*.

Brigadier, سرتیپ *sartip*.

Bright, روشن *rouʃan*, منور *monavvar*.

Brightness, روشنائی *rouʃanai*.

Brilliance, شعشعه *ʃa'ʃa'e*, درخشندگی *daraxʃandegi*, تابش *tabeʃ*.

Brilliant, مشعشع *moʃa'ʃa'*, درخشان *daraxʃan*, تابان *taban*.

Brim, لب *lab*.

Brimful, لبریز *labriʒ*.

Bring, to, آوردن *avardan*; to bring up, پرورش دادن *parvareſ dadan*, بار آوردن *bar avardan*; to bring out, بیرون آوردن *birun avardan*; to bring in (=to produce), حاصل کردن *hasel k.*; to bring together (persons), بهم نزدیک کردن *be ham naƶdik k.*

Brisk, to be (of a market), رواج داشتن *ravaj d.*

Broad, پهن *pahn*, پهناور *pahnavar*, وسیع *vasi'*, عریض *ariƶ*.

Broadcast, to, پخش کردن *paxſ k.*

Broadcloth, ماهوت *mahut*.

Brocade (cloth of gold, etc.), زرباف *ƶarbaſ*, زری *ƶari*.

Broker, دلال *dallal*.

Brokerage, دلالی *dallali*.

Bronze, مفرغ *mafraƴ*.

Brooch, سنجاق *sanjaq*; to wear a brooch, سنجاق زدن *sanjaq ƶadan*.

Broom, جارو *jaru*.

Broth, شوربا *ſurba*, آب گوشت *abguſt*.

Brothel, فاحشه خانه *faheſexane*.

Brother, برادر *bəradar*; داداش *dadaſ*.

Bruised, کوفته *kufte*.

Brush (clothes-), ماهوت پاک کن *mahutpakkon*.

Bubble, حباب *hobab*.

Bubble, to, جوشیدن *juſidan*.

Buck, to (of a horse), جفتک زدن *joſtak ƶadan*.

Bucket, سطل *satl*, دلو *dalv*.

Bud, غنچه *ƴonce*.

Budget, بودجه *budje*.

Buffalo, گاومیش *gamiſ*, *gavmiſ*.

Bug, ساس *sas*; سرخک *sorxak*.

Bugle, شیپور *ſeïpur*.

Bugler, شیپورزن *ſeïpurƶan*.

Bugloss, گل گاوزبان *gole gavƶaban*.

Build, to, بنا کردن *bana k.*, ساختن *saxtan*.

Building, عمارت *emarat*; (=act of building), ساختن *saxtan*.

Bulb, پیاز *piaƶ*.

Bull, گاو نر *gave nar*.

Bullet, گلوله *golule*.

Bunch (of grapes, corn, etc.), خوشه *xuſe*; (of flowers), دسته *daste*.

Bundle, بسته *baste*.

Burden, بار *bar*.

Burn, سوختگی *suxtegi*; to burn, سوختن *suxtan* (intrans.), سوزانیدن *suzanidan* (trans.).

Burning (subs.), سوزش *suzeſ*.

Burst, to (intrans.), ترکیدن *tarakidan*.

Bury, to, خاك کردن *xak k.*, دفن کردن *dafn k.*

Bush, بوته *bote*.

Business (=occupation), شغل *ſoyl*, کار *kar*.

Bustard, هوبره *hubare*.

Busy, مشغول *maſyul*.

But, اما *amma*, ولی *vali*, لکن *laken*, لیکن *liken*; but also (after a negative), بلکه *balke*.

Butcher, قصاب *qassab*.

Butcher's shop, قصابخانه *qassabxane*.

Butler, پیشخدمت *piſxedmat*.

Butter, کره *kare*; clarified butter, روغن *rōuyan*.

Butterfly, پروانه *parvane*.

Buttermilk, دوغ *duy*.

Button, دگمه *dogme*.

Buy, to, خریدن *xaridan*.

Buyer, خریدار *xaridar*.

By, از *az*, به *be*, با *ba*; by the time that, تا *ta*.

C

Cab, درشکه *doroſke*.

Cabbage, کلم *kalam*.

Cabinet (government), کابینه *kabine*; هیئت دولت *hēiate dōulat*.

Cabman, درشکهچی *doroſkeci*.

Cage, قفس *qafas*.

Cake: he wants to have his cake and eat it, هم خدارا میخواهد و هم خرمارا *ham xodara mixahad va ham xormara*.

Calamity, آفت *afat*, بلا *bala*, مصیبت *mosibat*, نکبت *nekbat*.

Calculate, to, حساب کردن *hesab k.*

Calculation, حساب *hesab.*

Calendar, تقويم *taqvim.*

Calf, گوساله *gusale.*

Calibre (of a gun), قطر دهنه *qotre dahane,* كاليبر *kalibr.*

Calico, چيت *cit,* قلمكار *qalamkar.*

Caliph, خليفه *xalife.*

Caliphate, خلافت *xelafat.*

Call, to, (زدن) صدا كردن *sada k.* (ʒadan); to call out, بانگ زدن *bang ʒadan;* to call upon someone (make a call), بديدن كسى رفتن *be didane kasi raftan;* to return a call, بباز ديد رفتن *be baʒdid raftan;* (=to name), اسم گذاشتن *esm goʒaʃtan,* ناميدن *namidan.*

Calligraphist, خوش نويس *xoʃnevis,* خطاط *xattat.*

Calligraphy, خوشنويسى *xoʃnevisi.*

Calm (adj.), آرام *aram,* ساكت *saket,* ساكن *saken;* to become calm, calm oneself, آرام گرفتن *aram gereftan.*

Calumniate, to, تهمت زدن *tohmat ʒadan.*

Calumny, تهمت *tohmat.*

Camel, شتر *ʃotor.*

Camel-driver, شتربان *ʃotorban.*

Camera, دوربين عكسى *durbine akkasi.*

Camp, اردو *ordu;* to camp, چادر زدن *cador ʒadan.*

Camphor, كافور *kafur.*

Camping-place, اردوگاه *ordugah.*

Can, see Able.

Canal, نهر *nahr,* جوى *jui.*

Canalization (of water supply), لوله كشى *lulekaʃi.*

Cancel, to, لغو كردن *laɣv k.,* فسخ كردن *fasx k.*

Cancellation, لغو *laɣv,* فسخ *fasx.*

Cancer, سرطان *saratan.*

Candid, see Frank and Sincere.

Candle, شمع *ʃam'.*

Candle-stick, شمع دان *ʃam'dan.*

Cannon, توپ *tup.*

Cap, كلاه كپى *kolahe kepi.*

Capability, لياقت *liaqat,* قابليت *qabeliyat,* استعداد *este'dad.*

Capable, لایق *layeq,* قابل *qabel,* قادر *qader,* با استعداد *ba este'dad.*

Capacity, ظرفیت *ẓarfiyat,* گنجایش *gonjayeʃ,* بارگیری *bargiri;* see also Capability.

Cape (of land), دماغه *damaɣe.*

Capital (city), پایتخت *paɪtaxt,* مرکز *markaẓ;* (money), سرمایه *sarmaye.*

Capitalism, سرمایه‌داری *sarmayedari.*

Capitalist, سرمایه‌دار *sarmayedar.*

Captain (military), سروان *sarvan;* (naval), ناخدا یکم *naxoda yakom.*

Captive, اسیر *asir;* to take captive, اسیرگرفتن *asir gereftan.*

Captivity, گرفتاری *gereftari,* بند *band,* قید *qeɪd,* اسارت *esarat,* حبس *habs.*

Car, ماشین سواری *maʃine savari.*

Caravan, کاروان *karvan.*

Caravanserai, کاروانسرای *karvansaraɪ.*

Carcase, لاش *laʃ,* لاشه *laʃe,* مردار *mordar.*

Card (visiting), کارت *kart;* (playing), ورق *varaq;* to card (cotton), حلاجی *hallaji k.,* پنبه زدن *pambe ẓadan.*

Cardamom, هل *hel.*

Care (=attention), توجه *tavajjoh,* اعتنا *e'tena;* (=caution), احتیاط *ehteyat;* (=anxiety, sorrow), غم *ɣam,* اندوه *anduh,* الم *alam;* (=tending), پرستاری *parastari;* to take care (=be cautious), خبردار بودن *xabardar b.,* بر حذر بودن *bar haẓar b.,* احتیاط کردن *ehteyat k.*

Careful, با احتیاط متوجه *motavvajeh,* هوشیار *huʃyar,* دقیق *daqiq,* با احتیاط *ba ehteyat.*

Careless, غافل *ɣafel,* لاقید *la qeɪd,* بی اعتنا *bie'tena,* بیپروا *biparva.*

Carelessness, غفلت *ɣeflat,* بی اعتنائی *bie'tenai,* بیپروائی *biparvai.*

Cargo, بار *bar.*

Carnation, میخک *mixak.*

Carpenter, نجار *najjar.*

Carpentry, نجاری *najjari.*

Carpet (=floor covering), فرش *farʃ;* (kind of coarse carpet), گلیم *gelim;* (fine carpet), قالی *qali;* (small carpet or rug), قالیچه *qalice;* (prayer carpet), سجاده *sajjade,* مصلا *mosalla;* to carpet, فرش کردن *farʃ k.*

Carpet-weaver, قالیباف *qalibaf.*

Carpet-weaving, قالیبافی *qalibafi.*

Carriage, کالسکه *kaleske.*

Carrier (=porter), حمال *hammal*; (muleteer), مكارى *mokari*.

Carrion, مردار *mordar*.

Carrot, زردك *ӡardak*; هويج *havij*.

Carry, to, بردن *bordan*; (=to transport), حمل كردن *haml k.*

Cart, گارى *gari*, چرخ *carx*.

Carter, گاريچى *garici*, چرخى *carxi*.

Cartilage, غضروف *yoӡruf*.

Cartridge, فشنگ *fefang*.

Case (=box), صندوق *sanduq*, جعبه *ja'be*; (=affair), امر *amr*, مطلب *matlab*, حال *hal*; in case, در صورتيكه *dar suratike*; in any case, در هر صورت *dar har surat*.

Cash, نقد *naqd*, پول نقد *pule naqd*.

Cash account, حساب نقدى *hesabe naqdi*.

Cashier, صندوقدار *sanduqdar*.

Caspian Sea, بحر خزر *bahre xaӡar*.

Cassation, Court of, ديوان تميز *divane tamiӡ*.

Castle, قلعه *qal'e*, قصر *qasr*; (in chess), رخ *rox*.

Castor-oil, روغن گرچك *rōyane garcak*.

Castrate, to, اخته كردن *axte k.*

Casualties, تلفات *talafat*.

Cat, گربه *gorbe*.

Catapult, منجنيق *manjaniq*.

Catarrh, زكام *ӡokam*.

Catch, to, گرفتن *gereftan*; (=to stick), گير كردن *gir k.*

Categorical, قطعى *qat'i*.

Cattle, گاو و گوسفند *gav o gusfand*; مواشى *mavafi*.

Cauldron, ديگ *dig*, پاتيل *patil*.

Cauliflower, گل كلم *gole kalam*.

Cause (=reason), سبب *sabab*, علت *ellat*; (=what causes), باعث *ba'es*, موجب *mujeb*.

Cautery, داغ *day*.

Cauterize, to, داغ كردن *day k.*

Caution, احتياط *ehteyat*.

Cave, غار *yar*.

Caviare, خاويار *xaviar*.

Cedar, سرو آزاد sarve azad, كاج kaj.

Cede, to, واگذار کردن vagozar k.

Ceiling, سقف saqf.

Celebrate, to (a holiday), عید گرفتن id gereftan; (a victory, etc.), جشن گرفتن jaʃn gereftan; (to give a feast in celebration of something), سور دادن sur dadan.

Celebrated, مشهور maʃhur, نامور namvar.

Celebration (of an occasion, etc.), جشن jaʃn.

Celery, کرفس karafs.

Cell (of a recluse), صومعه soumeʿe, زاویه zavie, تکیه tekie.

Cellar, زیر زمین zirzamin, سردابه sardabe.

Cement, سیمان siman.

Cemetery, قبرستان qabrestan, گورستان gurestan.

Census, سرشماری sarʃomari.

Central, مرکزی markazi.

Centralization, مرکزیت markaziyat.

Centre, مرکز markaz; (=the middle), وسط vasat, میانه miane.

Century, قرن qarn.

Ceremonial (adj.), تشریفی taʃrifi.

Ceremony, تعارف taʿarof, تشریفات taʃrifat; آئین ain; without ceremony, بدون تعارف bedune taʿarof; (=homely), خودمانی xodemani; master of ceremonies, رئیس تشریفات raʿise taʃrifat.

Certain, یقین yaqin; (=true), محقق mohaqqaq.

Certainly, یقیناً yaqinan; (=of course), البته albatte.

Certificate, تصدیق نامه tasdiqname, گواهی نامه gavahiname.

Chain, سلسله selsele; (=fetter), زنجیر zanjir.

Chair, صندلی sandali.

Chairman (of a delegation), رئیس هیئت raʿise heiʿat; (of a committee), رئیس کمیسیون raʿise komisiun.

Chairmanship, ریاست riasat.

Chalk, گچ gac.

Chamber of Commerce, اطاق تجارت otaqe tejarat.

Chamber of Deputies, مجلس مبعوثین majlese mabʿusin.

Chameleon, بوقلمون buqalamun.

Champion, پهلوان pahlavan.

Chance (=accident), اتفاق *ettefaq*; (=opportunity), فرصت *forsat*; (=fortune), تقدیر *taqdir*; by chance, اتفاقًا *ettefaqan*.

Change, تبدیل *tabdil*, تغییر *tayyir*; (=small money), پول خرد *pule xord*, پول سیاه *pule siah*; to change, عوض کردن *avaz k.*, تبدیل کردن *tabdil k.*, تغییر دادن *tayyir dadan*; (money), پول خرد کردن *pul xord k.*; to be changed, تغییر یافتن *tayyir yaftan*, تبدیل شدن *tabdil ʃ.*

Changeable, تغییر پذیر *tayyirpazir*.

Changeless, تغییر ناپذیر *tayyirnapazir*.

Channel: irrigation channel, جو *ju*, جوب *jub*; underground irrigation channel, قنات *qanat*, کاریز *kariz*.

Chaos, هرج و مرج *harj o marj*.

Chapter, باب *bab*.

Character (=disposition), اخلاق *axlaq*; (=reputation), شهرت *ʃohrat*, نام *nam*; (=writing), خط *xatt*, رقم *raqam*.

Characteristic, صفت *sefat*, خصلت *xeslat*, خاصیت *xasiyat*.

Characterized: to be characterized by, موصوف بودن (به) *mousuf b. (be)*.

Charcoal, زغال چوب *zoyale cub*.

Charge: to be in charge (of), عهده‌دار بودن *ohdedar b.*; charged (with a responsibility, etc.), مکلف *mokallaf*, موظف *movazzaf*.

Chargé d'Affaires, کاردار *kardar*.

Charitable, خیرخواه *xeirxah*.

Charity (=good works), خیریه *xeiriye*; to collect funds for charity, اعانه جمع کردن *e'ane jam' k.*

Charm (spell), جادو *jadu*, سحر *sehr*, افسون *afsun*, طلسم *telesm*.

Charter, منشور *manʃur*, فرمان *farman*.

Chaste, پاك دامن *pakdaman*, عفیف *afif*.

Chastity, عفت *effat*.

Cheap, ارزان *arzan*.

Cheapness, ارزانی *arzani*.

Cheat, حقه بازی کردن *hoqqebaz*; to cheat, تقلب کردن *taqallob k.*, حقه باز *hoqqebazi k.*

Check, to (=to prevent), منع کردن *man' k.*; (=to compare), تطبیق کردن *tatbiq k.*

Checkmate, مات *mat*.

Cheek, رخ *rox*, رخسار *roxsar*; see also Impudence.

Cheerful, بشاش baʃʃaʃ, شادمان ʃadman, شاد ʃad.

Cheerfulness, بشاشت baʃaʃat, شادی ʃadi.

Cheese, پنیر panir.

Cheetah, یوز yuʒ.

Chemical, شیمیائی ʃimiai.

Chemist (=druggist), دواساز davasaʒ, داروگر darugar, داروساز darusaʒ.

Chemistry, شیمی ʃimi.

Cheque, چك cek.

Cherry, گیلاس gilas.

Chess, شطرنج ʃatranj.

Chest (=breast), سینه sine; (=box), صندوق sanduq.

Chestnut: sweet chestnut, شاه بلوط ʃahbalut.

Chew, to, جویدن javidan; (the cud), نشخوار کردن neʃxar k.

Chicken, جوجه juje.

Chicken-pox, آبله مرغان abelemoryan.

Chick-pea, نخود noxod.

Chief (=chieftain), رئیس raʾis, سردار sardar, سالار salar; (chief of a group of tribes), ایلخانی ilxani; (=principal), عمده omde.

Chieftainship, ریاست riasat.

Child, بچه bacce, bace, کودك kudak, طفل tefl.

Childhood, بچگی baccegi, bacegi, کودکی kudaki.

Childish, بچگانه baccegane, bacegane.

Chill, سرماخوردگی sarmaxordegi; to catch a chill, چائیدن caidan.

Chimney, دودکش dudkaʃ.

Chin, چانه cane.

China (=porcelain ware), ظروف چینی ʒorufe cini; (adj.), چینی; (the country), چین cin.

Chivalry, جوانمردی javanmardi, فتوت fotovvat.

Choice (=decision), اختیار exteyar; (=selection), انتخاب entexab; the choice part of anything, نخبه noxbe, زبده ʒobde.

Cholera, وبا vaba.

Choose, to (=to decide), اختیار کردن exteyar k.; (=to select), برگزیدن bar goʒidan, انتخاب کردن entexab k.

Christ, حضرت مسیح haʒrate masih, حضرت عیسی haʒrate isa.

Christian, مسیحی masihi, عیسوی isavi, نصرانی nasrani.

Christianity, مسيحيت masihiyat, نصرانيت nasraniyat.

Christmas, عيد ميلاد ide milad.

Chronic, مزمن mozmen.

Chronology, تاريخ tarix.

Church, كليسا kalisa.

Churn, to (milk), چرخ كردن carx k.

Cigarette, سيگار sigar.

Cinnamon, دارچين darcin.

Circle, (دايره) دائره da'ere (dayere).

Circular (adj.), مدور modavvar, گرد gerd; (subs.), بخشنامه baxʃname.

Circulate, to (intrans.), گشتن gaʃtan, گرديدن gardidan; (of news, etc., intrans.), انتشار يافتن enteʃar yaftan.

Circulation, گردش gardeʃ; (of money), رواج ravaj; (of newspaper), تيراژ tiraʒ; (traffic), عبور و مرور obur o morur; to put into circulation (money), رواج دادن ravaj dadan.

Circumspect, ملاحظه‌كار molaheʒekar.

Circumspection, ملاحظه molaheʒe.

Circumstance, امر amr, حال hal, واقعه vaqe'e, وضعيت vaʒ'iyat; in these circumstances, در اين صورت dar in surat.

Cistern, حوض houʒ, آب انبار abambar, بركه berke.

Citadel, ارك ark.

City, شهر ʃahr.

Civil, كشورى keʃvari; (=polite), مؤدب mo'addab; civil law, حقوق مدنى hoquqe madani; civil war, جنگ داخلى jange daxeli.

Civility, ادب adab; مدارا modara, آداب adab, نزاكت neʒakat.

Civilization, تمدن tamaddon, مدنيت madaniyat.

Claim, طلب talab, مطالبه motalebe; (=pretension), ادعا edde'a; to claim, طلب كردن talab k., مطالبه كردن motalebe k.; (=to make pretensions to), ادعا كردن edde'a k.

Claimant, مدعى modda'i.

Clan, طائفه ta'efe, تيره tire.

Class, طبقه tabaqe; (in a school, etc.), كلاس kelas.

Classical (of language), فصيح fasih.

Classification, طبقه‌بندى tabaqebandi.

Claw, چنگ cang, چنگال cangal.

Clay, طين *tin*, گل رس *gele ros.*

Clean, پاك *pak*, پاكيزه *pakiƶe*, نظيف *naƶif*; to clean, پاك كردن *pak k.*; (= to tidy), لاروبی کردن *larubi k.*; to clean an irrigation channel, نظيف كردن *naƶif k.*

Cleanness, پاکيزگی *pakiƶegi*, نظافت *neƶafat.*

Clear, آشکار *aʃkar*, صاف *saf*, شفاف *ʃaffaf*, روشن *rōuʃan*; (= evident), واضح *vaƶeh*, هويدا *hoveida*, روشن *rōuʃan.*

Clerk, دبير *dabir*, کارمند *karmand*, منشی *monʃi.*

Clever, باهوش *bahuʃ*; (= smart), زرنگ *ƶarang.*

Climate, آب و هوا *ab o hava.*

Cling, to, چسبيدن *casbidan.*

Clinic, پزشك خانه *peƶeʃkxane*; travelling clinic, بهداری سيار *behdariye sayyar.*

Cloak, عبا *aba.*

Clock, ساعت *sa'at*; clock-maker, ساعت ساز *sa'atsaƶ.*

Clod, کلوخ *kolux.*

Close (= near), نزديك *naƶdik*; (of weather), خفه *xaffe*; to close (= to shut), بستن *bastan*; (= to block), مسدود کردن *masdud k.*

Closeness, نزديکی *naƶdiki.*

Cloth, پارچه *parce.*

Clothes, لباس *lebas*, رخت *raxt.*

Clothing, پوشاك *puʃak.*

Cloth-merchant, بزاز *baƶƶaƶ.*

Cloud, ابر *abr.*

Cloudy, گرفته *gerefte*, ابردار *abrdar*; (= turbid), تيره *tire.*

Clove, ميخك *mixak.*

Clover, شبدر *ʃabdar.*

Club, چماق *comaq*; (for recreation, etc.), باشگاه *baʃgah.*

Coach, كالسکه *kaleske*; (of a train), واگون *vagun.*

Coal, زغال سنگ *ƶoɣale sang.*

Coalition, ائتلاف *e'telaf.*

Coarse (= thick), ضخيم *ƶaxim*, کلفت *koloft*, درشت *doroʃt*, زبر *ƶebr.*

Coarseness (= thickness), درشتی *doroʃti*, زبری *ƶebri.*

Coast, ساحل *sahel*, کرانه *kerane.*

Coat, نيم تنه *nimtane*, كت *kot.*

Cobweb, تار عنکبوت *tare ankabut.*

Cock, خروس *xorus.*

Cocoa-nut, نارگیل *nargil.*

Cocoon, پیله *pile.*

Coffee, قهوه *qahve.*

Cog, دندانه *dandane.*

Coin, سکه *sekke.*

Cold (adj.), سرد *sard;* (subs.), سرما *sarma;* (=catarrh), زکام *zokam;* to catch cold, سرما خوردن *sarma xordan.*

Colic, قولنج *qulanj,* پیچ *pic.*

Collar, یقه *yaxe.*

Collate, to, تطبیق کردن *tatbiq k.*

Collect, to, جمع کردن *jam' k.*

Collection, جمع *jam',* مجموع *majmu',* مجموعه *majmu'e;* اجتماع *ejtema';* (=collecting), جمع آوری *jam'avari;* (=funds), اعانه *e'ane.*

College, دانشکده *danefkade.*

Collision, تصادم *tasadom,* تصادف *tasadof.*

Collusion, توطئه *toute'e,* دسیسه *dasise.*

Collyrium, کحل *kohl,* سرمه *sorme.*

Colonel, سرهنگ یکم *sarhang yakom.*

Colonial, استعماری *este'mari.*

Colonization, استعمار *este'mar.*

Colour, رنگ *rang.*

Column, ستون *sotun.*

Comb, شانه *fane.*

Combatant, مبارز *mobarez.*

Combination (=union), اتحاد *ettehad;* (=mixture), ترکیب *tarkib.*

Come, to, آمدن *amadan;* to come back, بر گشتن *bar gaftan;* to come up, بالا آمدن *bala amadan;* to come down, پائین آمدن *pain amadan.*

Comely, زیبا *ziba.*

Comet, ستاره دنباله‌دار *setareye dombaledar.*

Comfort, آسایش *asayef,* راحت *rahat;* (=consolation), تسلی *tasalli;* to comfort, تسلی دادن *tasalli dadan.*

Comfortable, راحت *rahat,* آسوده *asude.*

Coming (adj.), آینده ayande.

Command, حکم hokm, فرمان farman, امر amr; (of an army), فرماندهی farmandehi; High Command (of an army), فرماندهی عالی farmandehiye ali.

Commander (naval), ناخدا دوم naxoda dovvom.

Commander-in-Chief, فرمانده کل farmandehe koll.

Commemorate, to, یاد آوری کردن yadavari k.

Commentary, تفسیر tafsir.

Commentator, مفسر mofasser.

Commerce, داد و ستد dad o setad, تجارت tejarat.

Commercial, تجارتی tejarati, بازرگانی bazargani.

Commiseration, رحم rahm, شفقت safaqat.

Commissariat, مباشرت mobaserat, اداره ارزاق edareye arzaq.

Commit, to, (به) مرتکب شدن mortakeb ʃ. (be); (=to entrust), سپردن sepordan.

Committee, کمیسیون komisiun, هیئت heiʻat.

Common, عام amm; (=general, ordinary), عمومی omumi; (=joint), مشترک moʃtarak; common sense, ممیزی momaiyezi; شعور ʃoʻur.

Commotion, جار و جنجال jar o janjal, شلوق ʃoluq, هنگامه hengame, غوغا youya, janjal.

Communication, means of, وسائل ارتباطی vasaʻele ertebati.

Community, امت ommat, جامعه jameʻe.

Compact (adj.), جمع jamʻ; (subs.) see Agreement.

Companion, رفیق rafiq; (travelling companion), همراه hamrah.

Company (commercial), شرکت ʃerkat; (military), گروهان goruhan.

Compare, to, تشبیه کردن moqabele k., تطبیق کردن tatbiq k., مقابله کردن taʃbih k.; compared with, نسبت به nesbat be.

Comparison, تطبیق tatbiq, مقابله moqabele, تشبیه taʃbih.

Compass (mathematical), پرگار pargar; (mariner's), قطب نما qotbnama.

Compassion, رحمت rahmat, شفقت safaqat.

Compassionate, دلسوز delsuz.

Compel, to, مجبور کردن majbur k.

Compendium, مجمل mojmal.

Compensate, to, جبران کردن jobran k., تلافی کردن talafi k.

Compensation, تلافی talafi, جبران jobran, غرامت yaramat.

Compete, to, مسابقه کردن *mosabeqe k.*; (=to rival), رقابت کردن *reqabat k.*; (=to take part), شرکت کردن *ʃerkat k.*

Competence, صلاحیت *salahiyat*, کفایت *kefayat*, قابلیت *qabeliyat.*

Competition, مسابقه *mosabeqe*; (=rivalry), رقابت *reqabat.*

Competitive: competitive examination, کنکور *konkur.*

Complain, to, شکایت کردن *ʃekayat k.*, گله کردن *gele k.*; (=to moan), ناله کردن *nale k.*

Complaint, شکایت *ʃekayat*, گله *gele*; (=moan), ناله *nale*; (of injustice), تظلم *taʒallom*; see also Illness.

Complete, تمام *tamam*, کامل *kamel.*

Completely, بکلی *be kolli*, تماماً *tamaman.*

Completion, اتمام *etmam*, تکمیل *takmil.*

Complicated, پیچیده *picide*, بغرنج *boɣranj.*

Compliment, تعارف *ta'arof.*

Composed: to be composed of, مرکب بودن (از) *morakkab b. (aʒ).*

Composition (=mixture), ترکیب *tarkib*; (=essay), مقاله *maqale*; (=literary work), تصنیف *tasnif*, تألیف *ta'lif.*

Compositor, حروف‌چین *horufcin.*

Compound (=mixture), ترکیب *tarkib.*

Comprehend, to, ادراک کردن *edrak k.*, فهمیدن *fahmidan.*

Comprehending (=including), شامل *ʃamel.*

Comprehension, ادراک *edrak*, فهم *fahm.*

Comprehensive, جامع *jame'.*

Comprise, to, شامل بودن (از) *ʃamel b. (aʒ)*, عبارت بودن (از) *ebarat b. (aʒ).*

Compulsion: under compulsion, از روی اجبار *aʒ ruye ejbar.*

Compulsory, اجباری *ejbari.*

Computation, حساب *hesab.*

Comrade, رفیق *rafiq.*

Conceal, to, پنهان کردن *panhan k.*, مخفی کردن *maxfi k.*, قایم کردن *qayem k;* to be concealed, غائب شدن *ɣa'eb ʃ.*

Concealment, پنهانی *panhani*, نهانی *nehani*, غیبت *ɣeıbat.*

Conceit, خود پسندی *xodpasandi.*

Conceited, خود پسند *xodpasand.*

Concern: this does not concern you, این بشما ربط ندارد *in be ʃoma rabt nadarad*, این بشما مربوط نیست *in be ʃoma marbut nist.*

Concession, امتياز *emteyaz*; to make a concession (over something), پائين آمدن *pain amadan.*

Conciliatory, مصالحه آميز *mosaleheamiz.*

Conciliation, ستمالت *estemalat*, مصالحه *mosalehe.*

Conciseness, ايجاز *ijaz.*

Conclude, to (a treaty), منعقد ساختن *mon'aqed saxtan*, بستن *bastan*; see also Finish and Suppose.

Conclusion (of a treaty), انعقاد *en'eqad*; see also End.

Concord, موافقت *movafeqat*, هم آهنگى *hamahangi.*

Condemn, محکوم کردن *mahkum k.*

Condemnation, محکوميت *mahkumiyat.*

Condition (=state), حال *hal*, حالت *halat*, وضع *vaz'*; (=stipulation), شرط *fart*; condition of affairs, وضعيت *vaz'iyat*, اوضاع *ouza'.*

Conditional, شرطى *farti*; to be conditional upon, (بر) مشروط بودن *mafrut b. (bar).*

Condole, to, (دادن) تسليت گفتن *tasliat goftan (dadan).*

Condolence, تسليت *tasliat.*

Conduct, رفتار *raftar.*

Confectioner, قناد *qannad*, قنادى *qannadi*; شيرينى پز *firinipaz.*

Confectionery, شيرينى *firini.*

Confer, to (=discuss), مذاکره کردن *mozakere k.*; see also Bestow.

Confess, to, ايمان آوردن (به) اعتراف کردن *e'teraf k.*; (a faith) *iman avardan (be).*

Confession, اعتراف *e'teraf*; (of faith) شهادت *fahadat.*

Confidant, محرم *mahram.*

Confidence, اعتماد *e'temad*; to have confidence in, اعتماد داشتن (به) *e'temad d. (be).*

Confined (=imprisoned), محبوس *mahbus*, زندانى *zendani*; (=limited), محدود *mahdud*; to be confined (of a woman), در وضع حمل بودن *dar vaz'e haml b.*

Confinement (=imprisonment), حبس *habs*; (of a woman), وضع حمل *vaz'e haml.*

Confines (=limits), حدود *hodud.*

Confirm, to, تصديق کردن *tasdiq k.*

Confirmation, تصديق *tasdiq.*

Confiscate, to, ضبط کردن ـabt k., توقیف k. ـtouqif k.

Confiscation, ضبط ـabt, توقیف ـtouqif.

Conformity, متابعت motabe'at.

Confronted: to be confronted by, مواجه شدن (با) movajeh ſ. (ba), رو برو شدن (با) ru be ru ſ. (ba).

Confuse, to, خلط مبحث کردن maxlut k.; to confuse the issue, مخلوط کردن xalte mabhas k.

Confused, در هم و برهم dar ham o bar ham, پیچیده picide, مختل moxtall; (in mind), پریشان pariſan, حیران heiran, آشفته aſofte, دستپاچه dastpace.

Confusion, اختلال extelal; (of mind), پریشانی pariſani, آشفتگی aſoftegi, دستپاچگی dastpacegi.

Congeal, to, منجمد شدن monjamed ſ.

Congratulate, to, (به) تبریک گفتن tabrik goftan (be).

Conjecture, حدس hads; to conjecture, حدس زدن hads ـadan.

Conjunction (gram.), حرف عطف harfe atf; (of planets), قران qeran.

Conjurer, شعبده باز ſo'badebaـ.

Conjuring, شعبده بازی ſo'badebaـi.

Connect, to, متصل کردن mottasel k., وصل کردن vasl k., پیوستن peivastan; to be connected with (related to), نسبت داشتن (با) nesbat d. (ba).

Connexion, اتصال ettesal, پیوند peivand, وصل vasl; (relationship), نسبت nesbat.

Connoisseur, خبره xebre.

Conquer, to, غالب آمدن (بر) ـaleb amadan (bar), فتح کردن fath k., غلبه کردن ـalabe k.

Conqueror, فاتح fateh.

Conquest, فتح fath.

Consanguinity, خویشی xiſi, قرابت qarabat.

Conscience, وجدان vejdan.

Conscription (military), نظام وظیفه neـamvaـife.

Consecutive, متوالی motavali, متواتر motavater.

Consensus (of opinion), اتفاق آرا ettefaqe ara.

Consent, اجابت ejabat.

Consequence (=result), نتیجه natije.

Consequently, در نتیجه dar natije.

Conservatism, محافظه کاری mohafeـekari.

Conservative, محافظه‌کار mohafezekar.

Consider, to, تأمل کردن فکر کردن اندیشه کردن andiſe k., fekr k.,
ta'ammol k.; (to = count, reckon), شمردن ſomordan; to consider
necessary, لازم شمردن lazem ſomordan; (= be of opinion that), دانستن
danestan.

Consideration, اندیشه andiſe, فکر fekr, تأمل ta'ammol.

Consign, to, واگذار کردن تفویض کردن سپردن sepordan, tafviz k., vagozar k.; (merchandise, etc.), حمل کردن haml k., ارسال داشتن ersal d.

Consist, to, see Comprise.

Consolation, see Condolence.

Consort: to consort with, معاشرت کردن (با) mo'aſerat k. (ba).

Conspiracy, توطئه tōute'e, دسیسه dasise.

Conspirator, توطئه کننده tōute'e konande, دسیسه کار dasisekar.

Constant, دائمی da'emi; constantly, دائماً da'eman.

Consternation, وحشت vahſat, آشفتگی aſoftegi.

Constipation, یبوست yobusat, یبس yobs.

Constituency (electoral), حوضه انتخابی hōuzeye entexabi.

Constitution (form of government), مشروطیت maſrutiyat; (nature), نهاد
nehad, سرشت sereſt; (of the body), بنیه bonye, مزاج mezaj; (of a
society, etc.), نظام نامه nezamname.

Constitutional (of a government), مشروطه maſrute; (of the body), طبعی
tab'i, مزاجی mezaji.

Constitutionalist, مشروطه خواه maſrutexah.

Construction, ساختمان saxteman, ساختمانی saxtemani; construction department, اداره ساختمانی edareye saxtemani.

Consul, قنسل qonsol, کنسل konsol.

Consular, قنسلی qonsoli, کنسلی konsoli.

Consulate, قنسلخانه qonsolxane, کنسلخانه konsolxane.

Consul-General, سرقنسل sarqonsol, سرکنسل sarkonsol.

Consult, to, مشورت کردن maſvarat k.

Consultation, مشورت maſvarat.

Consume, to, صرف کردن sarf k., خوردن xordan.

Consumption, صرف sarf; (= disease), سل sell.

Consumptive, مسلول maslul.

Contagious, مسری mosri.

Contain, to, شامل بودن ʃamel b., مشتمل بودن (بر) moʃtamel b. (bar);
to be contained in, گنجیدن ganjidan, مندرج بودن mondarej b.

Containing, (بر) مشتمل moʃtamel (bar), (بر) شامل ʃamel (bar).

Contemporary, معاصر mo'aser.

Contempt, حقارت heqarat, تحقیر tahqir, خواری xari.

Contemptible, حقیر haqir, خوار xar, دون dun, پست past.

Contented, راضی raʒi, قانع qane'.

Contentment, رضایت reʒayat, قناعت qana'at.

Contents, مضمون maʒmun; list of contents (of book, etc.), فهرست مندرجات
fehreste mondarejat.

Continent, قاره qare.

Continual, see Constant.

Continuance, دوام davam, ادامه edame.

Continuation (of a serial story, etc.), بقیه baqiye, دنباله dombale.

Continue, to, ادامه دادن edame dadan.

Continuity, پیوستگی peivastegi.

Contraband, قاچاق qacaq; (adj.), قاچاقی qacaqi.

Contract, قرارداد qarardad.

Contractor, مقاطعه کار moqate'ekar.

Contradict, to, تکذیب کردن takʒib k., رد کردن radd k.

Contradiction, رد کلام radde kalam; (=inconsistency) ضد و نقیض ʒedd
o naqiʒ.

Contradictory, متناقض motanaqeʒ, متضاد motaʒadd.

Contrary, خلاف xelaf, مخالف moxalef, نقیض naqiʒ, متناقض motanaqeʒ; on
the contrary, بر عکس bar aks; contrary to, بر خلاف bar xelaf(e), بر
عکس bar aks(e).

Contrast (=opposites), ضد و نقیض ʒedd o naqiʒ.

Contribution, سهم sahm, امداد emdad.

Contributor, سهم دهنده sahm dehande.

Contrition, توبه toube, ندامت nedamat.

Control, نظارت neʒarat, اختیار exteyar; (=examination of documents),
بازدید baʒdid; to exercise control (supervise), نظارت کردن neʒarat k.;
see also Prevent.

Controller, بازبین baʒbin, بازرس baʒras.

Convenient, مناسب monaseb.

Conversation, گفتگو (گفتوگو) goftogu, محبت sohbat.

Converse, to, محبت کردن sohbat k.

Convex, محدب mohaddab.

Convince, to, قانع کردن qane' k.

Convoy: to travel in a convoy, دسته جمع حرکت کردن daste jam' harakat k.

Cook, آشپز aspaz, طباخ tabbax; to cook, پختن poxtan.

Cool, خنك xonak.

Co-operate, to, همکاری کردن hamkari k.

Co-operation, همکاری hamkari, تعاون ta'avon.

Co-operative, تعاونی ta'avoni; co-operative society, شرکت تعاونی serkate ta'avoni.

Copper, مس mes.

Coppersmith, مسگر mesgar.

Copy, پاکنویس کردن نسخه nosxe, سواد savad; to make a fair copy; paknevis k.; to copy (in writing), از رو نوشتن az ru nevestan, رو نویس runevis کردن k.

Copyist, مستنسخ mostansex.

Copyright, حق طبع haqqe tab'; copyright reserved, حق طبع محفوظ haqqe tab' mahfuz.

Coquetry, ناز naz, عشوه esve.

Coral, مرجان marjan.

Cord, ریسمان risman.

Cork, چوب پنبه cubpambe.

Corn, غله yalle.

Corner, گوشه; (in a road), پیچ pic.

Coronation, تاجگذاری tajgozari.

Corporal (army rank), سرجوخه sarjuxe.

Corporeal, جسمانی jesmani.

Corps (of an army), سپاه sepah.

Correct, صحیح sahih; to correct, اصلاح کردن eslah k.

Correction, تصحیح tashih; to make a correction, تصحیح کردن tashih k.

Correspond, to, مکاتبه کردن mokatebe k.; (=to be alike), شبیه بودن sabih b.

Correspondence, مکاتبه mokatebe; (=resemblance), مطابقت motabeqat.

Correspondent, مكاتب *mokateb*; newspaper correspondent, مخبر روزنامه *moxbere ruzname*.

Corresponding (to), مطابق *motabeq(e)*.

Corridor, دالان *dalan*.

Corroboration, اثبات *esbat*, تأييد *ta'yid*, تثبيت *tasbit*.

Corrupt, فاسد *fased*; (of a person), رشوه خور *refvexor*.

Corruption, فساد *fesad*, رشوه خورى *refvexori*; (of a text), تحريف *tahrif*.

Cost (= price), قيمت *qeimat*; (= outlay), خرج *xarj*; to cost, ارزيدن *arzidan*.

Cosy, دنج *denj*.

Cotton, پنبه *pambe*; (in the pod), جوزق *jouzaq*, غوزه *yuze*, كلوزه *koluze*; (= calico), چيت *cit*, چلوار *celvar*.

Cotton-dresser, حلاج *hallaj*, پنبه زن *pambezan*.

Cotton piece-goods, قماش *qomaf*.

Cotton-wool, پنبه *pambe*.

Cough, سرفه *sorfe*; to cough, سرفه كردن *sorfe k.*

Council, شورى *foura*.

Counsellor, راى زن *raizan*, مشاور *mofaver*.

Count, to, شمردن *fomordan*, حساب كردن *hesab k.*

Counter-attack, حمله متقابل *hamleye motaqabel*.

Counterfeit, جعلى *ja'li*, ساختگى *saxtegi*, تقلبى *taqallobi*.

Country, كشور *kefvar*, مملكت *mamlakat*; (opp. of town), دهات *dehat*.

Countryman, دهاتى *dehati*.

Couple (= pair), جفت *joft*; to couple (of animals), جفتگيرى كردن *joftgiri k.*

Couplet, بيت *beit*.

Coupon, برش *boref*, كوپن *kupon*.

Courage, شجاعت *foja'at*, دليرى *daliri*, دلاورى *delavari*, شهامت *fahamat*, مردانگى *mardanegi*.

Courageous, دلير *dalir*, شجاع *foja'*.

Course (of a river, etc.), مجرا *majra*; (of action), رفتار *raftar*; (of instruction), برنامه *barname*; of course, البته *albatte*; in the course of, در ظرف *dar zarf(e)*, ضمن *zemn(e)*, در ضمن *dar zemn(e)*.

Court (royal), دربار *darbar*; (of justice), دادسرا *dadsara*, دادگاه *dadgah*, محكمه *mahkame*; criminal court, محكمه جنائى *mahkameye janai*; (= attendants), خدم و حشم *xadam va hafam*, ملازمان *molazeman*; (= levée), سلام *salam*.

Courteous, مؤدب *mo'addab.*

Courtesy, نزاکت *nezakat.*

Courtyard, حیاط *hayat;* (of a mosque), صحن *sahn.*

Cousin (son or daughter of paternal uncle or aunt or of maternal uncle or aunt), پسرعمو *pesaramu,* دختر عمو *doxtaramu,* etc.

Covenant, عهد *ahd,* پیمان *peiman.*

Cover, سر *sar,* سرپوش *sarpuʃ,* پوشش *puʃeʃ;* (for note issue), پشتوانه *poʃtevane;* to cover, پوشیدن *puʃidan.*

Covet, to, طمع داشتن *tama' d.*

Covetous, طمعکار *tama'kar.*

Covetousness, طمع *tama'.*

Cow, ماده گاو *madegav,* گاو *gav.*

Cowherd, گاو چران *gavcaran.*

Cowl (of a chimney), بادگیر *badgir*

Crab, خرچنگ *xarcang.*

Cradle, گهواره *gahvare,* مهد *mahd.*

Craft (=trade), پیشه *piʃe.*

Craftsman, پیشه ور *piʃevar.*

Crane (machine), جر ثقیل *jarre saqil.*

Cream, خامه *xame;* سرشیر *sarʃir;* قیماق *qeimaq.*

Create, to, آفریدن *afaridan,* خلق کردن *xalq k.;* (=to produce), ایجاد *ijad k.,* تولید کردن *toulid k.*

Creation, آفرینش *afarineʃ,* خلقت *xelqat;* (=created beings), مخلوقات *maxluqat;* (=production), ایجاد *ijad,* تولید *toulid.*

Creator, خالق *xaleq,* آفریننده *afarinande;* (Creator of the world), خالق *xaleqe maxluqat,* جهان آفرین *jahanafarin.*

Credentials, اعتبار نامه *e'tebarname;* (of an ambassador), استوار نامه *ostovarname.*

Credit, اعتبار *e'tebar;* on credit, نسیه *nesie.*

Creditor, طلبکار *talabkar.*

Creek (=backwater), مرداب *mordab.*

Creep, to, خزیدن *xazidan.*

Crescent (moon), هلال *helal.*

Crew (of a ship), جاشوان *jaʃvan,* جاشو *jaʃu.*

Crier, جارچی *jarci.*

Crime, جنایت jenayat, جرم jorm.

Criminal (subs.), جانی jani, جنایت کار jenayatkar.

Crisis, بحران bohran.

Critical (=serious), بحران آمیز bohranamiz, باریك barik; (of an illness), خطرناك xatarnak; (=appraising), انتقادی enteqadi; (=carping), خرده گیر xordegir.

Criticism, انتقاد enteqad; (=complaint), ایراد irad.

Criticize, to, انتقاد کردن enteqad k.; (=to complain), ایراد گرفتن irad gereftan, خرده گرفتن xorde gereftan.

Crocodile, تمساح temsah.

Crooked, کج kaj, معوج mo'vajj.

Crop (=produce), محصول mahsul.

Cross (subs.), صلیب salib; he is cross, اوقاتش تلخ است ouqataʃ talx ast; to cross, (از) عبور کردن obur k. (az); to cross out, خط کشیدن xatt kaʃidan.

Crossbred (of a horse, etc.), دو رگه dorage.

Cross-examination, استنطاق estentaq, باز پرسی bazporsi.

Crossness, اوقات تلخی ouqate talxi.

Crow, کلاغ kalay, زاغ zay.

Crowd, ازدحام ezdeham, جمعیت jam'iyat; to crowd, ازدحام کردن ezdeham k.

Crown, تاج taj; crown land, خالصه xalese (pl. خالصجات xalesejat).

Crucial, حیاتی hayati.

Crucify, to, مصلوب ساختن maslub saxtan.

Cruel, بیرحم birahm, جفاکار jafakar.

Cruelty, بیرحمی birahmi, جفا jafa.

Cruiser, رزم ناو razmnav; battle cruiser, نبرد ناو nabardnav.

Crumb, ریزه rize.

Crust, قشر qeʃr, پوست pust.

Cry (=shout), بانگ bang, نعره na're, فریاد faryad; to cry out, فریاد (نعره، بانگ) زدن faryad (na're, bang) zadan; (=to weep), گریه کردن gerie k., گریستن geristan.

Crystal, بلور bolur.

Crystallographer, بلور شناس bolurʃenas.

Crystallography, بلور شناسی bolurʃenasi.

Cucumber, خیار xiar.

Cud: to chew the cud, نشخوار کردن *neʃxar k.*

Cul-de-sac, بن بست *bombast.*

Cultivate, to, زراعت کردن *ʒeraʿat k.*

Cultivated (of land), مزروع *maʒruʿ.*

Cultivation (=cultivated land), زراعت *ʒeraʿat,* كشت *keʃt.*

Cultivator, زارع *ʒareʿ.*

Cultural, فرهنگی *farhangi.*

Culture, فرهنگ *farhang.*

Cuneiform (subs.), خط میخی *xatte mixi.*

Cup, فنجان *fenjan,* پیاله *piale,* استكان *estekan;* to cup (bleed), حجامت کردن *hejamat k.*

Cupboard, قفسه *qafase,* دولابچه *dulabce.*

Cupola, گنبد *gombad.*

Cupping-glass, شاخ حجامت *ʃaxe hejamat.*

Curb (part of a bridle), لگام *legam.*

Curdle, to (of milk), بریدن *boridan.*

Curds, ماست *mast;* (dried), كشك *kaʃk.*

Cure, معالجه *moʿaleje,* درمان *darman,* شفا *ʃefa,* علاج *elaj,* چاره *care;* to cure, معالجه کردن *moʿaleje k.,* علاج کردن *elaj k.,* چاره کردن *care k.*

Curl, زلف *ʒolf.*

Currency (monetary), پول رایج *pule rayej.*

Current (subs.), جریان *jarian;* (adj.), جاری *jari,* رایج *rayej.*

Curse, لعنت *laʿnat;* to curse, لعنت کردن *laʿnat k.*

Curtain, پرده *parde.*

Cushion, نازبالش *nazbaleʃ.*

Custom, رسم *rasm,* عادت *adat.*

Customary, عادی *adi;* (of law), عرف *orfi.*

Customs, گمرک *gomrok,* گمركات *gomrokat.*

Customs-house, گمركخانه *gomrokxane.*

Cut (=wound), زخم *ʒakhm;* (of clothes) برش *boreʃ;* to cut, بریدن *boridan;* (=to interrupt), قطع کردن *qatʿ k.*

Cycle (of time), دور *dour,* دوره *doure.*

Cypher, رمز *ramʒ;* (=nought), صفر *sefr;* cypher department, اداره رمز *edareye ramʒ.*

Cypress (tree), سرو *sarv.*

D

Dagger, خنجر *xanjar.*

Dahlia, کوکب *koukab.*

Daily, روزانه *ruzane,* هر روز *har ruz.*

Dam, سد *sadd,* بند *band;* to dam, سدبندی کردن *saddbandi k.*

Damage, خسارت *xesarat.*

Damp, تر *tar,* نمناك *namnak;* (of climate) مرطوب *martub.*

Damson, آلوچه *aluce.*

Dance, رقص *raqs;* to dance, رقص کردن *raqs k.*

Dancer, رقاص *raqqas.*

Danger, خطر *xatar.*

Dangerous, خطرناك *xatarnak.*

Dare, to, جرأت داشتن *jor'at d.*

Dark, تاریك *tarik,* تیره *tire.*

Darkness, تاریکی *tariki,* تیرگی *tiregi.*

Darn, to, رفو کردن *rofu k.*

Date (time), تاریخ *tarix;* (fruit), خرما *xorma;* to date, تاریخ گذاشتن *tarix gozaʃtan;* (=to become old), کهنه شدن *kohne ʃ.*

Dated, مورخ *movarrax.*

Daughter, دختر *doxtar;* daughter-in-law, عروس *arus.*

Dawn, طلوع *tolu'.*

Day, روز *ruz;* the day before yesterday, پریروز *pariruz;* the day after tomorrow, پس فردا *pasfarda;* from day to day, روز بروز *ruz be ruz.*

Dead, مرده *morde.*

Deal (wood), صنوبر *senoubar.*

Dealer, تاجر *tajer.*

Dear (=beloved), عزیز *aziz;* (=expensive), گران *geran;* (=precious), گرانبها *geranbeha;* it will cost him dear, برای او گران تمام میشود *baraye u geran tamam miʃavad.*

Death, مرگ *marg,* فوت *fout,* وفات *vafat.*

Debate, مذاکره *mozakere,* مباحثه *mobahese;* to debate, مذاکره کردن *mozakere k.,* مباحثه کردن *mobahese k.*

Debauchee, عیاش *aiyaʃ.*

Debauchery, عیاشی *aiyaʃi.*

Debt, وام vam, دین dein, قرض qarʒ; to be in debt, مقروض بودن maqruʒ b.,
قرض داشتن qarʒ d.; (fig.), (به) مدیون بودن madyun b. (be).

Debtor, بدهکار bedehkar.

Decay, فاسد ʃ., زوال ʒaval; to decay, ضایع شدن xarab ʃ., خراب شدن ʒayeʻ ʃ.,
فاسد شدن fased ʃ.

Deceit, تقلب taqallob, مکر makr.

Deceitful, متقلب motaqalleb.

Deceive, to, فریفتن fariftan, فریب دادن farib dadan; گول زدن gul ʒadan;
to be deceived, گول خوردن gul xordan.

Decide, to, تصمیم گرفتن tasmim gereftan; to be decided (on a course of
action, etc.), بر آن بودن bar an b.; (= to be determined), مصمم شدن
mosammam ʃ.; (= to be fixed), مقرر بودن moqarrar b.

Decision, تصمیم tasmim.

Decisive, قطعی qatʻi, قاطع qateʻ.

Deck (of a ship), عرشه arʃe.

Declaration, اعلان eʻlan, اعلام eʻlam, اظهار eʒhar; (= a declaration form),
اظهار نامه eʒharname.

Declare, to, اظهار کردن eʒhar k., اعلام کردن eʻlam k., اعلان کردن eʻlan k.

Decline, to, see Decrease and Refuse.

Declivity, نشیب neʃib, شیب ʃib, سرازیری saraʒiri, سراشیب saraʃib.

Decorate, to, آراستن arastan, زینت دادن ʒinat dadan, تزیین کردن taʒyin k.

Decoration, آرایش arayeʃ, زینت ʒinat, تزیین taʒyin, پیرایش pirayeʃ.

Decrease, کاهش kaheʃ, تنزل tanaʒʒol; to decrease (intrans.), کاستن kastan,
تنزل کردن tanaʒʒol k.; (trans.), کم کردن kam k., کاستن kastan, کسر کردن
kasr k.

Decree, حکم hokm, امر amr.

Deduct, to, کسر کردن kasr k.

Deduction, استدلال estedlal; (= decrease), کسر kasr.

Deed: title deed, قباله qabale.

Deep, گود goud, ژرف ʒarf, عمیق amiq.

Defamation, هتک hatk.

Detame, to, هتک شرف کردن hatke ʃaraf k.

Defeat, شکست ʃekast, هزیمت haʒimat; to defeat, شکست دادن ʃekast
dadan; to be defeated, شکست خوردن ʃekast xordan.

Defect, عیب eib, نقص naqs.

Defective, معیوب ma'yub, ناقص naqes.

Defence, حفظ hefz, محافظت mohafezat, حمایت hemayat.

Defend, to, حفظ کردن hefz k., حمایت کردن hemayat k.

Defendant (at law), مدعی علیه modda'a aleih.

Deficiency, کسر kasr, نقص naqs.

Deficient, ناقص naqes.

Deficit, کسر kasr.

Defile (narrow pass), تنگه tange; to defile (=make unclean), نجس کردن nejes k.

Define, to (=to describe), تصریح کردن tasrih k.; (=to settle), تعیین کردن ta'yin k.

Definite, معین mo'ayyan.

Degree (=amount), قدر qadr, مقدار meqdar; (=rank), رتبه rotbe, درجه daraje; (=proportion), نسبت nesbat; (mathematical), درجه daraje; (university), دیپلوم diploum; by degrees, بتدریج be tadrij.

Delay (=stoppage), توقف tavaqqof; (=lateness), تأخیر ta'xir; (=respite), مهلت mohlat; without delay, بی درنگ bi darang.

Delegate, نماینده namayande.

Delegation, هیئت نمایندگی hei'ate namayandegi.

Deliberately, عمداً amdan.

Deliberation, تفکر tafakkor, تأمل ta'ammol.

Delicate, ظریف zarif, لطیف latif; (=weak), ضعیف za'if.

Delight, حظ hazz, لذت lezzat; to be delighted, محظوظ شدن mahzuz š., لذت بردن lezzat bordan.

Delineation, ترسیم tarsim.

Deliver, to (=surrender), تسلیم کردن taslim k.; (=hand over), تفویض کردن tafviz k., حواله کردن havale k., سپردن sepordan; (=cause to arrive), رساندن rasandan; (=set free), آزاد کردن azad k., خلاص کردن xalas k., نجات دادن nejat dadan.

Demand, تقاضا taqaza, در خواست darxast, مطالبه motalebe; to demand, مطالبه کردن motalebe k., در خواست کردن darxast k., تقاضا کردن taqaza k.; (=to require, 3rd pers. only), اقتضا کردن eqteza k.

Demagogue, عوام فریب avamfarib, هوچی houci.

Demagogy, عوام فریبی avamfaribi, هوچیگری houcigari.

Demolish, to, منهدم کردن (ساختن) monhadem k. (saxtan).

Demolition, انهدام *enhedam.*

Demonstration: to make a demonstration, تظاهرات کردن *tazahorat k.*

Denial, انکار *enkar,* تکذیب *takzib.*

Deny, to, انکار کردن *enkar k.,* تکذیب کردن *takzib k.;* (=to refuse), دریغ داشتن *dariy d.*

Department, اداره *edare,* شعبه *fo'be.*

Depend: to depend on (=be contingent upon), موقوف بودن (به) *mouquf b.* (be), منوط بودن (به) *manut b.* (be), بسته بودن (به) *baste b.* (be).

Dependence, بستگی *bastegi,* تعلق *ta'alloq.*

Dependencies, تعلقات *ta'alloqat,* توابع *tavabe'.*

Deploy, to (of an army), گستردن *gostardan.*

Deployment (of an army), گسترش سپاه *gostarefe sepah.*

Depopulated, ویران *veiran.*

Depose, to (=expel), اخراج کردن *exraj k.,* معزول کردن *ma'zul k.;* (=give testimony), شهادت دادن *fahada dadan,* گواهی دادن *gavahi dadan.*

Deposit, ودیعت *vadi'at,* سپرد *sepord,* امانت *amanat;* to deposit, سپردن *sepordan,* امانت گذاشتن *amanat gozaftan.*

Depositor, امانت گذار *amanatgozar,* سپارنده *separande.*

Deprive, to, (ساختن) محروم کردن *mahrum k. (saxtan).*

Deprivation, محرومیت *mahrumiyat.*

Depth, گودی *goudi,* عمق *omq.*

Deputize, to, وکالت کردن *vekalat k.,* معاونت کردن *mo'avenat k.*

Deputy, وکیل *vakil;* (=assistant), معاون *mo'aven,* نائب *na'eb.*

Derivative, فرعی *far'i,* مشتق *moftaqq.*

Derogation (of one's dignity), کسر شأن *kasre fa'n.*

Dervish, درویش *darvif.*

Descend, to (=to alight), پیاده شدن *piade f.;* (=to come down), پائین آمدن *pain amadan.*

Descendants, نسل *nasl,* خلف *xalaf,* اخلاف *axlaf.*

Descent, see Declivity.

Describe, to, شرح دادن *farh dadan,* بیان کردن *bayan k.,* تعریف کردن *ta'rif k.,* توصیف کردن *tousif k.*

Description, تعریف *ta'rif,* بیان *bayan,* شرح *farh,* توصیف *tousif.*

Desert, بیابان *biaban;* salt desert, کویر *kavir;* to desert, ترک کردن *tark k.*

Desertion, ترك *tark.*

Deserve, to, سزاوار بودن *sazavar b.,* مستحق بودن *mostahaqq b.*

Desirable, مرغوب *maryub,* مطبوع *matbu',* مقبول *maqbul.*

Desire, آرزو *arzu,* خواهش *xahef,* مراد *morad;* to desire, آرزو داشتن *arzu d.,* خواستن *xastan.*

Desirous, خواهان *xahan,* طالب *taleb,* آرزومند *arzumand.*

Desist, to, دست بر داشتن *dast bar d.*

Desolate, خراب *xarab,* ویران *veiran;* see also Grieved.

Desolation, خرابی *xarabi,* ویرانی *veirani;* see also Grief.

Despair, یأس *ya's,* نومیدی *noumidi (naomidi);* to despair, مأیوس بودن *ma'yus b.,* نومید بودن *noumid (naomid) b.*

Despicable, see Contemptible.

Despise, to, حقیر شمردن *haqir fomordan.*

Despot, مستبد *mostabedd.*

Despotic, مستبد *mostabedd,* استبدادی *estebdadi.*

Despotism, استبداد *estebdad.*

Destination, مقصد *maqsad.*

Destiny, تقدیر *taqdir,* قسمت *qesmat,* قضا *qaza;* (=future lot), سرنوشت *sar-neveft,* نصیب *nasib.*

Destitute, بینوا *binava,* مفلس *mofles.*

Destitution, بینوائی *binavai,* افلاس *eflas.*

Destroy, to, معدوم کردن *ma'dum k.,* (ساختن) منهدم کردن *monhadem k. (saxtan),* نیست و نابود کردن *nist o nabud k.*

Destroyer (ship), ناوشکن *navfekan.*

Destruction, انهدام *enhedam,* اعدام *e'dam.*

Detail, تفصیل *tafsil;* details, جزئیات *joz'iyat;* in detail, باتفصیل *ba tafsil.*

Detain, to, نگاه داشتن *negah d.,* باز داشتن *baz d.*

Detective, کارآگاه *karagah.*

Determination, عزم *azm,* جزم *jazm,* تصمیم *tasmim.*

Determine, to, see Decide.

Detriment, ضرر *zarar,* زیان *zian,* لطمه *latme.*

Devastation, خرابی *xarabi,* ویرانی *veirani.*

Develop, to (a film), ظاهر کردن *zaher k.;* see also Progress.

Development, تکامل *takamol;* see also Extension and Progress.

Deviate, to, منحرف شدن *monharef f.*

Deviation, انحراف *enheraf.*

Devil, the, شیطان *settan,* ابلیس *eblis.*

Devoid, عاری *ari.*

Devotion (to a cause, etc.), فداکاری *fedakari.*

Devout, دیندار *dindar,* باتقوی *bataqva.*

Dew, شبنم *sabnam.*

Dexterity, تردستی *tardasti.*

Dialect, لهجه *lahje,* زبان محلی *zabane mahalli.*

Diameter, قطر *qotr.*

Diamond, الماس *almas.*

Dice, طاس *tas.*

Dictionary, کتاب لغت *ketabe loɣat,* فرهنگ *farhang.*

Die, to, مردن *mordan,* وفات یافتن *vafat yaftan,* فوت کردن *fout k.*

Difference, فرق *farq,* تفاوت *tafavot,* توفیر *toufir,* اختلاف *extelaf;* to make a difference, فرق (تفاوت, توفیر, اختلاف) کردن *farq (tafavot, toufir extelaf) k.*

Different, مختلف *moxtalef,* متفاوت *motafavet,* متفرق *motafarreq.*

Difficult, مشکل *moskel,* دشوار *dosvar,* سخت *saxt,* صعب *sa'b.*

Difficulty, اشکال *eskal,* دشواری *dosvari,* سختی *saxti,* صعوبت *so'ubat;* to put difficulties (in the way of someone), اشکالتراشی کردن *eskaltarasi k.*

Diffidence, کمروئی *kamrui.*

Diffident, کمرو *kamru.*

Diffuse, to, پخش کردن *paxs k.,* منتشر کردن *montaser k.*

Diffusion, پخش *paxs,* انتشار *entesar.*

Dig, to, کندن *kandan,* بیل زدن *bil zadan.*

Digest, to, هضم کردن *hazm k.*

Digestion, هضم *hazm;* (=digestive faculty), هاضمه *hazeme.*

Dignified, متین *matin,* سنگین *sangin,* موقر *movaqqar,* وزین *vazin,* باوزن *bavazn*

Dignity, متانت *matanat,* وقار *vaqar;* شأن *sa'n.*

Diligence, اهتمام *ehtemam.*

Dimension, اندازه *andaze.*

Dinner (=supper), شام *sam;* (=lunch), نهار *nahar.*

Diploma, تصدیق نامه *tasdiqname,* دیپلوم *diploum;* (=decree), منشور *mansur,* سند *sanad.*

Diplomacy, امور سیاسی *omure siasi,* سیاست *siasat.*

Diplomatic, سیاسی *siasi*.

Direct, مستقیم *mostaqim*; to direct (=administer), اداره کردن *edare k.*;
(=to show the way), راهرا نشان دادن *rahra nefan dadan*.

Direction (=side), طرف *taraf*, سمت *samt*, جانب *janeb*; (=guidance),
راهنمائی *rahnamai*, هدایت *hedayat*; (=management), ریاست *riasat*.

Director, مدیر *modir*, رئیس *ra'is*.

Dirt, dirtiness, کثافت *kesafat*, چرکی *cerki*.

Dirty, کثیف *kasif*, چرك *cerk*.

Disagree, to, اختلاف نظر داشتن *extelafe nazar d.*

Disagreeable, ناپسند *napasand*, نامقبول *namaqbul*; (=cross) بدخلق *badxolq*.

Disagreement, اختلاف نظر *extelafe nazar*.

Disappear, to, غائب شدن *ya'eb f.*, ناپدید شدن *napadid f.*; (=come to an
end), از بین رفتن *az bein raftan*.

Disarm, to, خلع سلاح کردن *xal'e selah k.*

Disaster (=defeat), شکست فجیع *fekaste faji'*; see also Calamity.

Disband, to, منحل کردن *monhall k.*

Discern, to, دریافت کردن *daryaft k.*, فهمیدن *fahmidan*; (=to see),
مشاهده کردن *mofahede k.*

Discerning (adj.), با تمیز *batamiz*, با فراست *bafarasat*.

Discernment, تمیز *tamiz*, فراست *farasat*, بصیرت *basirat*.

Discharge, to, اخراج کردن *exraj k.*, معزول کردن *ma'zul k.*, بیرون کردن
birun k.; (a gun), در کردن *dar k.*, خالی کردن *xali k.*

Disciple, مرید *morid*, شاگرد *fagerd*; (of Christ), حواری *havari*.

Discipline, انتظام *entezam*, نظم *nazm*, انتظامات *entezamat*.

Disconnect, to, قطع کردن *qat' k.*

Discord, تفرقه *tafreqe*; to cause discord (in a group of people, etc.),
تفرقه انداختن *tafreqe andaxtan*.

Discordant, ناساز *nasaz*.

Discover, to, کشف کردن *kaff k.*, پیدا کردن *peida k.*

Discoverer, کشف کننده *kaff konande*.

Discovery, کشف *kaff*.

Discretion: age of discretion, سن بلوغ *senne boluy*.

Discuss, to, مذاکره کردن *mozakere k.*, بحث کردن *bahs k.*

Discussion, مذاکره *mozakere*, بحث *bahs*.

Disease, see Illness.

Disgrace, ننگ nang, رسوائی rosvai.

Disgust, نفرت nefrat, تنفر tanaffor, بيزاری bizari.

Dish, ظرف zarf, دوری duri; (=food), غذا yaza, خوراك xorak.

Dishonest, ناصالح nasaleh, نادرست nadorost, متقلب motaqalleb.

Dishonesty, نادرستی nadorosti, تقلب taqallob.

Disinfectant (adj.), ضد عفونی zedde ofuni, گندزدا gandzada.

Disinfection, گندزدائی gandzadai.

Dislocated, to become (of a limb), در رفتن dar raftan, جابجا شدن ja be ja ſ.

Dismiss, to, see Discharge.

Disobedience, نافرمانی nafarmani, سرکشی sarkaſi.

Disobey, to, نافرمانی کردن nafarmani k., سرکشی کردن sarkaſi k.

Disorder, شلوق ſoluq, بی نظمی binazmi; (violent disorder), اغتشاش eyteſaſ.

Displease, to, ناراضی کردن narazi k., رنجانيدن ranjanidan.

Dispense: to dispense with, صرف نظر کردن (از) sarfe nazar k. (az).

Disperse (trans.), to, متفرق کردن motafarreq k., پراكنده کردن parakande k.; (intrans.), متفرق (پراكنده) شدن motafarreq (parakande) ſ.

Disposal: to be at (one's) disposal, در اختيار بودن dar exteyar b.

Disposition, مزاج mezaj, طبعيت tab'iyat, اخلاق axlaq.

Dispute, منازعه monaze'e, دعوی da'va; to dispute, منازعه کردن monaze'e k., دعوی کردن da'va k.

Disquiet, آشفتگی aſoftegi.

Disrespect, بی احترامی biehterami.

Dissect, to, تشريح کردن taſrih k.

Dissection, تشريح taſrih.

Dissipate, to, پراكنده کردن parakande k., از هم پاشيدن az ham paſidan; (funds, etc.), بر باد دادن bar bad dadan.

Dissolve, to (trans.), منحل کردن monhall k.; (intrans.), حل شدن hall ſ.

Dissolved, منحل monhall.

Dissuade, to, منحرف ساختن monharef saxtan, بر گردانيدن bar gardanidan.

Distance, فاصله fasele; (=remoteness), دوری duri; it is a distance of 10 farsax from here, ده فرسخی اينجاست dah farsaxiye injast; what is the distance from here? از اينجا چقدر راه است az inja ce qadr rah ast.

Distant, دور dur, بعيد ba'id.

Distasteful, ناگوار nagavar.

Distil, to (spirits), عرق گرفتن araq gereftan.

Distinguish, to, تشخیص دادن *taʃxis dadan.*

Distinguished, برجسته *barjaste.*

Distracted, حیران *heïran,* سر گردان *sargardan,* برآشفته *baraʃofte.*

Distress, پریشانی *pariʃani,* اضطراب *eʒterab.*

Distressed, پریشان *pariʃan,* مضطرب *moʒtareb.*

Distribute, to, تقسیم کردن *taqsim k.,* پخش کردن *paxʃ k.*

Distribution, پخش *paxʃ,* تقسیم *taqsim.*

District, ناحیه *nahie,* محل *mahall.*

Disturb, to (=to agitate), برآشفتن *bar aʃoftan;* (=to disorder), مختل کردن *moxtall k.,* بر هم زدن *bar ham ʒadan.*

Disturbance, شلوق *ʃoluq,* اغتشاش *eɣteʃaʃ,* فتنه *fetne.*

Ditch, خندق *xandaq.*

Dive, غوطه کردن *ɣute;* شیرجه *ʃirje,* غوطه; to dive, شیرجه رفتن *ʃirje raftan,* غوطه *ɣute k.*

Divert, to (=to turn aside), بر گردانیدن *bar gardanidan,* منحرف کردن *monharef k.*

Divide, to, قسمت کردن *qesmat k.,* تقسیم کردن *taqsim k.*

Divine, الهی *elahi.*

Division, تقسیم *taqsim;* (of an army), لشکر *laʃkar;* (=department), شعبه *ʃo'be.*

Divisional Commander, سرلشکر *sarlaʃkar.*

Divorce, طلاق *talaq;* to divorce, طلاق دادن *talaq dadan.*

Divulge, to, فاش کردن *faʃ k.*

Dizzy, گیج *gij.*

Dizziness, گیجی *giji.*

Do, to, کردن *kardan.*

Doctor, طبیب *tabib,* پزشک *peʒeʃk,* حکیم *hakim;* doctor not qualified by examination, طبیب مجاز *tabibe mojaʒ.*

Document, سند *sanad.*

Dodge, to (=to avoid doing something), (رفتن) طفره زدن *tafre ʒaaan (raftan),* از زیر بار در رفتن *aʒ ʒire bar dar raftan.*

Dog, سگ *sag.*

Doll, عروسک *arusak.*

Dome, گنبد *gombad.*

Dominant, مسلط *mosallat;* (=predominant), حکمفرما *hokmfarma.*

Dominion, see Power and Government; (= part of an empire), مستملکه
mostamlake.

Donkey, خر xar, الاغ olaɣ.

Door, در dar.

Doorkeeper, دربان darban.

Dossier, پرونده parvande.

Dot, نقطه noqte.

Double, دولا dola; مضاعف moʐaʿaf.

Double-faced, دو رو doru.

Doubt, شبهه ʃobhe, شك ʃakk, تردید tardid; to doubt, (شبهه , شك) تردید
داشتن tardid (ʃakk, ʃobhe) d.

Doubtful (= questionable), مشکوك maʃkuk, مبهم mobham.

Dough, خمیر xamir.

Dove, کبوتر kabutar, کفتر kaftar.

Down (adv.), پائین pain, فرو foru, فرود forud.

Dowry, مهر mahr.

Draft (= plan, outline), شالوده ʃalude, طرح tarh; (of a letter, etc.), سواد
savad; (of money), حواله havale, برات barat.

Dragon, اژدها eʐdeha, اژدر aʐdar.

Drain, گذر آب goʐarab; to drain (land), زه کشیدن ʐeh kaʃidan.

Drainage (of land), زه کشی ʐehkaʃi; (of sewage), دفع فاضل آب dafʿe faʐelab.

Draper, بزاز bazzaʐ; draper's shop, بزازی bazzaʐi.

Draught (medicinal), شربت ʃarbat; (of air), کوران kuran, جریان هوا jariane
hava.

Draughtsman, طراح tarrah.

Draw, to (= pull), کشیدن kaʃidan; (a sword), بیرون کشیدن birun
kaʃidan; (= paint), کشیدن kaʃidan; to draw up (regulations), تنظیم
کردن tanʐim k.; to draw up a plan, نقشه کشیدن naqʃe kaʃidan.

Drawer (of a table), کشو keʃou; (of a cheque), برات کش baratkaʃ.

Drawers, زیر جامه ʐirjame, شلوار ʃalvar.

Dread, see Fear.

Dream, خواب xab; to dream, خواب دیدن xab didan.

Dredge, to, شن کشی کردن ʃenkaʃi k., لاروبی کردن larubi k.

Dredger, شن کش ʃenkaʃ.

Dredging, شن کشی ʃenkaʃi, لا روبی larubi.

Dregs, درد dord.

Drench, to, خیس کردن xis k.

Dress, لباس lebas, رخت raxt, جامه jame; to dress (intrans.), لباس پوشیدن lebas puʃidan, رخت پوشیدن raxt puʃidan; (a wound), بستن bastan; (victuals), حاضر کردن haẓer k.

Dressmaker, خیاط xayyat.

Dressmaking, خیاطی xayyati.

Drill (military), مشق maʃq.

Drill-ground, میدان مشق meidane maʃq.

Drink, مشروب maʃrub; to drink, خوردن xordan, آشامیدن aʃamidan, نوشیدن nuʃidan; to drink to the last drop, سرکشیدن sar kaʃidan.

Drinking-water, آب خوردنی abe xordani.

Drip, چکه ceke; to drip, چکیدن cekidan.

Dripping (fat), پیه pih, چربی carbi.

Drive, to, راندن randan.

Driving (a vehicle), رانندگی ranandegi.

Drizzle, to, نم نم باریدن nam nam baridan.

Drop, قطره qatre.

Drought, خشکی xoʃki, بیابی biabi, خشک سالی xoʃksali.

Drug, دارو daru, دوا dava.

Druggist, see Chemist.

Drum, طبل tabl.

Drunk, مست mast.

Dry, خشک xoʃk.

Dryness, خشکی xoʃki.

Duck, اردك ordak.

Due: to fall due, سر آمدن sar amadan.

Dull (= tedious), خنك xonak, خسته کننده xaste konande.

Dullness (of a market), کساد kasad.

Dumb, لال lal, گنگ gong.

Dung (of cows), سرگین sargin; (of horses), پهن pehen; (of sheep, deer camels, etc.), پشکل peʃkel.

Durability, دوام davam, پایداری paidari.

Durable, با دوام badavam, پایدار paidar.

During (=within the period of), در ظرف *dar ẓarf(e)*; (=in the course of), ضمن *ẓemn(e)*, در ضمن *dar ẓemn(e)*.

Dust, خاك *xak*, گرد *gard*, غبار *ɣobar*; to dust, گردگیری کردن گردگیری *gardgiri k.*

Dustman, رفته گر *roftegar*, سپور *sopur*.

Dusty, خاکی *xaki*.

Dutch, هلندی *holandi*.

Dutiful, وظیفه شناس *vaẓifeʃenas*.

Duty, وظیفه *vaẓife*; (=task), تکلیف *taklif*; to be on duty, کشیك داشتن *kaʃik d.*

Dwarf, کوتوله *kutule*.

Dwell, to, سکونت کردن *sokunat k.*

Dweller, ساکن *saken*.

Dwelling, سکونت *sokunat*.

Dye, رنگ *rang*; to dye, رنگ کردن (زدن) *rang k. (ẓadan)*.

Dyer, رنگرز *rangraẓ*.

Dyeing, رنگرزی *rangraẓi*.

Dynasty, سلسله *selsele*.

E

Each, هر یکی *har yaki*; each other, یك دیگر *yak digar*, هم دیگر *ham digar*

Eagle, عقاب *oqab*.

Ear, گوش *guʃ*.

Early, زود *ẓud*; early morning, سحر *sahar*; an early riser, سحر خیز *saharxiẓ*; you are (=have come) early, زود آمدید *ẓud amadid*.

Earn, to, کسب کردن *kasb k.*; (=to be entitled to), مستحق بودن *mostahaqq b.*

Earnest: in earnest, جدی *jeddi*.

Earnestness, جدیت *jeddiyat*.

Earnings, کسب *kasb*.

Ear-ring, گوشواره *guʃvare*.

Earth, زمین *ẓamin*; (=soil), خاك *xak*.

Earthquake, زلزله *ẓelẓele*.

Ease (=facility), آسانی *asani*, سهولت *sohulat*; (=repose), آسایش *asayeʃ*.

Easily, بآسانی *be asani*.

East, مشرق *mafreq*, شرق *farq*, خاور *xavar*; the East, مشرق زمين *mafreqʒamin*.

Eastern, شرق *farqi*, خاورى *xavari*.

Easterner, شرق *farqi*, اهل مشرق زمين *ahle mafreqʒamin*.

Easy, آسان *asan*, سهل *sahl*.

Eat, to, خوردن *xordan*.

Eclipse (of the sun), كسوف *kosuf*; (of the moon), خسوف *xosuf*.

Economic, اقتصادى *eqtesadi*.

Economical (of a thing), با صرفه *basarfe*; (of a person), صرفه جو *sarfeju*.

Economize, to, صرفه جوئى كردن *sarfejui k.*

Economy, اقتصاد *eqtesad*; (= care in expenditure), صرفه جوئى *sarfejui*.

Edge, لبه *labe*.

Edible, خوردنى *xordani*.

Edifice, ساختمان *saxteman*, عمارت *emarat*.

Edit, to (a book), تصحيح كردن *tashih k.*

Editor (of a newspaper), مدير روزنامه *modire ruzname*; (of a book), تصحيح كننده *tashih konande*.

Educate, to, پرورش دادن *parvaref dadan*, تربيت كردن *tarbiat k.*

Educated, درس خوانده *dars xande*, تربيت شده *tarbiat fode*.

Education, تعليم و تربيت *ta'lim o tarbiat*, آموزش و پرورش *amuʒef va parvaref*; Ministry of Education, وزارت فرهنگ *veʒarate farhang*, وزارت معارف *veʒarate ma'aref*.

Educational, فرهنگى *farhangi*, معارفى *ma'arefi*.

Effect, تأثير *ta'sir*, اثر *asar*; (= result), نتيجه *natije*; to this effect, از اين قرار *aʒ in qarar*.

Effective, مؤثر *mo'asser*.

Effort, كوشش *kufef*, سعى *sai*, تلاش *talaf*, جد و جهد *jedd o jahd*; to make an effort, تلاش كردن *talaf k.*, كوشش كردن *kufef k.*, كوشيدن *kufidan*, سعى كردن *sai k.*, جد و جهد كردن *jedd o jahd k.*

Egg, تخم *toxm*; (hen's egg), تخم مرغ *toxme morγ*.

Egg-plant, بادنجان *badenjan*.

Egypt, مصر *mesr*.

Egyptian, مصرى *mesri*.

Eight, هشت *haft*.

Eighteen, هيجده *hijdah, hejdah*.

Eighty, هشتاد *haftad*.

Either (of two or more), هر کدام *har kodam*; either...or, یا...یا *ya...ya*

Eject, to, see Turn.

Elastic (noun), کش *keʃ*; (adj.), کشدار *keʃdar*.

Elasticity, کشش *keʃeʃ*, کش *keʃ*.

Elder (subs.), ریش سفید *riʃsefid*.

Elect, to, بر گزیدن *bar goʒidan*, انتخاب کردن *entexab k.*

Election, انتخاب *entexab*; (political), انتخابات *entexabat*.

Electric, برق *barqi*.

Electricity, برق *barq*.

Elegance, لطافت *letafat*, ظرافت *ʒerafat*.

Elegant, لطیف *latif*, ظریف *ʒarif*.

Element, عنصر *onsor*.

Elementary, ابتدائی *ebtedai*.

Elephant, فیل *fil*.

Eleven, یازده *yaʒdah*.

Eliminate, to, حذف کردن *haʒf k.*

Elimination, حذف *haʒf*; (= turning out), استخراج *estexraj*.

Elm-tree, نارون *narvan*.

Eloquence, فصاحت *fasahat*, بلاغت *balaɣat*.

Eloquent, فصیح *fasih*, بلیغ *baliɣ*.

Emanate, to, صادر شدن *sader ʃ.*, ظهور کردن *ʒohur k.*

Emanation, صدور *sodur*, ظهور *ʒohur*.

Embark, to (on a ship), سوار (کشتی) شدن *savar(e kaʃti) ʃ.*

Embarrass, to, دست پاچه کردن *dastpace k.*, ناراحت کردن *narahat k.*

Embarrassment, دست پاچگی *dastpacegi*; to be an embarrassment (to someone), مزاحم بودن *moʒahem b.*

Embassy, سفارت *sefarat*; سفارت کبری *sefarate kobra*.

Embezzle, to, اختلاس کردن *extelas k.*

Embezzlement, اختلاس *extelas*.

Emblem, نشان *neʃan*, علامت *alamat*.

Embrace, to, در بغل گرفتن *dar baɣal gereftan*, بغل کردن *baɣal k.*, در بر گرفتن *dar bar gereftan*, در آغوش گرفتن *dar aɣuʃ gereftan*.

Embryo, رویان *ruyan*.

Embryologist, رویان شناس *ruyanʃenas*.

Embryology, رویان شناسی *ruyanʃenasi*.

Emerald, زمرد *ɀomorrod.*

Emergency, حالت غیرعادی *halate ɣeire adi*; in case of emergency, در موقع ضرورت *dar mouqe'e ɀarurat.*

Emery, سنباده *sombade.*

Emigrant, مهاجر *mohajer.*

Emigrate, to, مهاجرت کردن *mohajerat k.*

Emigration, مهاجرت *mohajerat.*

Eminent, برجسته *barjaste*, محترم *mohtaram*, مشهور *maʃhur.*

Emotion, احساسات *ehsasat*; (=agitation), هیجانی *hayajani.*

Emotional, احساساتی *ehsasati.*

Emphasis, تأکید *ta'kid.*

Emphasize, to, تأکید کردن *ta'kid k.*

Empire, امپراطوری *emperaturi*; (=rule), سلطنت *saltanat*, سلطه *salte.*

Employ, to, استخدام کردن *estexdam k.*; (=to use), ستعمال کردن *este'mal k.*, بکار بردن *be kar bordan.*

Employee, مستخدم *mostaxdem.*

Employer, کارفرما *karfarma.*

Employment, کار *kar*, شغل *ʃoɣl.*

Empty, خالی *xali*, تهی *tohi*; (=idle), پوچ *puc.*

Enamel, لعابی *la'abi*; enamel-work, میناکاری *minakari.*

Enchanter, جادوگر *jadugar*, افسونگر *afsungar.*

Enclose, to (=to surround), احاطه کردن *ehate k.*; (=to transmit as an enclosure), لفًا ارسال داشتن *laffan ersal d.*

Enclosure, محوطه *mohavvate*; (for cattle), آغل *aɣol*; (in a letter), ملفوفه *malfufe*, ضمیمه *ɀamime.*

Encounter, بر خورد *barxord*; to encounter, (به) بر خوردن *bar xordan (be).*

Encourage, to, تشویق کردن *taʃviq k.*

Encouragement, تشویق *taʃviq.*

Encyclopedia, دائرة العلوم *da'erat ol-olum.*

End (point, tip), سر *sar*, نوک *nuk*; (=conclusion), عاقبت *aqebat*, آخر *axer*, پایان *payan*, اتمام *etmam*, انتها *enteha*, ختم *xatm*, خاتمه *xateme*; in the end, آخر الامر *axer ol-amr*, عاقبت الامر *aqebat ol-amr*; to end (intrans.), بـاتـمـام رساندن *be tamam rasandan*, پایان یافتن *payan yaftan*; (trans.), تمام شدن *tamam ʃ.*, اتمام رساندن *etmam rasandan*, تمام کردن *tamam k.*, خاتمه دادن *xateme dadan*; to come to an end (=pass away), سپری شدن *separi ʃ.*

Endeavour, see Effort.

Endemic, متداول *motadavel*; (of diseases) ساریه *sarie*.

Endorse, to (a cheque, etc.), پشت نویس کردن *poſtnevis k.*

Endorsement (of a cheque, etc.), پشت نویسی *poſtnevisi*.

Endowment (=bequest), وقف *vaqf*, موقوفه *mouqufe*.

Endurance (=strength), طاقت *taqat*; (=toleration), تحمل *tahammol*.

Endure, to, طاقت کردن *taqat k.*; تحمل کردن *tahammol k.*

Enema, اماله *emale*.

Enemy, دشمن *doſman*, عدو *adu*.

Energetic, جدی *jeddi*, فعال *fa''al*.

Energy, جدیت *jeddiyat*, فعالیت *fa'aliyat*.

Engage, to (=to take into employment), استخدام کردن *estexdam k.*; (to do something), بر عهده گرفتن *bar ohde gereſtan*; to be engaged (=to be affianced) نامزد شدن *namʒad ſ.*; (=to be busy), مشغول بودن *maſɣul b.*

Engagement (taking into employment), استخدام *estexdam*; (=undertaking), عهده *ohde*; (=appointment), وعد *va'de*.

Engineer, مهندس *mohandes*.

Engine, ماشین *maſin*.

Engineering, مهندسی *mohandesi*.

England, انگلستان *englestan*, انگلیس *englis*.

English, انگلیسی *englisi*.

Enigma, معما *mo'amma*.

Enjoy, to, لذت بردن *lezzat bordan*, کیف کردن *keif k.*, حظ کردن *hazz k.*, متمتع شدن *motamatte' ſ.*; خوش گذشتن *xoſ goʒaſtan* (used impersonally) I enjoyed myself, بمن خوش گذشت *be man xoſ goʒaſt*.

Enjoyment, لذت *lezzat*, حظ *hazz*, کیف *keif*, تمتع *tamatto'*.

Enmity, دشمنی *doſmani*, عداوت *adavat*.

Enormous, عظیم *aʒim*.

Enough, بس *bas*, کافی *kafi*.

Enquiry, پرسش *porseſ*; (=investigation), تفتیش *taftiſ*, باز رسی *baʒrasi*, استنطاق *estentaq*, رسیدگی *rasidegi*, باز جوئی *baʒjui*.

Enter, to (intrans.), داخل شدن *daxel ſ.*, وارد شدن *vared ſ.*

Entertain, to, پذیرائی کردن *paʒirai k.*

Entertainment, مهمانی *mehmani*, پذیرائی *paʒirai*.

Entire, کامل *kamel*, تمام *tamam*, تام *tamm*.

Entrance, ورود *vorud,* دخول *doxul.*

Entrust, to, سپردن *sepordan.*

Envelope, پاکت *pakat.*

Envious, حسود *hasud.*

Environs, حوالی *havali,* نواحی *navahi,* اطراف *atraf.*

Envy, حسد *hasad.*

Equal, برابر *barabar,* مساوی *mosavi,* نظیر *naẓir.*

Equality, برابری *barabari,* مساوات *mosavat.*

Equator, the, خط استوا *xatte esteva.*

Equilibrium, موازنه *movaẓene.*

Equip, to, تجهیز کردن *tajhiẓ k.*

Equipped, مجهز *mojahhaẓ.*

Equipment, ساز و برگ *saẓ o barg,* یراق *yaraq.*

Equity, see Justice.

Era, عصر *asr,* دوره *dōure.*

Erase, to, محو کردن *mahv k.*

Erect, راست *rast.*

Ermine, قاقم *qaqom.*

Errata: list of errata, غلط نامه *ɣalatname.*

Error, اشتباه *eʃtebah,* غلط *ɣalat,* خطا *xata,* سهو *sahv,* خبط *xabt*; to make an error, اشتباه (خطا،غلط،سهو،خبط) کردن *eʃtebah (xata, ɣalat, xabt, sahv) k.*

Escape, خلاص *xalas,* نجات *najat,* رها *raha*; to escape, رستن *rastan,* نجات (خلاص، رها) یافتن *nejat (xalas, raha) yaftan.*

Especially, علی الخصوص *alal-xosus,* مخصوصًا *maxsusan,* خصوصًا *xosusan,* خاصه *xasse.*

Essence, عین *ein,* ذات *ẓat,* جوهر *jōuhar,* خلاصه *xolase,* عرق *araq.*

Essential, اساسی *asasi,* اصلی *asli.*

Essentially, اساسًا *asasan,* اصلاً *aslan.*

Establish, to, بر قرار کردن *bar qarar k.*; (a claim, etc.), اثبات کردن *esbat k.*

Established, مقرر *moqarrar.*

Establishment, دستگاه *dastgah*; (=firm), مؤسسه *mo'assese.*

Esteem, احترام *ehteram,* اخلاص *exlas*; to esteem, احترام گذاشتن (به) *ehteram goẓaʃtan (be).*

Estimate, بر آورد *baravard,* تخمین *taxmin,* اندازه *andaẓe*; to estimate, بر آورد کردن *baravard k.,* سنجیدن *sanjidan.*

Et cetera, وغيره va ɣeïre.

Eternal, جاويدان javidan, ابدى abadi, ازلى aʒali.

Eternally, الى الابد elal-abad, ابدى abadi.

Eternity (without beginning), ازل aʒal; (without end), ابد abad.

Ethical, اخلاق axlaqi.

Ethics, اخلاق axlaq.

Ethnologist, نژاد شناس neʒadʃenas.

Ethnology, نژاد شناسى neʒadʃenasi.

Eunuch, خواجه xaje, آغا aɣa.

Europe, اروپا orupa, فرنگ farang, فرنگستان farangestan.

European, اروپائى orupai, فرنگى farangi.

Evacuate, to, تخليه كردن taxlie k.

Evacuation, تخليه taxlie.

Evade, to (doing something), (رفتن) طفره زدن tafre ʒadan (raftan).

Evaluate, to, تقويم زدن taqvim ʒadan, بر آورد كردن baravard k.

Evaluation, تقويم taqvim, بر آورد baravard.

Evaporate, to (intrans.), تبخير شدن tabxir ʃ.

Evaporation, تبخير tabxir.

Evasive, طفره آميز tafreamiʒ.

Evasion, طفره tafre, گريز goriʒ; (=pretence), بهانه bahane.

Eve, شب ʃab.

Even, حتى hatta; (of numbers), جفت joft; (level), هموار hamvar; and even if, و لو اينكه va lou inke.

Evening, شب ʃab.

Event, واقعه vaqe'e, حادثه hadese, پيش آمد piʃamad, اتفاق ettefaq.

Ever, هرگز hargeʒ, هيچ وقت hic vaqt, گاهى gahi, اصلاً aslan; for ever, هميشه hamiʃe, الى الابد elal-abad.

Every, هر har.

Everyone, همه hame; هركس har kas.

Everywhere, هرجا harja, همه جا hameja.

Evidence (=witness), شهادت ʃahadat, گواهى gavahi; (=proof), دليل dalil, مدرك madrak.

Evident, ظاهر ʒaher, معلوم ma'lum.

Evidently, ظاهراً ʒaheran, معلوم از قرار aʒ qarare ma'lum.

Evil, شرّ *ʃarr*; (adj.), شرير *ʃarir*; to speak evil (of), بدگوئی کردن (از) *badgui k.* (*aʒ*).

Ewe, میش *miʃ*.

Ewer, آفتابه *aftabe*.

Exact, درست *dorost*, صحیح *sahih*, کامل *kamel*.

Exactitude, درستی *dorosti*, صحّت *sehhat*.

Exactly, عیناً *einan*; exactly like, عینه *einahu*.

Exaggerate, to, اغراق کردن *eɣraq k.*, مبالغه کردن *mobaleɣe k.*

Exaggeration, اغراق *eɣraq*, مبالغه *mobaleɣe*.

Exalt, to, سرافراز کردن *sarafraʒ k.*; (=lift up), بر افراشتن *bar afraʃtan*.

Exalted (=honoured), عالی *ali*, سرافراز *sarafraʒ*.

Examination, باز رسی *baʒrasi*, تفتیش *taftiʃ*, باز دید *baʒdid*; (=search), تجسّس *tajassos*, تفحّص *tafahhos*; (=test), امتحان *emtehan*, معاینه *mo'ayene*; (=school examination, etc.), امتحان *emtehan*.

Examine, to, تفتیش کردن *taftiʃ k.*, باز رسی کردن *baʒrasi k.*; (=to test), امتحان کردن *emtehan k.*, معاینه کردن *mo'ayene k.*; (at a school, etc.), امتحان کردن *emtehan k.*; to sit for an examination, امتحان دادن *emtehan dadan*.

Examiner, ممتحن *momtahen*; see also Inspector.

Example, نمونه *namune*, مثال *mesal*; for example, مثلاً *masalan*.

Excavate, to, حفر کردن *hafr k.*

Excavation, حفریات *hafriat*.

Exceed, to, تجاوز کردن (بر) *tajavoʒ k.* (*bar*); to exceed the limit, از حد گذشتن *aʒ hadd goʒaʃtan*.

Exceeding, متجاوز *motajaveʒ*.

Exceedingly, بنهایت *be nehayat*, بغایت *be ɣayat*.

Excel, to, برتری داشتن *bartari d.*

Excellence, خوبی *xubi*, فضیلت *faʒilat*.

Excellency, جناب *janab*, حضرت *haʒrat*.

Excellent, عالی *ali*, خوب *xub* فوق العاده *fouq ol-ade xub*.

Except, سوا(ی) *seva(ye)*, جز *joʒ*, بجز *bejoʒ*, غیر *ɣeir(e)*, غیر از *ɣeir aʒ*: مگر *magar*, الا *ella*.

Exception, استثنا *estesna*.

Excess, افراط *efrat*, مازاد *ma ʒad*, زیاده *ʒiade*, زیادی *ʒiadi*.

Excessive, از حد گذشته *aʒ hadd goʒaʃte*.

Exchange, تبدیل *tabdil,* مبادله *mobadele,* عوض *avaʒ*; (=rate of exchange), نرخ *nerx*; foreign exchange, ارز *arʒ*; to exchange, (عوض, مبادله) تبدیل کردن *tabdil* (*avaʒ, mobadele*) *k.*

Excite, to, بر انگیختن *bar angixtan.*

Excitement, هیجان *hayajan.*

Exciting, مهیج *mohaɩyej.*

Excrement, گه *goh,* فضله *faʒle.*

Excursion, گردش *gardeʃ*; to make an excursion, گردش رفتن *gardeʃ raftan.*

Excuse, عذر *oʒr,* معذرت *ma'ʒarat,* پوزش *puʒeʃ*; (=pretext), بهانه *bahane.*

Excuse, to, (معذرت) عذر بخشیدن *baxʃidan*; to ask to be excused, (معذرت) عذر خواستن *oʒr* (*ma'ʒarat*) *xastan*; to make an excuse, بهانه در آوردن *bahane dar avardan.*

Excused, معذور *ma'ʒur.*

Execute, to, سر بریدن *sar boridan,* اعدام کردن *e'dam k.*; (=put into practice), اجرا کردن *ejra k.*

Execution, اعدام *e'dam*; (=putting into practice), اجرا *ejra.*

Executioner, میر غضب *mirʒaʒab,* جلاد *jallad.*

Executive, اجرائی *ejrai,* مجری *mojri,* اداری *edari*; the Executive, قوه مجریه *qovveye mojrie*; executive committee, هیئت مدیره *heï'ate modire,* هیئت مجریه *heï'ate mojrie.*

Executor, مجری *mojri*; (of a will), وصی *vasi.*

Exempt, معاف *mo'af*; to exempt, معاف کردن *mo'af k.*

Exequatur, روا نامه *ravaname.*

Exercise, تمرین *tamrin*; (physical), ورزش *varʒeʃ*; to take exercise, ورزش کردن *varʒeʃ k.*

Exercise-book, دفتر *daftar.*

Exert, to (force, etc.), اعمال کردن *e'mal k.*; to exert oneself, کوشیدن *kuʃidan.*

Exertion, see Effort.

Exhausted (=fatigued), هلاك *halak.*

Exhaustion, در ماندگی *darmandegi*; فرسودگی *farsudegi.*

Exigency, اقتضا *eqteʒa.*

Exigent, مقتضی *moqtaʒi.*

Exile, تبعید *tab'id*; to exile, تبعید کردن *tab'id k.*

Existence, وجود vojud, هستی hasti; to bring into existence, بوجود آوردن be vojud avardan.

Existing, موجود mōujud.

Exit, خروج xoruj, مخرج maxraj.

Exonerate, to, تبرئه کردن tabre'e k.

Exoneration, تبرئه tabre'e.

Expand, to (intrans.), توسعه یافتن tōuse'e yaftan; (trans.), توسعه دادن tōuse'e dadan.

Expanse, فضا faẓa.

Expansion, توسعه tōuse'e.

Expect, to, انتظار کشیدن enteẓar kaʃidan; expectation, انتظار enteẓar.

Expedient, صلاح salah.

Expel, to, اخراج کردن exraj k., بیرون کردن birun k.

Expend, to, خرج کردن xarj k., صرف کردن sarf k.

Expenditure, خرج xarj.

Expensive, گران geran.

Experience, تجربه tajrebe.

Experienced, مجرب mojarrab, کار آزموده karaẓmude.

Experiment, آزمایش aẓmayeʃ; to experiment, آزمایش کردن aẓmayeʃ k.

Expert, متخصص motaxasses, خبره xebre.

Expiration, انقضا enqeẓa.

Expire, to (=to come to an end), منقضی شدن monqaẓi ʃ.

Explain, to, توضیح کردن (دادن) بیان کردن bayan k., شرح کردن ʃarh k., تۆضیح k. (dadan), تفسیر کردن tafsir k.

Explanation, بیان bayan, شرح ʃarh, تعبیر ta'bir, تفسیر tafsir, توضیح tōuzih.

Explode, to (intrans.) انفجار یافتن enfejar yaftan; (trans.), منفجر کردن monfajer k.

Explosion, انفجار enfejar.

Exploit, to, استثمار کردن estesmar k.

Exploitation, استثمار estesmar.

Export, to, صادر کردن sader k.; exports, صادرات saderat.

Expose, to (to), در معرض....نهادن dar ma'raẓ(e)...nehadan; (an abuse, etc.), پرده بر داشتن (از) parde bar d. (aẓ).

Express (of a train, etc.), سریع السیر sari' os-seīr; to express (=to state), اظهار کردن eẓhar k.

Expression, اظهار *ezhar*; (=idiom), اصطلاح *estelah*; (=facial expression), قيافه *qiafe*.

Expropriation, خلع يد *xal'e yad*.

Expurgation, تنقيح *tanqih*, تصفيه *tasfie*.

Extension, توسعه *touse'e*, امتداد *emtedad*.

Extent, وسعت *vos'at*; (=size), اندازه *andaze*.

Exterior (subs.), بيرون *birun*; (adj.), بيرونى *biruni*, خارجى *xareji*.

Exterminate, to, استيصال كردن *estisal k.*

Extermination, استيصال *estisal*.

External, خارج *xarej*; external affairs, امور خارجه *omure xareje*.

Extinguish, to, خاموش كردن *xamuʃ k.*

Extort, to, اجحاف كردن *ejhaf k.*

Extortion, اجحاف *ejhaf*.

Extra (=in excess), اضافى *ezafi*; (=superfluous) زائد *za'ed*; (=out of the ordinary), فوق العاده *fouq ol-ade*.

Extravagance, ولخرجى *velxarji*, اصراف *esraf*.

Extravagant, ولخرج *velxarj*.

Extreme (subs.), نهايت *nehayat*, غايت *yayat*.

Extremely, بنهايت *be nehayat*, بغايت *be yayat*.

Extremist, افراطى *efrati*.

Extremity, انتها *enteha*, غايت *yayat*, نهايت *nehayat*.

Exudation, تراوش *taravoʃ*.

Eye, چشم *caʃm, ceʃm*, ديده *dide*; eyebrow, ابرو *abru*.

F

Fable, افسانه *afsane*.

Face, رو *ru*, صورت *surat*, چهره *cehre*; to face, (با) رو برو بودن *ru be ru b.* (*ba*), to be faced with, (با) مواجه شدن *movajeh ʃ.* (*ba*).

Facilitate, to, تسهيل كردن *tashil k.*; facilities, تسهيلات *tashilat*; to provide facilities, وسايل فراهم كردن *vasa'el faraham k.*

Facing, (ى) رو برو(ى) *ru be ru(ye)*, مقابل *moqabel(e)*.

Faction (=associates), دسته *daste*, دار و دسته *dar o daste*.

Factor, عامل *amel*.

Factory, كارخانه *karxane*.

Fade, to, پژمردن pezmordan, خشك شدن xofk f.; this stuff has faded, این پارچه رنگش رفته است in parce rangef rafte ast.

Fail, to (=not to succeed), موفق نشدن movaffaq nafodan; (in an exam.), رفوزه شدن refuze f.

Failure, عدم موفقیت adame movaffaqiyat.

Faint, to, غش کردن gaf k., بیهوش شدن bihuf f.; see also Feeble.

Fair (of hair), بور bur; (of complexion), سفید sefid; (of wind), موافق movafeq; (=just), منصف monsef; the fair sex, جنس لطیف jense latif.

Fairy, پری pari.

Fairylike, پریوش parivaf.

Faith (=religion), مذهب mazhab, دین din; کیش kif (the last is not applied to Islam); (=belief), ایمان iman, اعتقاد e'teqad, اعتماد e'temad.

Faithful, با وفا bavafa, وفادار vafadar.

Faithfulness, صداقت sadaqat, وفا vafa, وفاداری vafadari.

Faithless, بی وفا bivafa.

Faithlessness, بی وفائی bivafai.

Falcon, باز baz, قوش quf.

Fall, افتادن part f., سقوط soqut; to fall, سقوط کردن soqut k., پرت شدن oftadan; to fall down, زمین خوردن zamin xordan; to fall back or behind, عقب افتادن aqab oftadan; (of prices), تنزل کردن tanazzol k.; they have fallen out, میانهاشان بهم خورد mianeyefan be ham xord.

Fallow (of land), آیش ayef, ناکاشته nakafte; (of land left fallow in alternate years), کار مکار kar makar.

False, دروغی doruyi, دغل dayal, قلبی qalbi; (=knavish), مکار makkar, حیلهباز hilebaz, خائن xa'en; (of coin), قلابی qollabi, قلبی qalbi.

Falsehood, دروغ doruy, کذب kezb.

Falsification, تقلبی taqallobi, دغل dayal.

Fame, شهرت fohrat, نام nam.

Familiar (=intimate), مأنوس ma'nus; (=acquainted), آشنا afna.

Familiarity (=intimacy), الفت olfat, انس ons; (=acquaintance), آشنائی afnai.

Family, خانواده xanevade, فامیل famil; (=descendants of a common ancestor), خاندان xandan, قوم qoum, آل al, دودمان dudman; of good family, نجیب najib, اصیل asil.

Famine, قطی qahti, غلاء yela.

Famous, نامدار namdar, معروف ma'ruf, مشهور maʃhur.

Fan, بادبزن bad beӡan.

Fanatic, متعصب mota'asseb.

Fanaticism, تعصب ta'assob.

Fancy, گمان gaman, خيال xial; to fancy, (بردن) گمان کردن gaman k. (bordan), خيال کردن xial k.

Far, دور dur, بعید ba'id, دور دست durdast.

Fare, کرایه keraye; see also Food.

Farmer (= peasant), دهقان dehqan; (=one who rents land), مستأجر mosta'jer; (=landowner), مالك malek.

Farming, زراعت ӡera'at; dry farming, زراعت دیمی ӡera'ate deīmi; irrigated farming, زراعت آبی ӡera'ate abi.

Farrier, نعلبند na'lband.

Farseeing, پیشبین piʃbin.

Farsightedness, پیشبینی piʃbini.

Fast (=quick), تند tond, سریع sari'; (of a watch), تند tond, جلو jelou; see also Firm; (=abstinence), روزه ruӡe; to fast, روزه گرفتن ruӡe gereftan; to break the fast at sunset in the month of Ramazan, افطار کردن eftar k.

Fasting (adj.), روزەدار ruӡedar.

Fat, پیه pih, چربی carbi; (adj.), فربه farbe, چاق caq; (=greasy), چرب carb.

Fatal, مهلك mohlek.

Fate, see Destiny.

Father, پدر pedar, والد valed, ابو abu, اب ab, ابوی abavi.

Father-in-law (of wife), پدرشوهر pedarʃouhar; (of husband), پدر زن pedar-ӡan.

Fatigue, خستگی xastegi, درماندگی darmandegi.

Fault, عیب eīb, تقصیر taqsir, خبط xabt, خطا xata; to commit a fault, خطا کردن xata k., خط کردن xabt k.; it is his fault, تقصیر با اوست taqsir ba ust کردن.

Faultless, بی عیب bieīb.

Favour, لطف lotf, التفات eltefat; to show favour, التفات کردن el tefat k. لطف کردن lotf k.; (=to prefer), ترجیح دادن (به) tarjih dadan (be).

Favourite, محبوب mahbub; (=intimate), ندیم nadim.

Fear, خوف haras, هراس tars, بیم bim, باك bak, دهشت dehʃat, هول houl, خوف xouf; to fear, ترسیدن tarsidan, (خوف، هول، دهشت، باك، بیم) ترس tars (bim, bak, dehʃat, houl, haras, xouf) d. داشتن.

Fearful (=fearing), ترسان tarsan, هراسان harasan; (=dreadful), ترسناك tarsnak, بیمناك bimnak, دهشتناك dehſatnak, هولناك hoūinak.

Fearless, بیباك bibak, بیترس bitars.

Feast, ضیافت ziafat, ولیمه valime, سور sur.

Feast-day, عید id, ēid.

Feather, پر par.

Federation, اتحاد ettehad.

Fee, مزد mozd, اجرت ojrat, حق haqq.

Feeble, ضعیف za'if, عاجز ajez.

Feebleness, ضعف za'f, عجز ajz.

Feel, to, حس كردن hess k., احساس كردن ehsas k.; see also Touch.

Feeling, حس hess, احساس ehsas.

Fellow (=one of a pair), لنگه lenge; (of a person, derog.), یارو yaru.

Fellow-countrymen, هم میهنان hammihanan.

Fellow-townsman, هم شهری hamſahri.

Fellow-traveller, هم سفر hamsafar.

Felt, نمد namad.

Female (of gender), مؤنث mo'annas; (=she-), ماده made.

Feminine, مؤنث mo'annas.

Fencing, شمشیر بازی ſamſirbazi.

Fenugreek, شنبلیله ſambelile.

Fermented, مخمر moxammar.

Ferry (place), معبر ma'bar.

Fertile, حاصلخیز haselxiz.

Festival, جشن jaſn.

Fetid, گند gand.

Feudal, ملوك الطوائفی moluk ot-tava'efi; feudal barons, ملوك الطوائف moluk ot-tava'ef.

Fever, تب tab; (=ague), تب و لرز tab o larz; (=intermittent fever), تب و نوبه tab o noūbe.

Few, چند cand.

Fidget, to, ور رفتن var raftan.

Fief, تیول toyul.

Field (cultivated), كشتزار keſtzar; (=meadow), چمن caman.

Field-Marshal, سپهبد sepahbod.

Fifteen, پانزده *panẓdah.*

Fifty, پنجاه *panjah.*

Fig, انجیر *anjir.*

Fight, see Battle; to fight, جنگ کردن *jang k.*

Fighter (aeroplane), هواپیمای شکاری *havapeimaye ʃekari.*

Figure (=form), شکل *ʃekl*; (=body), هیکل *heikal.*

File, سوهان *sōuhan*; (=dossier), پرونده *parvande*; to file, سوهان زدن
sōuhan ẓadan; (=to enter in a dossier), در پرونده نوشتن (گذاشتن) *dar
parvande neveʃtan (goẓaʃtan).*

Filter, صافکن *ʃafkon*; to filter, صاف کردن *ʃaf k.*

Filth, see Dirt.

Fin (of a fish), پر *par,* بال *bal.*

Final (=certain), قطعی *qat'i*; (=last), آخری *axeri,* آخر *axer.*

Finally, آخر الامر *axer ol-amr.*

Finance, امور مالی *omure mali*; Ministry of Finance, وزارت دارائی *veẓarate
darai.*

Financial, مالی *mali.*

Find, to, پیدا کردن *peida k.,* یافتن *yaftan*; (in past tenses only), جستن
jostan; (=to understand), ملتفت شدن *moltafet ʃ.* to find out, تحقیق کردن
tahqiq k.

Fine (=thin), نازك *naẓok*; (of weather), خوب *xub,* مساعد *mosa'ed*;
(=small), ریزه *riẓe*; (=mulct), جریمه *jarime,* مصادره *mosadere*; to fine,
جریمه کردن *jarime k.,* مصادره کردن *mosadere k.*

Finger, انگشت *angoʃt.*

Finger-print, انگشتنگار *angoʃtnegar.*

Finish, to (trans.), تمام کردن *tamam k.*; باتمام رساندن *be etmam rasandan.*

Fir, کاج *kaj,* صنوبر *senōubar.*

Fire, آتش *ateʃ*; to catch fire, آتش گرفتن *ateʃgereftan*; to set fire to, تش زدن
ateʃ ẓadan.

Fire-fighting service, آتش نشانی *ateʃneʃani.*

Fireman, آتش نشان *ateʃneʃan.*

Fireplace, بخاری *boxari.*

Fire-temple, آتش کده *ateʃkade.*

Firewood, هیزم *hiẓom.*

Firework display, آتش بازی *ateʃbaẓi.*

Firm (=company), شركت *ſerkat*; (=fast), محكم *mohkam*, پايدار *paɪdar*, قائم *qa'em*, استوار *ostovar*; (=hard), سفت *seft*.

Firmness, محكمى *mohkami*, پايدارى *paɪdari*, استوارى *ostovari*; (=hardness), سفتى *seftii*.

First, اول *avval*, نخست *naxost*, اولين *avvalin*, نخستين *naxostin*; first fruits of the season, نوبر *noubar*; at first, در ابتدا *dar ebteda*.

Firstly, اولاً *avvalan*.

Fish, ماهى *mahi*.

Fissure, شكاف *ſekaf*.

Fist, مشت *moſt*.

Fit (apoplectic), سكته *sakte*; to have a fit, سكته كردن *sakte k.*; (=suitable), سزاوار *saʒavar*, شايسته *ſayeste*, مناسب *monaseb*; (=trained), ورزيده *varʒide*; (=worthy), لايق *layeq*.

Fitness (=suitability), شايستگى *ſayestegi*; (=worthiness), لياقت *liaqat*.

Fitter (=mechanic), ماشين سواركن *maſinsavarkon*.

Five, پنج *panj*.

Fix, to (=to settle), تعيين كردن *ta'yin k.*, معين كردن *mo'ayyan k.*; (=to put up), نصب كردن *nasb k.*

Fixed, معين *mo'ayyan*; fixed price, قيمت مقطوع *qeɪmate maqtu'*.

Flag, see Banner.

Flame, شعله *ſo'le*.

Flaming (in flames), شعله ور *ſo'levar*, مشتعل *moſta'el*.

Flat, هموار *hamvar*, صاف *saf*; (=apartment), آپارتمان *aparteman*.

Flatter, to, تملق گفتن (كردن) *tamalloq goftan (k.)*.

Flatterer, متملق *motamalleq*, چاپلوس *caplus*.

Flattery, تملق *tamalloq*, چاپلوسى *caplusi*.

Flax, كتان *kattan*, الياف *alyaf*.

Flay, to, پوست كندن *pust kandan*.

Flea, كك *kak*.

Flee, to, فرار كردن *farar k.*, گريختن *gorixtan*.

Fleet (of foot), تيز رو *tiʒrou*; (naval) ناوگان *navgan*.

Flesh, گوشت *guſt*.

Flight, فرار *farar*, گريز *goriʒ*; (of a bird, etc.), پرواز *parvaʒ*; to put to flight, هزيمت دادن *haʒimat dadan*.

Flint, چخماق *caxmaq*.

Flippant, شوخ *ʃux*.

Flock (of cattle or sheep), گله *gɔlle*, رمه *rame*.

Flood, سیل *seil*, سیلاب *seilab*; the Flood, طوفان *tufan*.

Floor, زمین *ʒamin*, کف *kaf*.

Flotilla, ناوتیپ *navtip*.

Flour, آرد *ard*.

Flourish, to, see Prosper.

Flow (of tide), مد *madd*; to flow, جاری شدن *jari ʃ*.

Flower, گل *gol*.

Flower-bed, گلزار *golʒar*.

Flower-garden, گلستان *golestan*.

Flowing, روان *ravan*, جاری *jari*.

Flue, دودکش *dudkaʃ*.

Fluent, روان *ravan*.

Flute, نی *nei*.

Flutter, to (of the heart), طپیدن *tapidan*; (the wings), پر زدن *par ʒadan*.

Fly, مگس *magas*; to fly, پرواز کردن *parvaʒ k*.

Foal, کره *korre*.

Foam, کف *kaf*; to foam, کف کردن *kaf k*.

Fodder, علف *alaf*, علیق *aliq*.

Fog, مه *meh*, غبار *ɣobar*.

Fold, تا *ta*, لا *la*; (for cattle), آغل *aɣol*; to fold, تا کردن *ta k*.

Follow, to (someone's example), پیروی کردن *peirovi k.*; see also Pursue; as follows, از این قرار *aʒ in qarar*, از قرار ذیل *aʒ qarare ʒeil*.

Follower, تابع *tabeʻ*, پیرو *peirou*, مرید *morid*; followers (=attendants), ملازمان *molaʒeman*, متعلقین *motaʻalleqin*, خدم و حشم *xadam va haʃam*.

Fond: to be fond of, دوست داشتن *dust d.*; (=to be intimate with), انس داشتن *ons d.*; to become fond of (intimate with), انس گرفتن *ons gereftan*.

Fondle, to, ناز (نوازش) کردن *naʒ (navaʒeʃ) k*.

Food, خوراك *xorak*, غذا *ɣaʒa*, طعام *taʻam*.

Foodstuffs, خواربار *xarbar*.

Fool, foolish, احمق *ahmaq*, ابله *ablah*.

Foolishly, احمقانه *ahmaqane*.

Foot, پا *pa*; on foot, پیاده *piade*; see also Base.

Footstep (=pace), قدم *qadam*, گام *gam*; (imprint), جا پا *japa*.

For, برای baraye, از برای از baraye, بهر bahr(e), از بهر az bahr(e); for your sake, محض خاطر شما mahze xatere ſoma.

Forage, see Fodder.

Forbid, to, منع کردن man' k., نهی کردن nahy k., قدغن کردن qadayan k.

Forbidden, ممنوع mamnu', قدغن qadayan; (=contrary to the religious law), حرام haram.

Force, زور zur, قدرت qodrat, قوه qovve, نیرو niru; (=validity), اعتبار e'tebar; (=armed force), سر نیزه sarneize; to force (=to compel), وادار کردن vadar k., مجبور کردن majbur k.; (=to open), باز کردن baz k., مفتوح کردن maftuh k.; to put into force, اجرا کردن ejra k.

Forced (=compelled), مجبور majbur; forced labour, بیگاری bigari.

Forces: armed forces, قوای مسلح qovaye mosallah, نیروی مسلح niruye mosallah.

Ford, معبر ma'bar.

Fore-arm, بازو bazu.

Forefather, جد jadd.

Forego, to, (از) صرف نظر کردن sarfe nazar k. (az).

Forehead, پیشانی piſani, جبین jabin.

Foreign, foreigner, بیگانه bigane, غریب yarib, اجنبی ajnabi, خارجی xareji; Ministry of Foreign Affairs, وزارت امور خارجه vezarate omure xareje.

Foreleg, دست dast.

Foreman, سرعمله sar'amale.

Forenoon, پیش از ظهر piſ az zohr.

Forerunner, پیشرو piſrou.

Foresee, to, پیش بینی کردن piſbini k.

Foresight, پیشبینی piſbini, بصیرت basirat.

Forest, جنگل jangal.

Forester, جنگلبان jangalban.

Forestry, جنگلبانی jangalbani.

Foretell, to, پیش گوئی کردن piſgui k., غیب گوئی کردن yeibgui k.

Forge (of a blacksmith), کوره kure; to forge (a document), جعل کردن ja'l k.; (=to make), ساختن saxtan.

Forger, جعل کننده ja'l konande, قلاب qallab.

Forgery, جعل ja'l, قلب qalb, قلابی qollabi, qallabi.

Forget, to, فراموش کردن faramuſ k.

Forgetful, فراموش کار faramuʃkar.

Forgetfulness, فراموش‌کاری faramuʃkari, فراموشی faramuʃi.

Forgive, to, بخشیدن baxʃidan, عفو کردن afv k., معذور داشتن ma'zur d.

Forgiveness, عفو afv.

Fork, چنگال cangal.

Form, see Bench, Body and Figure; to form (= to set up), تشکیل دادن taʃkil dadan; (= to take shape), صورت بستن surat bastan; to be formed (= to be set up), تشکیل یافتن taʃkil yaftan.

Formalities, تشریفات taʃrifat.

Formation, تشکیل taʃkil.

Former, سابق sabeq, قدیم qadim, پیشین piʃin; the former, آن an (as opp. to the latter, این in); in former days, در ایام گذشته dar ayyame gozaʃte.

Formerly, سابقًا sabeqan, پیش از این piʃ az in.

Fort, قلعه qal'e, دژ dez.

Fortifications, استحکامات estehkamat, سنگر بندی sangarbandi.

Fortunate, نیکبخت nikbaxt, خوشبخت xoʃbaxt, بختیار baxtyar; (= blessed), خجسته xojaste.

Fortunately, خوشبختانه xoʃbaxtane.

Fortune (= Providence), روزگار ruzegar; (= good fortune), نیکبختی nikbaxti, اقبال eqbal.

Forty, چهل cehel.

Forward, جلو jelou, پیش piʃ; to bring forward (raise a matter for discussion), مطرح کردن matrah k.

Foster, to, پرورش دادن parvareʃ dadan; (a belief), پروراندن parvarandan.

Foster-mother, دایه daye, تایه taye.

Foul, to (= to make dirty), نجس کردن nejes k., آلودن aludan, کثیف کردن kasif k.

Found, to, تأسیس کردن ta'sis k.; (metal), ریختن rixtan.

Foundation, اساس asas, بنیاد bonyad, پایه paye.

Founded (on), مبنی (بر) mabni (bar).

Founder, مؤسس mo'asses; (= smelter), ریخته گر rixtegar.

Foundry, ریخته‌گرخانه rixtegarxane.

Fountain, فواره favare.

Four, چهار cahar.

Fourteen, چهارده cahardah.

Fowl (=bird), پرنده *parande*; (=hen), مرغ *morɣ*.

Fox, روباه *rubah*.

Fraction, کسر *kasr*, برخه *barxe*.

Fracture, شکستگی *ʃekastegi*, انکسار *enkesar*.

Frame (for a picture, etc.), قاب *qab*.

France, فرانسه *faranse*.

Frank, رك *rok*, رکگو *rokgu*; to speak frankly, صاف و پوست کنده حرف زدن *saf o pust kande harf ʒadan*.

Frankness, رکگوئی *rokgui*.

Fraternal, برادرانه *baradarane*.

Fraud, تقلب *taqallob*, دغل *daɣal*.

Fraudulent, متقلب *motaqalleb*, دغلباز *daɣalbaʒ*.

Freckle, خال *xal*, لکه *lake*.

Free, آزاد *aʒad*; to free, آزاد کردن *aʒad k.*, خلاص کردن *xalas k.*, رها کردن *raha k.*

Freedom, آزادی *aʒadi*, ازادگی *aʒadegi*.

Freely, آزادانه *aʒadane*.

Freeze, to (intrans.), یخ بستن *yax bastan*.

Freight, بار *bar*.

Freighter, بار کش *barkaʃ*.

French, فرانسوی *faransavi*.

Frequent, زیاد *ʒiad*, کثیر الوقوع *kasir ol-voqu'*.

Frequently, بارها *barha*, زیاد *ʒiad*.

Fresh, تازه *taʒe*; (of air), خنك *xonak*.

Freshness, تازگی *taʒegi*.

Friday, جمعه *jom'e*.

Friend, دوست *dust*, رفیق *rafiq*, یار *yar*.

Friendless, بی کس *bikas*.

Friendly, دوستانه *dustane*.

Friendship, دوستی *dusti*, رفاقت *refaqat*.

Frighten, to, ترساندن *tarsandan*.

Frightening, see Fearful.

Frivolity (=emptiness), هرزگی *harʒegi*, سبکی *saboki*.

Frivolous (=empty), هرزه *harʒe*, سبك *sabok*, پوچ *puc*, بی معنی *bima'ni*.

Frog, قورباغه *qorbaɣe*.

From, از‌ *az.*

Front, پیش‌ *piʃ,* جلو *jelou;* in front of, پیش(ه) *piʃ(e),* جلو(ه) *jelou(e).*

Frontier, سرحد *sarhadd,* مرز *marz.*

Frontier-guard, مرزدار *marzdar.*

Frost-bite, سرما زدگی‌ *sarmazadegi.*

Frost-bitten, سرمازده *sarmazade.*

Froth, کف‌ *kaf.*

Fruit, میوه *mive,* بر *bar,* بار *bar,* ثمر *samar;* dried fruit, خشك بار *xoʃke bar;* fresh fruit and vegetables, تره بار *tarebar.*

Fruiterer, میوه فروش‌ *miveforuʃ.*

Fry, to, سرخ کردن‌ *sorx k.*

Frying-pan, تاوه *tave.*

Fuel, سوخت‌ *suxt.*

Fugitive, فراری‌ *farari.*

Fulfil, to, انجام دادن‌ *anjam dadan,* بیرون آمدن (چیزی) از عهده *az ohde(ye cizi) birun amadan.*

Full, مملو *mamlovv,* پر *por;* see also Complete.

Fundamental, اساسی‌ *asasi.*

Fundamentally, اساسًا *asasan.*

Funeral, تشییع جنازه *taʃyi'e janaze.*

Fungus, قارچ‌ *qarc.*

Funny, مضحك‌ *mozhek.*

Furnace, کوره *kure.*

Furlough, مرخصی‌ *moraxxasi.*

Furnish, to, مبل کردن‌ *mobl k.,* فرش کردن‌ *farʃ k.*

Furniture, اثاثیه *asasiye,* مبل‌ *mobl.*

Furrow (in a field), شیار *ʃiar.*

Further, دورتر *durtar;* (=moreover), گذشته از این‌ *gozaʃte az in,* بعلاوه *be alave,* دیگر *digar.*

Fuse, to (intrans.), اتصال پیدا کردن‌ *ettesal peida k.*

Fusilage, تنه *tane.*

Fusion, ذوب *zoub.*

Fuss, هیاهو *hayahu.*

Futile, بیهوده *bihude,* بیفائده *bifa'ede.*

Future (subs. and adj.), آینده *ayande.*

G

Gain, see Benefit.

Gallop, تاخت *taxt*; at a gallop, بتاخت *be taxt*; to gallop, تاختن *taxtan*; to make one's horse gallop, تازانیدن *tazanidan*.

Gallows, دار *dar*.

Gamble, to, قمار کردن *qomar k.*; (=to bet), شرط بستن *ʃart bastan.*

Gambler, قمار باز *qomarbaz.*

Gambling, قمار بازی *qomarbazi.*

Game, بازی *bazi*; (=prey), شکار *ʃekar.*

Gangrene, غانقاریا *yanqaria.*

Gaol, زندان *zendan*, محبس *mahbas.*

Gaoler, زندانبان *zendanban.*

Garden, باغ *bay.*

Gardener, باغبان *bayban.*

Gardening, باغبانی *baybani.*

Gargle, to غرغره کردن *yaryare k.*

Garlic, سیر *sir.*

Garment, see Clothes.

Garrison, پادگان *padegan,* ساخلو *saxlou.*

Garrulity, روده درازی *rudedarazi,* پر حرفی *porharfi.*

Garrulous, روده دراز *rudedaraz,* پر حرف *porharf.*

Gate, دروازه *darvaze.*

Gate-keeper, دربان *darban.*

Gather, to (=to pluck), چیدن *cidan*; (the harvest), جمع کردن *jam' k.*

Gathering (of people), جمعیت *jam'iyat,* عده *edde.*

Gazelle, غزال *yazal,* آهو *ahu.*

Gear (of a car, etc.), دنده *dande.*

Geld, to, اخته کردن *axte k.*

Gelding, اخته *axte.*

Gendarme, ژاندارم *zandarm.*

Gendarmerie, ژاندارمری *zandarmeri,* امنیه *amniye.*

Genealogy, نسب *nasab.*

General (military), سپهبد *sepahbod*; (=usual), عمومی *omumi*; in general, عموماً *omuman.*

General Staff, ستاد كل ارتش *setade kolle arteʃ*.

Generally, عموماً *omuman*.

Generation, نسل *nasl*, پشت *poʃt*.

Generosity, سخاوت *saxavat*, سخا *saxa*, جوانمردی *javanmardi*.

Generous, سخی *saxi*, جوانمرد *javanmard*.

Genius, نبوغ *nobuɣ*; (a person), نابغه *nabeɣe*.

Gentle, ملايم *molayem*.

Gentleness, ملايمت *molayemat*.

Gently, آهسته *aheste*, يواش *yavaʃ*.

Geography, جغرافيا *joɣrafia*.

Geologist, زمين شناس *ʒaminʃenas*.

Geology, زمين شناسی *ʒaminʃenasi*.

Geomancer, رمال *rammal*.

Geomancy, رمل *raml*.

Geometry, هندسه *hendese*.

German, آلمانی *almani*.

Germany, آلمان *alman*.

Get, to, حاصل كردن *hasel k.*, يافتن *yaftan*, بدست آوردن *be dast avardan*; to get up, بلند شدن *b·land ʃ.*

Ghost, روح *ruh*; Holy Ghost, روح القدس *ruh ol-qodos*.

Giddy, see Dizzy.

Gift, عطا *a·a*, تحفه *tohfe*, هديه *hadiye*; (from an inferior to a superior), پيشكش *piʃkaʃ*; (brought back from a journey), سوغات *souɣat*; (from a superior to an inferior), انعام *en'am*.

Ginger, زنجفيل *ʒanjafil*.

Gipsy, كولی *kouli*, غربتی *ɣorbati*.

Gird: to gird up one's loins, كمر بستن *kamar bastan*.

Girdle, كمربند *kamarband*.

Girl, دختر *doxtar*.

Girth (of a saddle), تنگ *tang*.

Give, to, دادن *dadan*; (as a gift), بخشيدن *baxʃidan*, عطا كردن *ata k.*, ارزانی داشتن *arʒani d.*

Giver, دهنده *dehande*.

Glad, شاد *ʃad*, شادمان *ʃadman*, خوشوقت *xoʃvaqt*, مسرور *masrur*, مشعوف *maʃ'uf*, خرم *xorram*.

Gladness, شادی *ʃadi*, خوشوقتی *xoʃvaqti*, مسرت *masarrat*, شعف *ʃaʻf*.

Glance, نگاه *negah*, نـظر *naẓar*; to glance, نگاه کـردن *negah k.*, نظر انداختن *naẓar andaxtan*.

Glass, لیوان *livan*; (=mirror), آئینه *aine*; (=plate glass), شیشه *ʃiʃe*.

Glass-blower (glazier), شیشه بر *ʃiʃebor*.

Globe, کره *korre*.

Glorious, جلیل *jalil*, مجلل *mojallal*, مجید *majid*. با شکوه *baʃokuh*.

Glory, جلال *jalal*, مجد *majd*, ابهت *obbohat*, شکوه *ʃokuh*.

Glove, دستکش *dastkaʃ*.

Glue, سریشم *seriʃom*.

Glutton, شکمپرست *ʃekamparast*, شکمو *ʃekamu*.

Go, to, رفتن *raftan*; (of a watch, etc.), کارکردن *kar k.*; to let go, ول کردن *vel k.*, رها کـردن *raha k.*; to go down, پائین رفتن *pain raftan*; to go up, بالا رفتن *bala raftan*; to go in, تو رفتن *tu raftan*, داخل شدن *daxel ʃ.*; to go out, بیرون رفتن *birun raftan*.

Goad (=spur), مهمیز *mehmiẓ*; to goad (=to spur), مهمیز زدن *mehmiẓ ẓadan*.

Go-between, دلال *dallal*, میانجی *mianji*.

Goat, بز *boẓ*.

Goblet, جام *jam*.

God, خدا *xoda*, خداوند *xodavand*, یزدان *yaẓdan*, الله *allah*; God most high, خدای تعالی *xodaye taʻala*; O God! خدایا *xodaya*; God willing, ان شاء الله *en ʃa allah*; God forbid, خدا نکند *xoda nakonad*; praise be to God, الحمد لله *al hamdo lellah*; God preserve you, خدا حافظ شما *xoda hafeẓe ʃoma*.

Godliness, یزدانپرستی *xodaparasti*, خدا پرستی *dindari*, تقوی *taqva*, دینداری *yaẓdanparasti*.

Godly, یزدانپرست *xodaparast*, خدا پرست *dindar*, دیندار *ba taqva*, با تقوی *yaẓdanparast*.

Gold, زر *ẓar*, طلا *tala*; pure gold, زر خالص *ẓare xales*.

Gold-beater, زر کوب *ẓarkub*.

Golden, زرین *ẓarrin*, طلائی *talai*.

Goldsmith, زرگر *ẓargar*.

Golosh, گالش *galeʃ*.

Gonorrhœa, سوزاك *suẓak*.

Good, خوب *xub,* نيك *nik,* نيكو *niku.*

Goodbye, خدا حافظ *xoda hafeʒ;* to say goodbye, خدا حافظی کردن *xoda hafeʒi k.*

Good-natured, خوش اخلاق *xoʃaxlaq.*

Goodness, خوبی *xubi,* نيک *niki,* نيكوئی *nikui.*

Goods (=belongings), مال *mal,* اموال *amval;* (=merchandise), متاع *mata',* کالا *kala,* اجناس *ajnas;* goods and chattels, اسباب *asbab,* اثاثیه *asasiye.*

Goodwill, خیرخواهی *xeirxahi;* (of a business), سر قفلی *sarqofli.*

Goose, غاز *yaʒ.*

Gorge, تنگه *tange.*

Gospel, انجيل *enjil.*

Gossip, سخنچینی *soxancini;* (person), سخنچین *soxancin.*

Govern, to, حکمرانی کردن *hokmrani k.,* سلطنت کردن *saltanat k.,* حکومت کردن *hokumat k.,* فرمانروائی کردن *farmanravai k.,* فرمانفرمائی کردن *farmanfarmai k.;* (=to administer), اداره کردن *edare k.*

Government, حکمرانی *hokmrani,* حکومت *hokumat,* دولت *doulat;* (=governing), فرمانروائی *farmanravai,* فرمانفرمائی *farmanfarmai.*

Governor (of a province), فرماندار *farmandar,* استاندار *ostandar,* والی *vali;* (of a city), حاکم *hakem.*

Governorate, فرمانداری *farmandari.*

Governor-General, استاندار *ostandar.*

Governorate-General, استانداری *ostandari.*

Grace (=elegance), لطافت *latafat,* زیبائی *ʒibai;* (of God), توفیق *toufiq.*

Graceful, لطیف *latif,* زیبا *ʒiba.*

Gracious, کریم *karim.*

Gradation, درجه بندی *darajebandi.*

Grade, درجه *daraje,* پایه *paye.*

Gradual, تدریجی *tadriji.*

Gradually, بتدریج *be tadrij.*

Graduate, فارغ التحصیل *farey ot-tahsil.*

Graft, to (a tree or bush), پیوند زدن *peivand ʒadan.*

Grafted (of a tree or bush), پیوندی *peivandi.*

Grain (=corn), غله *yalle;* (=seed), بذر *baʒr;* (=a single grain), دانه *dane.*

Grammar, صرف *sarf.*

Grandchild, نوه *nave*; great grandchild, نبیره *nabire.*

Grandeur, عظمت *azamat.*

Grandfather, جد *jadd.*

Grandmother, جده *jadde.*

Grant, see Bestow; to take for granted, مسلم گرفتن *mosallam gereftan.*

Grape, انگور *angur.*

Grass, گیاه *giah,* علف *alaf.*

Grateful, سپاسگزار *sepasgozar,* شکرگزار *fokrgozar,* حقشناس *haqqfenas.*

Gratis, مفت *moft,* برایگان *berayegan,* رایگان *rayegan.*

Gratitude, سپاسگزاری *sepasgozari,* حقشناسی *haqqfenasi.*

Gratuity, انعام *en'am.*

Grave, قبر *qabr,* گور *gur*; (=solemn), موقر *movaqqar,* متین *matin.*

Grave-digger, گورکن *gurkan.*

Gravel, سنگریزه *sangrize.*

Gravestone, سنگ قبر *sange qabr.*

Gravity, ثقل *seql,* گرانی *gerani*; (=sedateness), وقار *vaqar.*

Graze, to (of cattle) (intrans.), چریدن *caridan*; (trans.), چراندن *carandan.*

Grease (=oil), روغن *rouyan*; see also Fat.

Great, بزرگ *bozorg*; (=worthy), بزرگوار *bozorgvar.*

Greatness, بزرگی *bozorgi*; (=worthiness), بزرگواری *bozorgvari.*

Grecian, یونانی *yunani.*

Greece, یونان *yunan.*

Greed, حرص *hers,* طمع *tama'*; (=gluttony), پرخوری *porxori.*

Greek, یونانی *yunani.*

Green, سبز *sabz.*

Greengage, گوجه زرد *goujeye zard.*

Greengrocer, بقال *baqqal.*

Greenness, سبزی *sabzi.*

Greet, to, سلام کردن *salam k.*

Greeting, سلام *salam.*

Grief, غم *yam,* الم *alam,* اندوه *anduh,* حزن *hozn,* حسرت *hasrat.*

Grieve, to (intrans.), غم خوردن *yam xordan,* رنجیدن *ranjidan.*

Grieved, غمگین *yamgin,* محزون *mahzun.*

Grimace, ادا *ada*; (of disgust, etc.), ترش رویی *torfrui.*

Grind, to, سائیدن saidan, سابیدن sabidan; (=to sharpen), تیز کردن tiz k.

Groan, ناله nale, آه و ناله ah o nale; to groan, ناله کردن nale k., آه و ناله کردن ah o nale k.

Grocer, بقال baqqal.

Groom, مهتر mehtar; head groom, میر آخور miraxor.

Gross (=not net), غیر خالص γeire xales.

Ground, زمین zamin.

Groundless (=false), بی اساس biasas, عاری از حقیقت ari az haqiqat.

Groundwork, زمینه zamine.

Group, دسته daste; (of people), گروه goruh, جماعت jama'at.

Grow, to (intrans.), رستن rostan, نمو کردن nomovv k., رشد کردن rofd k., بزرگ شدن bozorg f., نشو و نما کردن nafv o nama k.

Growl, to, غریدن γoridan.

Growth, رشد rofd, نمو nomovv, نشو و نما nafv o nama.

Grudge, to, حسد بردن hasad bordan.

Gruel, شوربا furba, شوروا furva.

Grumble, to, لند لند کردن lond lond k., غر غر کردن γor γor k.

Guarantee, کفالت kefalat, ضمان zaman; to guarantee, ضمانت کردن zamanat k.

Guarantor, ضامن zamen, کفیل kafil, تعهد کننده ta'ahhod konande.

Guard (a company of men), قراول qaravol, کشیك kafik; (=sentinel), کشیکچی kafikci, قراول qaravol, مستحفظ mostahfez, پاسبان pasban; to guard, حفاظت کردن hefazat k., حمایت کردن hemayat k.; to be on guard, پاس دادن pas dadan.

Guardhouse, قراولخانه qaravolxane; (=prison), محبس mahbas.

Guardian, وصی vasi, قیم qeiyem; (=protector), محافظ mohafez, حامی hami.

Guess, تخمین taxmin, حدس hads; to guess, تخمین زدن taxmin z., حدس زدن hads zadan.

Guest, مهمان mehman.

Guidance, راهنمائی rahnamai, هدایت hedayat.

Guide, راهنما rahnama, هادی hadi; (=spiritual guide), مرشد morfed, پیر pir; (someone to show the way), بلد balad; to guide, راهنمائی کردن rahnamai k., هدایت کردن hedayat k.

Guild, صنف senf.

Guilt, تقصیر taqsir, جرم jorm; (=condemnation), محکومیت mahkumiyat.

Guilty, مقصر *moqasser*; (=condemned), محکوم *mahkum*.

Guinea-worm, رشته *reʃte*.

Guitar, تار *tar*.

Gulf, خليج *xalij*.

Gum (=glue), چسب *casb*; (of mouth), لثه *lase*.

Gum tragacanth, کتیرا *ketira*.

Gun, تفنگ *tofang*; double-barrelled gun, تفنگ دو لول *tofange do lul*.

Gunboat, توپدار *tupdar*.

Gun-carriage, عراده *arrade*.

Gunfire, شلیك توپ *ʃelike tup*.

Gunpowder, باروت *barut*.

Gut, روده *rude*.

Gutter, جوب *jub*.

Gynaecologist, متخصص در امراض زنانه *motaxasses dar amraʒe ʒanane*.

Gypsum, گچ *gac*.

H

Haemorrhage, خونريزی *xunriʒi*.

Haemorrhoids, بواسیر *bavasir*.

Hail, تگرگ *tegarg*.

Hair, مو *mu*; (=locks), گیس، گیسو *gis, gisu*.

Hair-splitting (subs.), موشكافی *muʃekafi*.

Half, نیم *nim*, نصف *nesf*, نیمه *nime*.

Half-way, نیم راه *nimerah*.

Hall, ایوان *eivan*, تالار *talar*, دالان *dalan*.

Halter, افسار *afsar*.

Halve, to, نصف کردن *nesf k.*, دو نیم کردن *do nim k.*

Hammer, چکش *cakoʃ*.

Hammock, ننو *nanu*.

Hand, دست *dast*; to shake hands, دست دادن *dast dadan*; at hand, دم دست *dame dast*; (=ready), حاضر *haʒer*; to hand over, تحویل دادن *tahvil dadan*.

Handcuffs, دست بند *dastband*.

Hand-grenade, نارنجك *naranjak*.

Handkerchief, دستمال *dastmal*.

Handle, دسته daste.

Hand-made, دستى (كار) (kare) dasti.

Handsome, خوشگل xoʃgel.

Hang, to, آویزان کردن aviʐan k., آویختن avixtan; (=to execute), بدار کشیدن be dar kaʃidan.

Hang-over (from drink), خمار xomar.

Happen, to, اتفاق افتادن ettefaq oftadan.

Happening, see Event.

Happiness, see Gladness.

Happy, see Glad.

Harbour, بندر bandar.

Hard (=firm), سفت seft; see also Difficult.

Hard-hearted, سنگدل sangdel, بیرحمانه birahmane.

Hard-mouthed (of a horse), سرکش sarkaʃ.

Hardness (=firmness), سفتى sefti; see also Difficulty.

Hardship, سختى saxti, مصیبت mosibat.

Hard-working, زحمت کش ʐahmatkaʃ

Hare, خرگوش xarguʃ.

Harm, ضرر ʐarar.

Harmful, مضر moʐerr.

Harmonious, هم آهنگ hamahang.

Harmony, هم آهنگى hamahangi.

Harness, ساز و برگ saʐ o barg, برگ barg, یراق yaraq.

Harrow (agricultural implement), مازو maʐu; to harrow, مازو کردن maʐu k.

Harsh, سخت saxt, درشت doroʃt, زبر ʐebr.

Harshness, سختى saxti, درشتى doroʃti, زبرى ʐebri.

Harvest, خرمن xarman, محصول mahsul, درو derou; to harvest, خرمن جمع کردن xarman jam' k., محصول جمع کردن mahsul jam' k., درو کردن derou k., خرمن (محصول) بر داشتن xarman (mahsul) bar d.

Haste, تعجیل ta'jil, شتاب ʃetab, عجله ajale.

Hasten, to, عجله کردن ajale k., شتاب کردن ʃetab k.

Hasty, عجول ajul, تند tond.

Hat, کلاه kolah.

Hatchet, تبر tabar.

Hate, to, (از) تنفر داشتن *tanaffor d.* (az), (از) نفرت داشتن *nefrat d.* (az), (از) متنفر بودن *motanaffer b.* (az).

Hatred, تنفر *tanaffor,* نفرت *nefrat.*

Hatter, كلاه فروش *kolahforuʃ.*

Haughtiness, تكبر *takabbor.*

Haughty, متكبر *motakabber.*

Haulage, بار كشى *barkaʃi.*

Have, to, داشتن *daʃtan.*

Haversack, كوله بار *kulebar.*

Hawk, باز *baz.*

Hawker (=pedlar), دست فروش *dastforuʃ,* خرده فروش *xordeforuʃ.*

Hawking (=peddling), دست فروشى *dastforuʃi,* خرده فروشى *xordeforuʃi.*

Hay, علف خشك *alafe xoʃk.*

Hazel-nut, فندق *fondoq.*

He, او *u,* وى *vei.*

Head, سر *sar,* كله *kalle;* (=chief), رئیس *ra'is,* مدیر *modir.*

Headache, درد سر *darde sar,* سردرد *sardard,* تصدیع *tāsdi',* صداع *soda';* he has a headache, (گرفت) سرش درد میکند *sareʃ dard mikonad (gereft).*

Headman, رئیس *ra'is;* (of a village), كدخدا *kadxoda.*

Health, تندرستى *tandorosti,* صحت *sehhat,* سلامت *salamat,* سلامتى *salamati.*

Healthy, تندرست *tandorost.*

Heap, توده *tude;* to heap up, اندوختن *anduxtan,* انبوه كردن *ambuh k.*

Hear, to, شنیدن *ʃenidan,* شنفتن *ʃenoftan.*

Heart, دل *del,* قلب *qalb,* خاطر *xater;* to know by heart, حفظ داشتن *hefz d.;* to learn by heart, حفظ كردن *hefz k.*

Hearth, بخارى *boxari.*

Heartless, سنگدل *sangdel.*

Heartlessness, سنگدلى *sangdeli.*

Heat, گرما *garma,* گرمى *garmi,* حرارت *hararat.*

Heathen, كافر *kafer.*

Heaven (=paradise), بهشت *beheʃt,* فردوس *ferdous,* جنت *jennat;* the heavens, آسمان *asman,* سپهر *sepehr,* سما *sama,* فلك *falak.*

Heavenly, سماوى *samavi,* آسمانى *asmani;* (=of paradise), بهشتى *beheʃti.*

Heaviness, سنگینى *sangini,* گرانى *gerani.*

Heavy, سنگین *sangin,* گران *geran.*

Hebrew, عبرى *ebri.*

Heckle, to, هو کردن *hōu k.*

Heckler, هوچى *hōuci,* هوچيگر *hōucigar.*

Hedgehog, خارپشت *xarpoſt.*

Heed, see Attention.

Heel, پاشنه *paſne.*

Height, ارتفاع *ertefaʿ,* بلندى *bolandi.*

Heir, وارث *vares.*

Heir-apparent, ولى عهد *valiahd.*

Hell, دوزخ *duᶎax,* جهنم *jahannam.*

Help, مدد *madad,* کمک *komak,* مساعده *mosaʿede,* يارى *yari;* to help,
مدد (کمک, مساعده , يارى) کردن *madad (komak, mosaʿede, yari) k.*

Helper, مددکار *madadkar,* يار *yar.*

Helpless, بيچاره *bicare.*

Hem (=border), حاشيه *haſie.*

Hemistich, مصرع *mesraʿ.*

Hemp, کنف *kanaf;* hempseed, شاهدانه *ſahdane.*

Hen, مرغ *morᵧ.*

Hen-house (nest), لانه مرغ *laneye morᵧ.*

Hence (=from this place), از اينجا *aᶎ inja;* (=for this reason), ازاينجهت
aᶎ in jehat, لهذا *lehaᶎa.*

Henceforth, از اين بعد *aᶎ in be baʿd.*

Henna, حنا *hanna.*

Herald, جارچى *jarci.*

Herd, see Flock.

Herdsman, گله‌دار *galledar,* چوپان *cupan.*

Here, اينجا *inja.*

Hereditary, موروثى *mōurusi.*

Heresy, بدعت *bedʿat.*

Heretic, رافضى *rafeᶎi.*

Heretofore, قبل از اين *qabl aᶎ in,* پيش از اين *piſ aᶎ in.*

Heritage, ميراث *miras,* ارث *ers.*

Hernia, فتق *fatq.*

Hero, پهلوان *pahlavan.*

Hesitate, to, مردد بودن *moraddad b.,* ترديد داشتن *tardid d.*

Hesitation, تردید *tardid*; تأمل *ta'ammol*.

Hiccup, سکسکه *saksake*; to hiccup, سکسکه کردن *saksake k.*

Hidden, پنهان *panhan*, نهان *nehan*, نهفته *nehofte*, مخفی *maxfi*.

Hide, to, see Conceal.

High, بلند *boland*, مرتفع *mortafe'*, عالی *ali*.

High-minded, بلند نظر *bolandnazar*.

Highway, شاهراه *fahrah*, راه *rah*; highway robbery, راهزنی *rahzani*; highway robber, راهزن *rahzan*.

Hill, تپه *tappe*, تل *tall*.

Hinge, لولا *loula*.

Hint, اشاره *efare*; to hint, اشاره کردن *efare k.*, گوشه زدن *gufe zadan*.

Hip, کفل *kafal*.

Hire, اجرت *ojrat*, مزد *mozd*; (=rent), کرایه *keraye*, اجاره *ejare*; to hire (=to take on hire), کرایه کردن *keraye k.*, اجاره کردن *ejare k.*; (=to let out on hire), اجاره دادن *ejare dadan*, بکرایه دادن *be keraye dadan*; (=to hire labour), اجیر کردن *ajir k.*

Hireling, مزدور *mozdur*, اجیر *ajir*.

Historian, مورخ *movarrex*.

Historical, تاریخی *tarixi*.

History, تاریخ *tarix*.

Hit, to, زدن *zadan*; (a target), خوردن (به) *xordan (be)*.

Hitherto, تاحال *ta hal*, پیش از این *pif az in*, قبل از این *qabl az in*.

Hoard, اندوخته *anduxte*; to hoard, اندوخنن *anduxtan*, احتکار کردن *ehtekar k.*

Hoarder, محتکر *mohtaker*.

Hoarding, احتکار *ehtekar*.

Hoarse: he is hoarse, صداش گرفته است *sadaf gerefte ast.*

Hog, خوك *xuk*, گراز *goraz*.

Hold, to, نگاه داشتن *negah d.*; (=to take hold of), گرفتن *gereftan*; (=to contain), گنجیدن *gonjidan*.

Hole, سوراخ *surax*.

Holiday, تعطیل *ta'til*; (=feast-day), عید *id*; public holiday, تعطیل عمومی *ta'tile omumi*.

Holiness, تقدس *taqaddos*.

Holland, هلند *holand*.

Hollow, جوف *jŏuf*; (=empty), خالی *xali*, تهی *tohi*; (=rotten), پوك *puk*.

Hollyhock, گل خطمی *gole xatmi*.

Holy, مقدس *moqaddas*.

Home, خانه *xane*, منزل *manʒel*; to be at home, منزل بودن *manʒel b.*, خانه بودن *xane b.*

Homogeneity, تجانس *tajanos*.

Homogeneous, مجانس *mojanes*, متجانس *motajanes*.

Honest, صالح *saleh*, راست *rast*, درست كار *dorostkar*, امین *amin*.

Honesty, درستكاری *dorostkari*.

Honey, عسل *asal*.

Honour, شرف *ʃaraf*; see also Reputation, Respect; word of honour, قول شرف *qŏule ʃaraf*; in honour (of), بافتخار *be eftexar(e)*; he is held in honour, باو احترام میگذارند *be u ehteram migoʒarand*.

Hoof, سم *som*.

Hook, قلاب *qollab*.

Hooligans, اوباش *ŏubaʃ*.

Hoop, چنبر *cambar*.

Hope, امیدوار *omid d.*, امید *omid*, امیدواری *omidvari*; to hope, امید داشتن بودن *omid d.*, امیدوار بودن *omidvar b.*

Hopeful, امیدوار *omidvar*.

Hopeless, نومید *naomid, nŏumid*.

Hopelessness, نومیدی *naomidi, nŏumidi*.

Horizon, افق *ofoq*.

Horizontal, افقی *ofoqi*.

Horn, شاخ *ʃax*; (of a motor-car), بوق *buq*; to blow the horn, بوق زدن *buq ʒadan*.

Hornet, زنبور *ʒambur*.

Horoscope, طالع *tale'*, زایچه *ʒaice*, جدول *jadval*.

Horror, وحشت *vahʃat*, واهمه *vaheme*, هیبت *heibat*, هول *hŏul*.

Horse, اسب *asb*; spare (or led) horse, اسب یدك *asbe yadak*.

Horseback: on horseback, سوار *savar*.

Horseman (=good rider), سوارکار *savarkar*.

Horse-power: one (two) horse-power, یك (دو) اسبه *yak (do) asbe*.

Horse-shoe, نعل *na'l*.

Hospitable, مهماننواز *mehmannavaʒ*, مهماندوست *mehmandust*.

Hospital, مريضخانه marizxane, بيمارستان bimarestan, شفاخانه ſefaxane.

Hospitality, مهماننوازى mehmannavazi, مهماندوستى mehmandusti.

Host, ميزبان mizban, مهماندار mehmandar.

Hostage, نوا nava, گرو gerōu.

Hot, داغ day; (=pungent), تند tond, تيز tiz; a hot country, گرمسير garmsir; pertaining to a hot climate or country, گرمسيرى garmsiri.

Hotbed, كانون kanun.

Hotel, مهمانخانه mehmanxane, مسافرخانه mosaferxane.

Hour, ساعت saʿat; twenty-four hours (i.e. a day and a night), شبانهروز ſabaneruz.

House, منزل manzel, خانه xane.

Household, اهل خانه ahle xane, خانواده xanevade.

Housekeeping, خانهدارى xanedari.

Housewife, كدبانو kadbanu.

How, چگونه cegune, چطور cetour, بچه وجه be ce vajh; how much, چند cand; how many, چند cand; how long, چند وقت cand vaqt; (=until when), تا چند ta cand, تا كى ta kēī; how often, چند بار cand bar, چند دفعه cand dafʿe, چند مرتبه cand martabe; how far (of distance), چقدر راه ce qadr rah; (interjection), چه ce.

However, بارى bari; however much, هر چند كه har cand ke, هر قدر كه har qadr ke.

Hubble-bubble, قليان qalian.

Hue and cry, هياهو hayahu.

Hull, بدنه badane.

Human, بشرى baſari, آدمىزاد; human being, بشر baſar, انسان ensan, adamizad; human nature, انسانيت ensaniyat, بشريت baſariyat.

Humanitarian, بشر دوست baſardust, نوع پرست nōuʿparast.

Humanitarianism, نوع پرستى nōuʿparasti.

Humanity, انسانيت ensaniyat; (=generosity), مروت morovvat.

Humble, متواضع motavazeʿ.

Humiliate, to, تحقير كردن tahqir k.

Humility, تواضع tavazoʿ, فروتنى forutani.

Hump, قوز quz; (of a camel) كوهان kōuhan.

Hunchback, قوز پشت quzpoſt.

Hundred, صد sad.

Hunger, گرسنگی *gorosnegi*.

Hungry, گرسنه *gorosne*.

Hunt, to, شکار کردن *ʃekar k.*, صید کردن *seid k.*

Hunter, شکارچی *ʃekarci*, صیاد *saiyad*.

Hunting, شکار *ʃekar*.

Hurricane, گرد باد *gerdbad*, طوفان *tufan*.

Hurry: to be in a hurry, عجله داشتن *ajale d.*; hurry up, زود باشید *ʒud baʃid*; see also Haste.

Hurt, to, درد کردن *dard k.*; to be hurt (offended), رنجیدن *ranjidan*.

Husband, شوهر *ʃouhar*.

Husbandman, زارع *ʒareʻ*, کشاورز *keʃavarʒ*, برزگر *barʒegar*.

Hut, کلبه *kolbe*.

Hyacinth, سنبل *sombol*.

Hyena, کفتار *kaftar*.

Hygiene, بهداشت *behdaʃt*.

Hypocrisy, ریا *ria*, ریاکاری *riakari*, دو روئی *dorui*, نفاق *nefaq*.

Hypocrite, ریاکار *riakar*, منافق *monafeq*.

Hypocritical, دو رو *doru*, اهل نفاق *ahle nefaq*, اهل ریا *ahle ria*.

Hypothesis, فرض *farʒ*.

Hypothetical, فرضی *farʒi*.

I

I, من *man*; بنده *bande* (lit. slave).

Ibex, بز کوهی *boʒe kuhi*.

Ice, یخ *yax*; kind of pit for storing ice, یخچال *yaxcal*.

Ice-cream, بستنی *bastani*.

Ice-cream seller, بستنی فروش *bastaniforuʃ*.

Idea, خیال *xial*; (=thought), فکر *fekr*; (=opinion), عقیده *aqide*.

Ideal, ایدئال *ideal*; (adj.), کامل *kamel*.

Identical, to be, (با) یکی بودن *yaki b. (ba)*.

Identity, هویت *hoviyat*; identity card, سجل احوال *sejelle ahval*.

Ideological, مرامی *marami*.

Ideology, مرام *maram*.

Idiom, اصطلاح *estelah*.

Idol, بت *bot*.

Idolatry, بت پرستی botparasti.

If, اگر agar; and if not, و اگر نه va agar na, و الا va ella.

Ignoble, پست past, دون dun.

Ignominy, ننگ nang, رسوائی rosvai.

Ignorance, جهل jahl, نادانی nadani.

Ignorant, جاهل jahel, نادان nadan.

Ill, بیمار bimar, مریض mariz, ناخوش naxoſ.

Illegal, غیر قانونی ɣeire qanuni, خلاف قانون xelafe qanun; see also Forbidden.

Ill-fated, شوم ſum, بد بخت badbaxt.

Illiteracy, بیسوادی bisavadi.

Illiterate, بی سواد bisavad.

Ill-matched, ناجور najur.

Ill-nature, بد خوئی badxui.

Ill-natured, بد خو badxu.

Illness, مرض maraz, بیماری bimari, ناخوشی naxoſi.

Illustrious, مشهور maſhur.

Imaginary, خیالی xiali, موهوم mōuhum.

Imagination, خیال xial.

Imitation, تقلید taqlid.

Imitator, مقلد moqalled.

Immature, خام xam, نارس naras.

Immaturity, خامی xami, نارسی narasi.

Immediate, فوری fōuri.

Immediately, فوراً fōuran, فی الساعة as-sa'e, فی الفور fel-fōur.

Imminent, نزدیک nazdik.

Immoral, فاسد fased.

Immorality, فساد fesad, فساد اخلاق fesade axlaq.

Immortal, لا یموت la yamut, لایزال la yazal, فنا ناپذیر fananapazir.

Immortality, فنا ناپذیری fananapaziri.

Immovable, غیر متحرك ɣeire motaharrek; (of property), غیر منقول ɣeire manqul.

Immune, مصون masun.

Immunity, مصونیت masuniyat.

Impartial, بیطرف bitaraf.

Impartiality, بیطرفی *bitarafi.*

Impatience, بیصبری *bisabri.*

Impatient, بیصبر *bisabr,* بیحوصله *bihōusele.*

Impediment, منع *man'.*

Imperative, see Necessary; imperative mood, امر *amr.*

Imperfect, ناقص *naqes;* (=unfinished), ناتمام *natamam.*

Imperial, شاهی *ʃahi,* شاهنشاهی *ʃahenʃahi.*

Imperialism (=exploitation), استعماری *este'mari.*

Imperil, to, در خطر انداختن *dar xatar andaxtan.*

Impertinence, فضولی *foʒuli.*

Impertinent, فضول *foʒul.*

Import, to, وارد کردن *vared k.*

Importance, اهمیت *ahammiyat.*

Important, مهم *mohemm.*

Imports, واردات *varedat.*

Importunate: he was importunate, اصرار کرد *esrar kard.*

Importunity, اصرار *esrar.*

Impose, to, تحمیل کردن *tahmil k.;* to impose upon (=to deceive), گول زدن *gul ʒadan.*

Imposition (=burden), تحمیل *tahmil.*

Impossibility, عدم امکان *adame emkan.*

Impossible, محال *mohal,* غیر ممکن *ɣeire momken.*

Impostor, شیاد *ʃayyad,* شارلاتان *ʃarlatan.*

Impotence, عجز *ajʒ,* ناتوانی *natavani.*

Impotent, عاجز *ajeʒ,* ناتوان *natavan.*

Impregnable, منیع *mani'.*

Impression, تأثیر *ta'sir;* to make an impression, تأثیر کردن *ta'sir k.*

Imprint, اثر *asar,* نقش *naqʃ.*

Imprison, زندان کردن *ʒendan k.,* حبس کردن *habs k.*

Imprisoned, محبوس *mahbus.*

Improper, نامناسب *namonaseb,* ناشایسته *naʃayeste.*

Improve, to, بهتر کردن *behtar k.,* اصلاح کردن *eslah k.*

Improvement, اصلاح *eslah,* بهبودی *behbudi.*

Impudence, گستاخی *gostaxi,* پررویی *porrui.*

Impudent, گستاخ *gostax,* پررو *porru.*

Imputation, افترا *eftera,* تهمت *tohmat.*

In, در *dar,* (ی)تو *tu(ye).*

Inaccessible (=far), دور دست *durdast;* (=impregnable), منیع *mani'.*

Inattention, غفلت *yeflat,* غافلی *yafeli.*

Inattentive, غافل *yafel.*

Incapable, ناقابل *naqabel,* بیکفایت *bikefayat;* to be incapable (of doing something), از عهده بر نیامدن *az ohde bar nayamadan.*

Incapacity, بی‌کفایتی *bikefayati,* نا قابلیت *naqabeliyat.*

Incarnation, حلول *holul.*

Incautious, بی احتیاط *biehteyat.*

Incident, see Event.

Incite, to, تحریك كردن *tahrik k.,* بر انگیختن *bar angixtan.*

Inclination, میل *meil,* تمایل *tamayol.*

Incline, to (=to lean), تكیه دادن *tekie dadan;* to be inclined (to), میل داشتن (به) *meil d. (be),* تمایل داشتن (به) *tamayol d. (be).*

Inclined, متمایل *motamayel.*

Include, to (=to insert), ضمیمه كردن *zamime, k.,* درج كردن *darj k.;* to be included, شامل بودن *jamel b.;* including, من جمله *men jomle.*

Inclusion, ضمیمه *zamime.*

Income, در آمد *daramad,* عایدات *ayedat;* income-tax, مالیات بر در آمد *maliate bar daramad.*

Incompatibility, منافات *monafat.*

Incompatible, منافی *monafi.*

Incomplete, ناتمام *natamam.*

Incorporation (=joining), الحاق *elhaq.*

Incorruptible (=permanent), فنا ناپذیر *fananapazir;* (=not to be bribed), پاك پا کدامن *pak, pakdaman.*

Increase, افزایش *afzayej,* ازدیاد *ezdeyad,* زیادی *ziadi,* اضافه *ezafe;* to increase (trans.), افزودن *afzudan,* زیاد كردن *ziad k.,* اضافه كردن *ezafe k.*

Incumbent (of a duty), واجب *vajeb;* to be incumbent upon, واجب بودن *vajeb b. (bar).*

Incurable, لا علاج *la elaj,* معالجه ناپذیر *mo'alejenapazir.*

Indebted, مقروض *maqruz;* (fig.) مدیون *madyun.*

Indecent (=coarse), رکیك *rakik.*

Indefinite, غیر معین *yeire mo'ayyan.*

Indemnity, غرامت ɣaramat.

Independence, استقلال esteqlal.

Independent, مستقل mostaqell.

Index, فهرست fehrest.

India, هندوستان hendustan, هند hend.

Indian (adj.), هندی hendi; (subs.), هندی hendi, هندو hendu.

Indicate, to, اشاره کردن eſare k.

Indication, اشاره eſare.

Indigestible, سنگین sangin.

Indigo, نیل nil.

Indirect, غیر مستقیم ɣeire mostaqim.

Indispensable, ضروری ʒaruri, ناگزیر nagoʒir.

Indisposed, کسل kesel.

Indisposition, کسالت kesalat.

Individual (subs.), فرد fard; (adj.), فردی fardi.

Individually, فرد فرد fard fard, منفردًا monfaredan.

Industrial, صنعتی san'ati.

Industry, صنعت san'at.

Inevitable, چاره ناپذیر carenapaʒir.

Inexperienced, بی تجربه bitajrebe.

Infantry, پیاده نظام piade neʒam.

Infectious, مسری mosri; (of illness only), واگیر vagir.

Infidel, کافر kafer.

Infinite, بی انتها bienteha, بی پایان bipayan.

Infinitive, مصدر masdar.

Infirm, see Weak.

Inflation, تورم tavarrom.

Influence, نفوذ nofuʒ; to exercise influence (in a bad sense), اعمال نفوذ e'male nofuʒ k. کردن

Influential, صاحب نفوذ sahebnofuʒ, با نفوذ banofuʒ, متنفذ motanaffeʒ.

Influenza, گریپ grip.

Inform, to, خبر کردن (دادن) xabar k. (dadan), اطلاع دادن ettela' dadan.

Information, اطلاع ettela', خبر xabar.

Informed, مطلع mottale'.

Informer, see Spy.

Infringe, to, مخلف کردن *taxallof k.*

Infringement, تخلف *taxallof.*

Inglorious, شرم آور *farmavar*, ننگین *nangin.*

Ingot (of gold), شمش *femf.*

Ingratitude, کفر نعمت *kofre ne'mat*, حق ناشناسی *haqqnafenasi.*

Inhabitant, ساکن *saken*; inhabitants, ساکنین *sakenin*, اهالی *ahali.*

Inhabited: inhabited place, آبادی *abadi.*

Inherent, جبلی *jebelli*, فطری *fetri.*

Inherit, to, بارث بردن *be ers bordan.*

Inheritance, see Heritage.

Inheritor, وارث *vares.*

Initial (adj.), ابتدائی *ebtedai.*

Initiative, ابتکار *ebtekar.*

Initiator, مبتکر *mobtaker.*

Injure, to, (به) ضرر رساندن *zarar rasandan (be).*

Injured (a person), آسیب دیده *asibdide*, زخمی *zaxmi.*

Injurious, مضر *mozerr.*

Injury, ضرر *zarar*, آسیب *asib.*

Injustice, بی انصافی *biensafi*, بیداد *bidad.*

Ink, مرکب *morakkab*, جوهر *jouhar.*

Inkstand, دوات *davat.*

Inlaid (with jewels), مرصع *morassa'.*

Inner, داخلی *daxeli*, توئی *tui*, درونی *daruni*, باطنی *bateni.*

Innocence, بیگناهی *bigonahi.*

Innocent, بیگناه *bigonah.*

Innovation, بدعت *bed'at.*

Innumerable, بیشمار *bifomar.*

Inoculation, تزریق *tazriq.*

Inquiry, see Enquiry.

Insects, حشرات *hafarat.*

Inside, داخل *daxel*, تو *tu*; باطن *baten*; (adj.), داخلی *daxeli*, توئی *tui*,
باطنی *bateni*; (adv. and prep.), داخل *daxel(e)*, (تو)ی *tu(ye)*; inside out,
وارونه *varune.*

Insignificant, ناچیز *naciz.*

Insipid (=tasteless), بیمزه *bimaze*, بینمک *binamak*; (fig.), خنک *xonak.*

Insist, to, اصرار کردن esrar k., تأکید کردن ta'kid k., پافشاری کردن pafeʃari k.

Insistence, اصرار esrar, تأکید ta'kid, پافشاری pafeʃari.

Insoluble, لاینحل la yanhall.

Inspect, to, see Examine.

Inspection, see Examination.

Inspector, باز رس baʒras, باز پرس baʒpors, مفتش mofatteʃ.

Inspiration (divine), الهام elham.

Install, نصب کردن nasb k., بر قرار کردن bar qarar k.; to be installed (in a house, etc.), بجا شدن ja be ja ʃ.

Instalment, قسط qest.

Instant (=moment), لحظه lahʒe.

Instead, عوض avaʒ(e), (ی)بجا beja(ye).

Institute, بنگاه bongah.

Institution, مؤسسه mo'assese; see also Regulation.

Instrument, آلت alat; (=puppet), آلت دست alate dast; instruments, آلات alat, اسباب asbab.

Insult, اهانت ehanat; to insult, اهانت کردن (به) ehanat k. (be).

Insupportable, غیر قابل تحمل yeire qabele tahammol, تحمل ناپذیر tahammol-napaʒir.

Insurance, بیمه bime.

Insurrection, شورش ʃureʃ, فتنه fetne.

Intellect, عقل aql.

Intellectual, عقلی aqli; (a person), روشنفکر rouʃanfekr.

Intelligence, هوش huʃ.

Intelligent, باهوش bahuʃ.

Intention, مقصود maqsud, نیت niyat, قصد qasd.

Intercalary, کبیسه kabise.

Intercede, شفاعت کردن ʃefa'at k., وساطت کردن vasatat k.

Intercession, شفاعت ʃefa'at, وساطت vasatat.

Intercourse, معاشرت mo'aʃerat, آمد و رفت amad o raft.

Interest, علاقه alaqe; (on money), سود sud, ربا reba, ربح rebh; (=advantage), نفع naf'.

Interested, ذی نفع ʒinaf', ذی علاقه ʒialaqe.

Interesting, جالب توجه jalebe tavajjoh; (to read), خواندنی xandani; (to hear), شنیدنی ʃenidani; (to see), دیدنی didani.

Interfere, to, دخالت کردن dexalat k., مداخله کردن modaxele k., فضولی کردن foʒuli k.

Interference, دخالت dexalat, مداخله modaxele.

Interior (adj.), داخلی daxeli, درونی daruni; Ministry of the Interior, وزارت داخله veʒarate daxele, وزارت کشور veʒarate keʃvar.

Intermediary, واسطه vasete, میانجی mianji.

Intern, to, باز داشت کردن baʒdaʃt k., باز داشتن baʒ d.

Internal, داخلی daxeli.

International, بین المللی beīn ol-melali.

Interned, باز داشت شده baʒdaʃt ʃode.

Internees, باز داشت شدگان baʒdaʃtʃodegan.

Internment, باز داشت baʒdaʃt; (place of), باز داشت گاه baʒdaʃtgah.

Interpellate, to, استیضاح کردن estiʒah k.

Interpellation, استیضاح estiʒah.

Interpret, to, تعبیر کردن ta'bir k.

Interpretation, تعبیر ta'bir.

Interpreter, مترجم motarjem.

Interregnum, فترت fatrat.

Interrogate, to, استنطاق کردن estentaq k.

Interrogation, استنطاق estentaq.

Interrupt, to, قطع کردن qat' k.

Interruption, قطع qat', وقفه vaqfe; (=interval), فاصله fasele.

Interval, فاصله fasele; (=pause), تنفس tanaffos.

Intervene, to, دخالت کردن dexalat k.

Intervention, دخالت dexalat.

Interview, ملاقات molaqat.

Intestine, روده rude.

Intimate (subs.), محرم mahram; (=boon companion), ندیم nadim.

Into, تو(ی) tu(ye), به be.

Intolerable, تحمل ناپذیر tahammolnapaʒir.

Intoxicate, to, مست کردن mast k.

Intoxicated, مست mast.

Intoxication, مستی masti.

Intrigue, دسیسه dasise, دسیسه بازی dasisebaʒi, سعایت sa'ayat; to intrigue, دسیسه کردن dasise k., سعایت کردن sa'ayat k. دسیسه کردن

Intriguer, باز دسیسه dasisebaʒ, کار سعایت sa'ayatkar.

Introduce, to, کردن معرف mo'arrefi k.

Introduction, معرف mo'arrefi; (of a book), دیباچه dibace, مقدمه moqaddame.

Invent, to, کردن اختراع extera' k.

Invention, اختراع extera'.

Inventor, مخترع moxtare'.

Investigate, to, کردن رسیدگی rasidagi k.; (= to establish as true), تحقیق کردن tahqiq k.

Investigation, تحقیق tahqiq; (=enquiry), رسیدگی rasidegi.

Invitation, دعوت da'vat.

Invite, to, کردن دعوت da'vat k.

Involuntarily, اختیار بی biexteyar.

Involve, to, داشتن بر در dar bar d.; to be involved in, گرفتار بودن gereftar b.

Involved (=complicated), پیچیده picíde.

Iris, زنبق ʒambaq.

Iron, آهن ahan; (adj.), آهنی ahani; (=flat iron), اتو otu; to iron, اتو کردن otu k.

Iron-clad (ship), پوش زره ʒerepuʃ, دار زره ʒeredar.

Iron-smith, آهنگر ahangar.

Irrevocable, اعاده قابل غیر ناپذیر برگشت ɣeire qabele e'ade, bargaʃt-napaʒir.

Irrigate, to, کردن آبیاری abyari k., دادن آب ab dadan; to be irrigated (watered), شدن مشروب maʃrub ʃ.

Irrigated (of land cultivated by irrigation), آبی abi.

Irrigation, آبیاری abyari.

Irritable, عصبانی asabani, اخلاق تند tondaxlaq.

Islam, اسلام eslam; Islamic, اسلامی eslami.

Island, جزیره jaʒire.

Isolation, تجرد tajarrod, انزوا enʒeva.

Issue (=number), شماره ʃomare; (=children), اولاد ōulad, نسل nasl; to issue, کردن صادر sader k.; (=publish), کردن منتشر montaʃer k.

It, آن an; (obs.), او u.

Italy, ایتالیا italia.

Itch, خارش xareʃ; to itch, خراشیدن xaraʃidan.

Item, فقره *faqare*, قلم *qalam*.

Ivory, عاج *aj*.

Ivy, پیچك *picak*.

J

Jackal, شغال *ʃaɣal*.

Jacket, نیم تنه *nimtane*.

Jack-of-all-trades, همه كاره *hamekare*.

Jam, مربا *morabba*.

Jasmine, یاسمن *yasaman*, یاس *yas*.

Jaundice, زردی (مرض) *(maraʒe) ʒardi*.

Jaw, چانه *cane*.

Jesus, حضرت عیسی *haʒrate isa*, حضرت مسیح *haʒrate masih*.

Jetty, اسكله *eskele*.

Jew, Jewish, یهودی *yahudi*, كلیمی *kalimi*.

Jewel, جوهر *joūhar*, گوهر *goūhar*.

Join, to, پیوستن *peīvastan*, وصل كردن *vasl k.*, متصل كردن *mottasel k.*; (= to become allied to), ملحق شدن (به) *elhaq ʃ. (be)*, الحاق شدن (به) *molhaq ʃ. (be)*.

Joint (of a limb), بند *band*, مفصل *mafsal*.

Joke, شوخی *ʃuxi*; to joke, شوخی كردن *ʃuxi k.*

Jolt, تكان *tekan*; to jolt, (به) تكان دادن *tekan dadan (be)*; to be jolted, تكان خوردن *tekan xordan*.

Journalist, روزنامه نویس *ruʒnamenevis*, روزنامه نگار *ruʒnamenegar*.

Journey, سفر *safar*, مسافرت *mosaferat*; to journey, سفر كردن *safar k.*, مسافرت كردن *mosaferat k.*

Joy, see Gladness.

Judaism, یهودیت *yahudiyat*.

Judge, قاضی *qaʒi*, حاكم *hakem*, دادرس *dadras*; to judge, قضاوت كردن *qaʒavat k.*; to judge (at law), داوری كردن *davari k.*

Judgement, حكم *hokm*, داوری *davari*; (= opinion), قضاوت *qaʒavat*.

Judicature, دادگستری *dadgostari*, عدلیه *adliye*.

Judicial, قضائی *qaʒai*.

Juice, آب *ab*.

Juicy, پر آب *porab*.

Jump, to, جستن *jastan,* پريدن *paridan.*

Junction, اتصال *ettesal.*

Jurisdiction, حوزه *hōuʒe,* قلمرو *qalamrōu.*

Jurisprudence (Islamic), فقه *feqh.*

Jury, هیئت منصفه *hei'ate monsefe.*

Just (=equitable), عادل *adel,* منصف *monsef,* منصفانه *monsefane.*

Justice, عدالت *adalat,* داد *dad,* انصاف *ensaf;* Ministry of Justice, وزارت دادگستری *veʒarate dadgostari;* court of justice, دادستان *dadsetan.*

Juvenile, خرد سال *xordsal.*

K

Keep, to, نگاه داشتن *negah d.,* داشتن *daʃtan.*

Keeper, مستحفظ *mostahfeʒ,* نگهبان *negahban.*

Keepsake, یادگار *yadegar.*

Kernel, مغز *mayʒ,* هسته *haste.*

Kettle, کتری *ketri.*

Kettle-drum, نقاره *naqqare,* کوس *kus.*

Key, کلید *kelid,* مفتاح *meftah.*

Khaki, خاکی *xaki.*

Kick, لگد *lagad;* to kick, لگد زدن *lagad ʒadan.*

Kid, بزغاله *boʒyale.*

Kidney, قلوه *qolve,* کلیه *kolie.*

Kill, to, کشتن *koʃtan.*

Kind (=sort), نوع *nōu',* طور *tōur,* جنس *jens,* جور *jur,* گونه *gune,* قسم *qesm;* (=amiable), مهربان *mehraban;* (as opp. to cash), جنس *jens;* in kind, جنسی *jensi;* to be kind (to), (به) مهربانی کردن *mehrabani k. (be).*

Kindergarten, کودکستان *kudakestan.*

Kindness, مهربانی *mehræbani.*

King, شاه *ʃah,* پادشاه *padeʃah,* ملک *malek,* سلطان *soltan;* King of Kings, شاهنشاه *ʃahenʃah.*

Kingdom (=country), مملکت *mamlekat;* (=domain), ملک *molk.*

Kingship, پادشاهی *padeʃahi,* سلطنت *saltanat.*

Kinship, خویشی *xiʃi.*

Kiss, بوسه *buse,* بوس *bus,* ماچ *mac;* to kiss, بوسیدن *busidan,* ماچ دادن *mac dadan.*

Kitchen, مطبخ *matbax,* آشپزخانه *aſpazxane.*

Kitten, بچه گربه *baccegorbe.*

Knee, زانو *zanu.*

Kneel, to, زانو زدن *zanu zadan.*

Knife, کارد *kard;* (=pocket-knife), چاقو *caqu.*

Knit, to, بافتن *baftan.*

Knock: to knock on the door, در زدن *dar zadan;* to knock down, زمین انداختن *zamin andaxtan;* to knock to pieces, خرد کردن *xord k.*

Knot, گره *gereh;* to knot, گره زدن *gereh zadan.*

Know, to, دانستن *danestan;* (=to recognize), شناختن *ſenaxtan;* (=to understand), فهمیدن *fahmidan;* (a language, the way, etc.), بلد بودن *balad budan;* to let (someone) know (=inform), خبر دادن *xabar dadan.*

Knowledge, علم *elm,* دانائی *danai,* دانش *daneſ,* سر رشته *sarreſte.*

Known, معلوم *ma'lum.*

Knuckle, بند انگشت *bande angoſt.*

L

Label, بر چسب *barcasb.*

Laboratory, آزمایشگاه *azmayeſgah.*

Labour, see Work, Effort, Trouble.

Labourer, کارگر *kargar,* عمله *amale.*

Lack (=absence of), عدم *adam.*

Ladder, نردبان *nardeban.*

Lady, خانم *xanom,* بانو *banu.*

Lagoon, مرداب *mordab.*

Lake, دریاچه *daryace.*

Lamb, بره *barre.*

Lame, لنگ *lang,* شل *ſal;* to be lame, لنگیدن *langidan.*

Lameness, لنگی *langi.*

Lament, to, ناله کردن *nale k.,* گریه و زاری کردن *gerie va zari k.*

Lamentation, ناله *nale,* گریه و زاری *gerie va zari.*

Lamp, چراغ *ceray.*

Lance, نیزه *neīze;* to lance (=to spear), نیزه زدن *neīze zadan.*

Lance-corporal, جوخه‌یار *juxeyar.*

Lancet, نیشتر *niſtar.*

Land, see Earth, Ground, Country; dry land, خشکی *xoʃki*; to land (intrans.), پیاده شدن *piade ʃ*.

Landlord (of house), صاحب خانه *sahebxane*.

Landowner, مالك *malek*; (=large landed proprietor), عمده مالك *omde-malek*; (=small landowner), خرده مالك *xordemalek*.

Language (=tongue), زبان *ʒaban*.

Lantern, فانوس *fanus*; storm lantern, چراغ دستی *ceraɣe dasti*.

Lapis-lazuli, لاجورد *lajvard*.

Lapse, to (=to be no longer valid), از اعتبار افتادن *aʒ eʿtebar oftadan*, لغو شدن *laɣv ʃ*.; (=to run out), منقضی شدن *monqaʒi ʃ*.

Large, see Big.

Last, آخرین *axerin*, آخر *axer*; last week, هفته گذشته *hafteye goʒaʃte*; last night, دیشب *diʃab*; the night before last, پریشب *pariʃab*; to last (=be durable), دوام کردن (داشتن) *davam k. (d.)*, پایدار بودن *paidar b*.; (=to stay), ماندن *mandan*; (of time), طول کشیدن *tul kaʃidan*; a shoe-maker's last, قالب کفش *qalebe kaʃ*.

Late, دیر *dir*; to be late, دیر کردن *dir k*.; you are late, دیر کردید *dir kardid*.

Lateness, دیری *diri*.

Latrine, مستراح *mostarah*, مبال *mabal*.

Latter, این *in* (as opposed to the former, آن *an*).

Laugh, خنده *xande*; to laugh, خندیدن *xandidan*.

Laughing, Laughter, خنده *xande*.

Launch, to, بآب انداختن *be ab andaxtan*.

Law, قانون *qanun*; Mohammadan law, شرع *ʃarʿ*, شریعت *ʃariʿat*; science of Mohammadan law, فقه *feqh*; international law, حقوق بین المللی *hoquqe bein ol-melali*; civil law, حقوق مدنی *hoquqe madani*; criminal law, قانون جزائی *qanune jaʒai*; common law (=custom), عرف *orf*, قانون عرفی *qanune orfi*.

Law-court, محکمه *mahkame*.

Lawful, قانونی *qanuni*; (lawful according to Mohammadan law), واجب *vajeb*, فرض *farʒ* (i.e. lawful and imperative); مستحب *mostahabb* (i.e. desirable but the omission of which does not constitute a sin); مباح *mobah*, حلال *halal*, (i.e. the commission of which is not sinful but the performance of which is not meritorious); see also Unlawful.

Lawsuit, دعوی *da'va*, مرافعه *morafe'e*.

Lawyer, وکیل *vakil*.

Lax, سست *sost*.

Lay: to lay aside, کنار گذاشتن *kenar goẓaſtan*; to lay the table, میزرا چیدن *miẓra cidan*; to lay an egg, تخم کردن *toxm k.*

Laziness, تنبلی *tambali*, کاهلی *kaheli*.

Lazy, تنبل *tambal*, کاهل *kahel*.

Lead (metal), سرب *sorb*; to lead (=to show the way), هدایت کردن *hedayat k.*, رهنمائی کردن *rahnamai k.*

Leader, پیشوا *piſva*, سردار *sardar*, رئیس *ra'is*; (of a movement), علمدار *alamdar*.

Leadership, هدایت *hedayat*, ریاست *riasat*, پیشوائی *piſvai*.

Leaf, برگ *barg*, ورق *varaq*.

League (=federation), اتحادیه *ettehadiye*, اتحاد *ettehad*.

Leak, رخنه *rexne*, سوراخ *surax*; to leak, آب پس دادن *ab pas dadan*.

Lean, to, (به) تکیه کردن *tekie k. (be)*, (به) اتکا کردن *etteka k. (be)*; (=to be inclined), (به) مایل بودن *mayel b. (be)*.

Leap-year, سال کبیسه *sale kabise*.

Learn, to, آموختن *amuxtan*, یاد گرفتن *yad gereftan*.

Learned, دانا *dana*, عالم *alem*, فاضل *faẓel*, دانشمند *daneſmand*, عارف *aref*.

Learning, علم *elm*, فضل *faẓl*, دانش *daneſ*, معرفت *ma'refat*.

Lease, اجاره *ejare*; to lease out, اجاره دادن *ejare dadan*; to lease (take on lease), اجاره گرفتن *ejare gereftan*.

Least: at least, اقلاً *aqallan*, دست کم *daste kam*, لا اقل *la aqall*.

Leather, چرم *carm*; chamois leather, جیر *jir*.

Leathern, چرمی *carmi*.

Leave (=permission), اجازه *ejaẓe*, اذن *eẓn*; (=furlough), مرخصی *moraxxasi*; to leave (=to place), گذاشتن *goẓaſtan*; (=to abandon), ترک کردن *tark k.*; to take leave, وداع کردن *veda' k.*

Leaven, مایه *maye*, خمیر *xamir*.

Lecture, کنفرانس *konferans*; (=lesson), درس *dars*; to lecture, کنفرانس دادن *konferans dadan*; (=to teach), درس دادن *dars dadan*.

Leech, زالو *ẓalu*.

Leek, تره *tarre*.

Left, چپ cap; left over, باقی baqi, مانده mande, باقیمانده baqimande; on (to) the left, دست چپ daste cap.

Leg, پا pa, ساق saq.

Legacy, میراث miras.

Legal, see Lawful.

Legation, سفارت sefarat.

Legend, افسانه afsane.

Legendary, افسانه آمیز afsaneamiz.

Legible, خوانا xana.

Legislate, to, قانون وضع کردن qanun vaz' k.; قانون گذاری کردن qanungozari k.

Legislative, مقنن moqannen; legislative power, قوه مقننه qovveye moqannene.

Legislation, قانون گذاری qanungozari, وضع قوانین vaz'e qavanin; (=the laws), مجموع قوانین majmu'e qavanin.

Legislator, قانونگذار qanungozar, مقنن moqannen.

Legitimate (by birth), حلالزاده halalzade.

Leisure, فراغت farayat.

Lemon, لیمو limu.

Lend, to, قرض دادن qarz dadan.

Length, طول tul.

Lengthy (cf time), مدید madid.

Lentil, عدس adas.

Leopard, پلنگ palang.

Leper, مجذوم majzum.

Leprosy, جذام jozam.

Less (in quantity), کم kam, کمتر kamtar; (in rank), کهتر kehtar.

Lessee, اجاره دار ejaredar.

Lesson, درس dars; to take lessons (with), درس خواندن (پیش) dars xandan (piʃ(e)).

Lessor, اجاره دهنده ejare dehande.

Lest, مبادا mabada, مبادا که mabada ke.

Let, to, see Allow and Lease.

Letter (=epistle), نامه name, کاغذ kayaz, مکتوب maktub, مراسله morasele; (of the alphabet), حرف harf.

Lettuce, کاهو kahu.

Levée, سلام salam.

Level (adj.), هموار hamvar, مسطح mosattah; to level, هموار کردن hamvar k., مسطح کردن mosattah k.

Liaison, رابطه rabete; liaison officer, افسر رابط afsare rabet.

Liar, دروغگو doruɣgu, کاذب kaɀeb.

Libel, توهین toūhin; to libel, توهین کردن toūhin k.

Liberal, see Generous; (in politics), آزادیخواه aɀadixah.

Liberalism, آرادیخواهی aɀadixahi.

Liberality, see Generosity.

Liberate, see Free.

Liberator, منجی monji.

Liberation, رهائی rahai, تخلیص taxlis.

Liberty, see Freedom.

Librarian, کتابدار ketabdar.

Library, کتابخانه ketabxane.

Licence, اجازه ejaɀe, پروانه parvane.

Lichen, پیسه pise.

Lick, to, لیسیدن lisidan.

Lid, سر sar, سرپوش sarpuʃ.

Lie, دروغ doruɣ, کذب keɀb; to lie, دروغ گفتن doruɣ goftan; (= be situated) واقع شدن vaqe' ʃ.; to lie down, دراز کشیدن daraɀ kaʃidan.

Lieutenant (army), ستوان setvan; sub-lieutenant, ناوبان navban; lieutenant (naval), ناوسروان navsarvan.

Lieutenant-Colonel, سرهنگ دوم sarhang dovvom, نائب سرهنگ na'eb sarhang.

Lieutenant-Commander, ناخدا سوم naxoda sevvom.

Lieutenant-General, سرلشکر sarlaʃkar.

Life, زندگی ɀendegi, عمر omr, حیات hayat; standard of living, سطح زندگی sathe ɀendegi.

Lift, to, بر داشتن bar d., بلند کردن boland k.

Ligament, پیوند peivand.

Light (adj., = not dark), روشن roūʃan, منور monavvar; (= not heavy), سبک sabok, خفیف xafif; (noun), روشنائی roūʃana'i, نور nur.

Lighthouse, فانوس دریائی fanuse daryai, فنار fanar.

Lightness (=little weight), سبكی *saboki,* خفت *xeffat.*

Lightning, برق *barq.*

Like, چون *cun,* مانند *manand(e),* مثل *mesl(e)*; to like (=to be inclined to do something), میل داشتن *meil d.*; (a person or thing), دوست داشتن *dust d.*; to be like (=to resemble), شبیه بودن (به) *fabih b. (be),* شباهت داشتن (به) *fabahat d. (be).*

Likeness, شباهت *fabahat.*

Lilac, یاس *yas.*

Lily, سوسن *susan*; white lily, گل مریم *gole maryam.*

Limb, عضو *ozv.*

Lime, آهك *ahak.*

Limekiln, کوره آهکپزی *kureye ahakpazi.*

Limit, حد *hadd*; to limit, محدود کردن *mahdud k.*

Limited, محدود *mahdud.*

Limp, to, لنگیدن *langidan.*

Line, سطر *satr,* خط *xatt*; (of battle), صف *saff*; (=cord), ریسمان *risman*; to draw a line, خط کشیدن *xatt kafidan*; to draw up in line, صف کشیدن *saff kafidan.*

Linen, کتان *kattan.*

Lining (of a garment), آستر *astar.*

Link (in a chain), حلقه *halqe.*

Linseed, بزرك *bazrak.*

Lion, شیر *fir,* اسد *asad.*

Lioness, شیر ماده *fire made.*

Lip, لب *lab.*

Listen, to, شنیدن *fenidan,* گوش دادن *guf dadan.*

Literal, لفظی *lafzi,* تحت اللفظی *taht ol-lafzi.*

Literary, ادبی *adabi.*

Litter (camel litter), محمل *mahmel,* کجاوه *kajave*; (carried by mules), تخت روان *taxte ravan*; (=rubbish), آشقال *afqal,* خاك روبه *xakrube.*

Little (=small), کوچك *kucek,* خرد *xord,* صغیر *sayir*; (in quantity), اندك *andak,* کم *kam*; (subs.), اندکی *andaki,* کمی *kami,* قدری *qadri,* یک خرده *yak xorde,* جزئی *joz'i*; a little while, اندکی *andaki,* چندی *candi,* مدتی *moddati*; little by little, کم کم *kam kam,* رفته رفته *rafte rafte*; very little (in quantity), یك ذره *yak zarre.*

Live, to (=be alive), زیستن ҳistan, زنده بودن ҳende b.; (=to pass one's time), زندگی کردن ҳendegi k., بسر بردن be sar bordan; (=to dwell), سکونت داشتن sokunat d., ساکن بودن saken b.

Livelihood, معاش ma'aʃ, مدد معاش madade ma'aʃ, معیشت ma'iʃat.

Liver, جگر jegar, کبد kabed.

Living (=alive), زنده ҳende.

Lo! اینك inak.

Load, بار bar; to load, بار کردن bar k.; (a gun), پر کردن por k.

Loam, ماسه mase.

Loan, قرض qarҳ, وام vam, بدهی bedehi.

Lobby, دالان dalan.

Local, محلی mahalli.

Lock, قفل qofl; (of hair), زلف ҳolf to lock, قفل کردن qofl k.

Locksmith, قفلساز qoflsaҳ.

Locust, ملخ malax.

Logic, منطق manteq.

Logical, منطقی manteqi.

Loin, کمر kamar.

Loin-cloth, لنگ long.

Long, طولانی tulani; (of place), طویل tavil, دراز deraҳ, daraҳ; how long? خیلی وقت پیش cand vaqt, تاچند ta cand, تاکی ta kēi; long ago, چند وقت (از این) xēili vaqt piʃ (aҳ in); to take a long time, طول کشیدن tul kaʃidan; how long does it take? چقدر طول میکشد ce qadr tul mikaʃad; as long as, تا ta.

Long-suffering, بردبار bordbar; (subs.), بردباری bordbari.

Look, نگاه negah, نظر naҳar; to look, نگاه کردن negah, k., نظر کردن naҳar k.; (=to appear, impers.), بنظر آمدن be naҳar amadan; مانستن manestan (3rd pers. sing. present only); to look for (something), (چیزی) عقب aqab(e ciҳi) gaʃtan. گشتن

Loom, دستگاه نساجی dastgahe nassaji.

Loop-hole, راه گریز rahgoriҳ.

Loose (=slack), شل ʃol; (=wide), گشاد goʃad; (=undone), باز baҳ; (=not firm), لك lak; to loose, گشاد کردن goʃad k., گشادن goʃadan, باز کردن baҳ k.

Lord (=God), رب rabb; House of Lords, مجلس اعیان majlese a'yan.

Lorry, ماشین باری *mašine bari.*

Lose, to, گم کردن *gom k.*; (a game, etc.), باختن *baxtan.*

Loss, زیان *zian,* تلف *talaf;* losses (=casualties), تلفات *talafat;* to suffer loss, زیان دیدن *zian didan.*

Lost, گم *gom,* مفقود *mafqud.*

Lot: to draw lots, قرعه کشیدن *qor'e kašidan.*

Lottery, بخت آزمائی *baxtazmai.*

Loud, بلند *boland.*

Lounge, to, لمیدن *lamidan.*

Louse, شپش *šepeš.*

Love, عشق *ešq,* محبت *mohabbat,* حب *hobb,* وداد *vedad;* to love, محبت داشتن (به) *mohabbat d. (be),* دوست داشتن *dust d.;* to be in love (with), عاشق بودن (به) *ašeq b. (be).*

Lover, عاشق *ašeq.*

Low, پست *past;* (=quietly), آهسته *aheste;* to low (of a cow), بانگ زدن *bang zadan.*

Lower, to, پائین آوردن *pain avardan,* بزیر انداختن *be zir andaxtan.*

Loyal, با وفا *bavafa,* وفادار *vafadar,* صادق *sadeq.*

Loyalty, وفاداری *vafadari,* صداقت *sedaqat.*

Luck, شانس *šans;* see also Fortune and Destiny.

Lucky, see Fortunate; he is a lucky fellow, خوش بحال او *xoš be hale u*

Luggage, اسباب *asbab.*

Lump, بر آمدگی *baramadegi.*

Lunacy, دیوانگی *divanegi,* جنون *jonun.*

Lunar, قمری *qamari.*

Lunatic, دیوانه *divane,* مجنون *majnun.*

Lunch, ناهار *nahar.*

Lung, شش *šoš,* ریه *rie.*

Lust, شهوت *šahvat,* هوا *hava,* هوس *havas.*

Lustful, شهوت پرست *šahvatparast.*

Luxurious, باتجمل *batajammol;* (of a person) خوش‌گذران *xošgozaran,* عیاش *ayyaš.*

Luxury, تجمل *tajammol,* خوشگذرانی *xošgozarani,* عشرت *ešrat,* عیش *eiš.*

M

Mace (weapon), گرز gorz, چماق comaq.

Mace-bearer, گرز دار gorzdar, چماق دار comaqdar.

Machine-gun, مسلسل mosalsal.

Machine-tools, ماشین آلات maſinalat.

Machinery, ماشین آلات maſinalat, دستگاه ماشین dastgahe maſin.

Mad, see Lunatic.

Magazine (=periodical), مجله majalle.

Maggot, کرم kerm.

Magic, جادو jadu, سحر sehr.

Magician, جادوگر jadugar.

Magnet, آهن ربا ahanroba.

Magnetic, مقناطیسی meqnatisi.

Magpie, زاغ zaɣ.

Main (=principal), عمده omde; main road, شاهراه ſahrah.

Maize, ذرت zorrat, بلال balal.

Majesty: His Majesty, اعلیحضرت a'la haƶrat; Her Majesty, علیا حضرت olya haƶrat.

Major (mil.), سرگرد sargord; (obs.), یاور yavar.

Major-General, سرلشکر sarlaſkar.

Majority, اکثریت aksariyat.

Make, to, کردن kardan, ساختن saxtan, درست کردن dorost k.; made in, ساخته saxte(ye), کار kar(e); see also Create.

Malaria, تب و نوبه tab o nōube, مالاریا malaria.

Male, مذکر moƶakkar; (=he-), نر nar.

Malice, کین kin, بغض boɣƶ, بدخواهی badxahi.

Malign, to, بدگوئی کردن (از) badgui k. (az).

Malignant, بدخواه badxah; (of illness), خطرناک xatarnak, مهلک mohlek.

Malignity, بدخواهی badxahi, کینه kine, دشمنی doſmani.

Mallet, کلوخ کوب koluxkub.

Man (=mankind), انسان ensan, بنی آدم bani adam, بشر baſar; (=male person), مرد mard, آدم adam.

Manage, to (=direct), اداره کردن edare k.

Management, اداره *edare,* مديريت *modiriyat;* (=managing body), هيئت *hei'ate modire;* (=skill in management), حسن تدبير *hosne tadbir.*

Manager, مدير *modir.*

Mandate (=protectorate), قيمومیت *qeimumiyat;* to be under a mandate (of a country), تحت الحماية بودن *taht ol-hemaye b.*

Mane (of an animal), يال *yal.*

Mange, گر *gar.*

Manger, آخور *axor.*

Manliness, مردی *mardi,* مردانگى *mardanegi.*

Manner, طور *tour,* طريق *tariq,* منوال *menval,* رسم *rasm,* طرز *tarz.*

Manners, آداب *adab.*

Manual (=by hand), دستى *dasti.*

Manufacture, to, ساختن *saxtan.*

Manufacturer, سازنده *sazande;* (=owner of a factory), صاحب كارخانه *sahebe karxane.*

Manure, كود *kud;* to manure, كود دادن *kud dadan.*

Manuscript, نسخه خطى *nosxeye xatti;* (adj.), خطى *xatti.*

Many, بسيار *besyar,* خيلى *xeili,* زياد *ziad;* many a, بسى *basi;* how many, چند *cand;* twice as many (as), دو برابر *do barabar(e);* many times, بارها *barha.*

Map, نقشه *naqʃe.*

Marble, مرمر *marmar;* (adj.), مرمرى *marmari.*

March, to, قدم زدن *qadam zadan;* marches (=boundaries), مرز *marz,* سرحد *sarhadd.*

Mare, ماديان *madian.*

Margin, حاشيه *haʃie.*

Marine, دريائى *daryai,* بحرى *bahri.*

Mark, نشان *neʃan,* علامت *alamat;* (=brand), داغ *day;* to mark, علامت گذاشتن *alamat gozaʃtan;* (=to brand), داغ كردن *day k.*

Market, بازار *bazar.*

Marriage, ازدواج *ezdevaj,* عروسى *arusi;* temporary marriage, صیغه *siye;* marriage ceremony, عقد *aqd,* نكاح *nekah;* marriage contract, عقد نامه *aqdname;* marriage portion, مهر *mehr.*

Married, متأهل *mota'ahhel.*

Marrow (plant), كدو *kadu;* (of a bone), مغز *mayz.*

Marry, to, ازدواج کردن ezdevaj k., عروسی کردن arusi k.; (of a man), زن گرفتن zan gereftan; (of a woman), شوهر کردن souhar k.

Marsh, (بطلاق) باطلاق botlaq.

Martyr, شهید sahid.

Martyrdom, شهادت sehadat.

Marvel, عجب ajab.

Marvellous, عجیب ajib, عجب ajab.

Masculine, مذکر mozakkar.

Mass, توده tude; the masses, توده مردم tudeye mardom; to mass, جمع شدن jam' s.

Massacre, قتل عام qatle amm; to massacre, قتل عام کردن qatle amm k.

Mast, دگل dagal.

Master, آقا aqa, صاحب saheb; (=teacher), معلم mo'allem.

Masterpiece, شاهکار sahkar.

Match (=game), مسابقه mosabeqe; (=lucifer), کبریت kebrit; (=rival, equal), حریف harif; (=pair), جفت joft; (=marriage), عروسی arusi.

Material (=cloth), پارچه parce; (=matter), مطلب matlab; (adj.=not spiritual), مادی maddi.

Maternal, مادری madari.

Mathematical, ریاضی riazi.

Mathematician, ریاضی دان riazidan.

Mathematics, ریاضیات riaziyat.

Matter, see Affair and Material; it does not matter, عیب ندارد eib nadarad, ضرر ندارد zarar nadarad.

Matting, حصیر hasir.

Mattress, دوشك dosak.

Mature (of a thing), رسیده raside; (of a person), کامل kamel, پخته poxte; to mature, رسیدن rasidan, کامل شدن kamel s.

Maturity (of a thing), رسیدگی rasidegi; (of a person), کمال kamal, پختگی poxtegi; (=age of discretion), بلوغ boluy; (of a bill, etc.), سر رسید sarrasid.

Mausoleum, مقبره maqbare.

Mauve, بنفش banafs.

Mayor, شهردار sahrdar, رئیس بلدیه ra'ise baladiye.

Meadow, چمن caman, چمنزار camanzar, مرغزار maryzar.

Mean (=vile), پست *past,* دون *dun,* فرومایه *forumaye;* (=average, adj. and subs.), واسطه *vasete,* معدل *moʻaddel;* see also Avaricious.

Meaning, معنی *maʻni;* (=purpose), مقصود *maqsud.*

Meanness, see Avarice.

Means, وسیله *vasile;* by means of, بوسیله *be vasile(ye),* بواسطه *be vasete(ye);* by all means (=of course), البته *albatte;* by no means, بهیچ وجه *be hic vajh.*

Meanwhile, در ضمن *dar ʒemn,* ضمناً *ʒemnan,* در این بین *dar in beïn.*

Measles, سرخك *sorxak.*

Measure, میزان *miʒan,* پیمان *peïman,* اندازه *andaʒe;* (=a vessel for measuring), پیمانه *peïmane;* (=poetical metre), بحر *bahr;* beyond measure, میزان گرفتن زیاده از حد *ʒiade aʒ hadd;* to measure, پیمودن *peïmudan,* میزان گرفتن *miʒan gereftan,* اندازه گرفتن *andaʒe gereftan.*

Meat, گوشت *guʃt.*

Meddle, to, دخالت کردن *dexalat k.,* مداخله کردن *modaxele k.,* فضولی کردن *foʒuli k.*

Meddler, فضول *foʒul.*

Meddling (subs.), مداخله *modaxele,* فضولی *foʒuli.*

Mediation, وساطت *vesatat,* توسط *tavassot,* میانجیگری *mianjigari.*

Mediator, واسطه *vasete,* میانجی *mianji.*

Medical, طبی *tebbi,* پزشکی *peʒeʃki.*

Medicine, دارو *daru,* دوا *dava.*

Mediocre, متوسط *motavasset.*

Meditate, to, تفکر کردن *tafakkor k.,* فکر کردن *fekr k.*

Meditation, تفکر *tafakkor,* فکر *fekr.*

Meet, to, ملاقات کردن *molaqat k.;* (by chance), بر خوردن (به) *bat xordan (be);* to go out to meet (someone), استقبال کردن *esteqbal k.;* (of a committee), تشکیل شدن *taʃkil ʃ.*

Meeting, جلسه *jalse,* مجمع *majmaʻ;* (=encounter), ملاقات *molaqat.*

Melancholy, مالخولیا *malxulia,* افسردگی *afsordegi;* (adj.), افسرده *afsorde.*

Melody, نغمه *naɣme.*

Melon, خربوزه *xarbuʒe,* خربزه *xarboʒe,* گرمك *garmak,* طالبی *talebi.*

Melt, to (of snow, etc.), آب شدن *ab ʃ.;* (of metals, etc.), گداختن *godaxtan.*

Member, عضو *oʒv.*

Membership, عضویت *oʒviyat.*

Memorandum, یاد داشت *yaddaſt.*

Memorial, یادگار *yadegar.*

Memory, یاد *yad,* حفـظ *hefƶ,* خاطر *xater;* (=power of remembering), حافظه *hafeƶe.*

Mention, ذكر *ƶekr;* above-mentioned, فوق الذكر *foūq oƶ-ƶekr,* مشار اليه *moſaron eleīh.*

Mercantile, تجارتى *tejarati.*

Mercenary, مزدور *moƶdur.*

Merchandise, مال التجاره *mal ot-tejare.*

Merchant, تاجر *tajer.*

Merciful, رحيم *rahim.*

Mercury (=quicksilver), سيم آب *simab.*

Mercy, رحمت *rahmat,* رحم *rahm,* مرحمت *marhamat;* to have mercy, رحم كردن *rahm k.,* مرحمت كردن *marhamat k.*

Merely, فقط *faqat,* تنها *tanha,* صرفًا *serfan.*

Meridian, ظهر *ƶohr.*

Merit (=worth), لياقت *liaqat,* قابليت *qabeliyat,* قدر *qadr;* to merit, see Deserve.

Message, پيغام *peīɣam,* پيام *peīam;* to send a message, پيغام فرستادن *peīɣam ferestadan.*

Messenger, پيغامبر *peīɣambar,* پيامبر *peīambar,* قاصد *qased.*

Messiah, مسيح *masih.*

Metal, فلز *feleƶƶ;* metalled (of a road), شوسه *ſose.*

Metallic, فلزى *feleƶƶi.*

Metaphor, استعاره *este'are;* metaphorically, بطور مجاز *betoūr-e mojaƶ.*

Method, see Manner.

Metre, see Measure.

Microbe, ميكرب *mikrob.*

Microscope, ريزبين *riƶbin.*

Midday, ظهر *ƶohr.*

Middle, وسط *vasat,* ميان *mian,* ميانه *miane;* (=centre), مركز *markaƶ.*

Midnight, نصف شب *nesfe ſab.*

Midwife, قابله *qabele;* midwifery, قابلگى *qabelegi.*

Migrate, to, كوچ كردن *kuc k.;* see also Emigrate.

Migration, كوچ *kuc;* see also Emigration.

Milch-cow, گاو شيرده *gave ſirdeh.*

Mild, ملايم molayem, نرم narm.

Mildness, ملايمت molayemat, نرمی narmi.

Military, نظامی neӡami; military service, خدمت نظام xedmate neӡam.

Militia, جند jond, عسکر askar.

Milk, شیر ſir.

Milkman, شیری ſiri.

Mill, آسیا asia.

Millet, ارزن arӡan, ذرت ӡorrat.

Million, ملیون meliun.

Minaret, منار menar.

Mind, عقل aql; (=memory), خاطر xater; to call to mind, یاد آوردن yad avardan; to come to mind, یاد آمدن yad amadan.

Mine, معدن maʿdan, کان kan; (=an explosive), مین min.

Miner, معدنچی maʿdanci.

Mineral (adj.), معدنی maʿdani.

Mineralogist, معدنشناس maʿdanſenas.

Mineralogy, معدنشناسی maʿdanſenasi.

Minesweeper, مینروب minrub, کشتی مین جمع کن kaſtiye minjamʿkon.

Minister (of state), وزیر vaӡir.

Ministry, وزارت veӡarat.

Minor (adj., =under age), صغیر السن saγir os-senn, خرد سال xordsal.

Minority, اقلیت aqalliyat; (=being under age), خرد سالی xordsali, صغر السن seγar os-senn.

Mint, نعناع naʿnaʿ, پونه pune; (for coins), ضرابخانه ӡarrabxane.

Minus (in arithmetic), منها menha.

Minute (of time), دقیقه daqiqe; minutes of a meeting, صورت جلسه surate jalse.

Miracle, معجزه moʿjeӡe.

Miraculous, معجزه آمیز moʿjeӡeamiӡ.

Mirage, سراب sarab.

Mirror, آئینه aine.

Misappropriation, حیف و میل heif o meil, اختلاس extelas.

Miscarriage (med.), سقط جنین seqte janin.

Miscellaneous, مختلف moxtalef, متفرق motafarreq.

Miscellany, مجموعه majmuʿe.

Mischief (=wickedness), شرارت *ʃararat.*

Mischief-maker, دو بهم زن *dobehamʒan.*

Mischievous, شیطانی *ʃeitani.*

Mischievousness, شیطنت *ʃeitanat.*

Miser, see Avaricious.

Miserable, شکسته‌حال *ʃekastehal,* بی چاره *bicare,* مسکین *meskin.*

Misery, بیچارگی *bicaregi.*

Misfortune, بدبختی *badbaxti,* بلا *bala,* فلاکت *falakat.*

Miss (unmarried woman), دوشیزه *duʃize*; to miss (=regret the absence of someone), دلتنگ بودن (برای) *deltang b. (baraye).*

Mission, سفارت *sefarat*; (prophetic mission), رسالت *resalat.*

Mist, غبار *yobar,* مه *meh.*

Mistake, see Error.

Mistress (=teacher), معلم *moʻallem.*

Misuse, سوء استفاده *suʻe estefade*; to misuse, سوء استفاده کردن (از) *suʻe estefade k. (aʒ).*

Mix, to, مخلوط کردن *maxlut k.,* آمیختن *amixtan.*

Mixed, مخلوط *maxlut.*

Mixture, اختلاط *extelat,* ترکیب *tarkib.*

Moan, ناله *nale*; to moan, ناله کردن *nale k.,* آه و ناله کردن *ah o nale k.*

Mobile, متحرک *motaharrek.*

Mobilization, بسیج *basij*; general mobilization, بسیج عمومی *basije omumi.*

Mobilize, to, بسیج کردن *basij k.*; (capital), براه انداختن *be rah andaxtan.*

Mock, to, ریشخند کردن *riʃxand k.,* مسخره کردن *masxare k.*

Mockery, مسخره *masxare.*

Model, نمونه *namune.*

Moderate, معتدل *moʻtadel.*

Moderation, اعتدال *eʻtedal.*

Modern, متجدد *motajadded*; (=new), جدید *jadid,* تازه *taze.*

Modest, با حیا *bahaya,* با شرم *baʃarm.*

Modesty, حیا *haya.*

Modification, تعدیل *taʻdil.*

Moist, نمناك *namnak,* تر *tar.*

Moisture, نمی *nami,* تری *tari.*

Mole (animal), موش کور *muʃe kur*; (on the skin), خال *xal.*

Moment (of time), لحظه *lahze*, دم *dam*.

Monastery, دير *deīr*; (Sufi hospice), خانقاه *xaneqah*.

Monday, دو شنبه *do ſambe*.

Money, پول *pul*.

Money-changer, صراف *sarraf*.

Mongol, مغل *moɣol*.

Monkey, ميمون *meīmun*.

Monopolistic, انحصارى *enhesari*.

Monopoly, انحصار *enhesar*.

Monotonous, يكنواخت *yaknavaxt*.

Month, ماه *mah*.

Monthly, ماهيانه *mahiane*, ماهى *mahi*, ماهانه *mahane*, هر ماهه *har mahe*.

Moon, ماه *mah*.

Moonlight, ماهتاب *mahtab*, ماهتابى *mahtabi*, مهتاب *mahtab*, مهتابى *mahtabi*.

Moral, اخلاق *axlaqi*; (=spiritual), معنوى *ma'navi*.

Morale, روحيه *ruhiye*.

Morality, اخلاق *axlaq*.

Morals, اخلاق *axlaq*.

More, بيش *biſ*, بيشتر *biſtar*, زياده *ziade*; more or less, كم و بيش *kam o biſ*; neither more nor less, بى كم و زياد *bi kam o ziad*.

Moreover, see Further.

Morning, پيش از ظهر *piſ az zohr*, صبح *sobh*; (early morning, before daybreak), سحر *sahar*.

Mortar (implement), هاون *havan*; (=gun), خمپاره انداز *xompareandaz*; (=mixture of lime, etc.), ساروج *saruj*.

Mortgage, گرو *gerōu*, رهن *rahn*; to mortgage, رهن كردن *rahn k.*, گرو گذاشتن *gerōu gozaſtan*.

Mosque, مسجد *masjed*.

Mosquito, پشه *paſe*.

Moss, خزه *xaze*.

Most, بيشتر *biſtar*, اكثر *aksar*.

Moth, بيد *bid*; (=butterfly), پروانه *parvane*.

Mother, مادر *madar*.

Mother-in-law (of wife), مادر شوهر *madarſōuhar*; (of husband), مادر زن *madarzan*.

Motion, حرکت *harakat*, جنبش *jombeʃ*.

Motive (ulterior), غرض *ɣaraẕ*; to have an ulterior motive, غرض داشتن *ɣaraẕ d.*

Motto, شعار *ʃeʻar.*

Mould (=shape), قالب *qaleb.*

Mount, to (a horse, carriage, etc.), سوار شدن *savar ʃ.*

Mountain, کوه *kuh.*

Mountainous country, کوهستان *kuhestan*, کوهسار *kuhsar.*

Mounted, سوار *savar.*

Mourn, to, عزادار بودن *aẕadar b.*

Mourner, عزادار *aẕadar*; (professional mourner), نوحه خوان *nŏuhexan.*

Mourning, سوگواری *sŏugvari*, عزا *aẕa*, عزاداری *aẕadari.*

Mouse, موش *muʃ.*

Mouth, دهن *dahan*, دهان *dahan*; (of a river), دهنه *dahane.*

Move, to (intrans.), تکان خوردن *tekan xordan*, حرکت کردن *harakat k.*, جنبیدن *jombidan*; (trs.,= to transfer), انتقال دادن *enteqal dadan*; to move (house, etc.), نقل مکان کردن *naqle makan k.*

Moveable (of property), منقول *manqul.*

Movement, حرکت *harakat*, جنبش *jombeʃ*; (political, etc.), نهضت *nehẕat.*

Much, بسیار *besyar*, خیلی *xēili*, زیاد *ẕiad*; this much, این قدر *in qadr*; that much, آنقدر *an qadr*; how much, چقدر *ceqadr.*

Mucus, مخاط *moxat.*

Mud, گل *gel.*

Muddled, درهم و برهم *dar ham o bar ham.*

Muddy, گل آلود *gelalud.*

Mulberry (white), توت *tut*; (red), شاهتوت *ʃahtut.*

Mulct, جریمه *jarime*, مصادره *mosadere*; to mulct, جریمه کردن *jarime k.*, مصادره کردن *mosadere k.*

Mule, قاطر *qater.*

Muleteer, قاطرچی *qaterci*; مکاری *mokari*, چاروادار *carvadar.*

Mulla, آخوند *axond.*

Multiplication, ضرب *ẕarb.*

Mummy, مومیا *mumia.*

Mummification, مومیاکاری *mumiakari.*

Municipal council, انجمن شهرداری *anjomane ʃahrdari.*

Municipality, شهرداری‬ *ʃahrdari.*

Munitions, مهمات‬ *mohemmat.*

Murder, قتل‬ *qatl*; to murder, قتل کردن‬ *qatl k.*

Murderer, قاتل‬ *qatel.*

Murmur, همهمه‬ *hamhame.*

Muscle (of the body), عضله‬ *aʒole,* ماهیچه‬ *mahice.*

Museum, موزه‬ *muʒe.*

Mushroom, قارچ‬ *qarc.*

Music, موسیقی‬ *musiqi,* ساز و آواز‬ *saʒ o avaʒ.*

Musk, مشك‬ *meʃk,* نافه‬ *nafe.*

Musket, تفنگ‬ *tofang.*

Muslim, مسلمان‬ *mosalman.*

Muslin, ململ‬ *malmal.*

Must, باید‬ *bayad* (impers., with subjunctive).

Mustard, خردل‬ *xardal.*

Myologist, ماهیچه شناس‬ *mahiceʃenas.*

Myology, ماهیچه شناسی‬ *mahiceʃenasi.*

Mystery, رمز‬ *ramʒ,* سر‬ *serr,* راز‬ *raʒ.*

Mysterious, مرموز‬ *marmuʒ.*

Mystic (a person), اهل تصوف‬ *ahle tasavvof,* صوفی‬ *sufi.*

Mystical, تصوف آمیز‬ *tasavvofamiʒ,* عرفانی‬ *erfani.*

Mysticism, تصوف‬ *tasavvof,* عرفان‬ *erfan.*

N

Nail (of the body), ناخن‬ *naxon*; (=spike), میخ‬ *mix.*

Naked, see Bare.

Name, نام‬ *nam,* اسم‬ *esm*; to name, نامیدن‬ *namidan,* نام گذاشتن‬ *nam goʒaʃtan,* نام دادن‬ *nam dadan.*

Named (=called), موسوم (به)‬ *mōusum (be).*

Namely, یعنی‬ *ya'ni.*

Nap, چرت‬ *cort*; to take a nap, چرت زدن‬ *cort ʒadan.*

Nape, قفا‬ *qafa.*

Napkin, دستمال‬ *dastmal.*

Narcissus, نرگس‬ *narges.*

Narrate, to, حكايت كردن *hekayat k.*

Narration, Narrative, حكايت *hekayat.*

Narrow, تنگ *tang,* باريك *barik.*

Narrowness, تنگى *tangi,* باريكى *bariki.*

Nation, ملت *mellat,* قوم *qoūm.*

National, ملى *melli.*

Nationality, مليت *melliyat.*

Nationalize, to, دولتى كردن *doūlati k.,* ملى كردن *melli k.*

Native, بومى *bumi;* native land, وطن *vatan.*

Natural, طبيعى *tabiʻi;* (=innate), ذاتى *zati,* جبلى *jebelli;* (=original), اصلى *asli.*

Naturally, طبيعةً *tabiʻatan,* بالطبع *bet-tabʻ.*

Nature, طبيعت *tabiʻat;* (=disposition), طبع *tabʻ;* (=composition), سرشت *sereſt.*

Naughtiness, شيطنت *ſeitanat.*

Naughty, شيطان *ſeitan.*

Naval, بحرى *bahri,* دريائى *daryai.*

Navel, ناف *naf.*

Navigate, to, كشتى راندن *kaſti randan.*

Navigation, ناوبرى *navbari,* كشتى رانى *kaſtirani,* دريا نوردى *daryanavardi.*

Navigator, دريا نورد *daryanavard,* ناوبر *navbar.*

Navy, نيروى دريائى *niruye daryai.*

Near, نزديك *nazdik(e)* قريب *qarib(e).*

Nearly, تقريبًا *taqriban,* قريب *qarib(e),* نزديك *nazdik(e),* در حدود *dar hodud(e).*

Nearness, نزديكى *nazdiki,* مقاربت *moqarebat.*

Necessary, لازم *lazem,* ضرورى *zaruri,* واجب *vajeb,* مقتضى *moqtazi.*

Necessities, لوازمات *lavazemat;* (=exigencies), مقتضيات *moqtaziat.*

Neck, گردن *gardan.*

Necklace, گردن بند *gardanband.*

Nectarine, شليل *ſalil,* شفتالو *ſeftalu.*

Need, حاجت *hajat,* ضرورت *zarurat,* احتياج *ehteyaj;* to need, حاجت (احتياج, لازم) داشتن *hajat (ehteyaj, lazem) d.*

Needle, سوزن *suzan.*

Negative, منفى *manfi,* منكر *monker;* (gram., subs.), نفى *nafy.*

Neglect, Negligence, غفلت ɣeflat, اهمال ehmal; to neglect, عفلت کردن ɣeflat k., غافل بودن ɣafel b., اهمال ورزیدن ehmal varƶidan.

Negligent, غافل ɣafel.

Negotiable, در خور معامله darxore mo'amele.

Negotiate, to, معامله کردن mo'amele k.

Negotiation, معامله mo'amele; (=discussion), مذاکره moƶakere.

Negro, سیاه siah.

Neigh, شیهه ʃeihe; to neigh, شیهه زدن ʃeihe ƶadan.

Neighbour, همسایه hamsaye, مجاور mojaver.

Neighbourhood, مجاورت mojaverat, حوالی havali, اطراف atraf.

Neither...nor, نه...نه na...na.

Nephew (=brother's son), برادر زاده baradarƶade, پسر برادر pesar-baradar; (=sister's son), خواهر زاده xaharƶade, پسر خواهر pesarxahar.

Nerve, عصب asab.

Nervous (=fearful), ترسناك tarsnak.

Nest, آشیانه aʃiane, لانه lane.

Net (=mesh), تور tur, توری turi; net (of profit, etc.), خالص xales.

Nettle, گزنه gaƶane.

Neutral, بی طرف bitaraf.

Neutralize, to, خنثی کردن xonsa k.

Neutrality, بی طرفی bitarafi.

Never, هرگز hargeƶ, اصلًا aslan, ابدًا abadan, هیچ hic (all followed by a negative verb).

Nevertheless, با این همه ba in hame.

New, نو no͡u, تازه taƶe, جدید jadid.

News, خبر xabar, اخبار axbar; news agency, خبر گزاری xabargoƶari; good news, مژده moƶde.

Newspaper, روزنامه ruƶname.

New Year, نوروز no͡uruƶ.

Next (=coming), آینده ayande, دیگر digar, بعد ba'd.

Niece (=brother's daughter), دختر برادر doxtarbaradar, برادر زاده baradar-ƶade; (sister's daughter), دختر خواهر doxtarxahar, خواهر زاده xaharƶade.

Night, شب ʃab.

Nightingale, بلبل bolbol, هزاردستان haƶardastan.

Nightmare, کابوس kabus.

Night-watchman, پاسبان شب *pasbane ſab*, شب‌گرد *ſabgard*, عسس *asas*.

Nimble, چالاك *calak*, چابك *cabok*.

Nine, نه *noh*.

Nineteen, نوزده *nuzdah*.

Ninety, نود *navad*.

No, نه *na*, خیر *xeɪr*, نخیر *naxeɪr*.

Nobility, نجابت *nejabat*, شرافت *ſarafat*; (=the aristocracy), طبقه اشراف *tabaqeye aſraf*.

Noble, شریف *ſarif*, نجیب *najib*, اصیل *asil*.

Noise, صدا *sada*; (=clamour), داد و فریاد *dad o faryad*, غوغا *ɣouɣa*, هنگامه *hengame*.

Noisy, پر صدا *porsada*, با سر و صدا *ba sar o sada*.

Nomad, ایلیاتی *iliati*, خانه بدوش *xane be duſ*.

Nominate, to, نامزد کردن *namzad k*.

Nomination, معرفی *mo'arrefi*.

Nonsense, یاوه‌گوئی *yavegui*, چرند *carand*, مهملات *mohmalat*, مزخرفات *mozaxrafat*, حرف پوچ *harfe puc*, حرف مفت *harfe moft*; to talk nonsense, حرف مفت زدن *harfe moft zadan*, مهملات گفتن *mohmalat goftan*.

Noon, ظهر *zohr*.

No one, هیچ کس *hic kas* (followed by negative verb).

Noose, کمند *kamand*.

Normal, عادی *adi*.

North, شمال *ſamal*; north-east, شمال شرق *ſamale ſarqi*; north-west, شمال غربی *ſamale ɣarbi*.

Northern, شمالی *ſamali*.

Nose, بینی *bini*, دماغ *damaɣ*.

Nose-bag (of a horse), توبره *toūbare*.

Notary, وکیل *vakil*.

Notched, دندانه‌دار *dandanedar*.

Note, یاد داشت *yaddaſt*, تبصره *tabsere*; (=banknote), اسکناس *eskenas*.

Note-book, کتابچه *ketabce*.

Nothing, هیچ *hic*, هیچی *hici* (followed by negative verb).

Notice (=observation), ملاحظه *molaheze*; (=notification), اعلان *e'lan*, اعلام *e'lam*, آگهی *agahi*; to notice (=observe), ملاحظه کردن *molaheze k*.

Notification, see Notice.

Notify, to, آگهی دادن agahi dadan, اعلام کردن e‘lam k., اعلان کردن e‘lan k.

Notoriety, رسوائی rosvai.

Notorious, رسوا rosva.

Notwithstanding, با این همه ba in hame; notwithstanding that, با اینکه ba in ke, با وجودیکه ba vojudike.

Nought, صفر sefr.

Noun, اسم esm.

Nourish, to, پروردن parvardan, پرورش دادن parvare∫ dadan.

Novel (subs.), رمان roman.

Novice, نو آموز nōuamuʒ, مبتدی mobtadi.

Now, اکنون aknun, حالا hala, فعلاً fe‘lan, نقداً naqdan.

Nuisance, اذیت aʒiyat, زحمت اسباب asbabe ʒahmat; to be a nuisance, مزاحم بودن اذیت کردن aʒiyat k., زحمت بودن اسباب asbabe ʒahmat b., موزهم b.

Numb, بی حس bihess.

Number, شماره ∫omare, عدد adad, تعداد te‘dad; to number, see Count.

Nurse, پرستار parastar; to nurse, پرستاری کردن parastari k.

Nursing, پرستاری parastari.

Nut, جوز jōuʒ; nuts (in general), آجیل ajil.

Nutrition, تغذیه taʒʒie, غذا ʒaʒa.

O

Oak, بلوط balut.

Oar, پارو paru.

Oath, سوگند sōugand, قسم qasam; to swear an oath, سوگند (قسم) خوردن sōugand (qasam) xordan.

Obedience, اطاعت eta‘at, فرمانبرداری farmanbardari.

Obedient, مطیع moti‘, فرمانبردار farmanbardar.

Obelisk, میل mil, ستون sotun.

Object (=thing), چیز ciʒ; (=aim), مقصود maqsud; to object, اعتراض کردن e‘teraʒ k., معترض بودن mo‘tareʒ b.

Objection, اعتراض e‘teraʒ.

Obligation, تعهد ta'ahhod, وظیفه vaẓife; to be under an obligation, موظف بودن movaẓẓaf b., متعهد بودن mota'ahhed b.; to put (someone) under an obligation, (سرکسی) منت گذاشتن mennat goẓaʃtan (sare kasi).

Oblige, to, see Force.

Obliterate, to, محو کردن mahv k.

Obscene, فاحش faheʃ, زشت ẕeʃt.

Obscenity, فحش fohʃ, زشتی ẕeʃti.

Obscure, تار tar, تیره tire; (=unknown), مجهول majhul.

Observance, رعایت re'ayat.

Observation, مشاهده moʃahede.

Observatory, رصد خانه rasadxane.

Observe, to, رعایت کردن re'ayat k.; (=to see), مشاهده کردن moʃahede k.

Obsolete, متروك matruk.

Obstacle, مانع mane'.

Obstinacy, لجاجت lejajat, لجبازی lajjbaẕi.

Obstinate, لجوج lajuj, لجباز lajjbaẕ.

Obtain, see Acquire.

Occupancy, تصرف tasarrof.

Occupant, متصرف motasarref, ساکن saken.

Occupation, تصرف tasarrof; military occupation, اشغال eʃɣal; (=employment), شغل ʃoɣl, کار kar.

Occupied (=busy), مشغول maʃɣul; (of a country), اشغال شده eʃɣal ʃode.

Occupy, to, تصرف کردن tasarrof k.; (a country), اشغال کردن eʃɣal k.; to be occupied (=busy), مشغول بودن maʃɣul b.

Occur, to, see Happen.

Occurrence, see Event.

Ocean, اقیانوس oqianus.

Oculist, چشم پزشك caʃmpeẕeʃk.

Odd (of a number), طاق taq; see also Strange.

Ode (of five to eighteen couplets), غزل ɣaẕal; (of over eighteen couplets), قصیده qaside.

Of, از aẕ.

Off, از aẕ; far off, دور dur, بعید ba'id, دور دست durdast.

Offence, see Sin and Error.

Offend, to, آزردن *azordan*, رنجانیدن *ranjanidan*; (in 3rd pers. only), بر خوردن به *bar xordan be*; see also Sin; to be offended, رنجیدن *ranjidan*.

Offer (=proposal), پیش نهاد *pisnehad*; to offer (=propose), پیشنهاد کردن *pisnehad k.*; (=to present), تقدیم کردن *taqdim k.*

Offering, تقدیم *taqdim*; see also Gift and Sacrifice.

Office (place), دفتر *daftar*, اداره *edare*; (=public charge), منصب *mansab*, کار *kar*, مقام *maqam*, شغل *soyl*.

Officer, صاحب منصب *sahebmansab*, افسر *afsar*; petty officer, مهناوی *mehnavi*; chief petty officer, مهناوی یکم *mehnavi yakom*.

Official (adj.), رسمی *rasmi*; (noun), مأمور *ma'mur*.

Offspring, بچه *bacce*; اولاد *oulad*.

Often, بارها *barha*, بسا *basa*.

Oil, روغن *rouyan*; (=petroleum) نفت *naft*; heavy (diesel) oil, مازوت *mazut*; to oil, روغن زدن *rouyan zadan*.

Old (of persons), پیر *pir*, سالخورده *salxorde*, مسن *mosenn*; (of things), کهنه *kohne*; old age, پیری *piri*.

Olive (fruit), زیتون *zeitun*.

Omen, فال *fal*; to take an omen, فال گرفتن *fal gereftan*.

Omission (=fault), سهو *sahv*; (from a document), افتادگی *oftadegi*.

Omit, to (from a document), انداختن *andaxtan*.

On, بر *bar*, بر رو(ی) *bar ru(ye)*; on foot, پیاده *piade*; on horseback, سواره *savare*.

Once, یکدفعه *yak daf'e*, یکمرتبه *yak martabe*, یکبار *yak bar*; (=once upon a time), باری *bari*; at once, فوراً *fouran*.

One, یك *yak*, *yek*.

Onion, پیاز *piaz*; spring onion, پیازچه *piazce*.

Only (=one), یگانه *yagane*, تنها *tanha*; see also Merely.

Ooze, لجن *lajan*; to ooze, تراوش کردن *taravos k.*

Open, باز *baz*, مفتوح *maftuh*; to open, باز کردن *baz k.*

Openly (=publicly), آشکار *askar*, علناً *alanan*.

Operate, to, عمل کردن *amal k.*

Operation, عمل *amal*; surgical operation, عمل جراحی *amale jarrahi*.

Opinion, عقیده *aqide*, فکر *fekr*, رأی *ra'i*.

Opium, تریاك *taryak*; to smoke opium, تریاك کشیدن *taryak kasidan*.

Opium smoker, تریاکی *taryaki*; افیونی *afyuni*.

Opponent, مخالف *moxalef*.

Opportune, بموقع *be mouqe'*, بجا *be ja*.

Opportunity, فرصت *forsat*; to seize an opportunity, فرصترا غنیمت شمردن *forsatra yanimat fomordan*.

Oppose, to, (با) مخالفت کردن *moxalefat k.* (*ba*), (با) ضدیت کردن *zeddiyat k.* (*ba*).

Opposed, opposing, مخالف *moxalef*.

Opposite (=facing), (ی)روبرو *ruberu(ye)*, مقابل *moqabel(e)*.

Opposition, مخالفت *moxalefat*, ضدیت *zeddiyat*; the opposition (=those who oppose), مخالفین *moxalefin*; to be in opposition, مخالف بودن *moxalef b.*

Oppress, to, دست *dast*, جفا کردن *jafa k.*, ظلم کردن *zolm k.*, ستم کردن *setam k.*, دستدرازی کردن *dastderazi k.*, تعدی کردن *ta'addi k.* (all with prep. بر *bar*).

Oppression, تعدی *dastderazi*, دست درازی ستم *setam*, ظلم *zolm*, جفا *jafa*, *ta'addi*.

Oppressive, Oppressor, ظالم *zalem*, ستمکار *setamkar*, جفاکار *jafakar*.

Optimism, خوشبینی *xofbini*.

Optimistic, خوشبین *xofbin*.

Option, اختیار *exteyar*.

Or, یا *ya*; either...or, یا...یا *ya...ya*.

Oral, شفاهی *fefahi*.

Orange, پرتقال *portoqal*.

Orator, ناطق *nateq*.

Order (=arrangement), تنظیم *tanzim*, ترتیب *tartib*; (=rule), قاعده *qa'ede*, آئین *ain*, قانون *qanun*; (=command), امر *amr*, حکم *hokm*, فرمان *farman*, دستور *dastur*; in order (=arranged), منظم *monazzam*, مرتب *morattab*; to put in order (=to arrange), منظم کردن *monazzam k.*, مرتب کردن *morattab k.*; (=to put right), درست کردن *dorost k.*; (=to repair), تعمیر کردن *ta'mir k.*; out of order (=broken), خراب *xarab*; in order that, تا *ta*, که *ke* (with subjunctive present); to order, امر دادن *amr dadan*, حکم دادن *hokm dadan*, فرمان دادن *farman dadan*, فرمودن *farmudan*; standing orders, نظام نامه *nezamname*.

Orderly (=servant), امر بر *amrbar*; (=methodical), مرتب *morattab*, منظم *monazzam*.

Ordinary, عادی *adi*.

Organization, تشکیل *tafkil*, تشکیلات *tafkilat*, سازمان *sazman*.

Organize, to, تشکیل دادن *taʃkil dadan.*

Orientalist, خاورشناس *xavarʃenas.*

Origin, اصل *asl;* (=source), مبداء *mabda',* منبع *mamba'.*

Original, اصلی *asli.*

Ornament, زینت *ʒinat,* زیور *ʒivar,* آرایش *arayeʃ.*

Ornamented, مزین *moʒayyan.*

Orphan, یتیم *yatim.*

Orphanage, دارالایتام *dar ol-eitam,* پرورشگاه یتیمان *parvareʃgahe yatiman.*

Ostentation, خودنمائی *xodnamai,* تظاهر *taʒahor.*

Ostentatious, خودنما *xodnama.*

Osteologist, استخوانشناس *ostoxanʃenas.*

Osteology, استخوانشناسی *ostoxanʃenasi.*

Ostrich, شتر مرغ *ʃotormorʏ.*

Other, دیگر *digar;* (=different), غیر *ʏeir;* (=the rest of), سائر *sa'er.*

Otherwise, والا *va ella,* واگرنه *va agar na.*

Ottoman (Turkish), عثمانی *osmani.*

Ought (=should), باید *bayad* (impers., with subjunctive).

Out, بیرون *birun,* خارج *xarej;* to be out, بیرون بودن *birun b.;* (of a flower, etc.), باز شدن *baʒ ʃ.;* to set out, راه افتادن *rah oftadan,* حرکت کردن *harakat k.*

Outcry, داد و فریاد *dad o faryad,* غوغا *ʏouʏa.*

Outside, بیرون *birun,* خارج *xarej.*

Outstanding, بر جسته *barjaste.*

Outwardly, ظاهرًا *ʒaheran.*

Oven, تنور *tanur.*

Over (=above), (ی)بالا *bala(ye),* بر *bar,* (ی)بر رو *bar ru(ye),* بر سر *bar sar(e),* فوق *fouq(e),* فراز *faraʒ(e),* (ی)رو *ru(ye);* (=across), آنطرف *an taraf(e),* (ی)آنسو *an su(ye);* (=in excess), زاید *ʒayed;* (=remaining), باقی مانده *baqimande,* مانده *mande,* باقی *baqi;* (=finished), تمام *tamam;* to hand over, تحویل دادن *tahvil dadan;* to make over, واگذار کردن *vagoʒar k.*

Overcast, گرفته *gerefte.*

Overcoat, پالتو *paltou.*

Overcome, see Conquer and Defeat.

Overflow, to, لبریز شدن *labriʒ ʃ.;* (of a river), طغیان کردن *toʏian k.*

Overland, از راه خشكى *az rahe xoʃki.*

Overseer, ناظر *naẕer,* مباشر *mobaʃer.*

Overshadow, to, (دادن) تحت الشعاع قرار گرفتن *taht oʃ-ʃoʻa qarar gereftan (dadan).*

Oversight, سهو *sahv,* اشتباه *eʃtebah.*

Overtake, to, (به) رسیدن *rasidan (be),* (به) در رسیدن *dar rasidan (be).*

Overthrow, to, بر انداختن *bar andaxtan;* see also Conquer.

Overturn, to, سر نگون کردن *sarnegun k.,* وارونه کردن *varune k.*

Owl, بوم *bum,* جغد *joɣd.*

Own, to (= to possess), داشتن *daʃtan;* (= to admit), اعتراف کردن *eʻteraf k.*

Owner, مالك *malek,* صاحب *saheb.*

Ownership, مالكیت *malekiyat.*

Ox, گاو *gav.*

P

Pace (= step), قدم *qadam,* گام *gam;* (= speed), تندی *tondi.*

Pacify, to, فرو نشاندن *foru neʃandan.*

Pack, to, بستن *bastan.*

Package, بسته *baste.*

Pack-horse, یابو *yabu.*

Packing-needle, جوال دوز *javalduz.*

Pack-saddle, پالان *palan.*

Page (of a book, etc.), صفحه *safhe,* ورق *varaq;* to turn over the pages, ورق زدن *varaq zadan.*

Pail, دلو *dalv,* سطل *satl.*

Pain, درد *dard,* عذاب *azab,* الم *alam;* to give pain, درد کردن *dard k.*

Painstaking, زحمت کش *zahmatkaʃ.*

Paint, رنگ *rang;* to paint (of an artist), نقاشی کردن *naqqaʃi k.;* (a room, etc.), رنگ زدن *rang zadan.*

Painter (= artist), نقاش *naqqaʃ.*

Painting, نقاشی *naqqaʃi;* (= picture), تصویر *tasvir,* پرده نقاشی *pardeye naqqaʃi.*

Pair, جفت *joft;* one of a pair, لنگه *lenge.*

Palace, قصر *qasr,* کاخ *kax.*

Pale, زرد *ʒard*; he went pale, رنگش پرید *rangeʃ parid*.

Palm (of the hand), کف *kaff*; date palm, درخت خرما *daraxte xorma*, نخل *naxl*.

Pansy (flower), بنفشه *banaffe*.

Panther, یوز پلنگ *yuʒpalang*.

Pants, زیر شلوار *ʒirʃalvar*.

Paper, کاغذ *kaɣaʒ*; blotting-paper, کاغذ خشک کن *kaɣaʒe xoʃkkon*.

Parachute, چتر نجات *catre nejat*.

Parade, سان *san*; to parade (of an army), سان دادن *san dadan*.

Paradise, بهشت *beheʃt*, جنت *jennat*, فردوس *ferdous*.

Paralysis, فلج *falaj*.

Paralytic, افلیج *eflij*, فالج *falej*.

Paralyze, to, فلج کردن *falaj k*.

Paraphernalia, اسباب *asbab*.

Parasite (biol.), طفیل *tofeil*, انگل *angal*.

Parasitologist, انگل شناس *angalʃenas*.

Parasitology, انگل شناسی *angalʃenasi*.

Parcel, بسته *baste*.

Pardon, عفو *afv*; to pardon, عفو کردن *afv k.*, معاف کردن *moʻaf k.*, بخشیدن *baxʃidan*.

Parenthesis, جمله معترض *jomleye moʻtareʒ*.

Parenthetically, بطور معترضه *be toure moʻtareʒe*.

Parents, والدین *valedein*.

Parity, مساوات *mosavat*, برابری *barabari*.

Paroxysm, حمله *hamle*.

Parrot, طوطی *tuti*.

Parsley, جعفری *jaʻfari*.

Part (= piece), تکه *tekke*, قطعه *qetʻe*, جزء *joʒʻ*, حصه *hesse*, قسم *qesm*; (= side), جانب *janeb*, طرف *taraf*; on the part of, از جانب *aʒ janeb(e)*, طرف *taraf(e)*; for the most part, غالباً *ɣaleban*; to part (= to separate, trans.), جدا کردن *joda k.*

Partial (= biased), طرفدار *tarafdar*.

Partiality, طرفداری *tarafdari*.

Participate, to, شرکت جستن (کردن) *ʃerkat jostan (k.)*.

Participation, شرکت *ʃerkat*.

Particular, خاص *xass*, مخصوص *maxsus*, مختص *moxtass*; particulars, تفصيلات *tafsilat*; in particular, بخصوص *be xosus*, خصوصاً *xosusan*, مخصوصاً *maxsusan*, على الخصوص *alal-xosus*.

Partisan, هوادار *havadar*, طرفداز *tarafdar*; to be a partisan (of), هواداری (طرفداری) کردن (از) *havadari (tarafdari) k. (az)*.

Partner, شريك *farik*.

Partnership, شركت *ferkat*.

Partridge, كبك *kabk*.

Party (=social assembly), مهمانى *mehmani*; (=political party), حزب *hezb*; see also Group.

Pass (=permit), جواز *javaz*, پروانه *parvane*; (=mountain pass), تنگه *tange*, كتل *kotal*; to pass, گذر کردن *gozar k.*, گذشتن *gozaftan*, رد شدن *radd* (all with prep. از *az*); (=to pass through), عبور کردن (از) *obur k. (az)*; to pass an examination, قبول شدن *qabul f.*; to pass over (to connive at), اغماض کردن *eymaz k.*; to pass (a law), وضع کردن *vaz' k.*

Passage (=corridor), دالان *dalan*; (=literary extract), عبارت *ebarat*; (=journey), سفر *safar*; (=alley-way), تیمچه *timce*.

Passenger, مسافر *mosafer*; (adj., of a train), مسافربر *mosaferbar*.

Passport, گذر نامه *gozarname*, تذکره *tazkere*.

Past (former), گذشته *gozafte*, ماضى *mazi*; (=on the other side of), آن طرف *an taraf(e)*; the past, گذشته *gozafte*; (==past career), سابقه *sabeqe*.

Paste, خمير *xamir*, سريشم *serifom*.

Pasture, مرغزار *mary*, چراگاه *ceragah*, مرتع *marta'*, علفزار *alafzar*, مرغزار *maryzar*; to pasture (intrans.), چریدن *caridan*; to take to pasture, چرانيدن *caranidan*.

Patch, پینه *pine*, وصله *vasle*.

Patent, سند *sanad*; patent right, امتیاز انحصاری *emteyaze enhesari*; (=evident), آشکار *afkar*, هویدا *hoveida*, روشن *roufan*, بدیهی *badihi*.

Paternal, پدری *pedari*.

Patience, صبر *sabr*, حوصله *housele*, شکیبائی *fekibai*, طاقت *taqat*, تحمل *tahammol*, بردباری *bordbari*.

Patient, با طاقت *bataqat*, صبور *sabur*, بردبار *bordbar*, شکیبا *fekiba*, با تحمل *batahammol*, بطاقت.

Patriot, Patriotic, وطنپرست *vatanparast*.

Patriotism, وطنپرستى *vatanparasti*.

Patrol, كشيك *kašik*; (=section), جوخه *juxe*.

Patrol-leader, سرجوخه *sarjuxe*.

Patron, حامى *hami*.

Patronage, حمایت *hemayat*, سر پرستى *sarparasti*, توجه *tavajjoh*.

Patronymic, نسبت *nesbat*.

Pattern, نمونه *namune*, مثال *mesal*.

Pause, تنفس *tanaffos*, وقفه *vaqfe*; to pause, تنفس كردن *tanaffos k.*, وقفه كردن *vaqfe k.*

Pave, to, سنگفرش كردن *sangfarš k.*

Paving, سنگفرشى *sangfarši*.

Pavement, پیاده‌رو *piaderou*.

Pawn, رهن *rahn*, گرو *gerou*; (at chess), پیاده *piade*.

Pawnbroker, گروگیر *gerougir*.

Pay, see Wages; to pay, پرداختن *pardaxtan*.

Payee, گیرنده وجه *girandeye vajh*, برات گیر *baratgir*.

Payment, تأدیه *ta'diye*, پرداخت *pardaxt*; (=sum of money), وجه *vajh*, پول *pul*.

Pea (=chick-pea), نخود *noxod*; (=green pea), نخود فرنگى *noxode farangi*.

Peace, صلح *solh*, آشتى *ašti*; (=rest), آسایش *asayeš*, آرام *aram*, راحت *rahat*, رفاهیت *refahiyat*; to make peace, صلح كردن *solh k.*, آشتى كردن *ašti k.*

Peaceful (=peace-loving), صلح دوست *solhdust*.

Peach, هلو *holu*.

Peacock, طاؤس *ta'us*.

Pear, گلابى *golabi*.

Pearl, مروارید *morvarid*, لوءلوء *lo'lo'*, درّ *dorr*.

Peasant, زارع *zare'*, روستائى *rustai*, دهقان *dehqan*, رعیت *ra'iyat*.

Peculation, اختلاس *extelas*.

Peculiar, مختص *moxtass*, مخصوص *maxsus*; see also Strange.

Peculiarity, خاصیت *xassiyat*, خصوصیت *xosusiyat*.

Pedigree, نسب نامه *nasabname*.

Pedlar, دست‌فروش *dastforuš*, پیله‌ور *pilevar*, خرده فروش *xordeforuš*.

Peel, پوست *pust*, قشر *qešr*; to peel, پوست كندن *pust kandan*.

Peerless, بینظیر *binazir*.

Pellet (=shot), ساچمه *sacme*, گلوله *golule*.

Pen, قلم *qalam.*

Penal, جزائى *jaӡai;* penal law, حقوق جزائى *hoquqe jaӡai.*

Pencil, مداد *medad.*

Penetrate, to (= to go in), داخل شدن *daxel f.;* (= to acquire influence), نفوذ کردن *nofuӡ k.*

Penetration (= acuteness), فراست *ferasat.*

Peninsula, شبه جزیره *febhe jaӡire.*

Penitence, see Repentance.

Penknife, چاقو *caqu.*

Pen-nib, سرقلم *sarqalam.*

Pension, حقوق تقاعد *hoquqe taqa'od,* حقوق باز نشستگى *hoquqe baӡnefastegi.*

Pentateuch, تورات *tourat.*

People, مردم *mardom,* مردمان *mardoman,* اهالى *ahali;* the common people, عوام الناس *avamm on-nas,* عوام *avamm,* عامه *amme;* to people, آباد کردن *abad k.*

Pepper, فلفل *felfel;* to pepper, فلفل زدن *felfel ӡadan.*

Per cent: five per cent, صدى پنج *sadi panj.*

Perception, درک *dark,* ادراک *edrak.*

Perchance (= by chance), احیانًا *ahyanan,* اتفاقًا *ettefaqan;* (= perhaps), مگر *magar.*

Perfect, کامل *kamel,* تمام *tamam;* to perfect, کامل کردن *kamel k.*

Perfection, کمال *kamal.*

Perfume, عطر *atr.*

Perhaps, شاید *fayad.*

Period, مدت *moddat;* (= epoch), دوره *doure,* عصر *asr.*

Periodical (= magazine), مجله *majalle.*

Perish, to, هلاک شدن *halak f.,* تلف شدن *talaf f.*

Perishable, فانى *fani.*

Permanent, پایدار *paidar,* دائمى *da'emi.*

Permanently, دائمًا *da'eman.*

Permissible, مجاز *mojaӡ,* روا *rava,* حلال *halal.*

Permission, اجازه *ejaӡe,* اذن *eӡn.*

Permit, جواز *javaӡ,* پروانه *parvane;* to permit, see Allow.

Perpetrate, to, (به) مرتکب شدن *mortakeb f. (be).*

Perpetration, ارتکاب *ertekab.*

Perpetual, مدام *modam,* دائم *da'em.*

Perpetuity, مداومت *modavemat.*

Perplex, to, حیران کردن *hēiran k.,* متحیر ساختن *motahaïyer saxtan.*

Perplexed, حیران *hēiran,* متحیر *motahaïyer.*

Persecute, to, تعقیب کردن *ta'qib k.,* زجر کردن *zajr k.,* اذیت کردن *aziyat k.*

Persecution, تعقیب *ta'qib,* زجر *zajr,* اذیت *aziyat.*

Perseverance, مداومت *modavemat,* استقامت *esteqamat,* پشتکار *poʃtekar.*

Persevere, to, مداومت کردن *modavemat k.,* استقامت کردن *esteqamat k.,* پشتکار نشان دادن *poʃtekar neʃan dadan.*

Persevering (adj.), پشتکار *poʃtekar.*

Persia, ایران *iran.*

Persian, ایرانی *irani;* Persian (language), فارسی *farsi.*

Person, شخص *ʃaxs,* کس *kas,* آدم *adam,* نفر *nafar,* تن *tan;* in person, شخصًا *ʃaxsan.*

Personality, شخصیت *ʃaxsiyat.*

Personnel Department, کارگزینی *kargozini.*

Perspiration, عرق *araq.*

Perspire, to, عرق کردن *araq k.*

Persuade, to, وادار کردن *vadar k.,* ترغیب کردن *taryib k.,* متقاعد کردن *motaqa'ed k.*

Persuasion, ترغیب *taryib;* see also Faith.

Pertain, to, (به) مربوط بودن *marbut budan (be).*

Perverse, خودسر *xodsar,* متمرد *motamarred,* لجوج *lajuj.*

Perverseness, خودسری *xodsari,* تمرد *tamarrod,* لجاجت *lejajat.*

Pessimism, بدبینی *badbini.*

Pessimistic, بدبین *badbin.*

Pestilence, طاعون *ta'un.*

Pet, to, نوازش کردن *navazeʃ k.*

Petal, برگ *barg.*

Petition, عرض *arz,* عریضه *arize.*

Petitioner, عارض *arez.*

Petroleum, نفت *naft.*

Petrologist, سنگ شناس *sangʃenas.*

Petrology, سنگ شناسی *sangʃenasi.*

Pharmacologist, دارو شناس *daruʃenas.*

Pharmacology, دارو شناسی *daruʃenasi.*

Pharmacy, دواخانه *davaxane,* داروخانه *daruxane.*

Pheasant, قرقاول *qarqavol.*

Philosopher, فیلسوف *filsuf,* حکیم *hakim.*

Philosophy, فلسفه *falsafe,* حکمت *hekmat.*

Phoenix, هما *homa.*

Photograph, عکس *aks;* to photograph, عکس انداختن *aks andaxtan.*

Photographer, عکاس *akkas.*

Photographic studio, عکاسخانه *akkasxane.*

Photography, عکاسی *akkasi.*

Physical, طبیعی *tabi'i.*

Pick, to, see Gather and Choose.

Pickaxe, کلنگ *kolang.*

Pickles, ترشی *torʃi.*

Pickpocket, جیب بر *jibbor.*

Picture, تصویر *tasvir.*

Piebald, ابلق *ablaq.*

Piece, تکه *tekke,* پاره *pare,* قطعه *qet'e.*

Pier, اسکله *eskele.*

Pierce, to, سفتن *softan,* سوراخ کردن *surax k.*

Piety, تقوی *taqva,* دیانت *dianat.*

Pig, خوك *xuk;* (wild), گراز *goraʒ.*

Pigeon, کبوتر *kabutar,* کفتر *kaftar.*

Pigeon-fancier, کفتر باز *kaftarbaʒ,* کبوتر باز *kabutarbaʒ.*

Pigment, رنگ *rang.*

Pilgrim, زوار *ʒavvar,* زائر *ʒa'er;* (to Mecca), حاجی *haji, hajji.*

Pilgrimage, زیارت *ʒiarat;* (to Mecca), حج *hajj;* to make a pilgrimage, زیارت رفتن *ʒiarat raftan;* (to Mecca), حج رفتن *hajj raftan.*

Pill, حب *habb.*

Pillage, see Plunder.

Pillar, ستون *sotun.*

Pillow, بالش *baleʃ,* ناز بالش *naʒbaleʃ.*

Pilot (of a ship), کشتیبان *kaʃtiban;* (of an aeroplane), هوانورد *havanavard.*

Pimp, قرمساق *qoromsaq.*

Pimple, جوش *juʃ.*

Pin, سنجاق *sanjaq.*

Pinch, نیشگون *niʃgun;* to pinch, نیشگون گرفتن *niʃgun gereʃtan.*

Pink (colour), صورتی *surati.*

Pious, متقی *mottaqi,* متدین *motadayyen.*

Pipe, لوله *lule;* (musical), نی *neī;* (water-pipe for smoking), قلیان *qalian;* (short pipe for smoking), چپوق *copoq.*

Piper, نی زن *neīʒan.*

Pistachio-nut, پسته *peste.*

Pistol, طپانچه *tapance.*

Piston-rod, میله *mile.*

Pit, چاه *cah,* چال *cal,* چاله *cale* گود *gōud.*

Pitch: to pitch a tent, چادر زدن *cador ʒadan.*

Pitcher, کوزه *kuʒe.*

Pity, رحم *rahm,* شفقت *ʃafaqat;* to have pity, رحم کردن *rahm k.,* شفقت کردن *ʃafaqat k.;* it is a pity, حیف است *heīf ast;* what a pity! چه حیف *ce heīf.*

Pivot, محور *mehvar,* مدار *madar.*

Place, جا *ja,* مکان *makan,* محل *mahall;* to place, see Put; in place of, see Instead; out of place, بیجا *bija,* بیموقع *bimōuqeʿ.*

Plague, see Pestilence.

Plain, دشت *daʃt,* صحرا *sahra,* جلگه *jolge;* (=unornamented), ساده *sade.*

Plaintiff, مدعی *moddaʿi,* شاکی *ʃaki,* داد خواه *dadxah,* متظلم *motaʒallem.*

Plan, نقشه *naqʃe,* طرح *tarh;* to make a plan, نقشه کشیدن *naqʃe kaʃidan.*

Plane (carpenter's), رنده *rande;* (tree), چنار *cenar;* to plane (wood), رنده کردن *rande k.*

Planet, سیاره *saīyare.*

Plank, تخته *taxte.*

Plant, نبات *nabat;* to plant, کاشتن *kaʃtan,* نشاندن *neʃandan;* (trees), غرس کردن *ɣars k.*

Plantation, بیشه *biʃe.*

Plaster, گچ *gac;* (for a wound), مرهم *marham;* to plaster, گچ مالیدن *gac malidan,* سفید کاری کردن *sefidkari k.*

Plasterer, گچ کار *gackar.*

Plate, پشقاب *poʃqab.*

Platoon, دسته *daste.*

Play (theatrical piece), نمایش *namayeʃ*; (=game), بازی *baʒi*; to play
(=to give a play), نمایش دادن *namayeʃ dadan*; to play (a game,
a role, etc.), بازی کردن *baʒi k.*; (a musical instrument), زدن *ʒadan.*

Player, بازی کن *baʒikon.*

Playfellow, همبازی *hambaʒi.*

Plead, to (a suit), اقامه دعوی کردن داد خواهی کردن *dadxahi k.*,
eqameye da'va k.; (=to plead as an excuse), بهانه قرار دادن *bahane qarar
dadan.*

Pleasant, پسندیده *pasandide*, خوش *xoʃ*, با صفا *basafa.*

Please, to, خوشنود کردن *xoʃnud k.*, خوشوقت کردن *xoʃvaqt k.*; (3rd pers. only),
پسند آمدن *pasand amadan*, خوش آمدن *xoʃ amadan*; it pleases him,
اورا پسند میاید *ura pasand miayad*, خوشش میاید *xoʃeʃ miayad.*

Pleased, خوشوقت *xoʃvaqt*, خوشنود *xoʃnud.*

Pleasure, نشاط *neʃat*, لذت *lezzat*, حظ *hazz*; (=sensual pleasure), عیش *eiʃ*,
عشرت *eʃrat.*

Pleat, چین *cin.*

Pleated, چیندار *cindar.*

Pledge, گرو رهن *rahn*, گرو *gerōu*; to pledge, رهن گذاشتن *rahn goʒaʃtan.*,
گرو گذاشتن *gerōu goʒaʃtan.*

Plenteous, Plentiful, فراوان *faravan*, وافر *vafer.*

Plenty, فراوانی *faravani*, وفور *vofur.*

Plot (=intrigue), توطئه *tōute'e*; to plot, توطئه کردن *tōute'e k.*

Plum, آلو *alu*, الوجه *aluce*, گوجه *gōuje.*

Plumb-line, ریسمان کار *rismane kar*, شاقول *ʃaqul.*

Plunder, غارت *ɣarat*, غنیمت *ɣanimat*, یغما *yaɣma*; to plunder, غارت
کردن *ɣarat k.*, غنیمت کردن *ɣanimat k.*, یغما کردن *yaɣma k.*,
چپاول کردن *capavol k.*, چاپیدن *capidan*, بغارت بردن *be ɣarat bordan.*

Plunderer, غارتگر *ɣaratgar.*

Plural (subs.), جمع *jam'.*

Ply, لا *la*; three-ply, سه لا *se la.*

Pneumonia, ذات الریه *ʒat or-rie.*

Poached (of an egg), نیم رو *nimru.*

Pocket, جیب *jib.*

Pock-marked, آبله رو *abeleru.*

Poem, شعر *ʃe'r*; to compose a poem, شعر گفتن *ʃe'r goftan.*

Poet, شاعر ʃaʻer.

Poetical, شاعرانه ʃaʻerane.

Poetry, نظم naẕm.

Point, سر sar, نوك nuk; (=dot), نقطه noqte; (=nicety), نكته nokte; he was on the point of going, میخواست برود mixast beravad; to point (=to indicate position), نشان دادن neʃan dadan, اشاره کردن eʃare k.

Poison, زهر ẕahr, سم samm; to poison, سم (زهر) دادن samm (ẕahr) dadan.

Polar, قطبی qotbi.

Pole, قطب qotb; the north pole, قطب شمال qotbe ʃamal; the south pole, قطب جنوب qotbe jonub.

Police, شهربانی ʃahrbani, نظمیه naẕmiye; secret police, آگاهی agahi; police district, کلانتری kalantari; chief of police, رئیس شهربانی raʻise ʃahrbani.

Policeman, آژان aẕan, پاسبان pasban.

Police station, کلانتری kalantari.

Policy, سیاست siasat.

Polish, to, صیقل زدن seiqal ẕadan, زدودن ẕadudan.

Polished (=shining), براق barraq.

Polite, مؤدب moʻaddab.

Politeness, ادب adab, نزاکت neẕakat.

Political, سیاسی siasi.

Politics, سیاست siasat.

Pollen, گرده garde.

Pollute, to, آلودن aludan, پلید کردن palid k.

Polluted, پلید palid, آلوده alude, ناپاك napak.

Pollution, آلودگی aludegi.

Polytheism, شرك ʃerk.

Polytheist, مشرك moʃrek.

Pomegranate, انار anar.

Pomp, تکبر takabbor, تجمل tajammol.

Pompous, متکبر motakabber.

Pond, Pool, حوض hōuẕ.

Poor (=indigent), فقیر faqir, مسکین meskin, مفلس mofles, بینوا binava, مفلوك mafluk.

Poor-house, نوانخانه navanxane, مسکینخانه meskinxane.

Pope, پاپ pap.

Poplar, تبریزی tabriẓi, کبوده kabude.

Popular (=beloved), محبوب mahbub.

Population, جمعیت jam'iyat.

Populous, آباد abad.

Porcelain (adj. and subs.), چینی cini.

Porch, طاق taq.

Pore (of the skin), مسام masamm.

Port, بندر bandar.

Porter (=carrier), حمال hammal; (=doorkeeper), دربان darban.

Porterage, حمالی hammali.

Position, see Place; (=post), شغل ʃoɣl, کار kar; (=situation), وضعیت vaẓ'iyat, موقعیت mouqe'iyat.

Positive, مثبت mosbat; see also Sure.

Possess, to, داشتن daʃtan.

Possession, تصرف tasarrof, ضبط ẓabt; possessions, دارائی darai; (=movable property), اموال amval.

Possessor, مالك malek, صاحب saheb.

Possible, ممکن momken, امکان‌پذیر emkanpaẓir; to be possible, امکان داشتن emkan d., ممکن بودن momken b.

Post (of letters), پست post; see also Position; to post (a letter), پست کردن post k.

Postage stamp, تمبر tambr.

Posterity, خلف xalaf, اخلاف axlaf, اولاد ōulad.

Post-office, پستخانه postxane.

Pot (=saucepan), دیگ dig; (for flowers), گلدان goldan.

Potato, سیب زمینی sibe ẓamini.

Pot-herbs, سبزی sabẓi.

Pottage, آش aʃ.

Potter, کوزه‌گر kuẓegar.

Pottery (manufactory), کارخانه چینی سازی karxaneye cinisaẓi; (ware), ظروف چینی ẓorufe cini.

Pound (money), لیره lire; to pound, کوبیدن kubidan.

Pour, to, ریختن rixtan.

Poverty, فقر faqr, افلاس eflas, بینوائی binavai.

Powder, گرد gard.

Power, قوه qovve, زور zur, قدرت qodrat, اقتدار eqtedar, توانائى tavanai, نیرو niru; electric power, قوه برق qovveye barq; powers (=competence), اختیارات exteyarat.

Powerful, مقتدر moqtader, نیرومند nirumand, توانا tavana, زورمند zurmand, قوی qavi, moqtader.

Practical, عملى amali.

Practice, تمرین tamrin, مشق maʃq; (=custom), عادت aɖat, رسم rasm; to put into practice, عمل کردن amal k., اجرا کردن ejra k.

Practise, to, مشق کردن maʃq k., تمرین کردن tamrin k.; (of a doctor), طبابت کردن tebabat k.

Praise, مدح madh, تمجید tamjid, تحسین tahsin, ستایش setayeʃ, تعریف taʻrif; to praise, مدح (ستایش , تعریف , تحسین , تمجید) کردن ستودن setudan, madh (setayeʃ, taʻrif, tahsin, tamjid) k.

Praiseworthy, قابل تمجید qabele tamjid, قابل تحسین qabele tahsin.

Prawn, میگو meigu.

Pray, to, نماز خواندن namaz xandan, دعا کردن doʻa k.; (=to beseech), التماس کردن eltemas k., استدعا کردن estedʻa k., تمنا کردن tamanna k.

Prayer, نماز namaz, دعا doʻa; (=entreaty), التماس eltemas, استدعا estedʻa, تمنا tamanna.

Preach, to, وعظ کردن vaʻz k.

Preacher, واعظ vaʻez.

Preaching, وعظ vaʻz.

Precautionary, احتیاطى ehteyati.

Precedence, تقدم taqaddom.

Precedent, سابقه sabeqe.

Preceding, سابق sabeq, مقدم moqaddam.

Precious, عزیز aziz, گرانبها geranbaha, نفیس nafis, گرانمایه geranmaye.

Precipice, پرتاب partab.

Predecessor, سلف salaf, متقدم motaqaddem.

Predestination, تقدیر taqdir, قضا qaza.

Predicament: to be in a predicament, گیر کردن gir k.

Predict, to (the future), غیب گوئى کردن yeib-gui k., پیش گوئى کردن piʃgui k.

Predominance, استیلا estila, غلبه yalabe, برترى bartari.

Predominant, غالب yaleb, مستولى mostouli.

Predominate, to, غالب آمدن yaleb amadan, غالب شدن yaleb f., مستولى mostōuli f., برترى داشتن bartari d.

Preface, see Introduction.

Prefer, to, ترجیح دادن tarjih dadan, رجحان دادن rojhan dadan.

Preference, ترجیح tarjih, رجحان rojhan.

Pregnant, آبستن abestan, حامله hamele.

Premium (in banking), صرف برات sarfe barat.

Preparation, تدارك tadarok, آمادگى amadegi.

Preparatory, ابتدائى ebtedai.

Prepare, to, حاضر کردن haʐer k.

Prepared, حاضر haʐer, آماده amade.

Prescription, نسخه nosxe, دستور dastur.

Presence, حضور hoʐur; (= personality), شخصیت faxsiyat.

Present, حاضر haʐer; (= existing), موجود mōujud; (= present time), زمان حال ʐamane hal; at present, فعلاً fe'lan, حالا hala, اکنون aknun; see also Gift; to present (= to give), تقدیم کردن taqdim k.; (= to introduce), معرفى کردن mo'arrefi k.

Presently, عن قریب an qarib.

Preservation, محافظه mohafeʐe, حفظ hefʐ, حفاظت hefaʐat.

Preserve, to, محافظه کردن mohafeʐe k., حفظ کردن hefʐ k., حفاظت کردن hefaʐat k.

President, رئیس ra'is.

Press, the, مطبوعات matbu'at; to press, فشردن fefordan, affordan; (= to iron), اتو کردن otu k.; (= to insist), اصرار کردن esrar k.

Pressure, فشار fefar; to put pressure (on), فشار آوردن (به) fefar avardan (be).

Pretence (= excuse), بهانه bahane; (= claim), ادعا edde'a.

Pretend, to (= to make excuses), بهانه در آوردن bahane dar avardan; (= to claim), ادعا کردن edde'a k.

Pretention, ادعا edde'a.

Pretentious, پر ادعا poredde'a.

Pretext, بهانه bahane.

Prestige, وجهه vejhe.

Pretty, خوشگل xofgel.

Prevail, to (=to conquer), غالب شدن ɣaleb ʃ., استيلا يافتن estila yaftan, مستولى شدن mostōuli ʃ.; (=to induce), وادار كردن vadar k.; (=to be prevalent), حكمفرما بودن hokmfarma b., متداول بودن motadavel b.

Prevalence, حكمفرمائى hokmfarmai.

Prevalent, حكمفرما hokmfarma, متداول motadavel; to be prevalent, see Prevail.

Prevent, to, (از) منع كردن mane' ʃ. (aʒ), باز داشتن baʒ d., مانع شدن man' k., دفع كردن daf' k.

Prevention, منع man', دفع daf'.

Prey, see Game.

Price, قيمت qeimat, بها baha.

Pride, غرور ɣorur, نخوت nexvat, تكبر takabbor; (in a good sense), افتخار eftexar; to pride oneself (on), (به) افتخار داشتن eftexar d. (be).

Priest, كشيش kaʃiʃ.

Primary, ابتدائى ebtedai.

Prime Minister, نخست وزير naxostvaʒir.

Prince, شاهزاده ʃahʒade.

Principal, اول avval, عمده omde.

Principle, اصل asl; on principle, از روى عقيده aʒ ruye aqide.

Print, to, چاپ كردن cap k., طبع كردن tab' k.

Printed, چاپى capi, مطبوع matbu'.

Printer, چاپچى capci, طباع tabba'.

Printing-office, printing-press, چاپخانه capxane, مطبعه matba'e.

Priority, تقدم taqaddom.

Prison, زندان ʒendan, محبس mahbas.

Prisoner, زندانى ʒendani, محبوس mahbus; (of war), اسير asir; to take prisoner, اسير گرفتن asir gereftan; to be taken prisoner, اسير شدن asir ʃ.

Privacy, خلوت xalvat.

Private, خصوصى xosusi; (=soldier), سرباز sarbaʒ.

Privilege, امتياز emteyaʒ; to be privileged, امتياز داشتن emteyaʒ d.

Probability, احتمال ehtemal.

Probable, محتمل mohtamel; to be probable, احتمال داشتن ehtemal d., محتمل بودن mohtamel b.

Probation, كار آموزى karamuʒi.

Probationer, كار آموز karamuʒ.

Problem, مسئله *mas'ale*.

Process (legal), محاكمه *mohakeme*.

Proclamation, اعلامیه *e'lamiye*, بیانیه *bayaniye*.

Prodigality, اسراف *esraf*, گشادبازی *gofadbazi*.

Produce, محصول *mahsul*, حاصل *hasel*; to produce, بعمل آوردن *be amal avardan*, تولید کردن *toulid k.*

Production, تولید *toulid*.

Productive (=fertile), حاصلخیز *haselxiz*.

Profession, پیشه *pife*, حرفه *herfe*, شغل *foyl*; (of faith), شهادت *fahadat*; (=declaration), اظهار *ezhar*.

Professor, استاد *ostad*.

Profit, سود *sud*, نفع *naf'*, منفعت *manfa'at*, فائده *fa'ede*; to profit, نفع بردن *naf' bordan*, منفعت کردن *manfa'at k.*, فائده بردن *fa'ede bordan*.

Profitable, سودمند *sudmand*, نافع *nafe'*, مفید *mofid*.

Profligacy, هرزگی *harzegi*, ولخرجی *velxarji*.

Profligate, هرزه *harze*, ولخرج *velxarj*.

Profound, عمیق *amiq*.

Profundity, عمق *omq*.

Programme, برنامه *barname*.

Progress, ترقی (پیشروی) *taraqqi*, پیشروی *pifravi*; to progress, ترقی (پیشروی) کردن *taraqqi (pifravi) k.*

Progressive, مترقی *motaraqqi*.

Prohibit, to, منع کردن *man' k.*, قدغن کردن *qadayan k.*

Prohibition, منع *man'*, نهی *nahy*, ممانعت *momane'at*.

Proletariat, توده مردم *tudeye mardom*.

Prolong, to, تمدید کردن *tamdid k.*

Prolongation, تمدید *tamdid*.

Promise, وعده *va'de*, قول *qoul*; to promise, وعده دادن *va'de dadan*, قول دادن *qoul dadan*.

Promising (adj.), خوش آیند *xofayand*, نیك اختر *nikaxtar*.

Promontory, رأس *ra's*.

Promotion, ترفیع درجه (رتبه) *tarfi'e daraje (rotbe)*.

Prong, چنگال *cangal*, شاخه *faxe*.

Pronunciation, تلفظ *talaffoz*.

Proof, دلیل *dalil*, برهان *borhan*, حجت *hojjat*.

Prop, see Support.

Propaganda, تبليغ *tabliɣ*.

Propagate, to, تبليغ كردن *tabliɣ k.*; (= to diffuse), انتشار دادن *entefar dadan*, منتشركردن *montafer k.*; (= to procreate), توليد كردن *toulid k.*, زائيدن *ʒaidan*.

Propagation (= diffusion), انتشار *entefar*; (= procreation), تـوليـد *toulid*, تولد *tavallod*.

Propel, to, راندن *randan*.

Propeller, پره *pare*.

Proper (= fitting), شايسته *fayeste*, مناسب *monaseb*; (= peculiar), مخصوص *maxsus*.

Property (landed), ملك *melk*; (= quality), خصلت *xeslat*, صفت *sefat*.

Prophecy (= prophetic office), نبوت *nobovvat*.

Prophesy, to, غيبگوئ كردن *ɣeibgui k.*

Prophet, پيغمبر *peiɣambar*, نبى *nabi*; (Mohammad), رسول *rasul*.

Proportion, نسبت *nesbat*, تناسب *tanasob*, مناسبت *monasebat*; in proportion, بتناسب *be tanasob*, بمناسبت *be monasebat*.

Proposal, پيشنهاد *pifnehad*.

Propose, to, پيشنهاد كردن *pifnehad k.*

Proprietor, مالك *malek*, صاحب *saheb*.

Propriety, شايستگى *fayestegi*.

Prorogation, تعطيل *ta'til*, ختم *xatm*.

Prorogue, to, تـعـطيـل كـردن *ta'til k.*, خاتمه دادن *xateme dadan*; to prorogue a session, ختم جلسه كردن *xatme jalse k.*

Prose, نثر *nasr*.

Prosecute, to (legally), محاكمه كردن *mohakeme k.*

Prosecutor, public, مدعى العموم *modda'i ol-omum*, دادستان *dadsetan*.

Prosody, علم عروض *elme aruʒ*.

Prospect (= view), منظره *manʒare*, چشم انداز *cafmandaʒ*.

Prosper, to, كامياب شدن *kamyab f.*; his affairs prosper, كار و بارش خـوب است *kar o baref xub ast*.

Prosperity, سعادت *sa'adat*, اقبال *eqbal*.

Prosperous, سعادتمند *sa'adatmand*, كامران *kamran*, مسعود *mas'ud*.

Prostitute, فاحشه *fahefe*, جنده *jende*.

Protect, حفظ (حفاظت، حمايت، محافظت) كردن *hefʒ (hefaʒat, hemayat, mohafeʒat) k.*

Protection, حفظ *hefẓ*, حفاظت *hefaẓat*, محافظت *mohafeẓat*, حمايت *hemayat*.

Protector, حامى *hami*, حافظ *hafeẓ*.

Protectorate, قيموميت *qeimumiyat*, مملكت تحت الحماية *mamlekate taht ol-hemaye*.

Protégé, دستپرورده *dastparvarde*.

Protest, اعتراض *e'teraẓ*; to protest, اعتراض کردن *e'teraẓ k.*

Proud, مغرور *maɣrur*, متکبر *motakabber*.

Prove, to, دلالت کردن *dalalat k.*, ثابت کردن *sabet k.*

Proverb, مثل *masal*, ضرب المثل *ẓarb ol-masal*.

Provide, to, تهيه کردن *tahie k.*

Providence, روزگار *ruẓegar, ruẓgar*.

Provident, عاقبت بين *aqebatbin*.

Province, ولايت *velayat*.

Provincial, ولايتى *velayati*.

Provision, تدبير *tadbir*; provisions (of a law) مقررات *moqarrarat*.

Provisional, موقتى *movaqqati*.

Provisions, آذوقه *aẓuqe*, خواربار *xarbar*, غذا *ɣaẓa*, خوراك *xorak*.

Proxy (person), وکيل *vakil*.

Prudence, احتياط *ehteyat*.

Prudent, احتياطکار *ehteyatkar*.

Puberty, بلوغ *boluɣ*.

Public (adj.), عموم *omum*, عمومى *omumi*, عام *amm*; (subs.), مردم *mardom*; public opinion, افکار عمومى *afkare omumi*; public health, بهداشت عموم *behdaſte omum*; public works, فوائد عامه *fava'ede amme*.

Publication (=diffusion), انتشار *enteſar*.

Publicly, آشکار *aſkar*, علنًا *alanan*.

Publish, to, منتشر کردن *montaſer k.*, انتشار دادن *enteſar dadan*.

Publisher, ناشر *naſer*.

Publishing-house, see Printing-office.

Pull (=advantage), پارتى *parti*; to have 'pull', پارتى داشتن *parti d.*; to pull, کشيدن *kaſidan*.

Pulpit, منبر *membar*.

Pulse, نبض *nabẓ*; pulses (leguminous plants), حبوبات *hobubat*.

Pump, تلمبه *tolombe*; to pump, تلمبه زدن *tolombe ẓadan*; (a bicycle, etc.), باد کردن *bad k.*

Punctual, وقت شناس vaqtʃenas.

Punctually, سر وقت sare vaqt.

Punish, to, تنبیه کردن tambih k.

Punishment, تنبیه tambih, عقوبت oqubat.

Puppet, دست نشانده dastneʃande.

Puppy, توله سگ tuleye sag.

Purchase, خرید xarid, خریداری xaridari; to purchase, خریدن xaridan.

Purchaser, خریدار xaridar, مشتری moʃtari.

Pure, پاك pak, صاف saf, خالص xales.

Purgative, مسهل moshel.

Purification, تصفیه tasfie.

Purify, to, پاك کردن pak k., تصفیه کردن tasfie k.

Purity, پاکی paki, صفا safa.

Purple (adj.), ارغوانی arɣavani.

Purport, معنی maʻni, مفاد mofad.

Purpose, اراده erade, عزم aʒm; see also Intention; on purpose, عمداً amdan.

Purse, کیسه kise, کیف kif.

Pursue, to, تعقیب کردن taʻaqob k., دنبال کردن dombal k., تعاقب کردن
 taʻqib k.

Pursuit, تعقیب taʻqib, تعاقب taʻaqob.

Push, تکان دادن hol, تکان tekan; to push, هل دادن hol dadan, تکان دادن
tekan dadan.

Put, to, گذاشتن goʒaʃtan, نهادن nehadan; to put down, زمین گذاشتن ʒamin
goʒaʃtan; to put out (a light, etc.), خاموش کردن xamuʃ k.; (= to
eject), بیرون کردن birun k.; to put on, پوشیدن puʃidan; to put off
(= to postpone), تعویق انداختن taʻviq andaxtan.

Pyramid, هرم haram; the Pyramids, اهرام ahram.

Q

Qorʻan, قرآن qorʻan.

Quadrangular, مربع morabbaʻ.

Quadriliteral, رباعی robaʻi.

Quadruped, چهارپا caharpa.

Quadruple, چهارگانه cahargane.

Quality, خاصیت xassiyat, خصلت xeslat, صفت sefat.

Quantity, قدر qadr, مقدار meqdar, اندازه andaze, کمیت kamiyat; (great quantity), فراوانی faravani.

Quarantine, قرنتینه qarantine, قرنطینه qarantine.

Quarrel, دعوی da'va, نزاع neza', منازعه monaze'e, مشاجره mosajere, مناقشه monaqese; to quarrel, کردن (نزاع, منازعه, مشاجره, مناقشه) دعوی da'va (monaqese, mosajere, monaze'e, neza') k.

Quarrelsome, ستیزهجو setizeju.

Quarry (for stone, etc.), معدن سنگ ma'dane sang.

Quarter, ربع rob', چهار یك caharyak, چارك carak; (=region), دیار deyar; (of a town), محل mahall, محله mahalle.

Quarter-master, کار پرداز karpardaz.

Quatrain, رباعی roba'i.

Quay, اسکله eskele.

Queen, ملکه maleke.

Question, سؤال so'al, پرسش porses.

Questionnaire, پرسش نامه porsesname.

Quick (=soon), زود zud; (=rapid), تند tond, سریع sari'; (=nimble), چست cost, چابك cabok.

Quickly, زود zud, تند tond, سریع sari', بسرعت be sor'at.

Quickness, تندی tondi, سرعت sor'at; (=nimbleness), چابکی caboki.

Quicksand, ریگ روان rige ravan.

Quicksilver, سیماب simab, جیوه jive.

Quiet (adj.), ساکت saket, آرام aram; to quiet, تسکین کردن taskin k., آرام کردن aram k.; (an animal), رام کردن ram k.

Quilt, لحاف lehaf.

Quinine, گنه گنه ganegane.

Quittance, بهل behel.

Quorum, نصاب nesab.

Quotation, نقل قول naqle qoul.

Quote, to, نقل کردن naql k.

R

Rabid, هار *har.*

Race, مسابقه *mosabeqe;* (=nationality), نژاد *neʒad,* قوم *qoum.*

Race-course, میدان اسب دوانی *meïdane asbdavani,* اسپریس *esperis.*

Racing (horse-racing), اسب دوانی *asbdavani.*

Rack (torture), شکنجه *ſekanje.*

Radiation, تشعشع *taſaſʻ.*

Radical, اصلی *asli;* (political term), آزادی خواه *aʒadixah.*

Radiography, پرتونگاری *partounegari.*

Radiologist, پرتوشناس *partouſenas.*

Radiology, پرتوشناسی *partouſenasi.*

Radish, تربچه *torobce.*

Railroad, Railway, راه آهن *rahe ahan.*

Rain, باران *baran,* بارندگی *barandegi;* to rain, باران آمدن *baran amadan,* باریدن *baridan.*

Rainbow, قوس قزح *qouse qaʒah.*

Raincoat, بارانی *barani.*

Raise, to, بر داشتن *bar daſtan,* بلند کردن *boland k.,* افراختن *afraxtan,* افراشتن *afraſtan;* (an army), جمع کردن *jamʻ k.*

Raisin, کشمش *keſmeſ.*

Ram, غوچ *yuc,* قوچ *quc.*

Range (of hills), سلسله *selsele;* (of a gun), پرتاب *partab,* تیررس *tirras.*

Rank (=line), صف *saff,* ردیف *radif;* (=degree), درجه *daraje,* رتبه *rotbe.*

Ransom, فدا *feda,* تصدق *tasaddoq;* (=money), خونبها *xunbaha.*

Rapacious (of an animal), درنده *darande;* (=greedy), حریص *haris,* طمعکار *tamaʻkar.*

Rapacity (of an animal), درندگی *darandegi;* (=greed), حرص *hers,* طمع *tamaʻ.*

Rape, هتك ناموس *hatke namus;* to rape, ربودن *robudan,* هتك ناموس کردن *hatke namus k.*

Rape-seed, کنجد *konjed.*

Rare, نادر *nader,* کمیاب *kamyab.*

Rarely, ندرةً *nodratan,* کم *kam,* بندرت *be nodrat.*

Rarification, ترقیق *tarqiq.*

Rarity, نادره *nadere.*

Rat, موش *muʃ.*

Rate (of exchange, etc.), نرخ *nerx;* تعرفه *taʿrefe;* at the rate of, از قرار *aʒ qarar(e);* at any rate, در هر صورت *dar har surat.*

Rather, بیشتر *biʃtar.*

Ratification, تصویب *tasvib.*

Ratify, to, تصویب کردن *tasvib k.*

Ratio, نسبت *nesbat.*

Ration, جیره *jire;* to ration, جیره بندی کردن *jirebandi k.*

Rationing, جیره بندی *jirebandi.*

Raven, کلاغ *kalaɣ.*

Ravine, تنگه *tange.*

Ravishing (adj.), دلربا *delroba.*

Raw, خام *xam;* raw materials, مواد خام *mavadde xam.*

Rawness, خامی *xami.*

Ray, پرتو *partōu,* شعاع *ʃoʿaʿ.*

Raze: to raze to the ground, با خاك یکسان کردن *ba xak yaksan k.*

Razor, تیغ *tiɣ.*

Reach: within reach, در دسترس *dar dastras;* to reach, (به) رسیدن *rasidan (be).*

Reaction, واکنش *vakoneʃ,* عکس العمل *aks ol-amal;* (retrograde tendency in politics, etc.), ارتجاع *ertejaʿ.*

Reactionary, مرتجع *mortajeʿ.*

Read, to, خواندن *xandan,* مطالعه کردن *motaleʿe k.*

Reader, خواننده *xanande.*

Ready, حاضر *haʒer,* آماده *amade,* مهیا *mohaɪya;* to make ready (= to prepare), مهیا کردن *mohaɪya k.,* حاضر کردن *haʒer k.;* to get ready (trans.), حاضر کردن *haʒer k.;* to be ready, حاضر شدن *haʒer ʃ.*

Real, حقیقی *haqiqi,* واقعی *vaqeʿi.*

Realize, to (= to understand), فهمیدن *fahmidan;* (= to cash), نقد کردن *naqd k.*

Reality, حقیقت *haqiqat,* واقعیت *vaqeʿiyat.*

Really, فی الحقیقت *fel-vaqeʿ,* واقعاً *vaqeʿan,* حقیقةً *haqiqatan,* فی الواقع *fel-vaqeʿ,* fel-haqiqat.

Reap, to, درو کردن *derōu k.,* درودن *dorudan,* درویدن *deravidan.*

Reaper, دروگر *derōugar,* خرمنچین *xarmancin.*

Rear, to (= to educate), تربیت کردن *tarbiat k.*

Rear-Admiral, دریادار *daryadar.*

Reason, عقل *aql;* (= cause), سبب *sabab,* جهت *jehat,* موجب *mujeb;* for this reason, از این جهت *aჳ in jehat,* از این سبب *aჳ in sabab.*

Reasonable, معقول *ma'qul.*

Rebate, تخفیف *taxfif.*

Rebel, یاغی *yaɣi,* عاصی *asi;* to rebel, یاغی شدن *yaɣi ʃ.,* طغیان کردن *toɣian k.,* سرکشی کردن *sarkaʃi k.,* شورش کردن *ʃureʃ k.*

Rebellion, یاغیگری *yaɣigari,* طغیان *toɣian,* سرکشی *sarkaʃi,* شورش *ʃureʃ.*

Rebellious, سرکش *sarkaʃ,* عاصی *asi.*

Rebuke, گوشمالی *guʃmali,* سرزنش *sarჳaneʃ,* ملامت *malamat,* توبیخ *tōubix;* to rebuke, ملامت کردن *malamat k.,* توبیخ کردن *tōubix k.,* گوشمالی کردن *guʃmali k.,* سرزنش کردن *sarჳaneʃ k.*

Recall (= summons), احضار *ehჳar;* to recall, احضار کردن *ehჳar k.;* see also Remember.

Receipt, در یافت *daryaft;* (of a bill etc.), رسید *rasid,* قبض رسید *qabჳe rasid.*

Receipts, در یافتی *daryafti.*

Receive, to, گرفتن *gereftan,* حاصل کردن *hasel k.;* (a person), پذیرفتن *paჳiroftan.*

Reception, پذیرائی *paჳirai;* evening reception, شب نشینی *ʃabneʃini.*

Recipient, گیرنده *girande.*

Reckon, شمردن *ʃomordan,* حساب کردن *hesab k.*

Reckoning, حساب *hesab.*

Recline, to (= to lean), تکیه کردن *tekie k.;* (= to lie down), دراز کشیدن *deraჳ kaʃidan.*

Recluse, گوشه نشین *guʃeneʃin.*

Recognize, شناختن *ʃenaxtan;* (= to distinguish), تشخیص دادن *taʃxis dadan.*

Recollection, یاد *yad.*

Recommendation, سفارش *sefareʃ;* letter of recommendation, سفارش نامه *sefareʃname.*

Recompense, پاداش *padaʃ,* مکافات *mokafat,* جزا *jaჳa;* to recompense, پاداش دادن *padaʃ dadan,* مکافات کردن *mokafat k.*

Reconcile, to, اصلاح کردن *eslah k.*

Reconciliation, اصلاح *eslah,* آشتی *aʃti,* صلح *solh.*

Reconnaisance, اکتشاف *ekteʃaf.*

Reconsider, to, تجديد نظر کردن *tajdide naẓar k.*

Reconsideration, تجديد نظر *tajdide naẓar.*

Reconstruction, ترميم *tarmim.*

Record, to, ثبت کردن *sabt k.*

Records (=documents), آمار *amar.*

Recourse, توسل *tavassol,* التجا *elteja,* مراجعت *moraje'at*; to have recourse (to), متوسل شدن (به) *motavassel ʃ. (be).*

Recover, to (in health), شفا یافتن *ʃefa yaftan,* بهبودی یافتن *behbudi yaftan.*

Recovery (in health), بهبودی *behbudi,* شفا *ʃefa.*

Recreation, تفریح *tafrih.*

Rectification, تصحیح *tashih.*

Rectify, to, تصحیح کردن *tashih k.*

Rectitude, درستکاری *dorostkari,* صحت عمل *sehhate amal.*

Red, قرمز *qermeẓ,* سرخ *sorx.*

Redeem, to (=to take out of pawn), از گرو در آوردن *aẓ gerou dar avardan.*

Redeemer, منجی *monji,* نجات دهنده *nejat dehande.*

Redness, قرمزی *qermeẓi,* سرخی *sorxi.*

Redress: to ask redress, تظلم کردن *taẓallom k.*

Reduce, to, see Conquer and Decrease.

Reduction, تخفیف *taxfif.*

Redundant, زائد *ẓa'ed.*

Reed, نی *nei*; place full of reeds, نی زار *neiẓar,* نیستان *neiestan.*

Reel (for thread), قرقره *qerqere.*

Refer, to, (به) رجوع کردن *roju' k. (be).*

Reference, مراجعت *moraje'at,* رجوع *roju'*; with reference to, نسبت به *nesbat be.*

Referring (to), (به) راجع *raje' (be).*

Refine, to, تصفیه کردن *tasfie k.*

Refinery, پالایشگاه *palayeʃgah,* تصفیه خانه *tasfiexane.*

Reflect, to, منعکس کردن *mon'akes k.*; to be reflected, منعکس شدن *mon'akes ʃ.*

Reflection, انعکاس *en'ekas,* عکس *aks.*

Reform, اصلاح *eslah*; to reform, اصلاح کردن *eslah k.*

Refractory, سرکش *sarkaʃ.*

Refrain, to, صرف نظر کردن (از) *sarfe naẓar k. (aẓ),* خودداری کردن (از) *xoddari k. (aẓ).*

Refuge, پناه *panah,* پناهگاه *panahgah,* ملجا *malja;* to take refuge, پناه بردن *panah bordan,* ملتجی شدن *moltaji ʃ.*

Refusal, امتناع *emtenaʿ,* رد *radd.*

Refuse (=rubbish), آشغال *afɣal;* to refuse, رد کردن *radd k.,* امتناع کردن (از) *emtenaʿ k. (az).*

Refutation, رد *radd,* تکذیب *takʒib.*

Refute, to, رد کردن *radd k.,* تکذیب کردن *takʒib k.*

Regard, see Esteem and Reference; to regard, see Consider and Look.

Regent, نائب السلطنه *naʿeb os-saltane.*

Regiment, هنگ *hang,* فوج *fouj.*

Region, دیار *deyar;* in those regions, در آن اطراف *dar an atraf;* see also District.

Register, دفتر *daftar;* to register, ثبت کردن *sabt k.;* (= to enter one's name), اسم نویسی کردن *esmnevisi k.*

Registration, اسم نویسی *esmnevisi.*

Regret, تأسف *taʿassof,* اندوه *anduh,* پشیمانی *paʃimani,* غم *ɣam,* الم *alam,* حزن *hoʒn;* to regret, تأسف خوردن *taʿassof xordan,* محزون شدن *mahʒun ʃ.,* پشیمان شدن *paʃiman ʃ.,* افسوس خوردن *afsus xordan,* متأسف شدن *motaʿassef ʃ.,* پشیمان شدن *paʃiman ʃ.*

Regretful, متاسف *motaʿassef,* پشیمان *paʃiman.*

Regular, منظم *monaʒʒam,* مرتب *morattab.*

Regularly, منظماً *monaʒʒaman,* مرتباً *morattaban.*

Regulation, قاعده *qaʿede,* آئین *ain;* regulations (for the execution of a law), نظام نامه *neʒamname.*

Reign, سلطنت *saltanat,* پادشاهی *padeʃahi,* حکمرانی *hokmrani;* to reign, سلطنت (پادشاهی , حکمرانی) کردن *saltanat (padeʃahi, hokmrani) k.*

Rein (fig.), عنان *enan,* زمام *ʒemam.*

Reinforcements, قوه امدادیه *qovveye emdadiye.*

Reject, to, رد کردن *radd k.*

Rejection, رد *radd.*

Rejoice, to, شادی کردن *ʃadi k.*

Relate, to, حکایت کردن *hekayat k.;* to be related (to), خویشی داشتن (با) *xiʃi d. (ba),* نسبت داشتن (با) *nesbat d. (ba).*

Relation (= recounting), حکایت *hekayat,* روایت *revayat;* (= kindred), قوم و خویش *qoum o xiʃ,* قریب *qarib;* (= proportion), نسبت *nesbat* relations (= intercourse), مناسبات *monasebat,* روابط *ravabet.*

Relationship, خویشی *xiſi*.

Relative (adj.), نسبی *nesbi*.

Relatively, نسبةً *nesbatan*.

Release, خلاص *xalas*, رهائی *rahai*; to release, خلاص کردن *xalas k.*, رهائی کردن *rahai k.*

Reliable, معتبر *moʻtabar*, معتمد *moʻtamad*.

Reliance, اعتماد *eʻtemad*.

Relics (ancient), آثار قدیم *asare qadim*.

Religion, دین *din*, مذهب *maẓhab*; (not Mohammadan), کیش *kiſ*.

Religious, دیندار *dindar*, متدین *motadayyen*; religious classes, روحانیون *ruhaniyun*.

Rely, to (on), (به) اعتماد کردن *eʻtemad k. (be)*.

Remain, to, ماندن *mandan*.

Remainder, باق مانده *baqimande*, بقیه *baqiye*, مابق *ma baqi*.

Remediable, اصلاح پذیر *eslahpaẓir*, تدارک پذیر *tadarokpaẓir*.

Remedy, چاره *care*.

Remember, to, یاد داشتن *yad d.*; I remember, یادم میاید *yadam miayad*.

Remembrance, یاد *yad*.

Remind, to, تذکر دادن *taẓakkor dadan*, یاد آوری کردن *yadavari k.*

Reminder, تذکر *taẓakkor*, یاد آوری *yadavari*.

Remit, to, بخشیدن *baxſidan*.

Remote, دوردست *durdast*, بعید *baʻid*.

Removal, نقل *naql*, انتقال *enteqal*.

Remove, to, see Move and Take.

Remunerative, مفید *mofid*, نافع *nafeʻ*, سودمند *sudmand*.

Renew, to, تجدید کردن *tajdid k.*

Renewal, تجدید *tajdid*.

Renounce, to, انکار کردن *enkar k.*, ترک کردن *tark k.*

Rent, see Hire and Tear.

Repair, to, تعمیر کردن *taʻmir k.*, درست کردن *dorost k.*

Repeal, لغو *laɣv*, الغا *elɣa*; to repeal, لغو کردن *laɣv k.*, الغا کردن *elɣa k.*

Repeat, to, تکرار کردن *tekrar k.*

Repel, to, دفع کردن *dafʻ k.*

Repent, to, توبه کردن *tōube k.*

Repentance, توبه *tōube*.

Repentant, پشیمان pašiman, توبه کار toubekar.

Repetition, تکرار tekrar.

Reply, پاسخ pasox, جواب javab; to reply, پاسخ دادن pasox dadan, جواب دادن javab dadan.

Report, گزارش gozareš; to put in a report, to report, گزارش دادن gozareš dadan.

Repose, آسایش asayeš, استراحت esterahat, راحت rahat, راحتی, rahati; to repose, استراحت کردن esterahat k., راحت کردن rahat k.

Represent, to (= to petition), عرض کردن arz k.

Representative, نماینده namayande.

Representation (= being a representative), نمایندگی namayandegi; (= petition), عرض arz.

Reprisal, مکافات mokafat, انتقام enteqam, معارضه بمثل mo'areze be mesl.

Reproach, ملامت malamat; to reproach, ملامت کردن malamat k.

Republic, جمهوریت jomhuriyat; President of the Republic, رئیس جمهور ra'ise jomhur.

Republican (of a political doctrine), جمهوریخواه jomhurixah.

Repulse, دفع daf', رد radd; to repulse, دفع کردن daf' k., رد کردن radd k.

Reputable, معتبر mo'tabar, محترم mohtaram.

Reputation, نام nam, نیکنامی niknami, آبرو abru, حرمت hormat.

Request, در خواست darxast; to make a request, در خواست کردن dar-xast k.

Requital, مجازات mojazat, مکافات mokafat, جزا jaza.

Requite, to, مجازات کردن mojazat k.

Rescue, رهائی rahai, خلاص xalas, رها raha; to rescue, رهائی کردن rahai k., خلاص دادن xalas dadan, رها دادن raha dadan.

Research, کنجکاوی konjkavi, تحقیقات tahqiqat, تفحص tafahhos; to research, تحقیقات کردن tahqiqat k.

Resemblance, شباهت šabahat.

Resemble, to, شبیه بودن šabih b.

Resentment, کینه kine.

Reservation, قید qeid; (= appropriation), تخصیص taxsis.

Reserve (monetary), اندوخته anduxte; to reserve (= to keep), نگه داشتن negah d.

Reservoir, آب انبار abambar, مخزن آب maxzane ab.

Reside, to, ساكن بودن saken b., اقامت كردن eqamat k.

Residence, منزل manzel, مسكن maskan, اقامت eqamat.

Resident, مقيم moqim, ساكن saken.

Resign, to (office, etc.), استعفا دادن este'fa dadan.

Resignation (of office, etc.), استعفا este'fa; (to Providence), توكل tavakkol.

Resist, to, مقاومت كردن moqavemat k.; (to resist successfully), تاب آوردن tab avordan.

Resistance, مقاومت moqavemat.

Resolute, راسخ rasex, با عزم baazm, با جزم bajazm.

Resolution, Resolve, تصميم tasmim, عزم azm, نيت niyat; to resolve, تصميم گرفتن tasmim gereftan; to be resolved, مصمم شدن mosammam ʃ.

Respect, احترام ehteram; to respect, احترام گذاشتن (به) ehteram gozaʃtan (be), محترم داشتن mohtaram d.; with respect to, راجع به raje' be, در باب raje' be, در باره dar bab(e), در باره dar bare(ye).

Respectful, با احترام baehteram, احترام آميز ehteramamiz, مؤدب mo'addab.

Respiration, تنفس tanaffos.

Respite, مهلت mohlat.

Respondent (at law), حريف harif, مدعى عليه modda'i aleih.

Responsible, مسئول mas'ul.

Responsibility, مسئوليت mas'uliyat.

Rest, see Remainder and Repose.

Restless, ناراحت narahat.

Restrain, to, باز داشتن baz d.

Restraint (=self-restraint), خودداري xoddari.

Result, نتيجه natije, حاصل hasel; to result in, (به) منجر شدن monjer ʃ. (be); to obtain a result, نتيجه گرفتن natije gereftan.

Résumé, اختصار extesar, خلاصه xolase.

Resurrection, رستخيز rastexiz, قيامت qiamat.

Resuscitate, to, احيا كردن ehya k.

Resuscitation, احيا ehya.

Retail, to, خرده فروختن xorde foruxtan.

Retailer, خرده فروش xordeforuʃ.

Retaliate, to, مكافات كردن mokafat k., قصاص كردن qesas k.

Retaliation, قصاص qesas, مكافات mokafat, معاوضه mo'aveze, انتقام enteqam.

Retinue, خدم و خشم xadam va haʃam, موكب moukab, ملازمان molazeman.

Retire, to, متقاعد شدن motaqaʿed ʃ., باز نشستن baz neʃastan; see also Retreat.

Retired, متقاعد motaqaʿed, باز نشسته bazneʃaste.

Retirement, تقاعد taqaʿod, باز نشستگی bazneʃastegi; (=solitude), خلوت xalvat, گوشه نشینی guʃeneʃini.

Retreat, عقب نشینی aqabneʃini; (=place of retreat), خلوتگاه xalvatgah; to retreat, عقب نشینی کردن aqabneʃini k.

Retribution, جزا jaza, مجازات mojazat, مکافات mokafat.

Retrocession, واگذاری vagozari.

Retrogression, تنزل tanazzol, ترق معکوس taraqqiye maʿqus.

Return, to (=to come back), بر گشتن bar gaʃtan, مراجعت کردن morajeʿat k.; (=to give back), پس دادن pas dadan; return ticket, بلیت دو سره belite dosare.

Reveal, to, فاش کردن faʃ k., افشا کردن effa k., آشکار کردن aʃkar k.; (of divine revelation), الهام کردن elham k., وحی کردن vahy k.

Revelation (divine), الهام elham, وحی vahy.

Revenge, انتقام enteqam, کینه kine; to take revenge, انتقام کشیدن enteqam kaʃidan.

Revengeful, کینه‌جو kineju.

Revenue, در آمد daramad, عایدات ayedat; (=taxes), مالیات maliyat.

Reverence, تعظیم taʿzim, تکریم takrim.

Reverse (=defeat), شکست ʃekast; (=back of something), پشت poʃt; (=opposite), عکس aks, خلاف xelaf, ضد zedd; to reverse (=to turn upside down), وارونه کردن varune k.

Revise, to (=to reconsider), تجدید نظر کردن tajdide nazar k.

Revision, تجدید tajdid, تجدید نظر tajdide nazar.

Revival, احیا ehya, تجدید tajdid.

Revocable, قابل نسخ qabele nasx, بر گشت پذیر bargaʃtpazir.

Revocation, نسخ nasx, فسخ fasx, لغو lazv.

Revolt, see Rebellion.

Revolution, انقلاب enqelab; (=completing a cycle), گردش gardeʃ, دوران davaran.

Revolutionary, انقلابی enqelabi.

Revolve, to, گردش کردن gardeʃ k., گردیدن gardidan, دور زدن dour zadan, چرخیدن carxidan.

Reward, پاداش *padaʃ,* جزا *jaʒa;* to reward, پاداش دادن *padaʃ dadan,* جزا دادن *jaʒa dadan.*

Rhetoric, علم كلام *elme kalam,* بديع *badi',* معاني و بيان *ma'ani va bayan.*

Rhubarb, ريواس *rivas.*

Rhyme, قافيه *qafie;* to rhyme (intrans.), قافيه داشتن *qafie d.*

Rib, دنده *dande.*

Ribbon, روبان *ruban,* نوار *navar.*

Rice, برنج *berenj;* (in the husk), شـلـتـوك *ʃaltuk;* boiled rice, چلو *celoū;* rice pudding, شير برنج *ʃirberenj;* rice mixed with meat or vegetables, etc., پلو *poloū;* rice cultivation, برنج كارى *berenjkari.*

Rich, ثروتمند *servatmand,* متمول *motamavvel.*

Riches, مال *mal,* ثروت *servat,* تمول *tamavvol.*

Rid: to get rid of someone, كلك فلان كسرا كندن *kalake folan kasra kandan.*

Riddle, معما *mo'amma,* رمز *ramʒ.*

Ride, to, سوار شدن *savar ʃ.;* (a horse), اسب سوارى كردن *asbsavari k.*

Rider, سوار *savar.*

Ridicule, مسخره *masxare;* to ridicule, مسخره كردن *masxare k.*

Ridiculous, مسخره آميز *masxareamiʒ,* مضحك *moʒhek.*

Riding (a horse), اسب سوارى *asbsavari.*

Rifle, تفنگ *tofang.*

Rifle-man, تفنگچى *tofangci.*

Right (not left), راست *rast,* دست راست *daste rast;* (=correct), درست *dorost,* صحيح *sahih;* (=proper), شايسته *ʃayeste;* (=appropriate), بجا *beja;* (=lawful), روا *rava;* see also Justice.

Rigid, سخت *saxt,* سفت *seft;* (of a person), سختگير *saxtgir.*

Rind, پوست *pust.*

Ring, حلقه *halqe;* (for the finger), انگشتر *angoʃtar;* to ring (a bell), زنگ زدن *ʒang ʒadan.*

Ring-dove, فاخته *faxte,* قمرى *qomri.*

Ringlet, زلف *ʒolf.*

Rinse, to, شستن *ʃostan.*

Riot, بلوا *balva.*

Ripe, رسيده *raside;* (=mature, of a person), پخته *poxte.*

Ripen, to (intrans.), رسيدن *rasidan.*

Ripeness, رسيدگى *rasidegi;* (=maturity), پختگى *poxtegi.*

Ripple, to, موج زدن *mōuj ɣadan.*

Rise, to (=to get up), بر خاستن *bar xastan*, بلند شدن *boland ʃ.;* (of the sun), طلوع کردن *tolu' k.;* (of bread, etc.), بر آمدن *bar amadan.*

Rite (=custom), رسم *rasm,* ادب *adab;* (=religious sect), فرقه *ferqe.*

Ritual, آئین *ain,* رسم *rasm.*

Rival, حریف *harif,* رقیب *raqib;* to rival, (با) رقابت کردن *reqabat k. (ba).*

Rivalry, رقابت *reqabat.*

River, رود *rud,* رودخانه *rudxane.*

Rivet, پرچین *parcin;* to rivet, پرچین کردن *parcin k.*

Road, راه *rah,* جاده *jadde.*

Roan, قزل *qeɣel.*

Roar, غرش *ɣorreʃ;* to roar, غریدن *ɣorridan.*

Roast, to, بریان کردن *berian k.*

Rob, to, دزدیدن *doɣdidan,* دزدی کردن *doɣdi k.;* (highway robbery), راهزنی کردن *rahɣani k.*

Robber, دزد *doɣd;* (highway robber), راهزن *rahɣan.*

Robbery, دزدی *doɣdi;* (highway robbery), راهزنی *rahɣani.*

Robe, جامه *jame,* لباس *lebas,* کسوت *kesvat;* robe of honour, خلعت *xel'at.*

Rock, صخره *saxre,* سنگ *sang;* to rock (trans.), تکان دادن *tekan dadan,* جنبانیدن *jombanidan;* (intrans.), جنبیدن *jombidan,* تکان خوردن *tekan xordan.*

Rocket, فشفشه *feʃfeʃe.*

Roe (of fish), تخم ماهی *toxme mahi.*

Roll (=list of names), صورت *surat,* فهرست *fehrest;* (of paper), لوله *lule;* (of material), توپ *tup;* to roll (trans.), غلطانیدن *ɣaltanidan;* (intrans.), غلطیدن *ɣaltidan;* to roll up, پیچیدن *picidan;* to call the roll, حاضر و غائب *haɣer va ɣa'eb k.*

Roller (for rolling mud-roofs), بام غلطان *bamɣaltan,* سنگ غلطان *sangɣaltan.*

Roof, بام *bam;* flat surface of a roof, پشت بام *poʃte bam.*

Rook, کلاغ *kalaɣ.*

Room, اطاق *otaq.*

Root, بیخ *bix,* ریشه *riʃe;* بن *bon;* (=origin), اصل *asl;* to take root, ریشه زدن *riʃe ɣadan;* to root up, از بیخ کندن *aɣ bix kandan.*

Rope, رسن *rasan,* ریسمان *risman,* طناب *tanab.*

Rose, گل *gol*; large white rose, نسترن *nastaran*; red rose, گل سرخ *gole sorx*.

Rose-garden, گلستان *golestan*.

Rose-water, گلاب *golab*.

Rot, to (intrans.), پوسیدن *pusidan*, گندیدن *gandidan*.

Rotten (= worn out), پوسیده *puside*; (= fetid), گند *gand*, گندیده *gandide*.

Rottenness (= being worn out), پوسیدگی *pusidegi*; (= being fetid), گندگی *gandegi*.

Rough, درشت *doroſt*, زبر *ʒebr*; (= uneven), ناهموار *nahamvar*; (= rude), خشن *xaſen*; (of the sea), متلاطم *motalatem*.

Roughness, درشتی *doroſti*, زبری *ʒebri*; (= rudeness), خشونت *xoſunat*.

Round, گرد *gerd*, مدور *modavvar*.

Roundness, گردی *gerdi*.

Row, see Line; (= tumult), هنگامه *hengame*, غوغا *ɣouɣa*, شلوق *ſoluq*; to row (a boat), پارو زدن *paru ʒadan*.

Royal, شاهی *ſahi*, سلطنتی *saltanati*.

Royalist, شاهپرست *ſahparast*, سلطنت خواه *saltanatxah*.

Rub, to, مالیدن *malidan*, مالش کردن *maleſ k.*; (= to wear away), سائیدن *sa'idan*, سابیدن *sɔbidan*.

Rubbish, آشغال *aſɣal*, خاشاك *xaſak*; (= sweepings), خاکروبه *xakrube*.

Ruby, لعل *la'l*, یاقوت *yaqut*.

Rudder, سکان کشتی *sokkane kaſti*.

Rude, بی ادب *biadab*.

Rudeness, بی ادبی *biadabi*.

Rue (herb), اسفند *esfand*, اسپند *espand*.

Ruffian, اوباش *oubaſ*.

Rug (= carpet), فرش *farſ*; (= blanket), پتو *patu*; (= horse-rug), جل *jol*.

Ruin, خرابی *xarabi*; (= ruined place), ویرانه *vēirane*, ویرانی *vēirani*, خرابه *xarabe*; to ruin, خراب کردن *xarab k.*

Ruined, خراب *xarab*, ویران *vēiran*, منهدم *monhadem*, معدوم *ma'dum*; (in fortune), شکسته حال *ſekastehal*, مفلس *mofles*, مستأصل *mosta'sal*.

Rule, حکومت *hokumat*, سلطنت *saltanat*, حکمرانی *hokmrani*; see also Regulation; to rule, حکومت (سلطنت ,حکمرانی) کردن *hokumat (saltanat, hokmrani) k.*

Ruler, حکمران *hokmran*; (= instrument for drawing lines), خطکش *xattkaſ*.

Rumour, شهرت ʃohrat; rumours, اراجيف arajif.

Run, to, دويدن davidan; to run over (in a car, etc.), زير گرفتن ʒir gereftan.

Runaway, فرارى farari.

Rural, رستائى rostai.

Rush, see Reed and Attack; to rush upon, بر ريختن rixtan bar, هجوم آوردن بر hojum avardan bar.

Russia, روسيه rusie.

Russian, روسى rusi.

Rust, زنگ ʒang.

Rusty, زنگ زده ʒangʒade.

S

Sabbath, سبت sabt.

Sable, سمور sammur.

Sabotage, خرابكارى xarabkari.

Saboteur, خرابكار xarabkar.

Sack, جوال javal; to sack (=dismiss), جواب كردن javab k.; see also Plunder.

Sacrifice, قربان qorban, فدا feda, تصدق tasaddoq.

Sad, دلتنگ deltang, محزون mahʒun, غمگين ʒamgin.

Saddle, زين ʒin; to saddle, زين كردن ʒin k.

Saddle-bag, خورجين xorjin.

Saddle-cloth, نمد namad.

Saddler, سراج sarraj.

Sadness, دلتنگى deltangi, حزن hoʒn, غم ʒam.

Safe, امن amn; (=sound), سالم salem; (=a box), صندوق sanduq.

Safely, بسلامت be salamat.

Safety, امن amn; (=soundness), سلامت salamat.

Saffron, زعفران ʒa'faran.

Sail, بادبان badban.

Sailing-ship, كشتى بادى kaʃtiye badi.

Sailor, ناوى navi, ملاح mallah.

Sake: for the sake of, از براى aʒ baraye, محض خاطر mahʒe xater(e).

Salary, مواجب mavajeb.

Sale, فروش foruʃ; (by auction), حراج harraj.

Salmon, ماهی آزاد *mahiaɤad.*

Salt, نمك *namak;* (adj.), شور *ʃur.*

Salt-cellar, نمكدان *namakdan.*

Salt-desert, كوير *kavir.*

Saluki (dog), سگ تازی *sage taɤi.*

Salute, سلام *salam;* to salute, سلام كردن *salam k.;* salute of guns, شليك *ʃelik.*

Salvation, نجات *nejat,* رستگاری *rastegari.*

Same (=identical), همين *hamin,* همان *haman;* (=similar), يكسان *yaksan,* برابر *barabar,* نظير *naɤir.*

Sample, نمونه *namune.*

Sanatorium, آسايشگاه *asayeʃgah.*

Sanctuary, بست *bast;* to take sanctuary, بست نشستن *bast nafastan.*

Sand, ريگ *rig.*

Sap (of a plant, etc.), شيره *ʃire.*

Sapling, نهال *nehal.*

Sarcasm, هجو *hajv,* هجاء *heja,* استهزاء *estehɤa.*

Sarcastic, طعنه آميز *ta'neamiɤ.*

Satan, شيطان *ʃeītan,* ابليس *eblis.*

Satanic, شيطانی *ʃeītani.*

Satiate, to, سير كردن *sir k.*

Satiated, سير *sir.*

Satire, هجو *hajv,* هجاء *heja.*

Satirist, هجاگو *hejagu.*

Satirize, to, هجو كردن *hajv k.*

Satisfaction, رضايت *reɤayat.*

Satisfactory, رضايت بخش *reɤayatbaxʃ.*

Satisfied, راضی *raɤi.*

Satisfy, to, راضی كردن *raɤi k.*

Saturday, شنبه *ʃambe.*

Saucepan, ديگ *dig,* ديگچه *digce.*

Savage, وحشی *vahʃi;* (=cruel), جفاكار *jafakar,* بيرحم *birahm;* (of an animal), درنده *darande.*

Savagery, وحشيگری *vahʃigari.*

Savings, پس‌انداز *pasandaɤ,* اندوخته *anduxte.*

Saviour, منجى‎ *monji.*

Saw, اره‎ *arre;* to saw, اره کردن‎ *arre k.*

Say, to, گفتن‎ *goftan;* that is to say, یعنی‎ *ya'ni.*

Saying, گفتار‎ *goftar,* سخن‎ *soxan;* (=idiom), اصطلاح‎ *estelah.*

Scab (=mange), گر‎ *gar.*

Scaffold, چوب بست‎ *cubbast;* (for execution), دار‎ *dar.*

Scale, ميزان‎ *mizan,* درجه‎ *daraje;* (=one side of a balance), کف ترازو‎ *kaffe tarazu;* (of fish), پولک‎ *pulak,* فلس‎ *fels.*

Scales, ترازو‎ *tarazu,* ميزان‎ *mizan.*

Scaly, پولک دار‎ *felsdar,* فلسدار‎ *pulakdar.*

Scandal, افترا‎ *eftera,* ننگ‎ *nang,* رسوائى‎ *rosvai.*

Scarce, see Rare.

Scarcely, بسختى‎ *be saxti;* he had scarcely arrived when..., تازه رسیده بود که....‎ *taze raside bud ke....*

Scarcity, کمى‎ *kami;* (=famine), قط‎ *qaht,* غلاء‎ *yala.*

Scarecrow, مترسک‎ *matarsak.*

Scarf, گردن بند‎ *gardanband.*

Scatter, to (=to disperse), پراکندن‎ *parakandan,* متفرق کردن‎ *motafarreq k.;* (=to rout), تار و مار کردن‎ *tar o mar k.*

Scene, منظره‎ *manzare;* (of a play), پرده‎ *parde.*

Scenery, منظره طبیعى‎ *manzareye tabi'i.*

Scholar (=man of letters), عالم‎ *alem,* فاضل‎ *fazel.*

School, مدرسه‎ *madrase, madrese,* آموزشگاه‎ *amuzefgah;* (old-fashioned type of school), مکتب‎ *maktab;* primary school, دبستان‎ *dabestan;* secondary school, دبیرستان‎ *dabirestan.*

Schoolfellow, هم‌درس‎ *hamdars,* همشاگرد‎ *hamfagerd.*

Schoolmaster, see Teacher

Sciatic nerve, عرق النسا‎ *erq on-nesa.*

Science, علم‎ *elm,* فن‎ *fann.*

Scientific, علمى‎ *elmi.*

Scissors, قیچى‎ *qeici.*

Scold, to, سر زنش کردن‎ *sarzanef k.,* ملامت کردن‎ *malamat k.*

Scorn, تحقیر‎ *tahqir,* اهانت‎ *ehanat.*

Scorpion, کژدم‎ *kazdom,* عقرب‎ *aqrab.*

Scout: boy scout, پیش آهنگ‎ *pifahang.*

Scouting, پیش آهنگی *piʃahangi.*

Scout-master, سر رسد *sarrasad*; assistant scout-master, رسدیار *rasadyar.*

Scout-troop, رسد پیشاهنگی *rasade piʃahangi.*

Scratch, to, خراشیدن *xaraʃidan*; to scratch out (=to obliterate), محوکردن *mahv k.*

Screw, پیچ *pic.*

Screwdriver, آچار *acar*, پیچ کش *pickaʃ.*

Scribe, کاتب *kateb*, نویسنده *nevisande.*

Scythe, داس *das.*

Sea, دریا *darya*, بحر *bahr*; by sea, باکشتی *ba kaʃti*; sea-level, سطح دریا *sathe darya.*

Seal, مهر *mohr*; (animal), سگ ماهی *sagmahi*; to seal, مهرکردن *mohr k.*

Sealing-wax, لاک *lak.*

Seam, درز *darz*; (=hem), بخیه *baxiye.*

Seaman, ملاح *mallah*, ملوان *malvan*; ordinary seaman, ناوی *navi*; leading seaman, سرناوی *sarnavi.*

Search, جستجو, جستوجو *jostoju*, تجسس *tajassos*; (=examination), جستوجو (جستجو) *taftiʃ*, باز رسی *baʒrasi*; to search, جستن *jostan*, (جستجو) *jostoju k.*, تجسس کردن *tajassos k.*; (=to examine), تفتیش کردن *taftiʃ k.*, باز رسی کردن *baʒrasi k.*

Search-light, نور افکن *nurafkan.*

Season, فصل *fasl*, موسم *mōusem.*

Seat, نشیمن *neʃiman*, کرسی *korsi*; (=chair), صندلی *sandali*; to seat, نشاندن *neʃandan.*

Seclusion, عزلت *oʒlat.*

Secondary, فرعی *far'i.*

Secondly, ثانیًا *sanian.*

Secrecy, پنهانی *panhani.*

Secret, سر *serr*, راز *raʒ*; (adj.), سری *serri*, مخفی *maxfi*, مخفیانه *maxfiane.*

Secretariat, دبیرخانه *dabirxane.*

Secretary, دبیر *dabir*; (of an embassy, etc.), نائب *na'eb.*

Sect, فرقه *ferqe.*

Section (of a chapter, etc.), فصل *fasl*; (military), جوخه *juxe.*

Secular, دنیوی *donyavi.*

Secure, see Safe and Acquire.

Security, امنیت amniyat; (=bail), ضمانت ζemanat.

Sedative, مسکن mosakken.

Sediment (=silt), شن ʃen; (=dregs), درد dord.

Sedition, فتنه fetne, فساد fesad.

Seditious, فتنه انگیز fetneangiζ, مفسد mofsed.

Seduce, to, فریفتن fariftan, فریب دادن farib dadan; (a woman),
هتک عرض کردن hatke arζ k.

Seductive فریبنده faribande.

See, to, دیدن didan, مشاهده کردن moʃahede k., ملاحظه کردن molaheζe k.

Seed, تخم toxm; (=grain), دانه dane; (for sowing), بذر baζr; to seed
(intrans.), تخم کردن toxm k.

Seek, see Search and Attempt.

Seeker, جوینده juyande, طالب taleb.

Seem, to, بنظر آمدن be naζar amadan; (impers.), مانستن manestan.

Segment, قطعه qet'e, قسمت qesmat.

Seize, to (=to take), گرفتن gereftan; (=to take possession of), تسخیر
(ضبط, تصرف, غصب) تسخیر tasxir (ζabt, tasarrof, γasb) k.

Seizure, ضبط ζabt, تصرف tasarrof, غصب γasb.

Seldom, کم kam, بندرت be nodrat.

Select, to, بر گزیدن bar goζidan, انتخاب کردن entexab k.

Selection, انتخاب entexab.

Self, خود xod, خویش xiʃ, خویشتن xiʃtan; نفس nafs.

Self-control, خود داری xoddari.

Self-reliance, اعتماد بنفس e'temad be nafs.

Self-sacrifice, فداکاری fedakari.

Sell, to, فروختن foruxtan; (intrans.), بفروش رفتن be foruʃ raftan.

Seller, فروشنده foruʃande.

Send, to, فرستادن ferestadan, ارسال داشتن ersal d.; to send for (=to
summon), پس فرستادن خواستن xastan, احضار کردن ehζar k.; to send back,
پس فرستادن pas ferestadan, بر گرداندن bar gardandan.

Sense (=sensation), حس hess, احساس ehsas; (=meaning), معنی ma'ni,
فحوا fahva; (=understanding), فهم fahm.

Sensible (=intelligent), معقول ma'qul, باهوش bahuʃ, عاقل aqel; (=able
to be felt), محسوس mahsus; sensible of (=convinced of), قائل به
qa'el be.

Sensual, نفسانی *nafsani,* نفس پرست *nafsparast.*

Sensuality, شهوت *fahvat,* هوس *havas.*

Sentence (=phrase), جمله *jomle;* (legal), حکم *hokm;* to sentence, محکوم کردن *mahkum k.;* to pass sentence, حکم دادن *hokm dadan.*

Sentiment, احساس *ehsas.*

Sentry, قراول *qaravol,* کشیك *kafik.*

Separate, جدا *joda,* علیحده *ala hadde;* to separate, جدا کردن *joda k.,* علیحده کردن *ala hadde k.*

Separation, جدائی *jodai,* فراق *feraq,* دوری *duri.*

Sergeant, گروهبان *goruhban;* (of police), سرپاسبان *sarpasban.*

Sergeant-major, استوار *ostovar.*

Series, رشته *refte,* سلسله *selsele.*

Serious (=in earnest), جدی *jeddi;* (of an illness), سخت *saxt.*

Sermon, وعظ *va'z.*

Serpent, مار *mar.*

Servant, نوکر *noukar,* فراش *farraf,* خدمتکار *xedmatkar;* (female servant), کلفت *kolfat;* head servant, پیش خدمت *pifxedmat,* فراش باشی *farraf-bafi.*

Serve, to, خدمت کردن *xedmat k.*

Service, خدمت *xedmat;* to take into service, استخدام کردن *estexdam k.*

Servitude, بندگی *bandegi;* (legal), ارتفاق *ertefaq.*

Set: to set out, حرکت کردن *harakat k.,* راه افتادن *rah oftadan.*

Settle, to (=to take up one's abode in a country), توطن کردن *tavatton k.* (=to subside), نشستن *nefastan;* (a dispute), مصالحه کردن *mosalehe k.* see also Fix and Decide.

Settlement (of a dispute), اصلاح *eslah;* (=agreement), قرارداد *qarardad;* (of accounts), تصفیه *tasfie.*

Seven, هفت *haft.*

Seventeen, هیفده *hifdah, hefdah.*

Seventy, هفتاد *haftad.*

Several, چند *cand.*

Severe, شدید *fadid,* سخت *saxt.*

Severely, بشدت *be feddat,* بسختی *be saxti.*

Severity, شدت *feddat,* سختی *saxti.*

Sew, to, دوختن *duxtan.*

Sewage, فاضل‌آب *faʐelab*.

Sex, جنس *jens*.

Shade, Shadow, سايه *saye*.

Shady, سايه‌دار *sayedar*, سايه‌ور *sayevar*.

Shake, to (trans.), تكان دادن *tekan dadan*, جنبانيدن *jombanidan*; (intrans.), لرزيدن *larʐidan*, جنبيدن *jombidan*, تكان خوردن *tekan xordan*.

Shaky, متزلزل *motaʐalʐel*.

Shame, شرم *ʃarm*, شرمندگی *ʃarmandegi*, خجالت *xejalat*; (=disgrace), رسوائی *rosvai*, ننگ *nang*; to put to shame, مفتضح كردن *moftaʐah k*.

Shameful, شرم آور *ʃarmavar*, ننگين *nangin*.

Shameless, بيحيا *bihaya*, بيشرم *biʃarm*.

Shape, شكل *ʃekl*, تركيب *tarkib*.

Shapeless, بدتركيب *badtarkib*.

Share, سهم *sahm*, قسمت *qesmat*; to share, قسمت كردن *qesmat k*.

Share-holder, شريك *ʃarik*, سهيم *sahim*.

Shark, كوسه *kuse*, سگ ماهی *sagmahi*.

Sharp, تيز *tiʐ*, تند *tond*; (=clever), زيرك *ʐirak*, زرنگ *ʐarang*.

Sharpen, to, تيز كردن *tiʐ k*.

Shave, to, اصلاح كردن *eslah k.*, تراشيدن *taraʃidan*.

Shawl, شال *ʃal*.

She, او *u*.

Shears, مقراض *meqraʐ*.

Sheath, غلاف *ɣelaf*.

Sheep, گوسفند *gusfand*.

Sheep-fold, آغل *aɣol*.

Sheepskin coat, پوستين *pustin*.

Sheet, ملافه *malafe*; (of paper), ورق *varaq*.

Shelf, طاقچه *taqce*.

Shell, صدف *sadaf*, مهره *mohre*; (of nut), پوست *pust*; (explosive), خمپاره *xompare*; to shell, پوست كندن *pust kandan*; (=to fire on), بمباران كردن *bombaran k*.

Shelter, پناه *panah*, پناهگاه *panahgah*; to shelter (intrans.), پناه بردن *panah bordan*.

Sheltered, محفوظ *mahfuʐ*.

Shepherd, چوپان *cupan*.

Shield, سپر separ; to shield, حمايت كردن hemayat k., حفظ كردن hefẓ k.

Shine, to, درخشيدن daraxſidan, تابيدن tabidan.

Shining, درخشان daraxſan, تابان taban.

Ship, جهاز jahaẓ, كشتى kaſti, ناو nav; merchant ship, كشتى تجارتى kaſtiye tejarati; to go on board a ship, سوار كشتى شدن savare kaſti ſ.

Shirk, to, طفره زدن tafre ẓadan.

Shirt, پيراهن pirahan.

Shirting, چلوار celvar.

Shiver, to, لرزيدن larẓidan.

Shivering, لرزه larẓe.

Shock, تكان tekan; to shock, تكان دادن tekan dadan.

Shoe, كفش kaſſ, ارسى orosi.

Shoehorn, پاشنه كش paſnekaſ.

Shoelace, بند كفش bande kaſſ.

Shoe-maker, كفاش kaffaſ, كفش دوز kaffduẓ.

Shoot, to (=to fire a gun), تفنگ خالى كردن tofang xali k.; (=to hit with a missile), زدن ẓadan.

Shooting (=hunting), شكار ſekar.

Shop, دكان dokkan, مغازه maɣaẓe.

Shopkeeper, دكاندار dokkandar, مغازه‌دار maɣaẓedar.

Shore, ساحل sahel, كنار kenar.

Short, كوتاه kutah; (of stature), كوتاه قد kutahqadd.

Short-coming, قصور qosur.

Shortly, عن قريب an qarib, بزودى be ẓudi.

Shortness, كوتاهى kutahi.

Shortsighted, كوتاه‌نظر kutahnaẓar; (=near-sighted), نزديك بين naẓdikbin.

Shot (sound of a gun), صداى تفنگ sadaye tofang; (=range), پرتاب partab; (=ball), گلوله golule; (=small shot), ساچمه sacme; to be shot, تير (گلوله) خوردن tir (golule) xordan.

Shoulder, دوش duſ, شانه ſane; to shoulder, بر دوش گرفتن bar duſ gereftan.

Shout, بانگ bang; to shout, بانگ زدن bang ẓadan.

Shovel, بيل bil; to shovel, بيل زدن bil ẓadan.

Show, to, نشان دادن (نمودن) neſan dadan (namudan).

Shrewd, زيرك ẓirak, زرنگ ẓarang.

Shriek, فرياد faryad; to shriek, فرياد كردن faryad k.

Shrill, تیز tiẓ.

Shrine, زیارت گاه ẓiaratgah, قدمگاه qadamgah.

Shroud, کفن kafan.

Shrub, بوته bote, بنه bone.

Shrug, to (the shoulders), تکان دادن tekan dadan.

Shun, to, (احتراز کردن (از ehteraẓ ejtenab k. (aẓ), اجتناب کردن (از) k. (aẓ).

Shut, to, بستن bastan.

Shuttle (weaver's), ماکو maku.

Shy, خجالتی xejalati, خجل xejel; to shy (of a horse), رم کردن ram k.; to be shy, خجالت کشیدن xejalat kaſidan.

Sick, مریض mariẓ, بیمار bimar, ناخوش naxoſ.

Sicken, to, ناخوش شدن naxoſ ſ., بیمار شدن bimar ſ., مریض شدن mariẓ ſ.

Sickening (=disgusting), مکروه makruh, نفرت انگیز nefratangiẓ.

Sickle, داس das.

Sickness, بیماری bimari, مرض maraẓ, ناخوشی naxoſi.

Side, پهلو pahlu, کنار kenar, طرف taraf, جانب janeb; on all sides, از همه طرف aẓ hame taraf, از هر طرف aẓ har taraf.

Siege, محاصره mohasere.

Sieve, غربال ẓerbal, الك alak.

Sift, to, الك کردن alak k., غربال زدن ẓerbal ẓadan.

Sigh, آه ah; to sigh, آه کشیدن ah kaſidan.

Sight, نظر naẓar, دیدار didar, دیده diae; (=spectacle), تماشا tamaſa; (=seeing-power), بینائی binai; (of a gun), نشانه neſane.

Sightless, نابینا nabina, کور kur, اعما a'ma.

Sign, Signal, اشاره eſare, نشان neſan, علامت alamat; to sign (a document), امضا کردن emẓa k.; to make a sign, اشاره کردن eſare k.

Signatory, امضاکننده emẓa konande.

Signature, امضا emẓa.

Silence, خاموشی xamuſi, سکوت sokut; to keep silence, سکوت اختیار کردن sokut exteyar k.; to silence, ساکت کردن saket k.

Silent, خاموش xamuſ, ساکت saket.

Silently, آهسته aheste.

Silk, ابریشم abriſom, حریر harir; silken, ابریشمی abriſomi, حریری hariri.

Silkworm, پیله *pile,* کرم ابریشم *kerme abriſom.*

Silt, شن *ſen,* لای *lāi.*

Silver, نقره *noqre,* سیم *sim.*

Silversmith, زرگر *ʒargar.*

Similarity, شباهت *ſebahat.*

Simile, تشبیه *taſbih.*

Simple, ساده *sade.*

Simpleton, ساده لوح *sadelōuh.*

Simplicity, سادگی *sadegi.*

Sin, گناه *gonah;* to sin, گناه کردن *gonah k.*

Since (=because), چونکه *cun ke,* (که) زیرا *ʒira (ke);* (=from the time that), تا *ta,* از موقعیکه *aʒ mōuqeʿike.*

Sincere, صمیمی *samimi,* صادق *sadeq,* مخلص *moxles.*

Sincerity, صمیمیت *samimiyat,* اخلاص *exlas,* صداقت *sadaqat.*

Sinful, گناهکار *gonahkar.*

Sing, to, آواز خواندن *avaʒ xandan,* سرودن *sorudan.*

Singer, آوازه خوان *avaʒexan.*

Single, مفرد *mofred;* (=alone), تنها *tanha,* تك *tak;* (=one), یك *yak.*

Singular, مفرد *mofred.*

Sink, to (intrans.), فرو رفتن *foru raftan,* غرق شدن *ʒarq ſ.*

Sinner, گناهکار *gonahkar.*

Sir, آقا *aqa.*

Sister, خواهر *xahar,* همشیره *hamſire.*

Sit, to, نشستن *neſastan;* to sit cross-legged, چهار زانو نشستن *cahar ʒanu neſastan.*

Site, جا *ja,* وضع *vaʒʿ,* جایگاه *jāigah.*

Situated, واقع *vaqeʿ.*

Situation, موقعیت *mōuqeʿiyat;* (=appointment), کار *kar,* شغل *ſoyl.*

Six, شش *ſeſ.*

Sixteen, شانزده *ſanʒdah.*

Sixty, شصت *ſast.*

Size, اندازه *andaʒe;* (=glue), سریشم *seriſom.*

Skein, کلافه *kalafe.*

Skeleton, استخوان بندی *ostoxanbandi.*

Skewer, سیخ *six.*

Skiff, زورق ‎*q̄ouraq.*

Skilful, هنرمند *honarmand,* ماهر *maher.*

Skill, هنر *honar,* مهارت *maharat,* سر رشته *sarreſte.*

Skim, to, کف گرفتن *kaf gereftan.*

Skimmer, کفگیر *kafgir.*

Skin, پوست *puſt;* (for holding water, etc.), مشك *maſk,* خیگ *xig;* to skin, پوست کندن *puſt kandan.*

Skirmish, زد و خورد *q̄ad o xord.*

Skirt, دامن *daman;* (of a mountain), دامنه *damane.*

Skull, کله *kalle.*

Sky, آسمان *asman,* فلك *falak.*

Slack, سست *sost,* شل *ſol.*

Slackness, سستی *sosti.*

Slander, تهمت *tohmat,* افترا *eftera;* to slander, تهمت زدن *tohmat q̄adan.*

Slap (on the face), سیلی *sili;* to slap, سیلی زدن *sili q̄adan.*

Slate (for writing), لوح *lōuh.*

Slaughter-house, سلاخ خانه *sallaxxane,* مسلخ *maslax.*

Slave, بنده *bande,* عبد *abd,* حلقه بگوش *halqe be guſ,* غلام *ɣolam,* مملوك *mamluk,* برده *barde.*

Sleep, خواب *xab;* to sleep, خوابیدن *xabidan.*

Sleeplessness, بیخوابی *bixabi.*

Sleepy, خواب آلود *xabalud.*

Sleet, بوران *buran.*

Sleeve, آستین *astin.*

Sleight of hand, تر دستی *tardasti.*

Slender, نازك *naq̄ok,* باریك *barik.*

Slenderness, نازکی *naq̄oki,* باریکی *bariki.*

Slice, قاچ *qac.*

Slide, to, سر خوردن *sor xordan.*

Slime, لجن *lajan.*

Slip, to, لغزیدن *laɣq̄idan,* لیز خوردن *liq̄ xordan,* سریدن *soridan;* see also Error.

Slipper, کفش راحتی *kafſe rahati.*

Slipshod, لا قید *la q̄ēid,* بی ترتیب *bitartib,* شلخته *ſalaxte.*

Slipway, سرسره *sorsore.*

Sloop, ناوچه *navce.*

Slope, شیب *sib.*

Sloth, کاهلی *kaheli,* تنبلی *tambali.*

Slovenly, شلخته *salaxte.*

Slow, کند *kond.*

Slowly, آهسته *aheste.*

Slowness, آهستگی *ahestegi.*

Slump, بحران اقتصادی *bohrane eqtesadi.*

Sly, زیرك *zirak,* موذی *muzi.*

Slyness, زیرکی *ziraki,* موذیگری *muzigari.*

Small, کوچك *kucek,* خرد *xord,* قلیل *qalil,* صغیر *sayir.*

Smallness, کوچکی *kuceki.*

Smallpox, آبله *abele.*

Smash, to, خرد کردن *xord k.*

Smear, to, اندودن *andudan,* آلودن *aludan.*

Smell, بو *bu;* to smell (trans.), بوکردن *bu k.,* بو شنیدن *bu sonidan;* (intrans.), بو دادن *bu dadan.*

Smelt, to, گداختن *godaxtan,* ذوب کردن *zoub k.*

Smile, تبسم *tabassom;* to smile, تبسم کردن *tabassom k.*

Smoke, دود *dud;* to smoke (intrans.), دود کردن *dud k.;* (a cigarette, etc.), دود کشیدن *dud kasidan.*

Smooth, هموار *hamvar,* مسطح *mosattah,* صاف *saf;* to smooth (= to make flat), صاف کردن *saf k.,* مسطح کردن *mosattah k.*

Smoothness, همواری *hamvari.*

Smother, to, خفه کردن *xaffe k.*

Smuggle, to, قاچاق کردن *qacaq k.*

Smuggler, قاچاقچی *qacaqci.*

Snake, مار *mar.*

Snap, to (= to break, trans.), گسیختن *gosixtan.*

Snare, دام *dam,* تله *tale.*

Snatch, to, ربودن *robudan.*

Sneeze, عطسه *atse;* to sneeze, عطسه کردن *atse k.*

Snore, to, خرخر کردن *xorxor k.*

Snout, خرطوم *xortum,* پوز *puz.*

Snow, برف *barf;* to snow, برف باریدن *barf baridan.*

So (=thus), چنین *conin,* چنان *conan,* همچنین *hamconin,* همچنان *hamconan;* so much, چندان *candan,* چندین *candin;* so that, تا *ta,* که *ke;* so long as, تا *ta,* مادامیکه *madamike;* and so forth, علی هذا *ala haza,* و غیره *va yeire;* so-and-so, فلانی *folani.*

Soak, to, خیساندن *xisandan.*

Soaked (=wet through), خیس *xis.*

Soap, صابون *sabun.*

Sobriety, پرهیزکاری *parhizkari,* متانت *matanat.*

Social, اجتماعی *ejtema'i.*

Socialist (political term), کارگر *kargar.*

Society, اجتماع *ejtema',* جامعه *jame'e;* (=companionship), صحبت *sohbat,* معاشرت *mo'aserat;* (=commercial company), شرکت *serkat;* (=association), انجمن *anjoman.*

Sock, جوراب *jurab.*

Sofa, نیمکت *nimkat.*

Soft, نرم *narm,* ملایم *molayem.*

Softly, آهسته *aheste,* یواش *yavaf.*

Softness, نرمی *narmi.*

Soil, زمین *zamin,* خاك *xak.*

Sojourn, اقامت *eqamat.*

Solar, شمسی *famsi.*

Solder, لحیم *lahim;* to solder, لحیم کردن *lahim k.*

Soldier, سرباز *sarbaz.*

Solid (=firm), محکم *mohkam.*

Soluble, حل شدنی *hall fodani.*

Solution (of a problem), حل *hall.*

Solve, to, حل کردن *hall k.*

Some, بعضی *ba'zi,* چند *cand;* (=a little), قدری *qadri.*

Somebody, کسی *kasi,* شخصی *faxsi.*

Somersault, پشتك *poftak,* معلق *mo'allaq;* to turn a somersault, پشتك زدن *poftak zadan,* معلق زدن *mo'allaq zadan.*

Something, چیزی *cizi.*

Sometimes, گاهی *gahi,* گاه گاه *gahgah.*

Somewhere, جائی *jai.*

Son, پسر *pesar,* فرزند *farzand,* ابن *ebn.*

Song, سرود sorud.

Son-in-law, داماد damad.

Soon, زود ɀud, بزودی be ɀudi, عن قريب an qarib; as soon as, همينكه haminke, بمحض اينكه be maḥ̃ze inke, بمجرد اينكه be mojarrade inke, تا ta.

Sore (subs.), زخم ɀaxm, ريش riʃ; (adj.), دردناك dardnak; to be sore, درد كردن dard k.

Sorrow, see Grief.

Sorrowful, see Sad.

Sorry: to be sorry, افسوس خوردن afsus xordan, متأسف بودن mota‘assef b.

Sort, نوع nōu‘, جور jur, طور tōur, قسم qesm, جنس jens.

Soul, روح ruh, نفس nafs, جان jan.

Sound, see Safe; (=noise), صدا sada; (loud noise), بانگ bang; to sound (=to measure the depth), تعميق كردن andaze gereftan, اندازه گرفتن ta‘miq k.

Soup, آبگوشت abguʃt.

Sour, ترش torʃ.

Source, منشاء manʃa‘, مبداء mabda‘, منبع mamba‘.

South, جنوب jonub; south-east, جنوب شرقی jonube ʃarqi; south-west, جنوب غربی jonube ɣarbi.

Southern, جنوبی jonubi.

Souvenir, يادگار yadgar.

Sovereign, see King; sovereign government, دولت متبوع dōulate matbu‘.

Soviet (adj.), شوروی ʃōuravi.

Sow, to, كشتن keʃtan, كاشتن kaʃtan, تخم پاشيدن toxm paʃidan.

Space (=interval), فاصله fasele; (=extent), وسعت vos‘at; (of time), مدت moddat, فاصله fasele.

Spacious, وسيع vasi‘.

Spaciousness, وسعت vos‘at.

Spade, بيل bil; wooden spade, پارو paru.

Spain, اسپانيا espania.

Span (a measure), وجب vajab.

Spanner, آچار acar.

Spare, يدكی yadaki; spare parts, اسباب يدكی asbabe yadaki; to spare, see Forgive.

Sparrow, گنجشك *gonjeſk*.

Spasm, تشنج *taſannoj*.

Speak, to, حرف زدن *harf ʒadan*.

Speaker, گوینده *guyande*; (of the National Assembly), رئیس مجلس *ra'ise majles*.

Spear, نیزه *neiʒe*.

Special, خاص *xass*, مخصوص *maxsus*, مختص *moxtass*.

Speciality, خاصیت *xassiyat*, اختصاص *extesas*.

Specially, خاصه *xasse*, خصوصًا *xosusan*, مخصوصًا *maxsusan*, علی الخصوص *alal-xosus*, بویژه *be viʒe*.

Species, see Sort.

Specified, معین *mo'ayyan*.

Specify, to, تعیین کردن *ta'yin k*.

Speck, ذره *ʒarre*.

Spectacle, تماشا *tamaſa*.

Spectacles, عینك *einak*.

Spectator, تماشاچی *tamaſaci*.

Speculate, to (in business), سفته بازی کردن *seftebaʒi k*.

Speculation, سفته بازی *seftebaʒi*.

Speculator, سفته باز *seftebaʒ*.

Speech, گفتار *goftar*, نطق *notq*; to make a speech, نطق کردن *notq k*.

Speed, سرعت *sor'at*.

Speedometer, سرعت‌نما *sor'atnama*.

Spell, to, املا کردن *emla k*.

Spelling, املا *emla*.

Spend, to, خرج کردن *xarj k*., مصرف کردن *masraf k*., صرف کردن *sarf k*.; (time), بسر بردن *be sar bordan*, گذراندن *goʒarandan*.

Sphere (earthly), کره *korre*; (heavenly), سپهر *sepehr*, گردون *gardun*; (of action), حوزه *hōuʒe*.

Spice, ادویه *advie*.

Spider, عنکبوت *ankabut*; spider's web, تار عنکبوت *tare ankabut*.

Spill, to, ریختن *rixtan*.

Spin, to, ریشتن *riſtan*, رشتن *reſtan*.

Spindle, دوك *duk*.

Spiral, مارپیچ *marpic*.

Spirit, روح *ruh,* نفس *nafs,* جان *jan;* see also Courage; (=distilled liquor), عرق *araq.*

Spiritual, معنوی *ma'navi,* روحانی *ruhani.*

Spirituality, روحانیت *ruhaniyat.*

Spit (for cooking), سیخ *six;* to spit (= to expectorate), تف کردن *tof k.*

Spite, کینه *kine,* بغض *boɣ̇z,* بد خواهی *badxahi;* in spite of, علی رغم *ala raɣm(e);* in spite of the fact that, با وجودیکه *ba vojudike.*

Spiteful, بد خواه *badxah,* بد ذات *badzat.*

Spittle, تف *tof,* آب دهن *abe dahan.*

Splendid, درخشان *daraxʃan,* معظم *mo'azzam.*

Splendour, جلال *jalal,* رونق *roˉunaq.*

Splint, تخته استخوان بندی *taxteye ostoxanbandi;* (of a horse), استخوان ساق *ostoxane saq.*

Split, شکاف *ʃekaf,* شق *ʃaqq;* to split (trans.), شکافتن *ʃekaftan;* (intrans., = to burst), پاره شدن *pare ʃ.,* ترکیدن *tarakidan.*

Split peas, لپه *lape.*

Spoil, to, ضایع کردن *ża'ye k.;* (a child, etc.), لوس کردن *lus k.*

Spoilt (=damaged), ضایع *ża'ye,* معیوب *ma'yub;* (of a child), لوس *lus.*

Sponge, اسفنج *esfanj.*

Spool, قرقره *qerqere.*

Spoon, قاشق *qaʃoq.*

Sport (=plaything), بازیچه *baˉziче.*

Spot, لک *lakke;* see also Place.

Spout (of tea-pot, etc.), دهنه *dahane.*

Spread, to (a carpet, etc.), پهن کردن *pahn k.;* (=to scatter), پاشیدن *paʃidan;* to spread abroad, منتشر کردن انتشار کردن *enteʃar k., montaʃer k.;* to be spread abroad, انتشار یافتن شایع شدن *enteʃar yaftan, ʃaye' ʃ.*

Spring (season), بهار *bahar;* (mechanical), فنر *fanar;* (=leap), جست *jast,* پرش *pareʃ;* (of water), چشمه *caʃme;* hot spring, آب گرم *abe garm;* spring of mineral water, آب معدنی *abe ma'dani;* to spring, جستن *jastan,* پریدن *paridan;* (=to grow), رستن *rostan;* to spring from (= to issue from), صادر شدن از *sader ʃ. az.*

Sprinkle, to, پاشیدن *paʃidan.*

Spur (=goad), مهمیز *mehmiz;* to spur, مهمیز زدن *mehmiz zadan;* (=to incite), تحریک کردن *tahrik k.*

Spy, جاسوس *jasus.*

Squabble, نزاع *neẓa'*, ستیزه *setiẓe*; to squabble, نزاع کردن *neẓa' k.*, ستیزه کردن *setiẓe k.*

Squadron (naval), ناو گروه *navgoruh.*

Squander, to, اسراف کردن *esraf k.*

Square (adj.), مربع *morabba'*; (subs.), چهارگوشه *caharguʃe*; (of a city), میدان، *meïdan.*

Squeeze, to, فشردن *feʃordan.*

Squib (firework), موشك *muʃak.*

Squint, to, لوچ بودن *luc b.*

Stability, ثبات *sabat*, استواری *ostovari.*

Stable, طویله *tavile*; (=firm), استوار *ostovar*, ثابت *sabet*, بر قرار *bar qarar*, قرص *qors.*

Staff, عصا *asa*, چوب دستی *cubdasti*; (military), ستاد *setad*; General Staff, ستاد کل ارتش *setade kolle arteʃ*; Chief of the General Staff, رئیس ستاد کل ارتش *ra'ise setade kolle arteʃ.*

Stag, گوزن *gavaẓn.*

Stage (of a journey), منزل *manẓel*, مرحله *marhale.*

Stagnant, گندیده *gandide*; expanse of stagnant water, مرداب *mordab.*

Stain (=spot), لکه *lakke.*

Stained, لکه دار *lakkedar*; (fig.), آلوده *alude.*

Stair, پله *pelle*; stairs, پلکان *pellekan.*

Stalk (of a plant), ساقه *saqe.*

Stall (for cattle), آخور *axor.*

Stammer, لکنت زبان *loknate ẓaban*; he stammers, زبانش میگیرد *ẓabaneʃ migirad.*

Stamp (=seal), مهر *mohr*, سکه *sekke*; (=mark), علامت *alamat*, نشان *neʃan*; (postage), تمبر *tambr*; to stamp (=to seal), مهر زدن *mohr ẓadan*; (=to mark), علامت گذاشتن *alamat goẓaʃtan*; (with a postage-stamp), تمبر زدن *tambr ẓadan*; (the feet), پا زدن *pa ẓadan.*

Stand, to, ایستادن *istadan*; to stand up, بر پا شدن *bar pa ʃ.*, راست ایستادن *rast istadan.*

Standard (=level), پایه *paye*, سطح *sath*; see also Banner.

Star, ستاره *setare*, اختر *axtar*, کوکب *koukab*, نجم *najm.*

Starch, نشاسته *neʃaste*; to starch, نشاسته زدن *neʃaste ẓadan.*

Starling, سار *sar.*

Start, to, see Begin.

Startling (=striking), زننده زنـنـده *zanande;* (=frightening), وحشت انگیز *vahfatangiz.*

State, see Condition and Government; to state, اظهار کردن *ezhar k.*

Statement, اظهار *ezhar,* گفتار *goftar.*

Statesman, مدبر *modabber,* سیاستمدار *siasatmadar.*

Statesmanship, سیاستمداری *siasatmadari.*

Station, ایستگاه *istgah;* (=place), مکان *makan,* مقام *maqam,* جایگاه *jaigah.*

Stationer, خرازی فروش *xarraziforuf.*

Statistician, آمار شناس *amarfenas.*

Statistics, آمار *amar.*

Statue, مجسمه *mojassame.*

Stature, قد *qadd,* قامت *qamat,* اندام *andam.*

Status, وضعیت *vaz'iyat,* مقام *maqam.*

Stay, to, ماندن *mandan;* (=to stop), توقف کردن *tavaqqof k.;* (=to sojourn), اقامت کردن *eqamat k.*

Steal, to, دزدیدن *dozdidan.*

Steam, بخار *boxar.*

Steamer, کشتی بخاری *kaftiye boxari.*

Steel, فولاد *fulad,* پولاد *pulad.*

Steely, فولادی *fuladi.*

Steep, سراشیب *sarafib;* (of a descent), سرازیر *sarazir;* (of an ascent), سرابالا *sarabala;* to steep, آغشتن *ayeftan.*

Step, قدم *qadam,* گام *gam;* (of a stair), پله *pelle.*

Step-brother, نابرادری *nabaradari.*

Step-father, ناپدری *napedari.*

Step-daughter, نادختری *nadoxtari.*

Step-mother, نامادری *namadari,* زن پدر *zane pedar.*

Step-sister, ناخواهری *naxahari.*

Step-son, ناپسری *napesari.*

Sterile, عقیم *aqim;* (of land), بایر *bayer,* شوره *fure,* لم یزرع *lam yazra';* (of a tree), بی ثمر *bi samar.*

Stew, خورشت *xoreft.*

Steward, ناظر *nazer.*

Stick, to (= to adhere), چسبیدن *casbidan*; (trans.), چسبانیدن *casbanidan.*

Sticky, چسپناك *caspnak.*

Stiff (= tired), کوبیده *kubide.*

Stifle, to, خفه کردن *xaffe k.*

Stifling, خفه *xaffe.*

Still, see Quiet, Silent and Nevertheless; (= yet), هنوز *hanuz*, بازهم *baz ham*; to still, آرام کردن *aram k.*

Stimulate, to, بر انگیختن *bar angixtan.*

Stimulating, مهیج *mohaïyej.*

Sting, نیش *niʃ*; to sting, نیش زدن *niʃ zadan.*

Stir, to, بهم زدن *be ham zadan*; (intrans., = to move), جنبیدن *jombidan*; to stir up, بر انگیختن *bar angixtan.*

Stirrup, رکاب *rekab.*

Stitch, بخیه *baxiye.*

Stock (= reserve), ذخیره *zaxire*; (= merchandise), بضاعت *baza'at*; (= capital), سرمایه *sarmaye*; (= lineage), اصل *asl*, نسل *nasl*, نسب *nasab*; (flower), شب بو *ʃabbu.*

Stocking, جوراب *jurab.*

Stomach, معده *me'de*, شکم *ʃekam*; stomach-ache, دلدرد *deldard.*

Stone, سنگ *sang*; (of fruit), هسته *haste*; precious stone, جوهر *jouhar*; to stone (a person), سنگ زدن *sang zadan*, سنگسار کردن *sangsar k.*

Stone-cutting, سنگ تراشی *sangtaraʃi.*

Stone-mason, سنگتراش *sangtaraʃ.*

Stony, سنگلاخ *sanglax.*

Stony-hearted, سنگدل *sangdel.*

Stop, to (intrans.), ایستادن *istadan*, وا ایستادن *va istadan*; (= to wait; to sojourn, intrans.), توقف کردن *tavaqqof k.*; see also Prevent.

Stoppage (of work), تعطیل *ta'til*; (= prevention), منع *man'*, جلوگیری *jelougiri.*

Stopper (of a bottle), سر شیشه *sare ʃiʃe.*

Store, انبار *ambar*; (= stock), ذخیره *zaxire.*

Storekeeper, انباردار *ambardar.*

Storey, طبقه *tabaqe.*

Stork, لكلك *laklak*, لقلق *laqlaq.*

Storm, طوفان *tufan.*

Storm-lantern, چراغ دستی ceraɣe dasti.

Story, حكایت hekayat, قصه qesse, داستان dastan.

Storyteller, قصه گو qessegu.

Stout, قوی qavi.

Stove, بخاری boxari.

Straight, راست rast, مستقیم mostaqim.

Strain, to (= to filter), صاف کردن saf k.

Strainer, صاف کن safkon.

Straits, تنگه tange, بغاز boɣaz.

Strange, غریب ɣarib.

Stranger, غریب ɣarib, بیگانه bigane; (= non-Persian), اجنبی ajnabi.

Strangle, to, خفه کردن xaffe k.

Stratagem, حیله hile.

Strategic, سوق الجیشی souq ol-jeiʃi.

Stratum, طبقه tabaqe, چینه cine.

Straw, که kah.

Strawberry, توت فرنگی tute farangi.

Stream, جوی jui.

Street, کوچه kuce.

Strength, see Power.

Strengthen, to, مستحکم کردن mostahkam k.

Stress, تأکید ta'kid; (= pressure), فشار feʃar; to stress, تأکید کردن ta'kid k.

Stretch, to, کشیدن kaʃidan; to stretch oneself, دراز کشیدن daraz kaʃidan.

Strict, اکید akid, شدید ʃadid.

Strictly, اکیداً akidan, شدیداً ʃadidan.

Stride, قدم qadam.

Strike (= refusal to work), اعتصاب e'tesab; to strike, اعتصاب کردن e'tesab k.; (= to hit), زدن zadan; (of a ship, to strike a mine, rock, etc.), خوردن (به) xordan (be).

Striking, زننده zanande.

String, ریسمان risman; (of a musical instrument), زه zeh; to string (an instrument), زه کشی کردن zehkaʃi k.

Strip, to (= to take off one's clothes), برهنه شدن barahne ʃ., لخت شدن loxt ʃ.

368

Strive, to, سعی کردن *sāi k.*, کوشیدن *kuʃidan,* کوشش کردن *kuʃeʃ k.*, تلاش کردن *tallaʃ k.*; (=to contend), مجادله کردن *mojadele k.*, دعوای کردن *da'va k.*

Stroll, to, قدم زدن *qadam ʒadan.*

Strong, see Powerful.

Strong-box, صندوق *sanduq.*

Struggle, کشمکش *keʃmakeʃ*; to struggle, کشمکش کردن *keʃmakeʃ k.*, کشتی گرفتن *koʃti gereftan.*

Student, دانش آموز *daneʃamuʒ,* محصل *mohassel.*

Study, مطالعه *motale'e*; studies (at an educational institution), تحصیلات *tahsilat*; to study, مطالعه کردن *motale'e k.*, تحصیلی کردن *tahsil k.*

Stuff (=cloth, etc.), پارچه *parce.*

Stumble, to, لغزیدن *layʒidan,* سکندری خوردن *sekandari xordan.*

Stumbling-block, سنگ لغزش *sango layʒeʃ*; (fig.), مانع *mane'.*

Stump, کنده *konde.*

Stupefied, مبهوت *mabhut,* مدهوش *madhuʃ.*

Stupid, احمق *ahmaq,* کودن *koudan,* ابله *ablah,* خرفت *xereft.*

Stupidity, حماقت *hemaqat,* خریت *xariyat.*

Sturgeon, سگ ماهی *sagmahi.*

Style (literary), سبک *sabk.*

Subdivide, to, تقسیم جزء کردن *taqsime joʒ' k.*

Subject (of a country), تابع *tabe'*; (=topic), موضوع *mōuʒu'*; subject to (=under), تحت *taht(e).*

Subjection, تسلیم *taslim,* اطاعت *eta'at.*

Sublime, عالی *ali.*

Submarine (noun and adj.), زیر دریائی *ʒirdaryai.*

Submerge, to (trans.), فرو بردن *foru bordan*; (intrans.), فرو رفتن *foru raftan,* غوطه‌ور شدن *yutevar ʃ.*

Submission, تسلیم *taslim.*

Submit, to, تسلیم کردن *taslim k.*; (=to represent), عرض کردن *arʒ k.*

Subordinate (subs.), زیردست *ʒirdast.*

Subscription, اشتراک *eʃterak.*

Subside, to, فرو رفتن *foru raftan*; (of a rebellion, etc.), فرو نشستن *foru neʃastan.*

Subsistence, معیشت *ma'iʃat,* مدد معاش *madade ma'aʃ,* امر معاش *amre ma'aʃ.*

Substance (= essential part), اصل *asl.*

Substantiality, تجسم *tajassom,* جسمانيت *jesmaniyat.*

Substantiate, to, اثبات كردن *esbat k.*

Substitute, تبـديـل كردن كفيل *kafil;* to substitute, عوض كردن *avaz k.,* تبديل كردن *tabdil k.;* to act as a substitute, كفالت كردن *kefalat k.*

Subterranean, زير زمينى *zirzamini.*

Subtle, دقيق *daqiq,* باريك *barik.*

Subtlety, دقت *deqqat,* باريكى *bariki.*

Subtract, to, تفريق كردن *tafriq k.,* منها كردن *menha k.*

Subtraction, تفريق *tafriq.*

Suburb, حوالى *havali.*

Succeed, to, موفق بودن *movaffaq b.,* كامياب شدن *kamyab ʃ.;* (= to follow), جانشين شدن *janeʃin ʃ.*

Successful, موفق *movaffaq,* كامياب *kamyab.*

Successive, پى در پى *pei dar pei,* متوالى *motavali.*

Successor, جا نشين *janeʃin.*

Such, همچو *hamcu,* همچون *hamcun,* چندين *candin,* چندان *candan,* چنين *conin* چنان *conan.*

Suck, to, مكيدن *makidan.*

Sucking (of a child), شير خوار *ʃirxar.*

Suckle, to, شير دادن *ʃir dadan.*

Sudden, ناگاه *nagah.*

Suddenly, ناگاه *nagah,* ناگهان *nagahan,* يكدفعه *yak dafʿe,* بغتةً *baʏtatan.*

Suffer, to (= to tolerate), تحمل كردن *tahammol k.;* (= to allow), گذاشتن *gozaʃtan;* to suffer pain, رنج كشيدن *ranj kaʃidan.*

Suffering, رنج *ranj,* عذاب *azab,* درد *dard.*

Suffice, to, كفايت كردن *kefayat k.,* كافى بودن *kafi b.,* بس بودن *bas b.*

Sufficiency, كفايت *kefayat.*

Sufficient, كافى *kafi,* بس *bas.*

Suffocate, to (intrans.), خفه شدن *xaffe ʃ.*

Sugar (castor), شكر *ʃekar;* (lump), قند *qand;* sugar candy, نبات *nabat;* loaf of sugar, كله قند *kalleqand.*

Sugar-bowl, قنددان *qanddan.*

Suicide, نتـحار خـود كـشـى *xodkoʃi, entehar;* to commit suicide, انتحار كردن خود كشى كردن *xodkoʃi k., entehar k.*

Suit (of clothes), دست dast; (legal), دعوی da'va, مرافعه morafe'e; to suit
   (3rd pers. only), (به) ماندن mandan (be), (به) ساختن saxtan (be).

Suitability, شایستگی ſayestegi, مناسبت monasebat.

Suitable, شایسته ſayeste, مناسب monaseb.

Sulphur, گوگرد gugerd.

Sulphurous, گوگردی gugerdi.

Sultan, سلطان soltan.

Sultana (fruit), کشمش keſmeſ.

Sum (of money), مبلغ mablaɣ; (mathematical), حساب hesab.

Sumach, سماق somaq.

Summarize, to, مختصر کردن moxtasar k.

Summer, تابستان tabestan; summer quarters (hill station), ییلاق yeïlaq.

Summit, قله qolle, سر sar.

Summon, to, احضار کردن ehẓar k.

Summons, احضاریه ehẓariye, احضار ehẓar.

Sun, آفتاب aftab, خورشید xorſid.

Sunburnt, آفتاب زده aftabẓade.

Sunday, یکشنبه yak ſambe.

Sunflower, آفتاب گردان aftabgardan.

Sunrise, طلوع آفتاب tolu'e aftab.

Sunset, غروب آفتاب ɣorube aftab.

Sunshade (= parasol), چتر catr.

Superficial, سطحی sathi.

Superfluity, زیادی ẓiadi, زیادتی ẓiadati.

Superfluous, زاید ẓayed.

Superintend, to, نظارت کردن neẓarat k.

Superintendence, نظارت neẓarat.

Superintendent, ناظر naẓer.

Superior, برتر bartar, ما فوق ma fōuq, عالی ali.

Superiority, برتری bartari, تفوق tafavvoq.

Supernatural, ما وراء الطبیعت ma vara' ot-tab'iyat.

Superstition, موهومات mōuhumat, خرافات xorafat.

Supervise, to, see Superintend.

Supper, شام ſam; the Lord's Supper, عشاء ربانی aſa'e rabbani.

Supplies (food), آذوقه aẓuqe.

Support, پشتیبانی poſtibani, پشتی poſti, تکیه tekie; to support, پشتیبانی کردن poſtibani k.; (= to tolerate), تحمل کردن tahammol k.

Supporter, پشتیبان poſtiban.

Suppose, to, تصور کردن tasavvor k., گمان کردن gaman k., پنداشتن pandaſtan, فرض کردن farʒ k.

Supposition, تصور tasavvor, گمان gaman, فرض farʒ.

Suppress, to, توقیف کردن tōuqif k., موقوف کردن mōuquf k.; (= to conceal), پنهان کردن panhan k., مخفی کردن maxfi k.

Suppression, توقیف tōuqif; (= concealment), کتمان ketman.

Sure, یقین yaqin, محقق mohaqqaq, مسلم mosallam, حتمی hatmi.

Surety, ضمانت ʒamanat, گرو gerōu; (guarantor), ضامن ʒamen.

Surface, سطح sath, رو ru.

Surgeon, جراح jarrah.

Surgery, جراحی jarrahi; (= dispensary), مطب matabb.

Surgical, جراحی jarrahi.

Surplus (subs.), مازاد ma ʒad, زیادتی ʒiadati.

Surprise, تعجب ta'ajjob; to take by surprise, غافلگیر کردن ɣafelgir k.

Surrender, تسلیم taslim; to surrender (trans.), تسلیم کردن taslim k.; (intrans.), تسلیم شدن taslim ſ.

Surround, to, محاصره کردن mohasere k., احاطه کردن ehate k.

Survey, to, مساحت کردن masahat k., نقشه برداری کردن naqſebardari k.

Surveyor, مساح massah, نقشه بردار naqſebardar.

Susceptible, مستعد mosta'edd.

Suspect, to, (از) شبهه داشتن ſobhe d. (aʒ), (از) سوء ظن داشتن su'e ʒann d. (aʒ).

Suspected, متهم mottaham, مظنون maʒnun.

Suspend, to, see Hang; (a rule, etc.), تعطیل کردن ta'til k.

Suspension (of hostilities), متارکه motareke; (of a rule, etc.), تعطیل ta'til.

Suspicion, سوء ظن su'e ʒann.

Suspicious (of someone or something), ظنین ʒanin, دارای سوء ظن daraye su'e ʒann; (= ambiguous), مشکوک maſkuk.

Suture, درز darʒ, بخیه baxiye.

Swaddling clothes, قنداق qondaq.

Swallow, پرستوک parastuk; to swallow, فرو بردن foru bordan, بلعیدن bal'idan.

Swamp, باطلاق botlaq, مرداب mordab.

Swear, to, see Oath.

Sweat, عرق *araq*, خوی *xui*; to sweat, عرق کردن *araq k.*

Sweep, to, رفتن *roftan*, جاروکردن *jaru k.*

Sweet, شیرین *firin.*

Sweeten, to, شیرین کردن *firin k.*

Sweetmeat, شیرینی *firini.*

Sweetness, شیرینی *firini.*

Swell, to (intrans.), ورم کردن *varam k.*, بر آمدن *bar amadan*, باد کردن
bad k.

Swelling, ورم *varam*, بر آمدگی *baramadegi*, باد *bad.*

Swim, to, شنا کردن *fena k.*

Swimming, شنا *fena.*

Swindle, کلاه گذاری *kolahgoʒari*; to swindle (someone), (کسی) کلاه
kolah(e kasi) goʒaftan, بر داشتن (کسی) کلاه *kolah(e kasi) bar d.* گذاشتن

Swindler, کلاه گذار *kolahgoʒar*, بر دار کلاه *kolahbardar.*

Switch (stick), ترکه *tarke.*

Swoon, غش *ɣaf*; to swoon, غش کردن *ɣaf k.*, ضعف کردن *za'f k.*

Sword, شمشیر *famfir.*

Sympathetic, دلسوز *delsuʒ*, شفیق *fafiq.*

Sympathy, همدردی *hamdardi*, دلسوزی *delsuʒi.*

Synagogue, کنشت *keneft.*

Syntax, نحو *nahv.*

Syphilis, سفلیس *seflis.*

Syringe, آبدزدك *abdoʒdak.*

Syrup, شیره *fire.*

Systematic, مرتب *morattab*, منظم *monaʒʒam.*

T

Table, میز *miʒ.*

Table-cloth, سفره *sofre.*

Tablet, لوح *louh.*

Tail, دم *dom*; fat tail of a sheep, دنبه *dombe.*

Tailor, خیاط *xayyat.*

Taint: to be tainted, آلوده شدن *alude f.*

Take, to, گرفتن gereftan, ستادن setadan, اخذ کردن axƶ k.; to take away,
بر داشتن bar d., بردن bordan; to take off (clothes), کندن kandan; to
take back, پس گرفتن pas gereftan.

Talisman, طلسم telesm.

Talk (broadcast talk, public speech, etc.), سخنرانی soxanrani; to talk, صحبت
کردن sohbat k., حرف زدن harf ƶadan; (publicly), سخنرانی کردن soxanrani k.

Tall (of stature), بلند قد bolandqadd.

Tamarisk, گز gaƶ.

Tame, رام ram; to tame, رام کردن ram k.; to become tame, رام شدن
ram f., انس گرفتن ons gereftan.

Tan, to (leather), دباغی کردن dabbaƴi k.

Tangerine, نارنگی narangi.

Tangled, در هم و بر هم dar ham o bar ham.

Tank, تانك tank; (water-tank), آب انبار abambar, حوض hōuƶ.

Tanker, کشتی نفت کش kaftiye naftkaf.

Tanner, دباغ dabbaƴ.

Tap, شیر fir.

Tar, قیر qir.

Tarantula, رتیل rotēil.

Target, هدف hadaf, نشانه nefane.

Tariff, تعرفه ta'refe.

Tarragon, ترخان tarxan.

Taste (=flavour), مزه maƶe, طعم ta'm; (=appreciation, judgement), سلیقه
saliqe, ذوق ƶōuq; to taste, چشیدن cafidan.

Tautology, لغت پردازی loƴatpardaƶi.

Tax, مالیات maliyat, باج baj; extraordinary taxes, عوارض avareƶ; to tax,
مالیات بستن maliyat bastan; to impose taxation, مالیات وضع کردن maliyat
vaƶ' k.

Taxable, مالیات بده maliyatbedeh.

Taxation, مالیات maliyat.

Tax-collector, تحصیلدار مالیات tahsildare maliyat.

Tea, چای cāi; to drink tea, چای خوردن cāi xordan; afternoon tea, عصرانه
asrane.

Teach, to, تعلیم دادن ta'lim dadan, یاد دادن yad dadan; (=give lessons),
تدریس کردن tadris k.

Teacher, معلم *mo'allem*; secondary school teacher, دبیر *dabir*; primary school teacher, آموزگار *amuzegar*.

Teaching (=being a teacher), معلمی *mo'allemi*.

Tea-cup, فنجان *fenjan*.

Tear (from the eye), اشك *afk*; to shed tears, اشك ریختن *afk rixtan*.

Tear, to, پاره کردن *pare k.*

Tease, to, سر بسر گذاشتن *sar be sar gozaftan*.

Technical, فنی *fanni*.

Technician, متخصص فنی *motaxassese fanni*.

Technique, فن *fann*.

Telegraph, تلگراف *telegraf*; to telegraph, مخابره کردن *moxabere k.*, تلگراف زدن *telegraf zadan*.

Telegraph-office, تلگراف خانه *telegrafxane*.

Telephone, تلفون *telefun*; to telephone, تلفون کردن *telefun k.*

Telescope, دور بین *durbin*.

Tell, to, گفتن *goftan*.

Temperament, مزاج *mezaj*, طبع *tab'*, خو *xu*.

Temperance, پرهیزکاری *parhizkari*.

Temperate, معتدل *mo'tadel*; (of persons), پرهیزکار *parhizkar*.

Temple, معبد *ma'bad*; idol temple, بتخانه *botxane*.

Temporal, دنیوی *donyavi*.

Temporary, موقتی *movaqqati*.

Temptation (of the devil), وسوسه *vasvase*.

Ten, ده *dah*.

Tenant, مستأجر *mosta'jer*.

Tend, to (=to incline), متمایل بودن *motamayel b.*; (the sick), پرستاری کردن *parastari k.*; (flocks), چوپانی کردن *cupani k.*

Tendency, تمایل *tamayol*.

Tender (=soft), نرم *narm*; (=gentle), مشفق *moffeq*; (=offer), پیشنهاد *pifnehad*; to tender (=to offer), پیشنهاد کردن *pifnehad k.*

Tenderness (=softness), نرمی *narmi*; (=gentleness), شفقت *fafaqat*.

Tent, چادر *cador*, خیمه *xeime*.

Tent-peg, وتد *vatad*.

Tepid, شیر گرم *firgarm*.

Term (=space of time), مدت *moddat*; (=expression), اصطلاح *estelah*; (=condition), شرط *fart*, قرار *qarar*; (=name), نام *nam*, اسم *esm*; to term, نام گذاشتن *nam gozaftan*, اسم گذاشتن *esm gozaftan*.

Test, امتحان *emtehan*, آزمایش *azmayef*; to test, امتحان کردن *emtehan k.*, آزمودن *azmudan*.

Testament (=will), وصیت *vasiyat*; the Old Testament, تورات *tourat*; the New Testament, عهد جدید *ahde jadid*.

Testator, وصیت کننده *vasiyat konande*.

Text, متن *matn*.

Texture, بافت *baft*.

Than, از *az*, تا *ta*.

Thank, to, تشکر کردن *tafakkor k.*

Thanks, شکر *fokr*, تشکر *tafakkor*.

Thanksgiving, شکر گذاری *fokrgozari*, سپاسگذاری *sepasgozari*.

That (demon. pronoun), آن *an*; (conj.), که *ke*; so that, که *ke*, تا *ta*; in order that, که *ke*, تا *ta*; that is to say, یعنی *ya'ni*.

Theatre, تماشاخانه *tamafaxane*, تثاتر *teatr*.

Theft, دزدی *dozdi*, سرقت *serqat*.

Then, پس *pas*, آنوقت *an vaqt*, آنگاه *angah*.

Thence, از آن جهت از آنجا *az anja*; (=for that reason), از آن سبب *az an sabab*, از آن جهت *az an jehat*.

Thenceforward, از آن وقت *az an vaqt*, از آن ببعد *az an be ba'd*.

Theoretical, نظری *nazari*.

Theory, علم نظری *elme nazari*.

There, آنجا *anja*.

Thereafter, بعد از آن *ba'd az an*.

Therefore, پس *pas*, لهذا *lehaza*, بنا بر این *bana bar in*, از آن سبب *az an sabab*, از آن جهت *az an jehat*, از برای آن *az baraye an*.

These, اینها *inha*.

They, آنها *anha*, ایشان *ifan*.

Thick, کلفت *koloft*, درشت *doroft*; (of liquid), غلیظ *γaliz*, سفت *seft*.

Thickness, کلفتی *kolofti*, درشتی *dorofti*; (of liquid), سفتی *sefti*.

Thief, دزد *dozd*, سارق *sareq*.

Thigh, ران *ran*.

Thimble, انگشتانه *angoftane*.

Thin, لاغر layer, باريك barik.

Thing, چيز ciz, شىء fei; that is another thing, امر عليحده است amre ala hade ast.

Think, to, فكر كردن fekr k., انديشيدن andifidan.

Thinking, فكر fekr.

Third (subs.), ثلث sols, سه يك se yak.

Thirdly, ثالثًا salesan.

Thirst, تشنگى tefnegi.

Thirsty, تشنه tefne.

Thirteen, سيزده sizdah.

Thirty, سى si.

This, اين in.

Thorn, خار xar.

Thorny, خاردار xardar.

Those, آنها anha.

Thou, تو to.

Thought, فكر fekr, تفكر tafakkor.

Thoughtful, متفكر motafakker.

Thousand, هزار hazar; thousands upon thousands, هزاران هزار hazaran hazar.

Thread, نخ nax.

Threadbare, مندرس mondares, كهنه kohne.

Threat, تهديد tahdid.

Threaten, to, تهديد كردن tahdid k.

Three, سه se.

Threefold, سه لا se la, سگانه segane.

Three-ply, سه لا se la.

Three-sided, مثلث mosallas.

Thresh, to (grain), كوبيدن kubidan.

Threshing-floor, خرمن گاه xarmangah.

Threshing-machine, خرمن كوب xarmankub.

Threshold, آستانه astane.

Thrift, صرفه جوئى sarfejui.

Thrifty, صرفه جو sarfeju.

Throat, گلو galu, حلق halq; sore throat, گلو درد galudard.

Throne, تخت *taxt*; to ascend the throne, جلوس کردن، بر تخت نشستن *jalus k.,*
bar taxt nefastan.

Throng, ازدحام *ezdeham.*

Through, از *az*; see also Means.

Throw, انداختن *andaxtan*, افکندن *afkandan*; to throw away, دور انداختن
dur andaxtan.

Thumb, شست *fast.*

Thunder, رعد *ra'd.*

Thunder-bolt, صاعقه *sa'eqe.*

Thursday, پنجشنبه *panj fambe.*

Thus, چنین *conin*, چنان *conan*, اینطور *in tour*, آنطور *an tour.*

Ticket, بلیت *belit.*

Ticket-office, باجه *baje.*

Tide, جزر و مد *jazr o madd*: ebb-tide, جزر *jazr*; flood-tide, مد *madd*; to
go against the tide, بر خلاف جریان آب رفتن *bar xelafe jariane ab raftan.*

Tidings, اخبار *axbar*; good tidings, مژده *mozde.*

Tie (=necktie), کراوات *kravat*; to tie, بستن *bastan*, بند کردن *band k.*

Tiger, ببر *babr.*

Tight, تنگ *tang*; (=stiff), سفت *seft.*

Tightness, تنگی *tangi*; (=stiffness), سفتی *sefti.*

Tile, کاشی *kafi.*

Till, تا *ta*, الی *ela*; till when, تا کی *ta kei*; till now, تا حال *ta hal*; (with
negative verb), تا هنوز *ta hanuz.*

Till, to, زراعت کردن *zera'at k.*

Tillage, زراعت *zera'at.*

Timber, چوب *cub.*

Time, وقت *vaqt*, زمان *zaman*, زمانه *zamane*, هنگام *hengam*, مدت *moddat*;
by the time that, تا *ta*; from time to time, گاه بگاه *gah be gah*, گاه گاهی
gah gahi; a long time, مدت مدیدی *moddate madidi*, مدتی *moddati*; a
short time, مدت قلیل، اندکی *andaki*, قدری *qadri*, یکچندی *yak candi*,
moddate qalil; at the right time, سر وقت *sare vaqt*; at some time or
other, یک وقتی *yak vaqti*; at the same time, در همین حال *dar hamin hal*;
at the very time, در عین وقت *dar eine vaqt*; (=epoch), عهد *ahd*, دوره
doure, عصر *asr*; (=a time or occasion), مرتبه *martabe*, دفعه *daf'e*, بار
bar; (=hour), ساعت *sa'at*; what is the time? ساعت چند است *sa'at cand ast.*

Timid, ترسو *tarsu*.

Tin (metal), قلع *qal'*; (receptacle), حلبی *halabi*; small tin, قوطی *quti*;
  sheet tin, حلبی *halabi*.

Tiny, ریز *riz*.

Tip, سر *sar*, نوك *nuk*; (gratuity), انعام *en'am*; to tip, انعام دادن *en'am*
  dadan.

Tire, to (trans.), خسته کردن *xaste k.*

Tired, خسته *xaste*; tired out, در مانده *darmande*.

Tireless, خستگی ناپذیر *xasteginapazir*.

Tiresome, خسته کننده *xastekonande*.

Tithe, ده يك *dah yak*, عشر *ofr*.

Title (of a person), لقب *laqab*; (of a book), عنوان *envan*.

Title-deed, قباله *qabale*.

To, به *be*.

Tobacco, تنباکو *tambaku*, توتون *totun*.

Tobacconist, تنباکو فروش *tambakuforuf*, توتون فروش *totunforuf*.

Today, امروز *emruz*.

Toe, انگشت پا *angofte pa*.

Together, با هم *ba ham*, همراه *hamrah*.

Tolerate, to, تحمل کردن *tahammol k.*

Toleration, تحمل *tahammol*.

Toll, باج *baj*.

Tomato, گوجه فرنگی *goujeye farangi*.

Tomb, قبر *qabr*, مقبره *maqbare*, گور *gur*.

Tomorrow, فردا *farda*; the day after tomorrow, پس فردا *pasfarda*.

Tongs, انبر *ambor*.

Tongue, زبان *zaban*, لسان *lesan*; tongue of flame, زبانه *zabane*.

Tonight, امشب *emfab*.

Tonnage, ظرفیت *zarfiyat*.

Tonsils, لوزتین *louzatein*.

Too, زیاد *ziad*; (=also), نیز *niz*, هم *ham*.

Tool, آلت *alat*, افزار *afzar*.

Tooth, دندان *dandan*.

Toothbrush, مسواك *mesvak*.

Top, سر *sar*.

Topsy-turvy, زیر و رو *zir o ru*, زیر و زبر *zir o zabar*.

Torch, مشعل *maʃʻal*.

Torment, see Torture.

Torpedo, اژدر *azdar*.

Torpedo-boat, اژدر افكن *azdarafkan*.

Torrent, سیل *seil*, سیلاب *seilab*.

Tortoise, لاك پشت *lakpoʃt*.

Torture, شكنجه *ʃekanje*, عذاب *azab*, عقوبت *oqubat*; to torture, شكنجه کردن *ʃekanje k.*, عذاب دادن *azab dadan*, عقوبت کردن *oqubat k.*

Total, مجموع *majmuʻ*, جمع *jamʻ*; (=complete), تام *tamm*.

Touch, to, دست زدن *dast zadan*, لمس کردن *lams k.*

Touchstone, محك *mehakk*.

Tough (of meat), سفت *seft*; (=hard, of a person), سرسخت *sarsaxt*.

Tourist, جهانگرد *jahangard*.

Towards, سو(ی) *su(ye)*; بطرف *be taraf(e)*, بجانب *be janeb(e)*, سمت *samt(e)*.

Tow-boat, کشتی یدك كش *kaʃtiye yadakkaʃ*.

Towel, حوله *hoʊle*.

Tower, برج *borj*; (for exposing the dead), دخمه *daxme*.

Town, شهر *ʃahr*; small town, قصبه *qasabe*.

Townsman, شهری *ʃahri*.

Toy, بازیچه *bazice*, اسباب بازی *asbabe bazi*.

Toxicologist, سم شناس *sammʃenas*, زهر شناس *zahrʃenas*.

Toxicology, سم شناسی *sammʃenasi*, زهر شناسی *zahrʃenasi*.

Toxin, زهرابه *zahrabe*.

Trace (=vestige), سراغ *soraɣ*, اثر *asar*.

Track (=foot-marks), اثر *asar*, جاپا *japa*; (=path), جاده *jadde*.

Tractable (of a beast), رام *ram*; (of a person), مطیع *motiʻ*.

Trade, تجارت *tejarat*, سوداگری *soʊdagari*, داد و ستد *dad o setad*, معامله *moʻamele*; to trade, تجارت کردن *tejarat k.*

Trader, تاجر *tajer*, سوداگر *soʊdagar*.

Tradesman, كاسب *kaseb*.

Trade union, اتحادیه *ettehadiye*.

Trading-house, تجارتخانه *tejaratxane*.

Tradition (=story), روایت *revayat*; (=precedent), سابقه *sabeqe*; (of Mohammad), حدیث *hadis*.

Traffic, آمد و شد *amad o ſod,* عبور و مرور *obur o morur.*

Tragacanth (gum), كتيرا *katira;* (plant), گون *gavan.*

Tragedy, مرثیه *marsiye.*

Tragic, اسفناك *asafnak.*

Train (railway), ترن *tren;* to train, تربیت کردن *tarbiat k.;* to be in train (of a matter), در جریان بودن *dar jarian b.*

Training, تربیت *tarbiat.*

Traitor, خائن *xa'en.*

Trample: to trample upon, پامال کردن *pamal k.*

Transaction (=business deal), معامله *mo'amele.*

Transcribe, to, استنساخ کردن *estensax k.*

Transfer, انتقال *enteqal;* to transfer, منتقل کردن *montaqel k.;* transferred, منتقل *montaqel.*

Transfusion, تزریق *taʒriq.*

Transgress, to, تجاوز کردن *tajavoʒ k.*

Transgression, تجاوز *tajavoʒ.*

Transgressor, متجاوز *motajaveʒ.*

Transitory, فانی *fani.*

Translate, to, ترجمه کردن *tarjome k.*

Translation, ترجمه *tarjome.*

Translator, مترجم *motarjem.*

Transmigration (of souls), تناسخ *tanasox.*

Transmit, to, ارسال داشتن *ersal d.,* رساندن *rasandan.*

Transoxania, ما وراء النهر *ma vara on-nahr.*

Transport, حمل و نقل *haml o naql,* وسایط نقلیه *vasa'ete naqliye;* (=a ship), کشتی سرباز بر *kaſtiye sarbaʒbar;* to transport, حمل و نقل کردن *haml o naql k.,* حمل کردن *haml k.*

Trap, تله *tale,* دام *dam;* to trap, دام انداختن *dam andaxtan.*

Travel, سفر *safar,* مسافرت *mosaferat,* سیاحت *siahat;* to travel, سفر کردن *safar k.,* مسافرت کردن *mosaferat k.*

Traveller, مسافر *mosafer.*

Tray, سینی *sini.*

Treachery, Treason, خیانت *xianat.*

Treasure, گنج *ganj.*

Treasurer, خزانه دار *xaʒanedar.*

Treasury, خزینه xazine, خزانه xazane.

Treatise, رساله resale.

Treatment, رفتار raftar; (medical), معالجه mo'aleje.

Treaty, عهدنامه ahdname, قرارداد qarardad, پیمان peiman.

Tree, درخت daraxt.

Tremble, to, لرزیدن larzidan.

Trembling (subs.), لرزش larzef.

Trench, خندق xandaq.

Trial (legal), دادرسی dadrasi, محاکمه mohakame; see also Experiment.

Triangle, سه گوشه segufe, سه پایه sepaye.

Triangular, مثلث mosallas.

Tribal, ایلی ili, ایلیاتی iliati.

Tribe, ایل il, طائفه ta'efe, قبیله qabile.

Tribesman, ایلیاتی iliati.

Tribunal, محکمه mahkame, دادگاه dadgah.

Tribute, باج baj.

Trick, حیله hile, نیرنگ neirang, مکر makr.

Trickle, قطره qatre, چکه ceke; to trickle, چکیدن cakidan. چکه کردن ceke k., قطره کردن qatre k.

Trifle, امر جزئی amre joz'i.

Trifling (adj.), ناچیز naciz.

Trigger, پاشنه تفنگ pafneye tofang.

Triliteral, مثلث mosallas.

Tripe, شکنبه fekambe.

Triple, سگانه segane, مثلث mosallas.

Tripod, سه پایه sepaye.

Troop, دسته daste, گروه goruh; (military term), دسته daste.

Trooper, سوار savar.

Tropical, گرمسیر garmsir.

Trot, یورتمه yortme; to trot, یورتمه رفتن yortme raftan.

Trotters, پاچه pace.

Trouble, زحمت zahmat; to take trouble, زحمت کشیدن zahmat kafidan.

Trousers, شلوار falvar.

Trout, قزل آلا qezelala.

Trowel, ماله male.

Truce, متاركه motareke.

True, راست rast, حقيقى haqiqi; (=faithful), صديق sadiq.

Trumpet, بوق buq.

Trunk (of a tree), تنه tane; (of an elephant), خرطوم xortum.

Trust (=confidence), اعتماد e'temad; (in God), توكل tavakkol; (=deposit),
امانت amanat; to trust, اعتماد كردن e'temad k.; (in God), توكل
كردن tavakkol k.

Trustworthy, معتمد mo'tamad.

Truth, راستى rasti, حق haqq, حقيقت haqiqat.

Truthful, راستگو rastgu.

Truthfulness, راستگوئى rastgui.

Try, see Effort.

Tube, لوله lule.

Tubercular, مسلول maslul.

Tuberculosis, سل sell.

Tuesday, سه شنبه se ʃambe.

Tugboat, كشتى يدك كش kaʃtiye yadakkaʃ.

Tulip, لاله lale.

Tumult, هنگامه hengame, غوغا youya, شلوق ʃoluq.

Tune, آهنگ ahang, نغمه nayme, پرده parde; to tune (an instrument), كوك
كردن kuk k.

Turban, عمامه amame.

Turbid, مكدر mokaddar.

Turf, چمن caman.

Turk, ترك tork.

Turkey, تركيه torkiye; (bird), بوقلمون buqalamun.

Turkish, تركى torki.

Turmeric, زرد چوبه yardcube.

Turn, نوبت noubat; (=corner), پيچ pic; to turn (intrans.), گرديدن
gardidan; to turn back (trans.), بر گرداندن bar gardandan; (intrans.),
بر گشتن bar gaʃtan; to turn aside (trans.), منحرف كردن monharef k.,
منصرف كردن monsaref k.; to turn out, بيرون كردن birun k.,
اخراج كردن exraj k.; to turn with a lathe, خراطى كردن xarrati k.

Turnip, شلغم ʃalyam.

Turquoise, فيروزه firuʒe.

Twelve, دوازده davaʒdah.

Twenty, بیست bist.

Twice, دو بار do bar, دو مرتبه do martabe, دو دفعه do dafʿe.

Twig, ترکه tarke.

Twist to (trans.), پیچیدن picidan, پیچ دادن pic dadan; (intrans.), پیچیدن picidan, پیچ خوردن pic xordan.

Two, دو do; two hundred, دویست devist.

Twofold, دولا dola.

Type (print), چاپ cap.

Typesetter, حروف چین horufcin.

Typesetting, حروف چینی horufcini.

Typewriting, ماشین نویسی maʃinnevisi.

Typhoid, حصبه hasbe.

Typhus, تیفوس tifus, محرقه mohreqe.

Typist, ماشین نویس maʃinnevis.

Tyrannical, ظالم ʒalem, ستم گر setamgar.

Tyranny, ظلم ʒolm, ستم setam, جور jour, جفا jafa, تعدی taʿaddi.

Tyrant, ظالم ʒalem, ستمکار setamkar, جبار jabbar.

U

Ugliness, زشتی ʒeʃti; (of appearance), بدگلی badgeli.

Ugly, زشت ʒeʃt; (of appearance), بدگل badgel.

Ulcer, ناسور nasur, زخم ʒaxm.

Umbrella, چتر catr.

Unalterable, تغییر ناپذیر taɣyirnapaʒir.

Unanimous, متفق الرأی mottafeq or-raʿi.

Unavoidable, ناگزیر nagoʒir.

Unbeliever, کافر kafer.

Unceasing, مدام modam.

Uncle (paternal), عمو amu (for ammu); (maternal), دائی dat.

Unclean, ناپاک napak; (ceremonially), نجس nejes.

Unconditional, بدون شرط bedune ʃart.

Unconscious, بیهوش bihuʃ.

Uncultivated, لم یزرع lam yaʒraʿ, بائر baʿer.

Undecided, مردد *moraddad.*

Under, Underneath, زیر *zir(e)*, تحت *taht(e)*, پائین *pain(e).*

Under-Secretary (in a Ministry), معاون *mo'aven.*

Understand, to, فهمیدن *fahmidan,* ملتفت شدن *moltafet ʃ.,* در یافتن *dar yaftan,* حالی شدن *hali ʃ.*

Understanding, فهم *fahm,* عقل *aql.*

Undertake, to, بر عهده گرفتن *bar ohde gereftan.*

Undertaking (=promise to perform), تعهد *ta'ahhod.*

Unemployed, بیکار *bikar.*

Unemployment, بیکاری *bikari.*

Uneven, ناهموار *nahamvar.*

Unevenness, ناهمواری *nahamvari.*

Unexpected, غیر منتظر *ɣeire montaʒar.*

Unfit (=unworthy), نا لایق *nalayeq.*

Unfortunate, بدبخت *badbaxt.*

Unfortunately, بدبختانه *badbaxtane,* متاسفانه *mota'assefane.*

Ungrateful, ناسپاس *nasepas.*

Uninvited, ناخوانده *naxande.*

Union, اتحاد *ettehad.*

Unique, یکتا *yakta,* بینظیر *binaʒir.*

Unit, واحد *vahed.*

Unite, to, متحد کردن *mottahed k.,* وصل کردن *vasl k.;* (intrans.), متفق شدن *mottafeq ʃ.,* متحد شدن *mottahed ʃ.*

Unity, اتحاد *ettehad,* اتفاق *ettefaq.*

Universal, عمومی *omumi.*

Universality, عمومیت *omumiyat.*

University, دانشگاه *daneʃgah,* دار الفنون *dar ol-fonun.*

Unjust, بی انصاف *biensaf,* غیر منصف *ɣeire monsef,* جفاکار *jafakar,* ظالم *ʒalem.*

Unknown, مجهول *majhul,* نامعلوم *nama'lum.*

Unlawful, حرام *haram,* نامشروع *namaʃru'.*

Unless, مگر اینکه *magar inke,* تا *ta.*

Unnecessary, غیر لازم *ɣeire laʒem.*

Unofficial, غیر رسمی *ɣeire rasmi.*

Unpleasant, ناپسند *napasand,* نامرغوب *namarɣub.*

Unprofitable, بی فائده *bifa'ede.*

Unreliable, غیر قابل اعتماد *ɣeire qabele e'temad.*

Unrest, بینظمی *binaʒmi,* اغتشاش *eɣtefaf.*

Unripe, نارس *naras,* خام *xam.*

Unseemly, ناشایسته *nafayeste.*

Unserviceable, نابکار *nabekar.*

Untie, to, باز کردن *baʒ k.*

Until, تا *ta.*

Unveil, to (= abolish the veil), رفع حجاب کردن *raf'e hejab k.* ; (= discover), کشف کردن *kaff k.*

Unworthy, نالایق *nalayeq.*

Up, بالا *bala.*

Upon, بر *bar,* بر رو(ی) *bar ru(ye),* رو(ی) *ru(ye).*

Upper, بالا *bala.*

Uproot, to, از بیخ کندن *aʒ bix kandan.*

Upset, to (something), وارونه کردن *varune k.,* بر گردانیدن *bar gardanidan.*

Upside-down, وارونه *varune,* واژگون *vaʒgun,* سر نگون *sarnegun.*

Urban, شهری *fahri.*

Urgency, فوریت *fouriyat.*

Urgent, فوری *fouri.*

Urine, شاش *faf,* ادرار *edrar.*

Usage, عادت *adat,* معمول *ma'mul.*

Use, استعمال *este'mal;* to use, بکار بردن *be kar bordan.*

Used, مستعمل *mosta'mal.*

Useful, مفید *mofid.*

Useless, بی فائده *bifa'ede.*

Usufruct, انتفاع *entefa'.*

Usury, ربح *rebh.*

Utensils, اسباب *asbab,* افزار *afʒar.*

Utmost, منتها *montaha.*

V

Vacancy, جا *ja.*

Vacant, خالی *xali.*

Vacate, to, خالی کردن *xali k.*

Vaccinate, to, آبله کوبیدن *abele kubidan.*

Vaccination, آبله کوبی *abelekubi,* مایه زنی *mayeɣani.*

Vaccine, مایه آبله *mayeye abele,* مایه *maye.*

Vain (=useless), باطل *batel,* بی فائده *bifa'ede;* (=conceited), مغرور *maɣrur,* خود پسند *xodpasand;* in vain, بی خود *bixod.*

Valid, دارای اعتبار *daraye e'tebar.*

Valley, دره *darre.*

Valuable, گرانبها *geranbaha,* عزیز *aɣiɣ,* نفیس *nafis,* قیمتی *qeĩmati.*

Value, قیمت *qeĩmat,* ارزش *arɣeʃ;* to value (=appraise), قیمت کردن *qeĩmat k.*

Vanity (=conceit), غرور *ɣorur,* خود پسندی *xodpasandi.*

Vapour, بخار *boxar.*

Variable, متغیر *motaɣaĩyer,* متلون *motalavven.*

Variegated (of colour), رنگارنگ *rangarang,* بوقلمونی *buqalamuni.*

Various, مختلف *moxtalef,* گوناگون *gunagun.*

Varnish, to, روغن زدن *rõuɣan ɣadan.*

Vegetable (adj.), نباتی *nabati.*

Veil, حجاب *hejab,* رو پوش *rupuʃ;* (long black veil), چادر *cador;* (long veil of coloured material worn in the house), چادر نماز *cadornamaɣ;* to veil, چادر پوشیدن *cador puʃidan;* to veil the face, رو گرفتن *ru gereftan.*

Vein, رگ *rag.*

Velvet, مخمل *maxmal.*

Venereal diseases, امراض مقاربتی *amraɣe moqarebati.*

Vengeance, see Revenge.

Verb, فعل *fe'l.*

Verbal, لفظی *lafɣi.*

Verify, to, تصدیق کردن *tasdiq k.*

Verminous, موذی *muɣi.*

Verse (=poetry), شعر *ʃe'r,* نثر *nasr;* (=couplet), بیت *beĩt.*

Vertebra, فقره *faqare,* مهره *mohre.*

Vertigo, سرگیجی *sargiji.*

Very, بسیار *besyar,* خیلی *xeĩli,* نهایت *nehayat,* غایت *ɣayat;* this very, همین *hamin;* that very, همان *haman;* not very, نه چندان *na candan,* چندان...نه *candan...na.*

Vessel (receptacle), ظرف *ɣarf;* see also Ship.

Vest, زیر پیراهن *ɣirpirahan.*

Veterinary surgeon, بیطار *beĩtar,* دام پزشک *dampeɣeʃk.*

Vex, to, رنجانیدن *ranjanidan*, مکدر ساختن *mokaddar saxtan*.

Vexation, کدورت *kodurat*.

Vice-admiral, دریابان *daryaban*.

Vice-consul, کنسل یار *konsolyar*.

Viceroy, نائب السلطنه *na'eb os-saltane*.

Vicious, شریر *ʃarir*.

Victim, قربانی *qorbani*.

Victor, فاتح *fateh*.

Victorious, فاتح *fateh*, غالب *ɣaleb*, مظفر *moʒaffar*, فیروز *firuz*, پیروز *piruz*.

Victory, فتح *fath*, ظفر *ʒafar*, پیروزی *piruzi*.

View (=outlook), منظره *manzare*, چشم‌انداز *caʃmandaz*; (=opinion), عقیده *aqide*; to keep in view, در نظر داشتن *dar nazar d*.

Vigorous, جدی *jeddi*.

Vigour, جدیت *jeddiyat*.

Village, ده *deh*, آبادی *abadi*; village headman, کدخدا *kadxoda*.

Villager, دهاتی *dehati*.

Vine, تاك *tak*, رز *raz*, مو *mōu*.

Vinegar, سرکه *serke*.

Violent, شدید *ʃadid*.

Virgin, دوشیزه *duʃize*, باکره *bakere*.

Virtue, فضل *fazl*; (=accomplishment), هنر *honar*; (=chastity), عصمت *esmat*.

Visa, روا دید *ravadid*.

Visible, هویدا *hovēida*, آشکار *aʃkar*, نمودار *namudar*, پدید *padid*, پدیدار *padidar*, نمایان *namayan*, مرئی *mar'i*.

Vision (=dream), رؤیا *ro'ya*.

Visit, زیارت *ziarat*; (to the sick), عیادت *eyadat*; return visit, باز دید *bazdid*; to visit, زیارت کردن *ziarat k.*, بدیدار رفتن *be didar raftan*; to exchange visits, دید و باز دید کردن *did o bazdid k*.

Vital, حیاتی *hayati*.

Vitriol, زاج *zaj*, زاگ *zag*, توتیا *tutia*.

Voice, آواز *avaz*, صدا *sada*.

Volcano, کوه آتش فشان *kuhe ateʃfeʃan*.

Volley (of guns), شلیك *ʃelik*; to fire a volley, شلیك کردن *ʃelik k.*

Volume (=book), جلد jeld.

Volunteer, داوطلب davtalab.

Vomit, to, استفراغ کردن estefraɣ k.

Vote, رأی ra'i; to vote, رأی دادن ra'i dadan; to take a vote, رأی گرفتن ra'i gereftan.

Vow, نذر naẓr; to vow, (بستن) نذر کردن naẓr k. (bastan).

Vulgar (=unseemly), رکیک rakik.

Vulture, کرکس karkas, لاش‌خور laʃxor.

W

Wag, to (trans.), جنبانیدن jombanidan.

Wages, مواجب mavajeb, حقوق hoquq.

Wail, ناله nale; to wail, ناله کردن nale k.

Waist, کمر kamar.

Wait, to, ماندن mandan, صبر کردن sabr k., منتظر بودن montaẓer b.

Waiting-room, اطاق انتظار otaqe enteẓar.

Wake, to (intrans.), بیدار شدن bidar ʃ.; (trans.), بیدار کردن bidar k.

Wakefulness, بیداری bidari.

Walk, گردش gardeʃ; to walk, راه رفتن rah raftan; (to go on foot), پیاده رفتن piade raftan; to walk about, گشتن gaʃtan; to go for a walk, گردش رفتن gardeʃ raftan.

Wall, دیوار divar.

Walnut, گردو gerdu.

Wander, to (=be lost), آواره گردیدن avare gardidan, گمراه شدن gomrah ʃ.

Want (=wish), خواهش xaheʃ, آرزو arẓu; (=need), احتیاج ehteyaj, حاجت hajat; to want (=to wish), خواستن xastan; (=to need), لازم داشتن laẓem d.

War, جنگ jang, رزم raẓm, حرب harb; Ministry of War, وزارت جنگ veẓarate jang; munitions of war, مهمات mohemmat; to wage war, جنگیدن jangidan, جنگ کردن jang k.

Warehouse, انبار ambar.

War-front, جبهه جنگ jebheye jang.

Warlike, جنگجو jangju.

Warm, گرم garm.

Warmth, گرما garma.

Warning (=example), عبرت *ebrat*; (of danger), اعلان خطر *e'lane xatar*;
to take warning, عبرت گرفتن *ebrat gereftan*.

Warship, ناو جنگی *nave jangi*.

Wash, شست وشو *ʃostoʃu*; to wash, شستن *ʃostan*, شست وشوکردن *ʃostoʃu k.*;
(the dead), غسل کردن *ɣosl k.*

Washerman, گازر *gazor*, رختشو *raxtʃu*.

Wash-house, رختشوخانه *raxtʃuxane*, گازرخانه *gazorxane*.

Wasp, زنبور *zambur*; wasp's nest, چال زنبور *cale zambur*.

Waste, to, تلف کردن *talaf k*.

Waste-land, ویرانه *vēirane*, شوره زار *ʃurezar*.

Watch (=time-piece), ساعت *sa'at*; (=guard), پاس *pas*, کشیك *kaʃik*; to
keep watch, پاس دادن *pas dadan*.

Watchman, کشیكچی *kaʃikci*, پاسبان *pasban*, دیده‌بان *dideban*, مستحفظ *mostahfez*,
kaʃikci.

Water, آب *ab*; to water, آب دادن *ab dadan*; (=to irrigate), آبیاری کردن
abyari k.

Water-carrier, سقا *saqqa*, آبی *abi*.

Water-course, جوی *jūi*, جوب *jub*; (subterranean), کاریز *kariz*, قنات *qanat*.

Waterfall, آبشار *abʃar*.

Water-fowl, مرغابی *moryabi*.

Watering-can, آب پاش *abpaʃ*.

Water-lily, نیلوفر *nilufar*.

Water-meadow, مرغزار *maryzar*.

Water-melon, هندوانه *hendevane*.

Water-pipe, لوله *lule*, تنبوشه *tambuʃe*; (for smoking), غلیان *yalian*.

Water-pot, آفتابه *aftabe*.

Wave (of water), موج *mōuj*.

Wax, موم *mum*.

Waxen, مومی *mumi*.

Way, راه *rah*, طریق *tariq*; (fig.), سبیل *sabil*, مسلك *maslak*, طریقه *tariqe*; see
also Manner.

We, ما *ma*.

Weak, ضعیف *za'if*, ناتوان *natavan*.

Weakness, ضعف *za'f*, ناتوانی *natavani*.

Wealth (=riches), ثروت *servat, sarvat*.

Wealthy, ثروتمند servatmand, sarvatmand.

Weapon, سلاح salah, حربه harbe; weapons, اسلحه aslehe.

Wear, to, پوشیدن pušidan; to wear (= to rub), سائیدن saidan, سابیدن sabidan.

Weather, هوا hava.

Weave, to, بافتن baftan.

Weaver, بافنده bafande, نساج nassaj.

Weaving, بافندگی bafandegi, نساجی nassaji.

Wednesday, چهار شنبه cahar ʃambe.

Weed, علف خودرو alafe xodru.

Week, هفته hafte.

Weep, to, گریه کردن gerie k.

Weeping (subs.), گریه gerie.

Weevil, شپشه ʃepeʃe.

Weft, تار tar.

Weigh, to, وزن کردن vaʒn k., سنجیدن sanjidan.

Weight, وزن vaʒn, سنگ sang.

Welcome, to (a person), خوش‌آمد گفتن xoʃamad goftan.

Weld, to, جوش کردن juʃ k.; to be welded, جوش خوردن juʃ xordan.

Welder, ریخته‌گر rixtegar.

Welding, ریخته‌گری rixtegari.

Welfare, سعادت sa'adat; public welfare, بهداری عمومی behdariye omumi.

Well (= pit), چاه cah; (in health), تندرست tandorost, سالم salem; (= good) خوب xub.

Well-being, خیر xeir, سلامت salamat.

Well-wisher, خیر خواه xeirxah.

West, مغرب mayreb, غرب yarb; (adj.), غربی yarbi; the West, مغرب زمین mayrebzamin.

Western, غربی yarbi.

Wet, تر tar; (of weather), بارانی barani; to wet, تر کردن tar k.

Wetness, تری tari.

Whale, نهنگ nahang.

What (= that which), آنچه ance; (interrog.), چه ce.

Whatever, هرچه har ce; (adj.), هر har.

Wheat, گندم gandom.

Wheel, چرخ carx.

When (interrog.), کی kei, چوقت ce vaqt; (conj.), وقتیکه vaqtike, آنگاه که angah ke, هنگامیکه hengamike, موقعیکه mouqeike.

Whenever, هروقتیکه har vaqtike, هرگاه که hargahke.

Where, کجا koja.

Whereas, درصورتیکه dar suratike.

Wherever, هرجا har ja.

Whether...or, خواه...خواه xah...xah, چه...چه, ce...ce; (interrog.), یا...آیا, aya...ya.

Whey, دوغ duy.

Which (interrog.), چه ce; (of two or more), کدام kodam; (relative), که ke.

Whichever, هرکدام har kodam.

While (=as long as) مادامیکه ma damike, تا ta; a while, مدتی moddati; a long while, مدت مدیدی moddate madidi.

Whine, ناله nale; to whine, ناله کردن nale k.

Whip, تازیانه taʒiane, شلاق ʃallaq; to whip, تازیانه زدن taʒiane ʒadan, شلاق زدن ʃallaq ʒadan.

Whirlpool, گرد آب gerdab.

Whirlwind, گردباد gerdbad.

Whisper, to, آهسته گفتن aheste goftan.

Whistle, سوت sut; to whistle, سوت زدن sut ʒadan.

White, سفید sefid.

Whiteness, سفیدی sefidi.

Who (interrog.), که ke, کی ki; (relat.), که ke; whoever, هرکه har ke.

Whole, see Entire; the whole, تمام tamam; on the whole, روی هم رفته ruye ham rafte.

Wholly, مطلقًا motlaqan, کلیةً kolliatan, تمامًا tamaman, بکلی be kolli.

Whooping-cough, سیاه سرفه siahsorfe.

Whore, فاحشه faheʃe.

Why, چرا cera, از برای چه aʒ baraye ce.

Wick, فتیله fetile.

Wide, پهناور pahnavar, پهن pahn, وسیع vasi', عریض ariʒ.

Widow, بیوه bive.

Width, پهنا pahna, وسعت vos'at, عرض arʒ.

Wife, زن ʒan, زوجه ʒouje, عائله a'ele.

Wild, وحشی *vahſi*.

Wilful, خودسر *xodsar*.

Wilfulness, خودسری *xodsari*.

Will, اراده *erade*; see also Testament.

Willow, بید *bid*; weeping willow, بید مجنون *bide majnun*.

Win, to, بردن *bordan*.

Wind, باد *bad*; to wind (of a road, etc.), پیچیدن *picidan*; (a watch, etc.), کوك کردن *kuk k.*

Windlass (used in cleaning wells, etc.), چرخ چاه *carxe cah*.

Window, پنجره *panjare*.

Window-pane, شیشه *ſiſe*; window-sill, طاقچه *taqce*.

Wine, شراب *ſarab*; to drink wine, شراب خوردن *ſarab xordan*.

Wing, بال *bal*, پر *par*, جناح *janah*; (of an army), جناح *janah*.

Wink, چشمك *caſmak*; to wink, چشمك زدن *caſmak ẓadan*.

Winnow, to, باد دادن *bad dadan*.

Winter, زمستان *ẓamestan*; winter quarters, قشلاق *qeſlaq*.

Wire, سیم *sim*.

Wireless, بی سیم *bisim*.

Wisdom, خرد *xerad*, حکمت *hekmat*, دانش *daneſ*.

Wise, خردمند *xeradmand*, دانشمند *daneſmand*, عاقل *aqel*.

Wisely, عاقلانه *aqelane*.

Wish, آرزو *arẓu*, مراد *morad*; to wish, آرزو کردن *arẓu k.*, خواستن *xastan*.

Wishbone, جناغ *janaɣ*.

Wit, ظرافت *ẓerafat*, لطافت *letafat*; see also Intelligence.

With, با *ba*; (together with), همراه *hamrah(e)*.

Withhold, to (=to grudge), دریغ داشتن *dariɣ d.*, باز داشتن *baẓ d.*, مضایقه کردن *moẓayeqe k.*

Within, (ی)تو *tu(ye)*, داخل *daxel(e)*.

Without, بی *bi*, بدون *bedun(e)*, بلا *bela*; (=outside), خارج *xarej(e)*, بیرون *birun(e)*.

Witness, شاهد *ſahed*, گواه *gavah*; (=evidence), شهادت *ſehadat*, گواهی *gavahi*; to bear witness, گواهی دادن *gavahi dadan*, شهادت دادن *ſehadat dadan*.

Witticism, لطیفه *latife*.

Witty, ظریف *ẓarif*, لطیفه گو *latifegu*.

Wolf, گرگ gorg.

Woman, زن ẓan, ضعیفه ẓa'ife.

Wonder, تعجب ta'ajjob, عجب ajab; to wonder, تعجب کردن ta'ajjob k., متعجب بودن mota'ajjeb b.

Wonderful, عجیب ajib.

Wood (=timber), چوب cub; (=firewood), هیزم hiẓom; (=forest), جنگل jangal; (=spinney), بیشه bife.

Wooden, چوبی cubi.

Woof, پود pud.

Wool, پشم pafm.

Woollen, پشمی pafmi, پشمینه pafmine.

Word, کلمه kaleme, سخن soxan, لفظ lafẓ.

Work, کار kar; to work, کار کردن kar k.

Worker, کارگر kargar.

Workers' union, اتحادیه کارگران ettehadiyeye kargaran.

Work-house, see Poor-house.

Workshop, کارخانه karxane, کارگاه kargah.

World, جهان jahan, عالم alam, دنیا donya, گیتی giti.

Worldly, دنیوی donyavi; (=materialistic), مادی maddi.

Worm, کرم kerm.

Worship, عبادت ebadat, پرستش parastef; to worship, پرستیدن parastidan.

Worth, ارزش arẓef, قیمت qeimat, بها baha, قدر qadr; to be worth, ارزیدن arẓidan, قیمت داشتن qeimat d.

Worthiness, لیاقت liaqat, قابلیت qabeliyat.

Worthy, لایق layeq, قابل qabel, سزاوار saẓavar, مستحق mostahaqq, شایسته fayeste.

Wound, زخم ẓaxm, ریش rif; to wound, زخم کردن ẓaxm k.

Wounded, زخمی ẓaxmi, مجروح majruh.

Wrap, to, پیچیدن picidan.

Wrapper, Wrapping, لفاف laffaf.

Wrestle, to, کشتی گرفتن kofti gereftan.

Wrestler, کشتی گیر koftigir.

Wrestling, کشتی kofti.

Wrist, مچ دست moce dast, بند دست bande dast.

Writ, حکم hokm.

Write, to, نوشتن *neveſtan*; مرقوم داشتن *marqum d.*, نگاشتن *negaſtan*; (= to compose), تأليف كردن *ta'lif k.*, تصنيف كردن *tasnif k.*

Writer, نويسنده *nevisande.*

Writing (= handwriting), خط *xatt.*

Y

Yard (court), حياط *haiyat*; (approx. 40 in.), ذرع *ʒar'*, گز *gaʒ.*

Yawl, زورق *ʒouraq.*

Year, سال *sal*; this year, امسال *emsal*; last year, پارسال *parsal*; the year before last, پيرارسال *pirarsal*; next year, سال آينده *sale ayande.*

Yearn, to, اشتياق داشتن *eſteyaq d.*

Yearning, اشتياق *eſteyaq.*

Yeast, مايه *maye.*

Yellow, زرد *ʒard.*

Yellowness, زردى *ʒardi.*

Yes, بلى *bali*, بله *bale*, آرى *ari, are.*

Yesterday, ديروز *diruʒ*; the day before yesterday, پريروز *pariruʒ.*

Yet (= till now), تا حال *ta hal*; not yet, نه هنوز *na hanuʒ*, هنوز...نه *hanuʒ...na.*

Yoke, يوغ *yuʒ.*

You, شما *ſoma.*

Young, جوان *javan*, خردسال *xordsal*, جاهل *jahel.*

Youth, جوانى *javani*; (= a young man), جوان *javan.*

Z

Zeal, غيرت *ʒeirat*, همت *hemmat.*

Zenith, اوج *ouj.*

Zephyr, نسيم *nasim.*

Zero, صفر *sefr.*

Zinc, روى *rui.*

Zodiac, برج *borj.*

Zone, منطقه *mantaqe.*

Zoroaster, زردشت *ʒardoſt.*

Zoroastrian, زردشتى *ʒardoſti*, گبر *gabr*, گبرى *gabri.*